How images mean

Iconography and meta-iconography

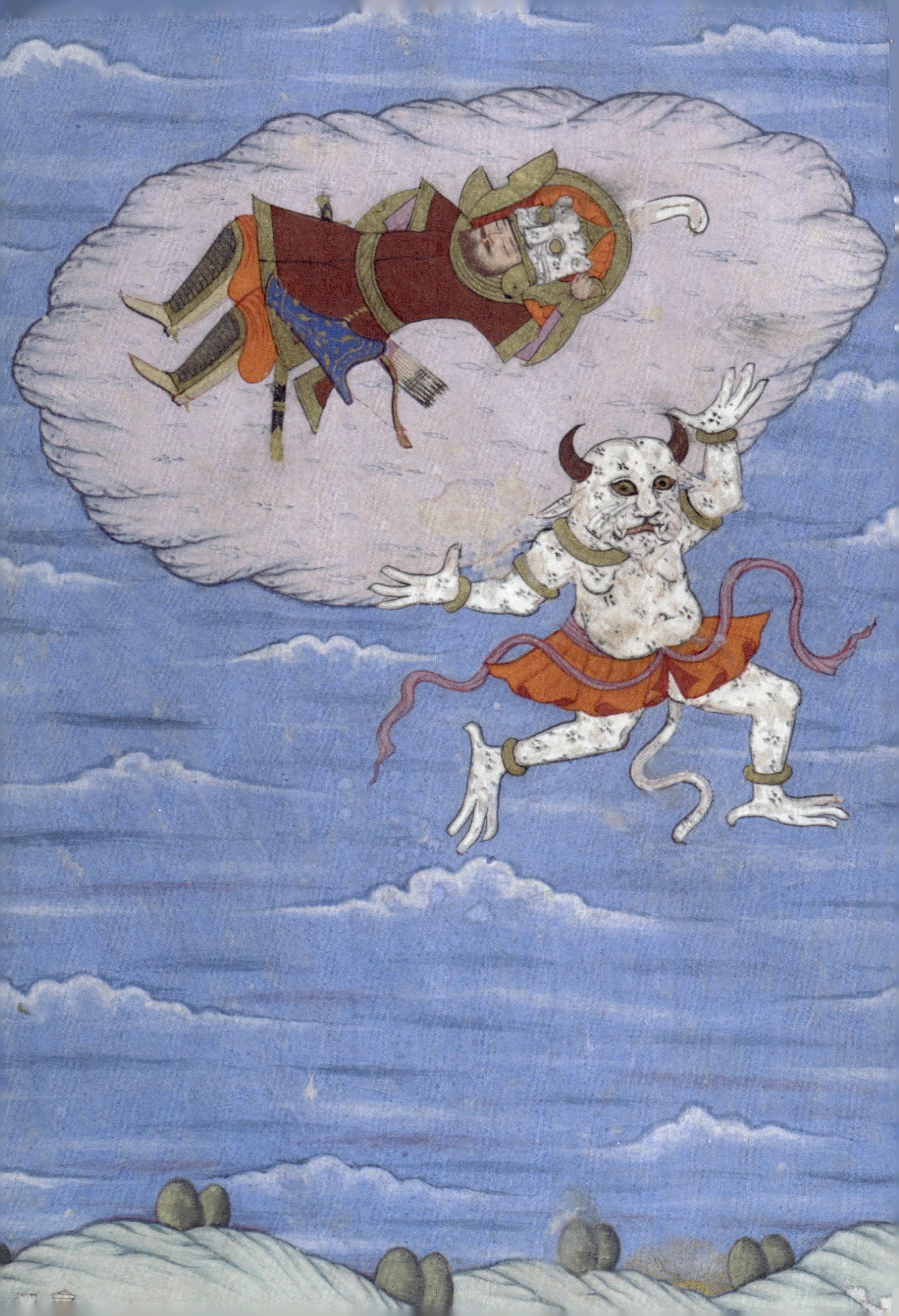

How images mean

Iconography and meta-iconography

Paul Taylor

Paul Holberton Publishing

For Charles and Liz

First published 2025

ISBN 978-1-915401-13-7

British Library Catalogue in Publishing Data

A CIP record of this publication is available from the British Library

Produced by Paul Holberton Publishing
One Kingdom Street, London, W2 6BD
paulholberton.com

Designed by Laura Parker

Distributed by Yale University Press,
New Haven and London

Printed by Gomer Press, Llandysul, Wales

Authorized Representative in the EU: Easy Access System Europe, Mustamäe tee 50, 10621 Tallinn, Estonia, gpsr.requests@easproject.com

Cover: details of figs. 4.33, 5.2, 5.5, 5.9, 6.17
Frontispiece: detail of fig. 5.26
Contents: detail of fig. 3.14

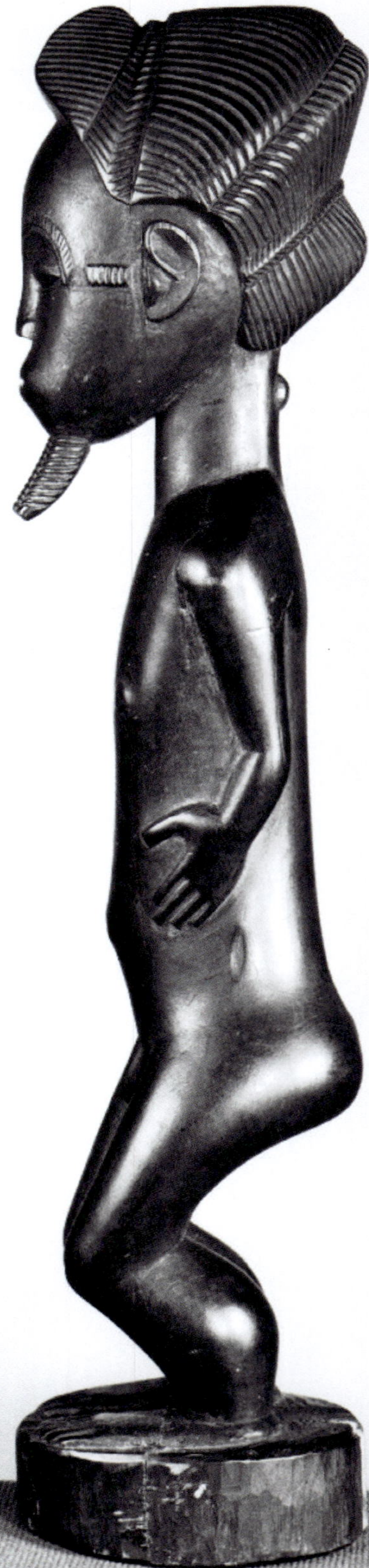

Contents

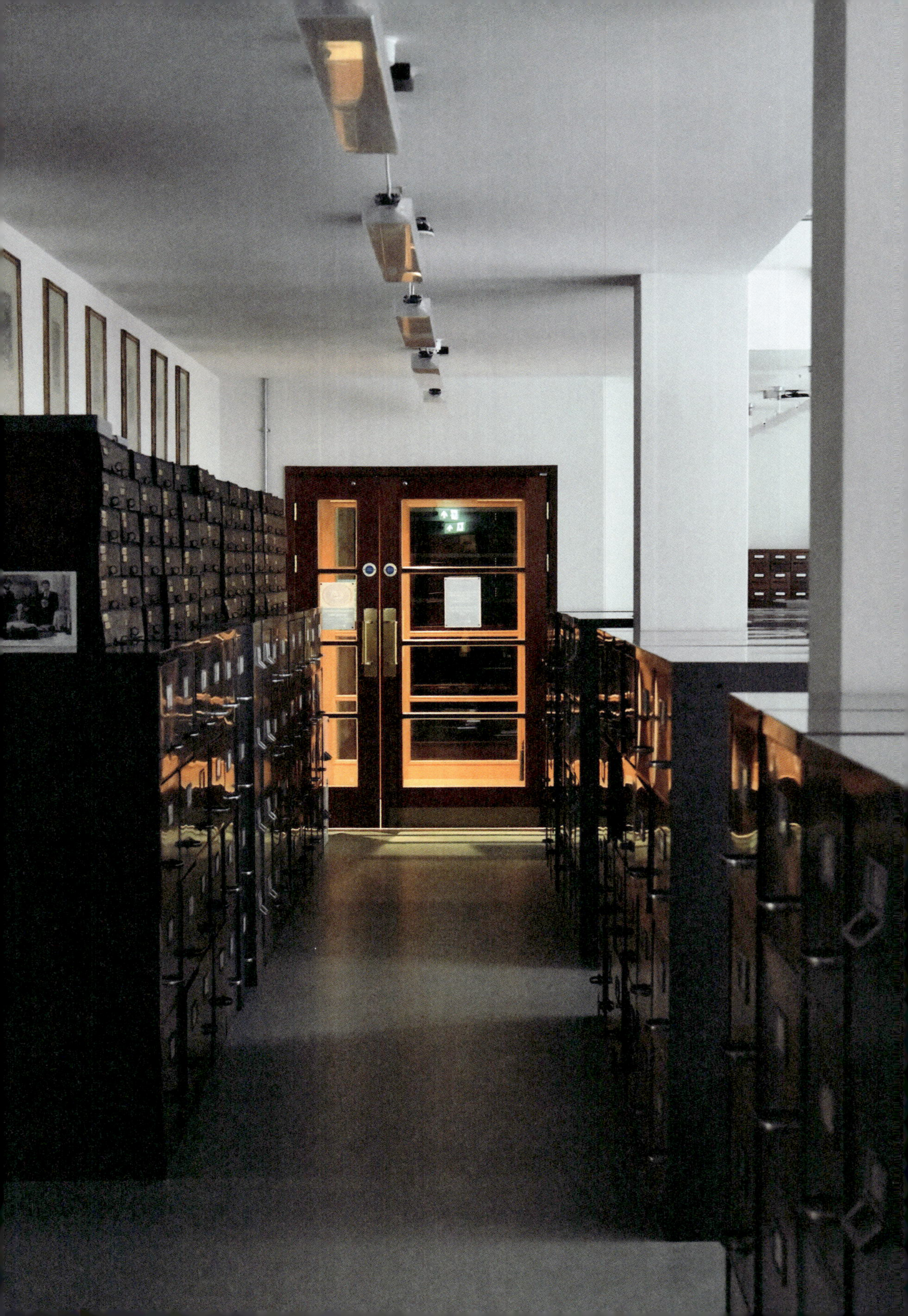

Preface

This book has grown out of my day job. For over thirty years I have worked in the Photographic Collection of the Warburg Institute in London. The drawers of the filing cabinets in this room contain around 18,000 folders enclosing over 400,000 photographs of paintings, sculptures, drawings and prints, all filed away 'iconographically', by the subject represented in the image. We have folders on Bacchus and Ariadne, the allegory of Prudence, the suicide of Lucretia, portraits of Elizabeth I, the miracles of St Dominic and so on. These subjects are made findable by the overall structure of the collection, with sections devoted to mythology, allegory, history, portraiture, religion: broader categories that are organized in ways that make locating subcategories (fairly) straightforward. We have built a visual library of the different iconographies recognized by people in the past, and while we do not claim to have a complete collection, we have managed (after 130 years of collecting) to put together a useful sample.[1]

When I arrived at the Photographic Collection in 1991 it was devoted almost exclusively to European imagery, but there were two little-consulted filing cabinets on Mesopotamian, Egyptian and early Buddhist art; unlike most of the Collection these were not filed iconographically. Since I was interested in non-European art, I decided to devote some months to reordering these peripheral sections by subject (Taylor 2006b). Once I had completed this task as well as I could, I went on to create entirely new sections on Asian, African, Oceanic and American iconography.

It was during my work on these new sections that I was struck by some fundamental differences of what might be called 'iconographic structure' between Eurasian and non-Eurasian imagery.[2] European and Asian imagery could be filed away on analogous principles, but I found it impossible to create a similar iconographic taxonomy for African, Oceanic and much of Amerindian art. This was due in part to the sheer number and variety of non-Eurasian cultures and to the scarcity of reliable iconographic information about some of them, but it was also due – although I was unaware of it at the time – to the difference between 'singles' and 'multiples', of which the reader will hear more in due course.[3]

In considering these issues I began to think about the theory of iconography, and I published a few studies on the subject (Taylor 2006a; 2006b; 2008a; 2010). However, the idea of devoting a book to the topic only occurred to me in 2014, when

1 On the history of the Photographic Collection see Mazzucco 2002; Mazzucco 2012; Fan 2022; Taylor 2022b.

2 It would be more accurate to talk of 'meta-iconographic structure'; see p. 11 below.

3 See pp. 79–86 below.

Mónica Uribe Flores of the Department of Philosophy at the University of Guanajuato in Mexico invited me to give a lecture series on iconography. The fifteen lectures I gave approached iconographic issues using concepts – denotation, reference, truth conditions, propositions, assertion – I had learned twenty years earlier, when I had studied analytical philosophy as an undergraduate. Since the audience was appreciative, I thought it would not be too difficult to turn the lectures into a book. The following year I had an eight-month honorary fellowship at the University of Wisconsin-Madison, and I devoted as much of it as I could to writing up my lectures. I managed to put down 45,000 words, but I was not happy with the result. It seemed to me that what I had written had insufficient theoretical direction; so I decided to bury the result in my computer.

I might never have returned to the project had it not been for two art historians, Elizabeth McGrath and Alexander Marr, and two philosophers, John Kulvicki and Jens Ziska, who asked to see the abandoned text and were kind enough to say that they thought I should continue with it. I have not followed their advice, preferring to start the book all over again, but I am very grateful to them for their encouragement.

Since giving my Mexican lectures, my way of thinking about these matters has become less philosophical and more historical, and I tried out papers in the new style at conferences honouring the retirements of my former supervisor, Jean Michel Massing, and of an iconologist whose work I have always admired, Jeroen Stumpel.[4] I then attempted an essay in a similar style at a meeting of philosophers of the image at Dartmouth College in New Hampshire. My thanks to the audience that day for giving me an easy ride, in particular to Catharine Abell, Roberto Casati, Gabriel Greenberg, Robert Hopkins, John Kulvicki and Dawn Wilson.

In 2019 I was invited to give a series of lectures at the China Academy of Art in Hangzhou, and used it as an opportunity to try out some ideas on the iconography of world art. I received much useful feedback, especially from Bao Liming, Cao Yiqiang, Fan Baiding, Jin Yuanhan, Kong Lingwei, Wang Youyou and Yang Zhenyu. On the last day of the series several distinguished European and American scholars, who were in town for a conference on the work of E.H. Gombrich, came to my lecture, and I thank Elisabeth de Bièvre, Whitney Davis, Carlo Ginzburg, John Onians and Nick Penny for their sharp questions.

In the spring of 2020 John Kulvicki was meant to come to the Warburg Institute for a three-month stay 'to find out more about iconography', as he put it, but before he could arrive Britain went into lockdown for the Coronavirus. So, instead, John stayed at home and the two of us had a long discussion about iconography over email. In some ways that was more useful to me than talking face to face, since I now have a record of our discussion, which has been of great help as I tried to unpack the issues discussed in this book.

Another unexpected outcome of the virus was that I was asked by the Warburg's Director, Bill Sherman, to give an online course called 'How Images Mean'. I am grateful to him for organizing the course, which forced me to put my ideas in order, as well as for suggesting the title of this book. The course was attended by over sixty people from all five continents, who gave me much helpful feedback and encouragement.

4 The first is published as Taylor 2022a, the second is cannibalized in pp. 79–86 below.

Most of this book was written on a nine-month Solmsen Fellowship in 2020–21, funded by the Institute for Research in the Humanities of the University of Wisconsin-Madison. Unfortunately, due to travel restrictions associated with Coronavirus, I was unable to travel to America, but I was able to join the institute's research seminars via video link from London and received support, technological and moral, from the institute's Director, Steve Nadler, and his assistants, Ann Harris and Lizzie Neary. I am very conscious of the fact that without the generous support of the IRH this book would never have been written.

A number of friends and colleagues kindly read some or all of the typescript at various stages of completion, and drew my attention to bad prose and muddled thinking; I thank Houra Adel, Ilaria Bernocchi, Brendan Cassidy, Richard Davies, Paul Holberton, John Kulvicki, Jacek Jaźwierski, Luciana Marcelino, Alexander Marr, Léa Monteil, David Stork, Jeroen Stumpel, Tanya Tiffany, Wang Yuxuan and Jens Ziska.

This is the third book I have published with Paul Holberton Publishing, and the process has again been a pleasure. It has been exceptionally easy to work with my editor, Ilaria Bernocchi, since she had already given me much generous editorial feedback before she took up her post.

Many other people have helped and encouraged me during the long gestation of this book, and I would like to thank Adeyemi Akande, Saba Alkuwari, Jonathan Allen, Marina de Angelis, Linda Báez Rubí, Robert Bagley, Paul Bahn, Kurt Behrendt, Madisson Brown, Emilie Carreón, Roberto Casazza, Elliott Christie, Gemma Cornetti, Nedal Haj Darwich, Timothy Demetris, Rembrandt Duits, Ludovica Fracassi, David Freedberg, Lorenza Gay, Sabine Gieben, Mariana Giovino, Maria Golovteeva, Steve Haggard, Felicity Harley-McGowan, Ian Karp, Ulrike Kern, Nataliia Kyva, Jill Kraye, Berthold Kress, James Laidlaw, Li Hanzhi, Christopher Lu, Sara Makari-Aghdam, Nico Mann, Behailu Mihirete, Eva Miller, Johannes von Müller, Andy Neale, John Nicoll, Anthony Ossa-Richardson, Martin Percy, Francesco Pierini, Katherine Reinhart, Juhyung Rhi, Ksenija Rozman, Carole Russell, Elizabeth Savage, Ursula Sdunnus, Sonia Sedivy, Paulo Silveira, Barry Smith, Tere Suárez, Aušra Vasiliauskienė, Hugo van der Velden, Marina Warner, Thijs Weststeijn, Greta Winckler, Irene Winter, Richard Woodfield, Yao Yuchen, Mahnaz Yousefzadeh, Ewa Zakrzewska and most of all my wife, Sara Trevisan.

This book is dedicated to Elizabeth McGrath and Charles Hope, who taught me iconography, and much else.

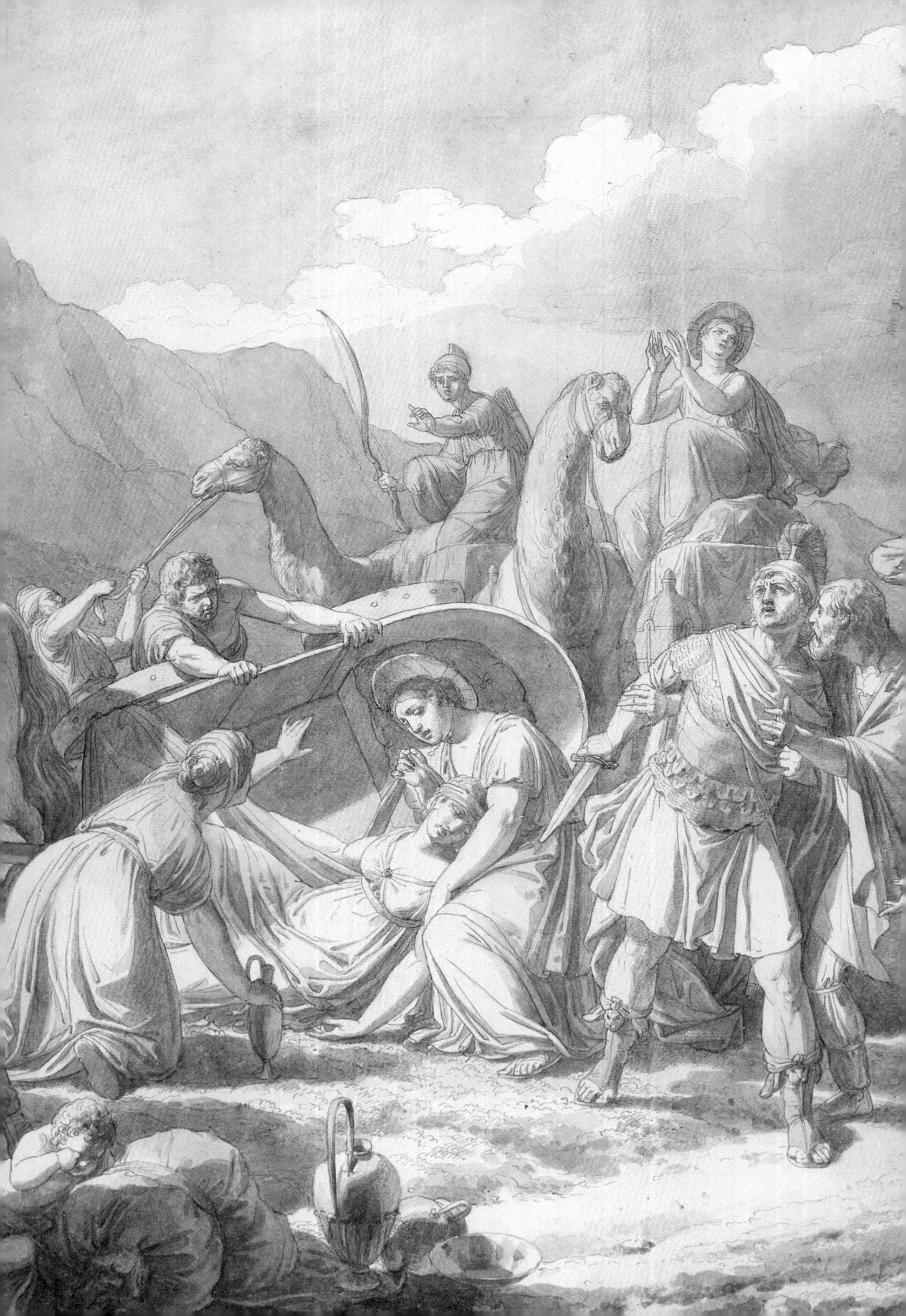

Introduction

Iconographers are a small group of experts who find out what images mean. Give them a picture of an unintelligible allegory, an unidentified historical scene or a nameless saint and they will try to discover what or who the image was once thought to represent. The detail of fig. 1.6 opposite provides an example of the kind of query an iconographer can receive. Who are these figures? What are they up to? It can take long hours of research to answer such questions. The solution of this particular iconographic riddle will be revealed in Chapter 1, but there are many other works that iconographers have still not managed to interpret.

Iconography, then, is concerned with *what* images mean, but the title of this book is *How Images Mean*. That is because it has a rather different aim. It is not an attempt to practise iconography; it is a book about iconography. It asks: what does iconography do? And how does it do it? How do we discover what images mean? What are the procedures that we need to go through to achieve this knowledge? How do images encode information to allow us to interpret their meanings? These are the types of question that will concern us in what follows, rather than the practical problems of historical detective work faced by the iconographer.

The ugly neologism 'meta-iconography', which appears in the subtitle of the book, is meant to refer to the kind of procedure in which we will be engaged. Among philosophers of language, the word 'metasemantics' was recently coined to refer to the study of "claims about the basis for ascribing a certain meaning to a word or phrase" (Kaplan 1989). In this it is distinguished from semantics, which is said to be concerned with "the fact that a word or phrase has a certain meaning" (Kaplan 1989). This distinction has proved useful, and metasemantics has become a subdiscipline with its own publications and conferences (Burgess and Sherman 2014). We might think of iconography as corresponding to semantics, and meta-iconography as corresponding to metasemantics; perhaps one day meta-iconography too will generate academic literature and events. At any rate, I will be making use of the word meta-iconography on occasion in the pages that follow.

Talk of the meanings of images leads to a thorny problem. Some scholars have denied that images have meanings, or have said that, if they do, these meanings are of limited interest (Kjørup 1978; Gell 1998; Hyman 1993). Images, it is claimed, cannot be said to have meanings in the way that words do. This philosophical position reflects a widely held point of view. If we take a photo of a horse (fig. 0.1) and compare it to some words for 'horse' in a selection of the world's languages – *bhiza, ló,* حصان, *hoiho, kawallu,*

Franz Caucig, Scene to be identified (detail of fig. 1.6)

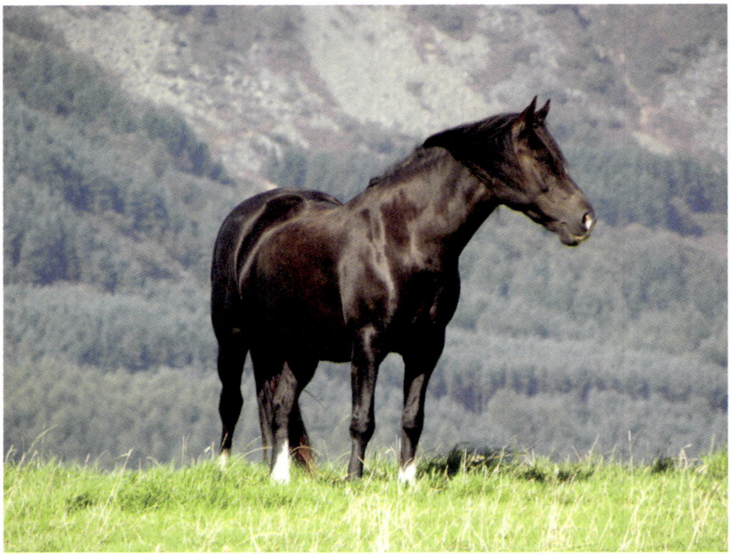

0.1 | Photograph of a stallion in Derbyshire

ẹṣin, лошадь, សេះ, *nguurru, tȟašúŋke*[5] – we can see a clear difference straight away. Few of the speakers of these languages are aware that the other words in this list mean 'horse', but they can all look at the picture and recognize a horse (or a *bhiza, kawallu, ẹṣin*, etc.). Languages you do not know are unintelligible unless you go to the considerable trouble of learning them, and since our lives are short and our memories limited, even gifted linguists can only understand a smattering of the world's 6,000+ languages. Images, on the other hand, have, or seem to have, an immediate and universal power of communication. They do not need to be learned in the way that words need to be learned. And what one is learning, when one learns a word, is its meaning; so, if images do not need to be learned, that is because (the argument runs) they do not have meanings of the kind that language does.

The argument runs further, claiming that images are not just universally intelligible, they also represent the world in a way that is unlike that of language. The variety in the list of words for 'horse' shows that any sound or symbol will succeed in referring to a horse so long as the group of people who use it agree about its meaning. Words do their work by linking signs and meanings by convention. Images, however, are said to be no more conventional than mirrors. An image resembles the thing of which it is an image; indeed, if it is made with a camera, it is causally linked to it. Light emanates from some object in the world and imprints its appearance on to the film or sensor. Whether the shutter release button is pressed by a speaker of Shona or Arabic or Quechua is completely irrelevant: the visual result will be the same, even though each photographer will think about the image in different words. Meanings are linked to

5 Shona, Hungarian, Arabic, Maori, Quechua, Yoruba, Russian, Khmer, Thiin and Lakota.

words by convention, and since images (on this view) are not conventional, they do not have meanings attached to them.

These ideas may seem self-evident, but for the past half century philosophers of the image have felt the need to defend them, or rather, versions of them, repeatedly. One reason for this reiterated defence is that a heretical philosopher, Nelson Goodman, published a book (1976) arguing that most common-sense views of images should be rejected. For Goodman, images do not need to resemble their objects; resemblance is in any case an incoherent notion; and the relationship between images and their objects is as conventional as the relationship between words and the world.

Goodman attracted a host of opponents, but the opponents soon found that, while disagreeing with Goodman was easy, proving him wrong was more difficult. A great deal of ingenuity has gone into arguing that the relationship between images and their objects is not conventional, and that there are essential differences between pictures and language; but the fact that the debate is ongoing only shows that the issues Goodman raised are surprisingly deep and difficult (Kulvicki 2014a; Hyman and Bantinaki 2017).

Goodman did not claim that images have meanings, since he had individual views on meaning, too. He believed that words refer directly to the world, unmediated by meanings, and wrote witheringly of "the dismal search through Never-Never land for some ghostly entities called 'meanings'" (1949, 4). Perhaps it was because of this aversion to the concept of 'meaning' that he had nothing to say about iconography, which had been defined by its most famous proponent, Erwin Panofsky (1939, 3), as "that branch of the history of art which concerns itself with the subject matter or meaning of works of art, as opposed to their form". And yet if he had taken an interest in iconography, Goodman would have added a powerful weapon to his armoury, because iconography gives strong support to the idea that images relate to the world in conventional ways.

Goodman's critics show more awareness of iconography than he did, but they would not agree with the bold assertion I made in the previous sentence. Philosophers of the image think of iconography as an oddity that only pertains to certain images, mostly traditional works of art, and only to some of them; they do not think of it as a universal feature of imagery (Hermeren 1969; Kjørup 1978; Schier 1986; Walton 1990; Hyman 1993; Lopes 1995; Casati 2004; Bantinaki 2008; Kulvicki 2020). It is not surprising that they think this, since it was a view shared by Panofsky himself, as we will see in the next chapter. In this book, however, I shall be arguing that all images, from ancestor figures to passport photos, can be said to have iconographic meanings: and that iconographic meanings are conventional.

To talk about iconography, we need to introduce a few technical terms that will allow us to differentiate the various forms of iconographic meaning. The first two chapters will be devoted exclusively to this task, but we will continue to feed in more terms as we proceed. Anyone who browses the later sections of the book without having read the first two chapters will find the discussion hard to follow, since it involves many words that have been explained earlier in the text.

'Iconography' is a word with more than one meaning. Panofsky defined it, as we have just seen, as "that branch of the history of art which concerns itself with the subject matter or meaning of works of art", but he then proceeded to give it a second, more restricted sense, as referring to the "conventional subject matter" of a work of art. He contrasted this concept with two other words he adopted for the purpose, 'pre-iconography' and 'iconology'. Leonardo's Last Supper[6] is at one level a depiction of thirteen men around a dinner table (pre-iconography); which would be read within the culture of its time as a representation of Christ's Last Supper (iconography); and which is revealing of Leonardo's personality, the culture of the High Renaissance and the religious thought of the time (iconology). I devote most of Chapter 1 to expounding Panofsky's three concepts and arguing that they ought to be rethought and revised. Panofsky wrote that his three levels formed a sequence from pre-iconography up to iconology; I argue that the sequence can be read in both directions, a phenomenon I call 'iconographic feedback'.

In Chapter 2 I focus on Panofsky's concepts of 'pre-iconography' and 'iconography' and argue that it is useful to split them into four different concepts: resemblance, conceptual depiction, indexical depiction and representation. 'Resemblance' and 'depiction' together correspond to Panofsky's 'pre-iconography', while 'representation' corresponds to Panofsky's 'iconography', although, as we will see, it is not synonymous with it.

At the end of Chapter 2 I introduce the concept of 'iconographic devices', the means by which meanings are attached to images. Although I call these means of semantic attachment 'iconographic devices', they might more accurately be termed 'meta-iconographic devices', or 'meta-iconographic mechanisms' – but 'iconographic devices' is easier on the ear.[7] The subsequent four chapters consider four principal types of iconographic device: designation, attributes, narrative and likeness. I do not claim that these are the only iconographic devices, and indeed three others – context, text and statistical assumption – will be discussed in a section of Chapter 4. The book argues that while devices can be used to identify figures, most often they act not as identifiers but as transmitters of identities; and that all iconographic devices are ultimately reliant on designation, the ascription of sense to an image.[8] These opaque remarks will, I hope, become clearer as the chapters proceed, and especially once we have unpacked the concept of 'designation' in Chapter 3. There is nothing obscure about the concept, as will emerge from the discussion of concrete examples.

The theory that designation is fundamental to iconographic devices weaves through much of the book, and running alongside it is another theory, that different forms of iconographic device emerge as a response to the increasing complexity of societies. The larger the population of image-users, the more iconographic types they will need, and new methods of generating those types must be invented in response to this iconographic demand. Whereas a small-scale society can make do with little more than pure designation, in societies of millions or billions of people further devices will be needed to generate the iconographic types required. This theory will be referred to on occasion in the chapters on iconographic devices, but it will be dealt

---

6 Readers may wonder why 'Last Supper' is not in italics. That is because, until the nineteenth century, images very rarely had titles; they were referred to by their content, like photographs; see McGrath 1998; Yeazell 2015. In this book I only use italicized titles if it is probable that the precise wording of the description was deliberately chosen by the person responsible for the making of the image.

7 'Devices' makes it sound as if the aim of these mechanisms is to assign iconographic identities, when sometimes, as we will see in pp. 115–16 below, iconographic identification is only a side product of the mechanism.

8 Bal and Bryson 1991, 191 may put forward a similar view.

with more directly in Chapter 7, which contains a discussion of iconographic diversity and demography.

The examples used in this book are taken from all five continents. In this I am following the trend in linguistics, where the number of languages discussed grows constantly. The standard textbook on pragmatics 40 years ago discussed a little over thirty languages, whereas a more recent textbook on the same topic discusses over three hundred (Levinson 1982; Huang 2014). This increasingly global scope is due to the complexity and variety of the world's languages. To understand the ways in which pragmatics operates in human speech, linguists must appreciate the intricate diversities of global grammar.

In the history of art, approaches tend to be more local; researchers on European or Chinese or African imagery talk to colleagues in their own fields. As Jeroen Stumpel (1996, 124) once observed, "Comparative art history, let alone comparative iconology, has apparently not yet got off the ground". And yet, as in linguistics, if we want to understand how human iconography works, we need to look across continents. Several concepts that will be central to this study, such as designation, singles and polysemy, are most revealingly instantiated in African and Oceanic art, but have implications for imagery in other parts of the globe.

1. Iconographic feedback

Panofsky and his predecessors

The 'Introductory' to Erwin Panofsky's collection of essays *Studies in Iconology* (1939) is cited by almost every author who intends to discuss the basic concepts of iconography.[1] Nothing would be gained by breaking with that tradition here. Panofsky's introduction is the ideal starting point for this discussion, not only because it sets up the argument in a very clear way, but also because it makes several statements with which we can fruitfully disagree.

Panofsky's name is so closely associated with iconography that his readers could be forgiven for thinking that he invented the subject himself – especially since he did not mention any of his predecessors in the 'Introductory'. But iconography had been in existence as a self-conscious academic discipline for a century before Panofsky wrote his introduction, and it had grown out of an older tradition of research stretching back to the sixteenth century (Białostocki 1963). Renaissance texts about antiquities often discussed the attributes of the deities and allegorical figures found on Roman coins and reliefs (e.g. Vico and Zantani 1548; Du Choul 1556; Erizzo 1568; Le Pois 1579), and by the eighteenth century this kind of study had come to be known as 'iconology' (*iconologia*, *iconologie*; see Sandrart 1680; Chambers 1728; Lacombe 1752; Prézel 1756).[2]

In the *Encyclopédie* edited by Diderot and d'Alembert, *iconologie* is said to be a term pertaining in particular to classical antiquities (1765, 488), but in the second quarter of the nineteenth century a new generation of scholars turned their attention from ancient to Christian art, changing the name of the subject as they did so from 'iconology' to 'iconography'.[3] A reason for the new emphasis on Christianity was given by one of the first of these iconographers, Georg Helmsdörfer:

1 A slightly rewritten and expanded version of the 'Introductory' was published as the first part of Panofsky 1955. The key difference is terminological: Panofsky talks of 'iconological interpretation' in the later introduction, whereas he wrote of 'iconographical interpretation in a deeper sense (iconographical synthesis)' in the earlier version. In what follows I shall mostly use the 1955 version. For discussions of Panofsky's essay and further literature, see Holly 1984; Hart 1993; De Vries 1999; Winter 2000; Recht 2013; Wuttke 2017; Kalinowski 2024; Sears 2024.

2 There was a parallel tradition of books with 'iconology' in the title that provided allegorical figures for the use of artists and poets. The first and most famous of these was Ripa 1593, with numerous subsequent editions. For more on the early meanings of 'iconology' and 'iconography', see Heck 1999; Recht 2013; Kalinowski 2024.

3 Not everyone approved of this new term, since 'iconography' was already in use to refer to collections of images and portraits; Cahier 1867, 6.

Let us be open about it: heathen antiquity is closer to us, is more intelligible to us, than our Christian past; and what emerged from a Christian way of thinking is stranger to us than those productions of the Greeks and Romans, on which we can bring to bear masses of antiquarian and mythological knowledge.
(Helmsdörfer 1839, xi)[4]

In this he was not exaggerating; after three centuries of research into antiquity a great deal was known about Greek and Roman imagery, but much of Christian iconography had been forgotten (Jameson 1848, 1:xxii; Ruskin 1851–53, 3:109–10). This was particularly true of the iconography of the saints, of whom there are tens of thousands in European churches and who, by the early nineteenth century, were mostly unidentifiable.[5]

Helmsdörfer's book on Christian iconography, published in 1839, despite an interesting and perceptive introduction, was little more than a checklist of the attributes of the best-known saints, and in this resembled the books on iconology of the eighteenth century, which were dictionaries of deities, personifications and symbols. In the 1840s, however, iconography transformed itself into a serious academic discipline, with in-depth investigations of individual monuments illuminated by research into theological and literary sources. Footnotes provided learned quotations in support of the text, and pertinent illustrations were included to form the focus of discussion. Much of this new scholarly impetus came from France, where two energetic iconographers, Adolphe Napoléon Didron and Charles Cahier, laid the foundation for the next 60 years of research (Bober 1978; Maraszak 2017). Didron set up a journal, the *Annales Archéologiques*, which was largely devoted to medieval iconography, and which was still being consulted long into the twentieth century – for example, by Panofsky (1955, 151, 264).

The most intensive work in iconography in the nineteenth and early twentieth centuries was on Christian imagery (Le Blant 1878; Kraus 1882; Mâle 1898; Mâle 1908; Mâle 1922; Kurz 1939; Ambrose 2017), but the subject also expanded into other fields, and by the time Panofsky came to write his introduction to iconographic method important work of lasting significance had been published on Mesopotamian (Delaporte 1920), Buddhist (Cunningham 1879; Foucher 1900; Foucher 1905; Foucher 1918; Foucher 1922), Hindu (Gopinatha Rao 1914–16), Mexican (Seler 1902–04; Seler 1908; Schellhas 1904), Northwest Coast Indian (Boas 1927) and secular European iconography (Schlosser 1896; Giehlow 1915; Van Marle 1931–32; Warburg 1932). Panofsky was well aware of the research on Europe, but not of work on the rest of the world, and his thinking about iconographic theory betrays his Eurocentric interests.

4 Helmsdörfer's book is the second known to me with 'iconography' in the title; the first is Radowitz 1834. In both *Ikonographie* may still have had something of its older sense as 'collection of portraits', but the word was in transition. Didron 1843 mostly uses the word to refer to the imagery of a period or region (*iconographie chrétienne, païenne, égyptienne*) but also uses it to refer to the study of subject matter (*"une iconographie des sibylles ne serait pas sans intérêt"*, 317).

5 To be precise, most of the types were unidentifiable, but most of the tokens were identifiable. On types and tokens see Lyons 1977, 13–18. You and I are both tokens of the type 'human being'. Since the most popular saint types – e.g. Peter, Mary Magdalene, Francis, Catherine – were still identifiable, and the least popular saints were the least identifiable, anyone walking into a church would be able to recognize most of the saint-tokens on the wall.

If iconography was a subject with a long tradition, theorizing about iconography was much rarer, and with his introduction to *Studies in Iconography* Panofsky made an original contribution not only to the history of art but also to the philosophy of images.[6] Not that his style in the essay is rigorous and philosophical; it was aimed at his Anglophone art historical colleagues, and for the most part uses the plain, descriptive language they expected in a learned article. An earlier version of the essay, published in German (Panofsky 1932), was more theoretical: there he felt free to include a discussion of a passage from Heidegger's *Kant und das Problem der Metaphysik*, but this analysis was jettisoned for the English-language publication. Panofsky's audience needed to be told what iconography was, and an excess of German philosophy was inappropriate in this context. As well as expounding the main concepts of iconography, Panofsky also tried to argue for the kinds of iconographic reading that he favoured, and which he later decided to christen with, as he put it, "the good old word 'iconology'" (Panofsky 1955, 32; cf. Kubler 1962, 4). Since the early nineteenth century 'iconology' had been little used in art history, so Panofsky felt entitled to appropriate it.[7] At the same time, he gave the word 'iconography' a more limited and precise sense than it had enjoyed to date. He also coined a new term, 'pre-iconography', which, as we shall see, was both useful and problematic.[8]

Pre-iconography and iconography

Panofsky laid out his ideas in the 'Introductory' while discussing several paintings, of which Leonardo da Vinci's Last Supper was the most frequently referenced (fig. 1.1). To explain the opposition between 'pre-iconography' and 'iconography', he invited the reader to imagine "an Australian bushman"[9] gazing at Leonardo's fresco:

> Iconographical analysis, dealing with images, stories and allegories instead of with motifs, presupposes, of course, much more than that familiarity with objects and events which we acquire by practical experience. It presupposes a familiarity with specific themes or concepts as transmitted through literary sources, whether acquired by purposeful reading or by oral tradition. Our Australian bushman would be unable to recognize the subject of a Last Supper; to him, it would only convey the idea of an excited dinner party. To understand the iconographical meaning of the picture he would have to familiarize himself with the content of the Gospels. When it

---

6 Charles Clermont-Ganneau, Salomon Reinach and G.J. Hoogewerff drew theoretical distinctions between 'iconography' and 'iconology' before Panofsky, see Recht 2013; Sears 2024. Panofsky's new concept of 'pre-iconography' allowed him to be more precise about the scope of 'iconography'.

7 'Iconology', however, was a word often used in conversation by Aby Warburg, see Wuttke 1979, 630–33; Sears 2015, 81; Huisstede 2017, 79–80. The idea that either iconography or iconology or both stem from the work of Aby Warburg remains persistent, see Wind 1931; Gombrich 1986, 312; Didi-Huberman 2002, 50. Even Panofsky claimed this to be so, although he certainly knew better, see Recht 2013, 9–10.

8 In fact, Panofsky never uses 'pre-iconography', but always 'pre-iconographical description', but since he frequently writes 'iconology' and 'iconography' it is hard to think that he could object to the noun. The term does not appear in Panofsky 1932.

9 By 'Australian bushman' he meant an Aboriginal Australian, rather than (in the Australasian context) a man, usually white, who lives in the Australian or New Zealand bush (*OED*, s.v. 'Bushman', 2). 'Bushman' has also been used to refer to the San people of southern Africa (*OED*, s.v. 'Bushman', 1; Gordon and Douglas 2000, xvi–xvii, 4–8). Although some Aboriginal peoples live in the Australian bush, they are not usually called bushmen, and were not so called in Panofsky's day either.

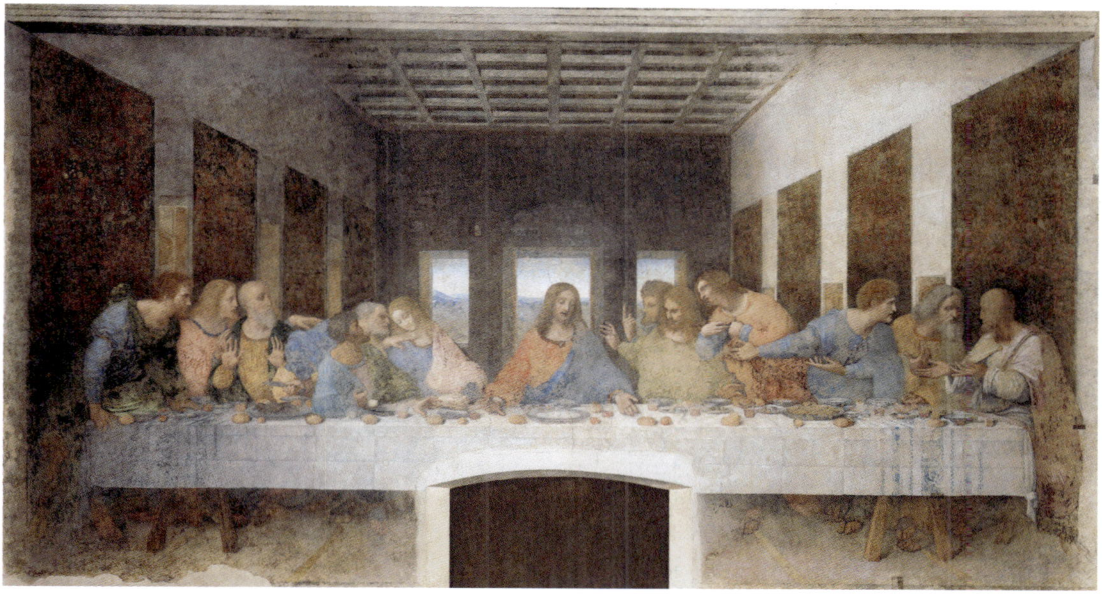

1.1 | Leonardo da Vinci, The Last Supper, 1495–98. Santa Maria delle Grazie, Milan

comes to representations of themes other than Biblical stories or scenes from history and mythology which happen to be known to the average 'educated person', all of us are Australian bushmen.
(Panofsky 1955, 35)

Clearly, Panofsky was right to say that an Aboriginal Australian, if we imagine him never to have had contact with European culture, would be unable to recognize the subject of a Last Supper. How can one recognize a scene showing Christ and his twelve disciples if one has never heard of Christ? And how could one know that this scene represents the last supper shared by this unknown group of men before the central figure was taken away and killed? That the man fourth from the left has betrayed the central figure for money? Not to mention all the layers of theological significance concerning the central figure being the Son of God, whose death will redeem humankind from sin.

However, if Panofsky thought, quite rightly, that an Aboriginal viewer would be unable to recognize the cultural and religious aspects of the narrative, he thought that some elements of the scene were cross-cultural. In particular, he thought that, to the Australian, the scene would "convey the idea of an excited dinner party". This assumption underlies Panofsky's concept of 'pre-iconographical description'. Our everyday experience of life, in Panofsky's view, allows us to recognize many of the creatures and things we see depicted in paintings. As he puts it, "Everybody can recognize the shape and behaviour of human beings, animals and plants, and everybody can tell an angry face from a jovial one" (33). This much all humans share, and since we know familiar things and familiar human expressions in the real world, Panofsky thought, we can distinguish them in images that depict the world in a realistic fashion. Paintings that employ a great deal of stylization, on the other hand, such as medieval illuminations, require prior knowledge of pictorial conventions. When looking at an Ottonian manuscript we might expect the Australian to find certain features, especially of spatial depiction, harder to interpret (34).[10] Panofsky appears to think, however, that the perspectival space of Leonardo's Last Supper is so lucid and self-evident that an Aboriginal beholder would have no problems in deciphering the motifs depicted.

Some aspects of a (realistic) painting can be recognized by any observer, but other aspects require a knowledge of particular narratives, texts or symbols, a knowledge that is culture-specific. Only someone who is aware of Christian beliefs can be expected to understand a scene of Christ's Crucifixion, only someone who has read Shakespeare's *Hamlet* can be expected to see what is taking place in an image that represents a scene from it, only someone who knows something of European allegorical symbols can be expected to recognize an image of Prudence, and so on. To identify themes of this kind, for which some textual knowledge is needed, is to engage in what Panofsky calls 'iconographical analysis'. Iconographical analysis relies on a knowledge of cultural conventions, and Panofsky makes convention part of his concept of iconography. He tells us that iconographical analysis has as its object of interpretation "*secondary* or *conventional* subject matter, constituting the world of images, stories and allegories", and that in this regard it is contrasted with pre-iconographical description, which is concerned with "*primary* or *natural* subject matter – (A) factual, (B) expressional – constituting the world of artistic motifs" (40–41).

We will discuss the pre-iconography/iconography distinction further in a moment, but first we should introduce the third of Panofsky's categories: iconology.

Iconology

'Iconology' is a term that has caused some confusion, as Panofsky himself acknowledged towards the end of his life (Lavin 1993; Wuttke 2017; Kalinowski 2024), and it has also attracted considerable criticism (Holly 1984, 161–73). Part of the problem has been that, although Panofsky decided to downplay German philosophy for the English essay, it was still there in the background, and because he did not want to burden his Anglophone audience with theoretical discussions, he often failed to explain the abstract terms he nevertheless decided to use. It was when he came to explain his concept of iconology, in particular, that he made use of philosophical concepts, and his prose was dotted with statements that were unintelligible to anyone who had not studied philosophy at a German university, e.g. "In thus conceiving of pure forms, motifs, images, stories and allegories as manifestations of underlying principles, we interpret all these elements as what Ernst Cassirer has called 'symbolical' values". In 1939, when *Studies in Iconology* was first published, Cassirer's neo-Kantian theories were barely known in Anglo-American philosophy departments, let alone among the art historians who might have been expected to read Panofsky's book.

10 I am putting words into Panofsky's mouth here; he does not introduce the Australian in his discussion of medieval style.

Not that any familiarity with Cassirer's philosophy is necessary for an understanding of most of what Panofsky tries to convey with the word 'iconology':

> As long as we limit ourselves to stating that Leonardo da Vinci's famous fresco shows a group of thirteen men around a dinner table, and that this group of men represents the Last Supper, we deal with the work of art as such, and we interpret its compositional and iconographical features as its own properties or qualifications. But when we try to understand it as a document of Leonardo's personality, or of the civilization of the Italian High Renaissance, or of a peculiar religious attitude, we deal with the work of art as a symptom of something else which expresses itself in a countless variety of other symptoms, and we interpret its compositional and iconographical features as more particularized evidence of this 'something else'. The discovery and interpretation of these 'symbolical' values (which are often unknown to the artist himself and may even emphatically differ from what he consciously intended to express) is the object of what we may call 'iconology' as opposed to 'iconography'.
> (Panofsky 1955, 31)

Despite the mention of 'symbolical values', there is nothing here that commits us to any of Cassirer's views on culture and history. To suggest that Leonardo's fresco may document the artist's personality (the fact that it is nearly falling off the wall certainly reflects his obsessive tendency to experiment with paint media), or the Italian High Renaissance (a painting of this particular appearance could hardly have been made a hundred years earlier, or later), or a peculiar religious attitude (the idea that sacred figures should be depicted in such a naturalistic manner would seem peculiar to most traditional sculptors in Africa) does not seem very controversial. That we might want to talk about the ways in which works of art reflect their makers, their times and the ideologies of those who made and beheld them also does not seem controversial. 'Iconology', in much of Panofsky's essay, is a straightforward notion, which hardly deserves the criticism it has received.

Another part of the problem with 'iconology', however, was that the word soon became associated with Panofsky's art historical practice, and with the practice of his followers. Panofsky's analyses of works of art frequently involved close readings that assumed that the artwork was conveying ideas through 'disguised symbols' (Panofsky 1934; Panofsky 1953) or making learned allusions to philosophical doctrines (Panofsky 1939; Panofsky 1969). Art historians ignored what Panofsky had written about iconology in the 'Introductory' and looked instead at what he did. Thus, 'iconology' began to be interpreted as an approach that involved giving intricate, erudite readings to works of art. Creighton Gilbert was speaking for many when he wrote, "[Iconology] is a method of study which we may agree to define by its general practice, rather than by the more complex statement of its best-known proponent" (Gilbert 1952, 202). Gilbert provided a reference here to the introduction to *Studies in Iconology*, which he proceeded cheerfully to ignore. In the early fifties, when Gilbert wrote these lines, Panofsky's method was at the height of its fame and prestige. To quote Gilbert again: "No technique of research in Renaissance art has recently had more success – or more deserved it – than iconology".

With time, however, Panofsky's method and its reputation began to wane. In part this was because, as with any academic fashion, scholars felt the need to move on and try new approaches. But iconology was not merely abandoned, it was also attacked. A number of Panofsky's readings of works of art have been sharply criticized as overintellectual and underdocumented, and 'iconology' has come to be associated with the interpretative excesses of his school (Hope 1980; Bedaux 1986; Kidson 1987; Lane 1988; Cassidy 1993; Van der Velden 1997; Rose 2022).

The term 'iconology' as it was defined by Panofsky in his theoretical introduction did not have to be taken to refer to the practice of Panofskian art history; it was much vaguer than that. And yet it was tarred with the same brush. When I arrived at the Warburg in the 1990s the word had been banished from the institute, and the 'Introductory' to *Symbolic Images* was considered ideologically suspect, due in part to its use of an apparently historicist phrase, "essential tendencies of the human mind" – historicism having received sharp criticism from the dominant intellectual influence in the Warburg at the time, E.H. Gombrich (Gombrich 1979; Burke 2014).

It seems to me that Panofskian practice, historicism and the theories of Cassirer can all be extracted from the concept of 'iconology', and that what is left is still a useful notion. For one thing, the contrast between 'iconology' and 'iconography' brings out a revealing difference between texts and images. 'Iconological interpretations' have their counterpart in literary history and criticism, but 'iconographic analyses' do not. To give an example: the literary scholar Lawrence Green (2016) has discussed the gravediggers' scene in *Hamlet* against the background of burial practices in Shakespeare's England. At the time it was common for new corpses to be buried in ground where other corpses had been buried not long before, leading to a general disruption of skeletons and a mixing-up of skulls and bones. Few people were left to rest in peace in contemporary churchyards, and in the gravediggers' scene in *Hamlet* the skull of Yorick, the king's jester, is dug out of the earth and handed to a bystander (Hamlet) so that the drowned Ophelia can be buried in the same ground. The practice of breaking up graves was one on which Shakespeare himself seems to have held strong opinions, if the epitaph on his grave was his own invention:

> GOOD FRIEND FOR JESUS' SAKE FORBEAR,
> TO DIG THE DUST ENCLOSED HERE:
> BLESSED BE THE MAN THAT SPARES THESE STONES,
> AND CURSED BE HE THAT MOVES MY BONES.

This kind of interpretation corresponds exactly to Panofsky's formulation of iconology: "But when we try to understand *the gravediggers' scene* as a document of *Shakespeare's* personality, or of the civilization of *Elizabethan England*, or of a peculiar religious attitude, we deal with the work of *drama* as a symptom of something else which expresses itself in a countless variety of other symptoms".[11]

But although literary historians often engage in interpretations that correspond to Panofsky's iconology, they do not engage in anything that might correspond to iconography. If the print by Eugène Delacroix in fig. 1.2 is shown to people who have never read *Hamlet* and have no knowledge of its plot, they find it impossible to identify the subject, or to understand what is happening. Someone reading the scene as it

11 Italicized terms mine.

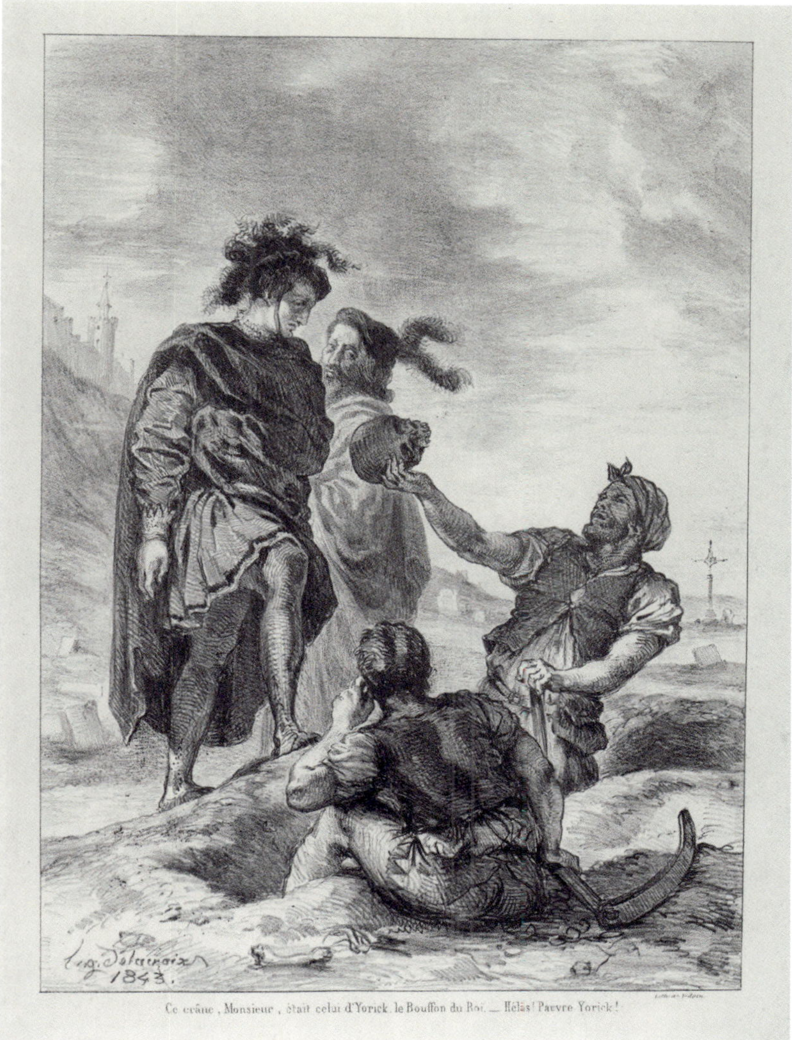

1.2 | Eugène Delacroix, Gravedigging scene from *Hamlet*, 1843.
The Metropolitan Museum of Art, New York

appears in the play, however, could work out a great deal of what is going on from the words of the passage, even if they had not read the rest of the tragedy. The image is much less informative, because gesture and expression tell us too little about cognition and intention. How can we know, just by looking at the print, who these people are, what has just happened, or what is about to happen? Is the skull being passed from one person to another, and if so from whom to whom? What is the name of the skull's owner? Did any of the people depicted know the owner's name? What thoughts arose at the sight of that skull? These questions are answered in the relevant passage in the play, even if the other complexities of the plot are still unknown.

Clown. Here's a skull now. This skull hath lain yon i' th' earth three-and-twenty years.
Hamlet. Whose was it?
Clown. A whoreson, mad fellow's it was. Whose do you think it was?
Hamlet. Nay, I know not.
Clown. A pestilence on him for a mad rogue! 'A pour'd a flagon of Rhenish on my head once. This same skull, sir, was Yorick's skull, the King's jester.
Hamlet. This?
Clown. E'en that.
Hamlet. Let me see. [*Takes the skull*.] Alas, poor Yorick! I knew him, Horatio. A fellow of infinite jest, of most excellent fancy. He hath borne me on his back a thousand times. And now how abhorred in my imagination it is! My gorge rises at it. Here hung those lips that I have kiss'd I know not how oft. Where be your gibes now? your gambols? your songs? your flashes of merriment that were wont to set the table on a roar? Not one now, to mock your own grinning? Quite chap-fall'n? Now get you to my lady's chamber, and tell her, let her paint an inch thick, to this favour she must come. Make her laugh at that.

There are many articles in art historical journals trying to identify the subjects of paintings, but none in literary journals trying to identify the subjects of plays. To learn what a play is about, one can read or watch it. Looking at a picture, however, does not reveal its subject; there is always the need for further evidence, external to the picture itself. Much more will be said about that last claim in what follows, but I hope the reader will already agree that Panofsky's iconography/iconology distinction is putting its finger on something revealing. It is interesting too for another reason, in that it forms part of the concept of 'iconographic feedback'; but before we can discuss this, we need to return to our Aboriginal Australian looking at the image of Leonardo's Last Supper.

Radical iconography

As we have seen, Panofsky rightly argued that an Aboriginal Australian with no knowledge of European culture would find it impossible to interpret the iconographic subject of Leonardo's fresco. He did, however, think that the pre-iconography of the image would be identifiable by the Australian, and that the scene would "convey the idea of an excited dinner party".

It is far from clear that Panofsky was right about this. For a start, the Australian might have had difficulties in seeing much in the painting at all. It is not just that it is in terrible condition; there is a certain amount of ethnological evidence that suggests that some people who have little experience of such images find it hard to interpret perspectival drawings and black and white photographs, although they can usually learn to recognize them quite swiftly (Layton 1977; Wright 1992; Deręgowski 2017; Forge 2017c). But even if we assume that the Australian had no difficulty in making out the contents of the image in front of him, he can hardly have seen the fresco as a depiction of "an excited dinner party". Indigenous Australians did not go to 'dinner parties'. They did not make tables, or tablecloths, either, so our observer would have had difficulty recognizing the long shape in the foreground as a support for a meal, especially when the objects on the table, the glasses, the plates, the knives, the bread, were unfamiliar to him. The straight-edged shapes around the figures would also have been hard to understand: Aboriginal Australians did not make architecture (Spencer 1914, 31). And most Aboriginal peoples did not wear clothes, so the coloured shapes enveloping the thirteen figures would not have been easy to interpret (Williams 1985, 38–41; Dyer 2005, 23–37; Gilligan 2008).

Panofsky might insist that the Australian would at least recognize the figures as fellow human beings and would understand their expressions. To take the last point first: some expressions are natural and universally recognizable – tears, laughter – but it is not always easy to know what they mean in a particular context. People pretend to laugh and to cry, and even when they are sincere, there are different meanings depending on what these expressions of emotion are about – tears of sadness, tears of laughter, tears of joy, tears of rage. Emotions are not simply sensations, they have referents – we laugh about this, cry about that – and they have their own character too – we laugh scornfully at enemies, lovingly at children.[12] Quite what the expressions on the faces of Leonardo's figures mean would have been hard enough for his Italian contemporaries to gauge, and there is no reason to think the Australian could have understood them. Using the gospels and iconographic tradition we can feel sure that Leonardo has represented the moment when Christ announces his impending betrayal:

> And as they did eat, he said, Verily I say unto you, that one of you shall betray me. And they were exceeding sorrowful, and began every one of them to say unto him, Lord, is it I? And he answered and said, He that dippeth [his] hand with me in the dish, the same shall betray me. The Son of man goeth as it is written of him: but woe unto that man by whom the Son of man is betrayed! it had been good for that man if he had not been born. Then Judas, which betrayed him, answered and said, Master, is it I? He said unto him, Thou hast said.
> (Matthew 26.21–25)[13]

The hands of Jesus and Judas are both reaching towards the same dish, but it is impossible to understand the significance of those gestures without reading the gospel. The same is true of the expressions of the disciples, who are all responding to a particular situation, which is unintelligible until we know the story so far: and that story is not visible in the fresco. Thus, unless we already know the story, we cannot understand the meanings of the expressions; and the same is true of the gestures. A very small number of gestures seem to be, if not universal, then geographically widespread – nodding, pointing, denoting size – but most are culturally specific (Kendon 2004). As it happens, many Aboriginal peoples in Australia use complex sign languages, so the varied gestures of the figures in Leonardo's painting could only have intrigued and baffled our imaginary viewer (Kendon 1988).

An Aboriginal beholder, then, would have found it very difficult to understand the expressions and gestures in the painting; and, even if he guessed them correctly, he could not have known that he had done so. Panofsky might, however, argue that, whatever problems these aspects of the painting may have caused, the Australian would at least have been able to see that the figures were humans; but this is not clear either.

12 Aby Warburg's well-known theory of the 'Pathos formula' begs the question: which pathos? Didi-Huberman 2002, 224–48.

13 Leonardo appears to have incorporated details from all four gospels; see Kurz 1939, 73–81.

The figures in Leonardo's painting do not look much like indigenous Australians, and our observer might think that they were meant to be powerful spirits or primordial ancestors. This is not simply a case of coming across beings that seem unfamiliar. Panofsky acknowledges that observers cannot recognize objects that are outside the range of their practical experience, "for instance when we find ourselves confronted with the representation of an obsolete or unfamiliar tool, or with the representation of a plant or animal unknown to us", as he puts it (33). But it is not only a matter of experience and recognition; it is also a matter of interpreting artistic intentions. The Aboriginal viewer would know that what he is looking at is an image, and would know, from his own cultural traditions, that images are used to depict all kinds of beings, and in particular ancestral spirits of various kinds (Carroll 1977; Hoff 1977; Layton 1985; Munn 1986). The question then would be, what the intentions of the makers were, and of course the Australian would only be able to speculate about this, in the absence of any information on the question.

So how much of Panofsky's 'pre-iconographical interpretation' could the hypothetical Aboriginal viewer, unaware of Western traditions, have been expected to grasp? Very little. He could not have known he was looking at a dinner party, or a table, or a room, and he could not even have known that he was looking at a group of humans, let alone what they were thinking or feeling. He could have seen that the parts of the figures emerging from the clothes *resembled* human faces and hands, but resemblance does not settle questions of identity. What looks like a human being can be a god or a spirit or a statue. Consider another painting, by a contemporary of Leonardo, Giovanni Bellini (fig. 1.3). In this painting the figures are supposed to be gods, but they do not look any less like humans than Christ and his disciples. If we think that one group is made up of gods and the other is made up of humans, that is because we can recognize the subjects of both paintings: one is a Feast of the Gods, the other is a Last Supper. Our pre-iconographic interpretations are guided by our iconographic analyses.

Panofsky's idea that iconographic aspects of a painting are conventional, while pre-iconographic aspects are natural, is not well supported by a thorough application of his own thought experiment. The aim of the experiment was to provide an example of radical translation as applied to images, but in Panofsky's hands it was not radical enough.[14] The truth is not that some elements of the content are natural and that others are conventional, but rather that all the elements are conventional and that different aspects of a painting will be intelligible to different people depending on their familiarity with the conventions involved. This is expressed in diagrammatic form in fig. 1.4. Our Aboriginal observer can only be sure about the most generic of the categories here; he knows that he is looking at beings that resemble humans. Whether he is looking at humans, rather than statues or spirits or deities, he cannot know for sure. He will not recognize their clothes, or the room they are sitting in, or the table they are seated behind, or the food on the table. Subtleties like the fact their costumes show they live in the past, and specifically that they are early Christians, will be lost on him. He will

14 The phrase 'radical translation' postdates Panofsky: Quine 1960, 1987. Panofsky's thought experiment differs from Quine's in that it assumes no interlocutor; it is more like trying to translate the script of a language that appears to have no known relatives. I am aware that Quine's concept of radical translation is applicable to the discussion of 'designation' in Chapter 3: how can we be sure of what is being designated from an ostensive definition? I leave it to my colleagues in philosophy to wrestle with this problem.

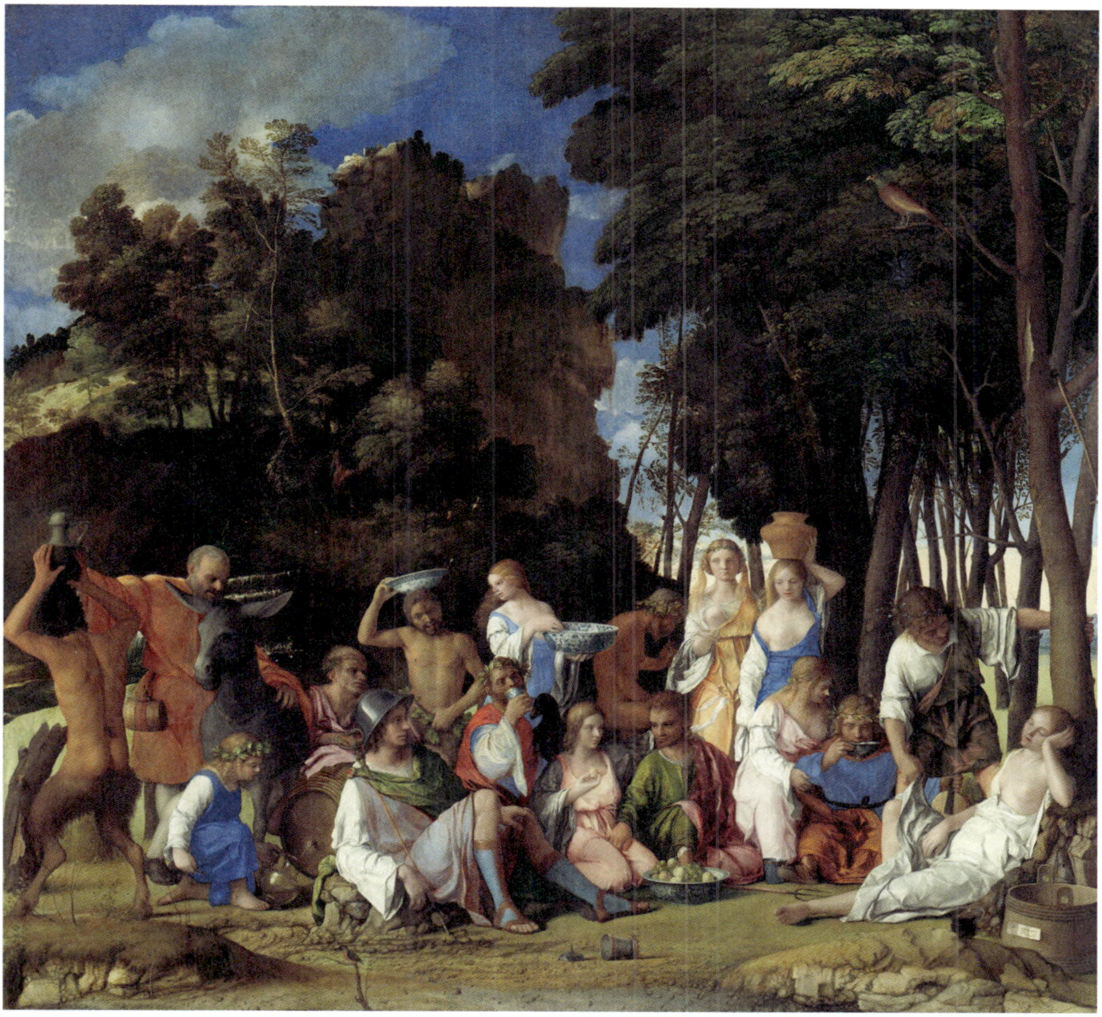

1.3 | Giovanni Bellini and Titian, The Feast of the Gods, 1514/1529. National Gallery of Art, Washington, D.C.

not recognize Christ and his disciples, nor will he know that this event is described in the Bible. Of course, he does not know that he is looking at a representation of the Last Supper.

If Panofsky were to be placed in front of Aboriginal paintings, he would face very similar difficulties. He might be able to see that some figures resembled humans and others particular animals – although even to do this much is not always easy for those who do not understand the iconic conventions of Aboriginal painting[15] – but he would not know that some were ancestral beings, and that specific myths were being recounted

15 See the brief discussion of the experience of N.W.G. Macintosh on p. 228 below. For the meaning of the word 'iconic' as used in this book, see Chapter 2, ftn. 16.

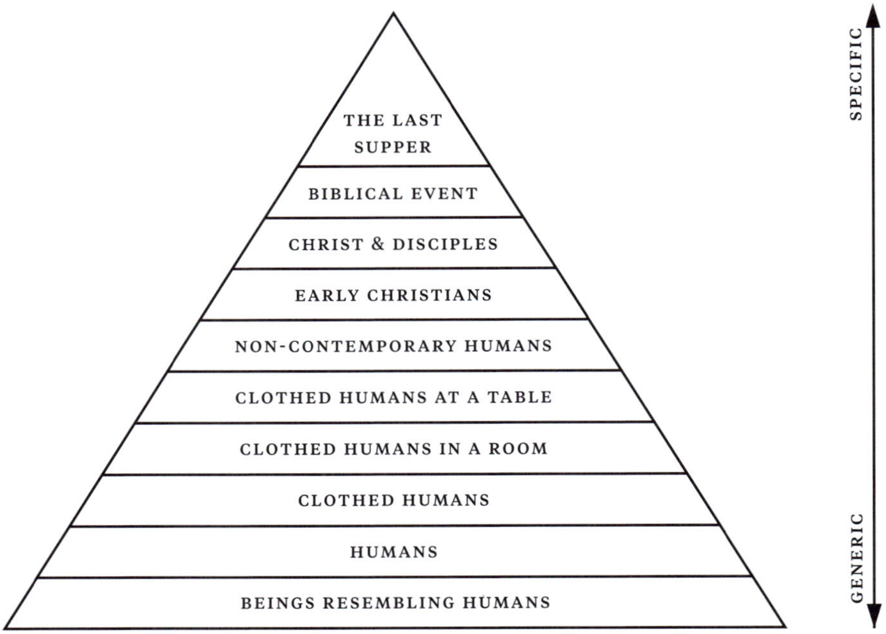

1.4 | Triangle of Content for Leonardo's Last Supper

that, like the Last Supper, outsiders could not have heard. This difficulty in interpreting images from an unfamiliar culture is something of which many Aboriginal peoples are aware. A key conceptual opposition in certain Australian languages is between 'outside' and 'inside', which refer to levels of cultural knowledge:

> For example, *mikararn* is the outside word for a particular species of snake. *Mundukul* is an inside word for the same snake. It is not a secret word but the one most often used when talking about the snake as an ancestral being. Although both words have as their referent 'death adder', *mundukul* refers specifically to the ancestral snake as the creator of thunder and lightning.
> (Morphy 1991, 79)

> Paintings also reflect this dual reality. Children gradually learn to see the more esoteric meanings of paintings as they gain knowledge of ancestral activities. … there is a continuous movement between the understanding of the secular and the sacred which Kunwinjku express as a movement from understanding the 'outside' to 'inside' meanings of things.
> (Taylor 1996, 153)

When Kunwinjku artists today sell their works to strangers, they expect the buyers to be able to see the most outside meanings of the paintings, to recognize the motifs at a superficial level, but to have no understanding of the layers of mythological, ancestral and spiritual knowledge available to those who understand the inside meanings (Taylor 1996, 16). In fact, there are levels of outside and inside also within clans, with children and women knowing more than strangers, male adults knowing more than women and children, and artists and senior clan members having the most developed understanding of imagery. When looking at a painting such as that in fig. 1.5, Panofsky would have identified two animals and a bird, and he might (if he was lucky) have classed the animals as possums; but he could not have known that the bird was a koel cuckoo (*guwak*), that the animals were ancestral beings (*wangarr*), or what was taking place, without knowing the myth portrayed:

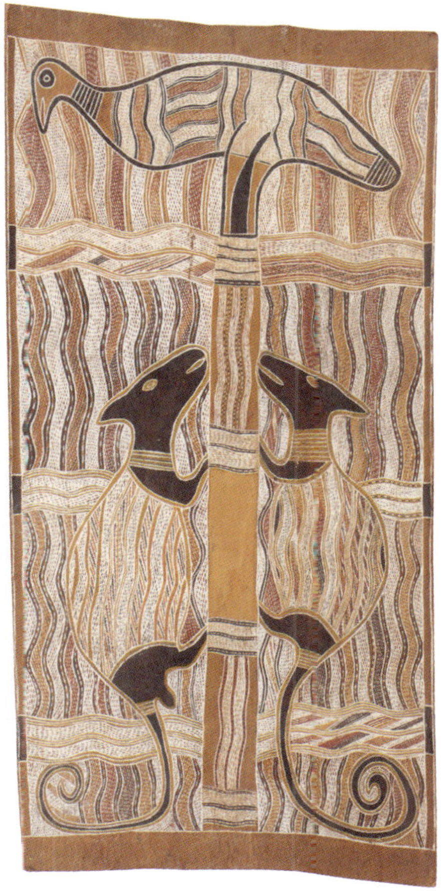

1.5 | Narritjin Maymuru, *The Marrawili Tree*, 1977. National Museum of Australia, Canberra

> Two guwak, two possums, two emus, and a number of other wangarr ancestors set out on a journey .... Each night they camped, and the guwak would sit on top of a native cashew tree (*ganyawu*) and eat its fruit. The possum would climb the tree ... spinning its fur into lengths of string. When he had spun a certain length, which differed from place to place, the guwak would tell him to stop. That length of string was given to the clan in whose country they were and subsequently became the length of the possum-fur string used by that clan .... The guwak and the possum ... talked to Barrama, a mythical being, and told him they were looking for a land to settle in. Barrama told them to keep walking southeast to a country by the sea, where the sand was white-hot and there was plenty of seafood. When they got there they would find a *marrawili* tree, and under it they should make their camp. When they got there they found that it was as Barrama had said; the *marrawili* tree was there, but otherwise the landscape was featureless.
> (Morphy 1991, 220)

This myth concerns how the land of the Manggalili clan was formed in the Dreamtime, and within the clan the story as told above is considered 'outside'; but, for Panofsky, it would have been very much 'inside' (Morphy 1991, 221–44). The situation is entirely analogous to that of an Aboriginal Australian asked to view the Last Supper with no knowledge of the 'inside' meanings of European culture.

Iconographic feedback

One might think that when trying to interpret a painting with an unfamiliar subject one begins by working out what is visible in the picture, the figures and the objects, then one looks for a subject that will fit this particular constellation of creatures and things, and only then will one be able to appreciate its significance within the culture that produced it. Panofsky seems to have thought of the iconological process along these lines; he laid out a set order of interpretation, leading up from pre-iconography to iconology: "as the correct identification of motifs is the prerequisite of their correct iconographical analysis, so is the correct analysis of images, stories and allegories the prerequisite of their correct iconological interpretation" (32). Yet from our analysis of what the Australian might have been expected to understand from the contemplation of Leonardo's Last Supper, and what Panofsky might have been expected to understand from Manggalili bark painting, it seems that the identification of motifs is dependent on the painting's iconographic meaning. A viewer cannot know that figures are meant to be human without knowing the story in which they are involved. And as we try to ascertain iconographic meaning, iconological significance is of key importance.

When we decide that Leonardo's painting represents a Last Supper, we are basing our identification on assumptions about what sort of iconography to expect, or not to expect, in late fifteenth-century Italy. It is after all logically possible that this picture does not represent the Last Supper, but rather a scene from a story that Leonardo himself invented, involving a group of characters who like to make ceramic facsimiles of foodstuffs that they enter into competitions, and that what we are witnessing here is the judge of the competition, in the centre, announcing the winner. And perhaps too it was only meant to represent this scene on Mondays, Wednesdays and Fridays, but on the other days of the week Leonardo intended it to mean a scene from a different story, in which the man in the centre is expelled from a dining club. Now, of course, this is a ridiculous interpretation of a fifteenth-century fresco painted for the refectory of a Dominican convent in Milan. In the European art of the time subjects do not just arbitrarily change on different days of the week. The scenario I have just sketched is one we might expect from a conceptual artist today, but not from Leonardo da Vinci. And it is equally impossible to imagine that Leonardo would dare, or would want, to paint one (or two) of his own narrative inventions in the dining hall of a Dominican convent. He would certainly have respected decorum and represented a Christian scene in a space built for an Order of Christian friars (Gombrich 1972a, 7–8). To do otherwise at the time could have been dangerous – the Holy Inquisition was largely run by the Dominicans.

This is all undeniable, but it makes our point; for these are iconological assumptions, concerning personality, religious attitudes and what we expect within a particular culture in a certain era. What we are doing here is using our knowledge of Renaissance civilization to delimit the possibilities of what Leonardo can plausibly be thought to have represented. We use iconological interpretation to support our iconographical analysis; and our iconographical analysis allows us to identify the motifs in the image. It is because we know that the image is a Last Supper that we know the figures are human and that the objects are simple material objects (Gombrich 1941, 'Introduction', 1–3; Baxandall 1988, 35–36; Casati 2004, 168; Taylor 2006a, 4). If the story were some magical tale, the walls might be made of cloud, and the food might be able to speak.

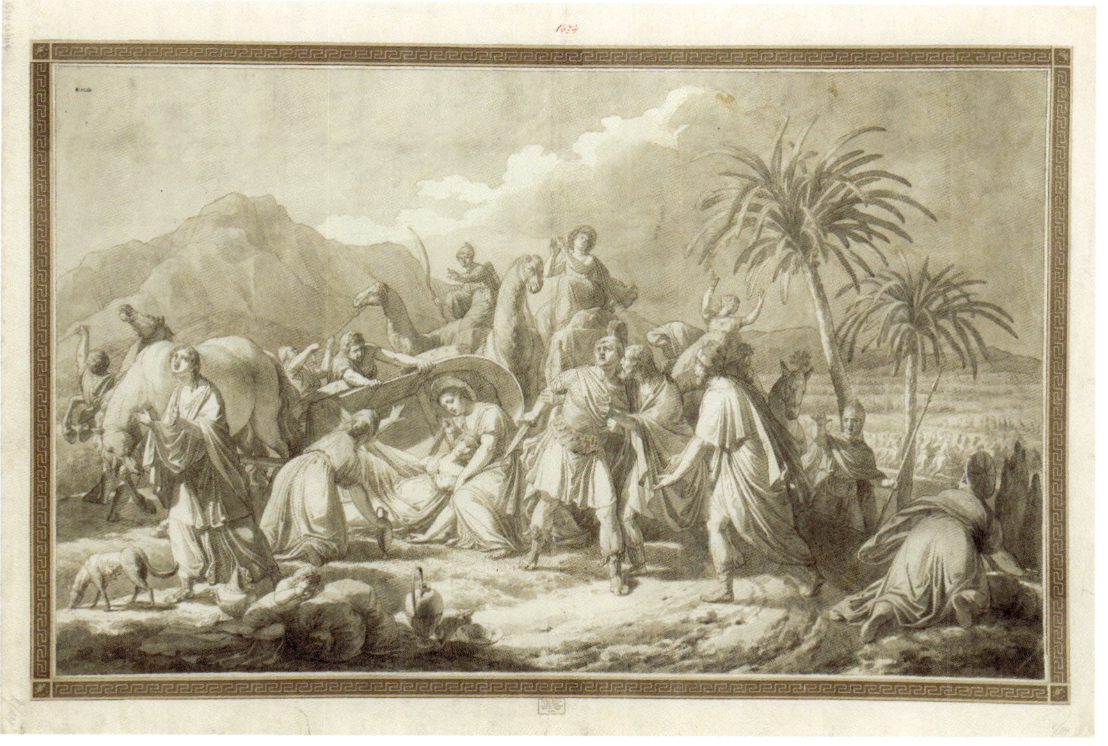

1.6 | Franz Caucig, Scene to be identified. Akademie, Vienna

The direction of interpretation here seems to be going from iconology via iconography to pre-iconography – the opposite of what Panofsky suggested. In an actual case of iconographic decoding, however, the intuitive assumption that one begins with the pre-iconography and proceeds from there to the iconography can seem (perhaps one should say 'feel') correct. Take the image in fig. 1.6, for example. I was asked to identify the narrative represented in this drawing, which was made by the Slovene Neoclassicist Franz Caucig (1755–1828). I began by trying to understand what things were depicted in the image. Before I tell you how I went about it and the answer I eventually managed to find, you might like to study the image yourself, to see if you can work out what is going on.

Some of the content was easy to decipher – mountains, horses, a dog, palm trees, dromedaries, people in ancient dress – and of course I took the last three to be significant clues; clearly this event had not taken place in southern Europe in the artist's time: it looked like a scene from the Near East in the Greco-Roman period. Then there were two aspects of the image that were harder to read. There was the curving shape to the left of centre, with a woman reclining in front of, or within it; and there was the man nearby who was holding a sword. I was not sure what he wanted to do with it.

The drawing was sent to me shortly after the beginnings of the internet, and I would not have been able to identify the subject in preceding years except by happening to read the book it illustrates – an event that would probably have occurred years later.[16] But now there was this new and powerful tool, and so I set to work typing words into a search engine. I decided after a while that the curved shape might be an overturned waggon, and that the woman lying in front of it might have been wounded in an accident; and I thought – though it was only one possibility among several – that the man with the sword might be trying to kill himself. After feeding different combinations of words into the search box, I eventually hit on a passing reference in an online history lecture, which said that King Herod once tried to kill himself after witnessing his mother wounded in a waggon accident. Knowing that the ancient historian who would be most likely to describe an event involving Herod was Flavius Josephus, I went to consult a copy of his *Antiquities of the Jews*, and found this passage:

> [Herod was] once almost going to kill himself, upon the overthrow of a waggon, and the danger his mother was then in of being killed; and this on two accounts, because of his great concern for her, and because he was afraid lest, by this delay, the enemy should overtake him in the pursuit: but as he was drawing his sword, and going to kill himself therewith, those that were present restrained him, and being so many in number, were too hard for him; and told him that he ought not to desert them, and leave them a prey to their enemies, for that it was not the part of a brave man to free himself from the distresses he was in, and to overlook his friends that were in the same distresses also.
> (Flavius Josephus, *Antiquities of the Jews*, 13.8)

It was only after reading this passage that I noticed two important 'pre-iconographic' elements: the man's hand resting on Herod's arm, restraining his action; and the army in the middle distance, which I could now read as Herod's troops, fleeing their enemies.

Here, then, I identified (most of) the pre-iconographic elements before I identified the iconography. Or did I? Some of my readings were conjectural and were only confirmed once I had found the key to the whole composition. I did not know that the man in the crested helmet was trying to kill himself – he might have been trying to kill someone else or just idly waving his sword about – and I did not know that the curved shape was an overturned waggon, I just thought that it might be. These were conjectures waiting for an explanation that would make sense of them. But even the easily identifiable parts of the pre-iconography were conjectures, too. They seemed less hypothetical because I had a sense of when the drawing was made, and what kinds of events the artist was likely to have been trying to represent. An artist around 1800 was clearly not representing a scene from science fiction, and so the creatures in the drawing could not have been intergalactic beings, talking trees or robot dogs. I did not even bother to consider such options, of course, even though there was nothing in the image itself that would have made such a reading impossible (cf. Eco 1976, 190). I might also have tried out readings based on fairy stories, or epic romance, with wizards and magical

16 Gombrich 1941, 'Introduction', p. 9: "And this is really the advice given by all scholars who were successful in establishing the subjects of their particular field of works of art: to impress the content of the pictures in question as clearly and firmly as possible into the memory and then to occupy oneself as much as possible with the literature favoured by this period – waiting for the happy chance that the particular constellation of protagonists may finally turn up".

beings. But I knew the iconological profile of the artist, Franz Caucig, and knew that, like many of his European contemporaries, he tended to represent episodes from ancient literature. This particular image looked like a scene from ancient history, so I felt sure that his horses would be real horses, his camels real camels, his landscape on planet Earth.

What I was attempting to find was a coherence between the iconology, the pre-iconography and the iconography, in which none was a 'prerequisite', as Panofsky put it. The manner of depiction suggested a scene from ancient history, and this coheres with what I knew about Caucig's art. The scene then cohered with the narrative of Josephus, although it is always possible to find more than one narrative to fit an image, as we will see in Chapter 5. Pre-iconography, iconography and iconology are all assumptions, and the aim is to find the best possible fit between assumptions; this best possible fit will form our best guess about the actual iconography and pre-iconography of the image.

Despite his statement about 'prerequisites', Panofsky himself seems to have been aware that pre-iconography, iconography and iconology feed back into one another:

> But we must bear in mind that the neatly differentiated categories, which ... seem to indicate three independent spheres of meaning, refer in reality to aspects of one phenomenon, namely, the work of art as a whole. So that, in actual work, the methods of approach which here appear as three unrelated operations of research merge with each other into one organic and indivisible process.
> (Panofsky 1955, 32)

This appears to be a contradiction of his earlier suggestion that the levels of meaning form a sequence, and perhaps it is. Like any good writer, Panofsky may have been trying to convey his ideas to his readers in intelligible stages, even if that undermined an internally consistent philosophical position (Hart 1993, 29).

The scope of iconography

The quotation I gave at the beginning of the previous section, in which Panofsky suggested that his three 'spheres of meaning' were arranged in a sequence, was part of a larger statement in which he delimited the scope of iconography:

> And as the correct identification of motifs is the prerequisite of their correct iconographical analysis, so is the correct analysis of images, stories and allegories the prerequisite of their correct iconological interpretation – unless we deal with works of art in which the whole sphere of secondary or conventional subject matter is eliminated and a direct transition from motifs to content is effected, as is the case with European landscape painting, still life and genre, not to mention 'non-objective' art.
> (Panofsky 1955, 32)

Panofsky argued that iconography concerns itself with some kinds of representation but not with others. The iconographer, in Panofsky's view, is concerned with the identification of attributes, symbols, allegories and narratives:

> *Secondary or conventional subject matter* ... is apprehended by realizing that a male figure with a knife represents St Bartholomew, that a female figure with a peach in her hand is a personification of veracity, that a group of figures seated at a dinner table in a certain arrangement and in certain poses represents the Last Supper, or that two figures fighting each other in a certain manner represent the Combat of Vice and Virtue. In doing this we connect artistic motifs and combinations of artistic motifs (compositions) with themes or concepts. Motifs thus recognized as carriers of a secondary or conventional meaning may be called images, and combinations of images are what the ancient theorists of art called *invenzioni*; we are wont to call them stories and allegories. The identification of such images, stories and allegories is the domain of what is normally referred to as 'iconography'.
> (Panofsky 1955, 29)

These statements by Panofsky have led to the impression that iconography is a subject with which only art historians need concern themselves, and indeed only art historians who study a particular style of imagery, in which attributes, symbols and narratives are predominant. As noted in the Introduction (p. 13 above), philosophers tend to think of iconography as a feature of a sub-class of images, especially of traditional works of art, and it is not surprising they should think this, given what Panofsky himself wrote in the standard introduction to the subject. But Panofsky was I think wrong to limit the scope of iconography in this way. Landscape, still life, genre and abstract art should be thought of as possessing iconographic senses, and so too – although Panofsky does not mention them – should photographs.

Take for example a painting that Panofsky would presumably think of as one "in which the whole sphere of secondary or conventional subject matter is eliminated and a direct transition from motifs to content is effected", Paul Cezanne's *Trees and Houses* (fig. 1.7). Panofsky would presumably argue that since this painting depicts some trees and some houses, and is presented as a representation of some trees and some houses, no more, then the conventional subject matter has been 'eliminated'. But making an image of this kind is certainly conventional. Imagine what his Aboriginal observer would have made of it; he would be asking himself why these trees had been depicted, and what the unfamiliar shape in the distance might be. What was the significance of the trees? Did they form part of some ancestral story? Were they meant to represent tree totems (Howitt 1904)? Were they perhaps supposed to be images of the arboreal mothers of 'tree people' (Munn 1986)? Or were they trees inhabited by spirit children (Spencer 1914)? The Aboriginal viewer would cast hypotheses back and forth as he tried to make sense of the image. And if he eventually learned that these trees were not spirits, nor ancestors, nor totems, but just trees, then that might surprise him, since making images that have no inside meaning at all is not something that is done in Aboriginal society.[17] Simply to make a picture of a tree with no possible further significance would seem to an indigenous Australian – and indeed to most other people outside Eurasia before the era of globalization – to be an odd thing to do.

---

17 In some contexts, however, images are made more for their 'outside' than their 'inside' significance; see Taylor 1996, 17–20.

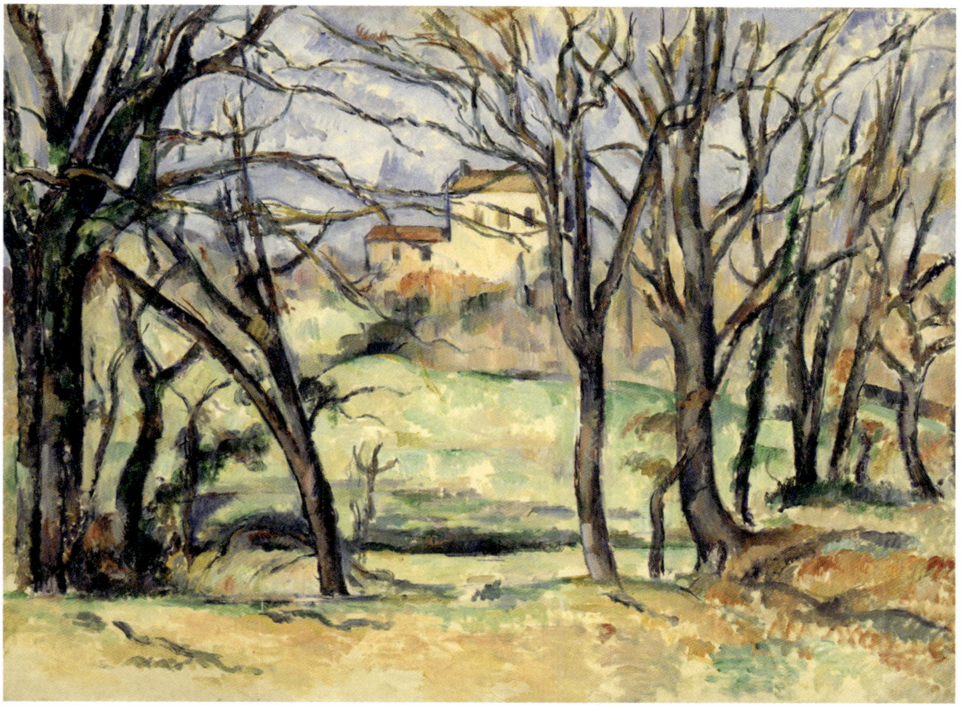

1.7 | Paul Cezanne, *Trees and Houses near the Jas de Bouffan*, 1885–86.
The Metropolitan Museum of Art, New York

If we find images of trees, just trees and nothing more, normal and unexceptional, that is because we have become used to a particular cultural practice of our society. The spirit-free landscapes of Western art, which emerged in ancient Rome and were revived in the European Renaissance (Gombrich 1966), are a telling indicator of the secular world view of those who made and bought them. Which is the same thing as to say that painting 'just trees' is a cultural convention, and so we can hardly say that, in images of this sort, the conventional subject has been eliminated. It may be easier to learn how to read landscapes than to learn how to read allegories or scenes from literature, but we do need to learn how to do it.

Since landscapes have conventional meanings, they have iconographies in the Panofskian sense, and the same can be said for still lifes.[18] Simple objects may be 'dead nature' as far as European cultures are concerned, but they come alive in other cultural contexts. In areas of Africa and pre-Columbian America, spirits were thought capable of entering into things – stones, pots, tusks, fruit, vegetables – and granting material objects the power to feel, decide and act (Cobo [1653] 1990, 45–46; MacGaffey 1994, 123–31; Curtis 2018, 20). Images of vegetables were made as ceramic bottles in ancient

18 Some still lifes have been given allegorical readings, but many others seem to be representations of 'just' objects; I discussed both varieties in Taylor 1995.

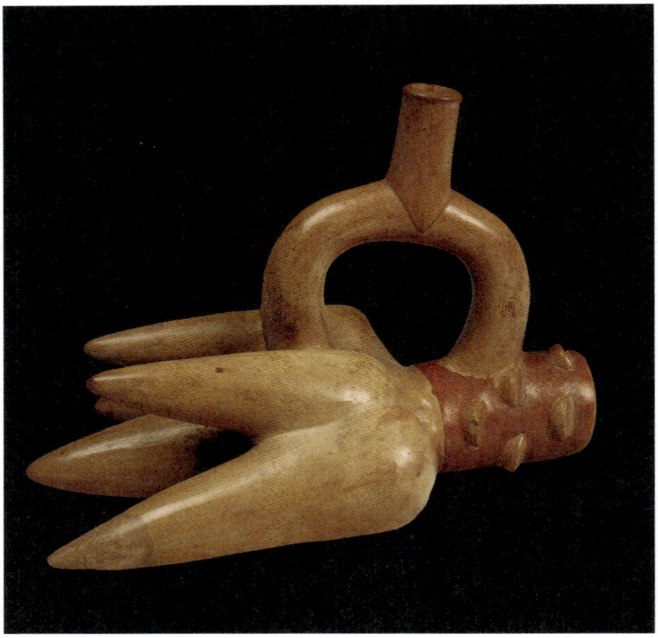

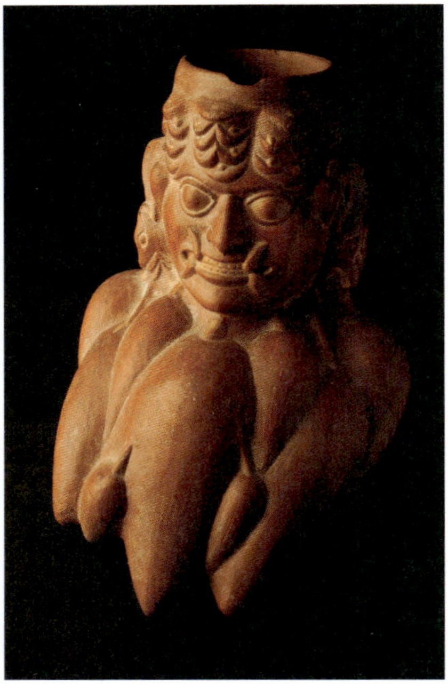

1.8, 1.9 | Moche, Cassava bottles, 1–800 AD. Museo Larco, Lima

Peru (fig. 1.8), but it is unlikely that they were thought of as nothing more than 'still lifes'; on other bottles we see fanged heads on top of the vegetables, turning an ordinary cassava into a supernatural being (fig. 1.9) (Donnan 1978, 153; Taylor 2008b). Compare this with a European painting of the same botanical specimen (fig. 1.10): here the artist has tried to describe the appearance of the tuberous roots as carefully as he can, to convey their appearance to people in Europe who had not seen this plant before. He does not think that the cassava is supernatural. This painting shows a cassava plant just as a cassava plant, and to make images of this kind is to follow a cultural convention. Even if deities do not live in cassava roots, making images of 'just cassava roots' is to adopt what we can call an iconographic position, and one that an anthropologist from a distant culture would need to learn.

That genre paintings, anonymous scenes of daily life, have iconographies is also clear. To make pictures of individuals who are unnamed, who have no specific identities, is rare in world imagery. The rise of the anonymity of the subject is in fact one of the most striking aspects of image-making over the past five centuries, and it is all the more remarkable that this phenomenon should have carried over into the age of photography, which by its very nature reproduces the specific, not the generic. For any painting, and for any photograph, we can ask: are these individuals/objects named or anonymous? Specific or generic? Our answers to these questions are inevitably iconographic.

As for non-objective art, here too we can argue that to paint a pattern that is thought to have no depictive content at all is to engage in a culturally specific, conventional activity. Patterns that look abstract to Westerners can be read in representational terms

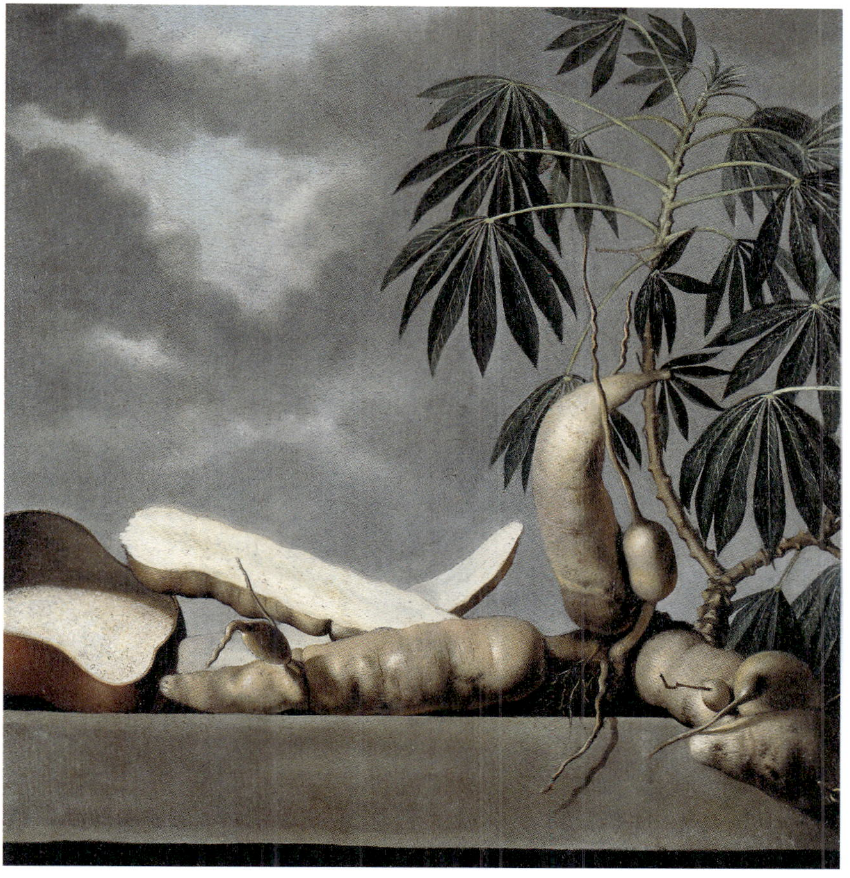

1.10 | Albert Eckhout, Cassava roots, 1643. Nationalmuseet, Copenhagen

in other cultures. Franz Boas brought together numerous examples of this phenomenon from the Americas, Oceania and Africa in his famous study, *Primitive Art* (1927).[19] There is no reason why abstract paintings by Wassily Kandinsky or Clifford Styll could not be given similar representational readings: it is just a matter of symbolic ingenuity (Goodman 1978, 61). If these works are presented as rigorously non-depictive, then that too is an iconographic position (although we can think of it as a position outside iconography), one which is typical of our culture. Panofsky's restriction of the scope of iconography does not seem justified on his own definition of the term as 'conventional subject matter'.

19 For more examples of the phenomenon, see Basedow 1925; Rattray 1927; Griaule 1963; Faris 1972; Munn 1973; Gombrich 1984; Le Quellec 2004; Beran 2011; Forge 2017b. For decoration that has many layers of meaning but apparently no representational intent, see Strathern and Strathern 1971. For words of caution on the stability of symbolical meanings over time, between and within regions, see Spooner 1988.

2. Resemblance, depiction and representation

Resemblance

The terms that will be introduced in this chapter, 'resemblance', 'depiction' and 'representation', have much in common with Panofsky's concepts of pre-iconography and iconography.[1] 'Representation', as we will use it here, has a meaning close to that of 'iconography', in Panofsky's narrow sense of 'secondary or conventional subject matter', while 'resemblance' and 'depiction' divide up Panofsky's concept of 'pre-iconography'. Even though these words add only so much to Panofsky's terminology, they provide us with several advantages. One is that they are grammatically more versatile; all three spawn verbs, 'resemble', 'depict' and 'represent', and these make talking about images easier. What is more, the verbs are transitive, they take objects – an image depicts a woman, represents Cleopatra – and, as we will see in Chapter 3, this allows us to introduce distinctions that are hard to make using Panofsky's terms, for example the idea of an image that has an iconography and can be said to depict, but which does not represent. And we will also be taking the word 'depiction' and dividing it in two, into 'conceptual depiction' and 'indexical depiction', a distinction that will allow us to talk about the differences between photographs and other kinds of image.

'Resemblance', 'depiction' and 'representation', as we ordinarily use them, are words with broad ranges of meaning. 'Depiction' and 'representation', when they are used to discuss images, are often used as synonyms, and 'representation' is also often used in connection with signs that are not images, such as diagrams, names or sentences. In this book, however, I will always use them in the senses outlined in this chapter, except when I am quoting or paraphrasing others; in fact, I have been doing so throughout the book up till now.

When Nelson Goodman wrote witheringly of "the most naïve view of representation" his criticism was based on the fact that, if "A represents B to the extent that A resembles B", then A will always resemble more things than it represents:

> An object resembles itself to the maximum degree but rarely represents itself; resemblance, unlike representation, is reflexive. Again, unlike representation, resemblance is symmetric: B is as much like A as A is like B, but while a painting may represent the Duke of Wellington, the Duke doesn't represent the painting. Furthermore, in many cases neither one of a pair of very like objects represents the

1 I first used these terms in Taylor 2008a.

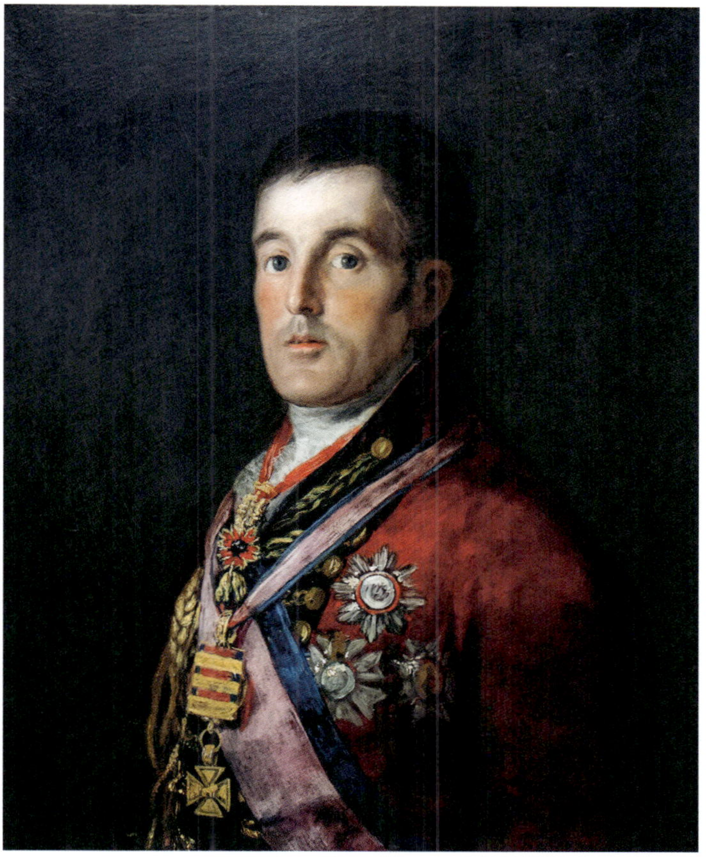

2.1 | Francisco de Goya, Portrait of the Duke of Wellington, 1812–14.
The National Gallery, London

> other: none of the automobiles off an assembly line is a picture of any of the rest; and a man is not normally a representation of another man, even his twin brother. Plainly, resemblance in any degree is no sufficient condition for representation.[2] (Goodman 1976, 4)

It is hard to disagree with this; resemblance and representation are two different things, and just because A *resembles* B, we cannot deduce that A *represents* B. The Duke of Wellington's reflection in his mirror and the Duke of Wellington's brother both resemble him, but they do not represent him. What is more, Goya's portrait of the Duke of Wellington (fig. 2.1) resembles plenty of other men; in fact, there is a good chance that

2 The words 'sufficient' and 'necessary' in what follows are standard terms in logic, see Brennan 2017: "For example, without water and oxygen, there would be no human life; hence these things are necessary conditions for the existence of human beings. Cockneys, according to the traditional definition, are all and only those born within the sound of the Bow Bells. Hence birth within the specified area is both a necessary and a sufficient condition for being a Cockney."

it resembles a number of men more than it resembles the duke, since it does not give the impression of being a very good likeness. And we can say that it resembles all men, and women, more closely than it resembles a dog or a lizard; also, that it resembles a dog or a lizard more than it resembles a spider.

Resemblance is a sliding scale, and Wellington's portrait resembles pretty much anything, to some degree. Added to which, the duke's portrait, even if it is the most exact likeness of its sitter, could also be a representation of his imaginary twin brother, or of a man who looked a lot like the duke, or of another portrait of the duke (the illustration of the duke's portrait in this book is an image of the portrait in the National Gallery, London), or of the duke's spirit, or of the virtue of Valour.[3] So when Goodman writes that "the plain fact is that a picture, to represent an object, must be a symbol for it, stand for it, refer to it; and that no degree of resemblance is sufficient to establish the requisite relationship of reference" (5), he is surely right.[4] Everything resembles something, but that does not make everything an image; to use Goodman's example, a car is not an image of another car of the same model, even though it resembles it exactly (although a conceptual artist could present a car as an image of a car).[5]

For something to be an image of something else, there must be an iconic *intentionality*, as philosophers put it.[6] I will be using this word again, and should introduce it here:

> Intentionality is the power of minds and mental states to be about, to represent, or to stand for, things, properties and states of affairs. To say of an individual's mental states that they have intentionality is to say that they are mental representations or that they have contents. Furthermore, to the extent that a speaker utters words from some natural language or draws pictures or symbols from a formal language for the purpose of conveying to others the contents of her mental states, these artifacts used by a speaker too have contents or intentionality.
> (Jacob 2019)

A car off a production line does not have intentionality, it just looks like other cars. A car presented as an image of other cars by a conceptual artist does have intentionality, bestowed on it by the artist. The difference between something that looks like something else and something that is an image of something else is precisely this property of intentionality (Jonas 1961, 163; Blumson 2014, 139–58). Note that intentionality is not being used here (or anywhere else in this book) to mean 'having intentions'.

Resemblance will always *underdetermine* representation (and depiction) (Grzankowski 2015, 6–7). Which means that a portrait of the Duke of Wellington resembles the duke, but since it also resembles the duke's brother etc., we cannot

---

3 To be pedantic, Goya's portrait represents the Marquess of Wellington, since Wellington was not yet a duke when it was painted.

4 Although, as I argue below, it is not clear that images should be thought of as referring to objects; see also the discussion of 'naming' and 'conceptual depiction' later in this chapter.

5 Hans Jonas (1961) argued that an image cannot be a perfect copy because "if I copy a hammer in every respect, I get another hammer, not an image of the hammer" (163). I think it depends on the intention of the hammer copier.

6 On 'iconic', see ftn. 16 below.

know, purely by considering its resemblance, what it is supposed to mean (depict, represent). So, when we are trying to establish the meaning of an image, we cannot rely on resemblance alone; there must be other indicators, which allow us to decide the image's content. In the particular case of the portrait by Goya, we think that it represents the Duke of Wellington, rather than, say, a man Goya knew who looked like the duke and whom the artist portrayed in a general's uniform for a joke, because we assume that it would hardly be in the National Gallery in London if Wellington had not been led to believe that it was a portrait of him; and while that does not in itself disprove the scenario of Goya's joke, it makes it even less likely than it was already. Why would Goya want to engage in such a convoluted and pointless prank? Here again we are using iconological arguments to establish the iconography, as we did in the discussion of Leonardo's Last Supper in the previous chapter, and as we always must, for any image.

There are parallels here with current arguments in the philosophy of language, and without wanting to stray too far into a complex and contested area of enquiry, it may be useful to gesture at some of the similarities. Just as we are claiming that resemblance underdetermines depiction and representation, so philosophers and linguists note that 'literal meaning' can underdetermine 'speaker meaning'. As John Searle has put it:

> Suppose I go into the restaurant and order a meal. Suppose I say, speaking literally, "Bring me a steak with fried potatoes." Even though the utterance is meant and understood literally, the number of possible misinterpretations is strictly limitless. I take it for granted that they will not deliver the meal to my house, or to my place of work. I take it for granted that the steak will not be encased in concrete, or petrified. It will not be stuffed into my pockets or spread over my head. But none of these assumptions was made explicit in the literal utterance.
> (Searle 1992, 180)

Here Searle is talking about background assumptions, but one could also note the ambiguity of the words themselves. Anyone uttering this sentence assumes that the steak will be made of beef, not lamb or horse or elephant, that the potatoes will not be sweet potatoes, that they would be sliced before they were cooked, and would be fried in butter and/or vegetable oil rather than linseed or engine oil. We mean much more than we say. Whether this is true of every sentence in a language, or of many or of some, is still a matter of debate in philosophy. Those who believe that every or nearly every sentence in a language needs to be interpreted with the help of assumption and context are called radical contextualists (e.g. Searle 1978; Travis 1997; Recanati 2010), while those who believe that the phenomenon of context-dependence is very limited are called semantic minimalists (e.g. Borg 2004; Cappelen and Lepore 2005; Bach 2006). The reader will have noticed that this book tends toward a position of radical contextualism with respect to images.

Before we continue to argue for that position, we should stock up with two more technical terms from current linguistic theory. In the philosophy of language and linguistics a distinction is drawn between 'pragmatics' and 'semantics'. Pragmatics is the analysis of all those aspects of communication that are needed to bridge the gap between literal meaning and speaker's meaning, e.g. presupposition, implication, relevance, reference (deixis) and so forth. Semantics, on the other hand, is the analysis of literal meaning. This at least is one way of thinking about the difference between

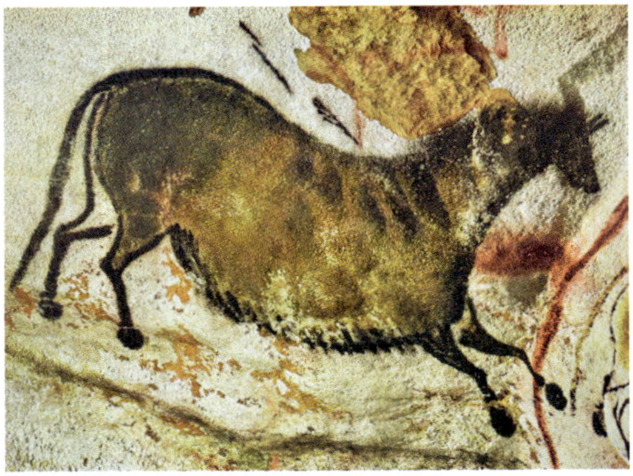

2.2 | 'Chinese' horse no. 1, c. 15,000–10,000 BC.
Caves of Lascaux, France

semantics and pragmatics, but drawing the distinction has proved hard to do, and there are several competing versions (Recanati 2004; Ezcurdia and Stainton 2013). One thing that everyone is agreed on is that in the study of language both pragmatics and semantics are needed; the disagreement concerns their relative importance, and how the two can be taken to relate to one another (Borg 2012; Korta and Perry 2020).

There is one more complication: sometimes 'semantics' is used to refer to the study of meaning in its entirety, so that semantics (in the narrow sense) is part of semantics (in the broad sense), just as iconography (in the narrow sense) is part of iconography (in the broad sense). But whereas iconography (in the broad sense) is closely related to semantics (in the broad sense), since both are the general subjects that study meaning in their respective fields, the narrow senses of semantics and iconography bear little relation to one another.

Depiction

Any image resembles many things, some closely, some only vaguely, and what the beholder needs to do is to establish which of those things a particular image *depicts*. Resemblance presents a range of options, from which the beholder must select the content of the image. An image will resemble many things, but it will (usually) depict one thing, or a set of things.

For Panofsky, pre-iconography was a matter of common experience, and when looking at an image like the one in fig. 2.2, from the cave of Lascaux, he would have said that it simply depicts a horse.[7] It does indeed resemble a horse, no doubt about that, and perhaps it was meant to depict a horse. But this is not an inevitable conclusion. It might have been intended to depict, say, a spirit in the form of a horse (Frazer 1912, 343–46), or the totem of a clan (Frazer 1910, 221, 234, 238, 248, 251, 274, 292, 314),[8] or the recently departed spirit of a member of a horse clan (Evans-Pritchard 1937, 24), or a horse-shaped

7 I am again putting words into Panofsky's mouth, but for a robust attitude towards Palaeolithic images that look like horses, see Stumpel 1993; Stumpel 1995.

8 The word 'totem' was famously attacked by Claude Lévi-Strauss (1964) but survived the assault. See Gunn 1992, 114–21; Ingold 2000; Rose 2013.

fetish (McGaffey 1990, 55) and so on. Since we know nothing about the world view of the Palaeolithic people who painted this horse, we can do no more than speculate about their depictive intentions. Here, as Panofsky would have said, "all of us are Australian bushmen". But while he took this phrase to apply to the iconographic level of meaning in the image, it also applies to the pre-iconographic level, or rather the depictive aspect of the pre-iconographic level.

Our horse-like painting in Lascaux resembles a horse but also a number of other beings, and it would be interesting to know which of them it was intended to depict at the time. As has often been observed, especially by literary critics, in talking about intentions we need to tread carefully; sometimes questions about the intentionality of images can be settled by asking what the maker of the image meant or intended, but there are other times when the maker of the image will not know the answer to the question (Barthes 1968; Burke 1998; Friend 2017). It is possible that the painter of this horse was asked by clan elders to paint an image that looked like a horse, but which the elders then interpreted as a spiritual being in a mythological story of which the painter was ignorant. In a case like this, the painter would not be expected to know the meaning of his or her own image.[9]

Quite what an image is taken to depict in any particular context will vary depending on the nature of the society, its semantic customs and its relations of power. Among the Palaeolithic people who went down into the cave of Lascaux at the time fig. 2.2 was painted, it is possible that painters were valued members of society whose authority was widely respected, and who would be questioned about the iconographies of the images they had made. Alternatively, it may be that paintings were made on behalf of clans, and that the clans decided what they depicted, perhaps without revealing their decisions either to the artist or to other clans. It is also possible that there were disagreements, with different groups reading images in different ways; and this scenario becomes more likely with the passage of time. The paintings in Lascaux were in place for two or three millennia before the end of the Ice Age, and might have been interpreted differently by people who went down into the cave over the centuries.

This is all just speculation, but it shows that the meanings of images can be generated in a variety of ways. Whether the meaning is grounded in the intention of the artist, or of the commissioner, or of some of their contemporaries, or of strangers living millennia later, the motifs of the image are likely to be specified. A viewer from any period looking at fig. 2.2 could theoretically see it as a cluster of possible resemblances – horse/spirit/fetish/totem and so on – but they may prefer to see it as a depiction of a horse, or a spirit, or a fetish, or a totem. They will select an intentionality, and they may well suppose that this is *the* intentionality of the image. This is a common enough response to an image, in any culture. There are examples of images changing their depictive identities – we will discuss some in Chapter 3 (p. 94) – but for the most part images are thought to depict just one thing at a time.[10]

Suppose that a particular viewer, living at the period when the painting was made, saw the image as a depiction of a horse. Then the next question will be: which horse?

9 For similar scenarios in Africa and Melanesia, see Biebuyck 1973, 227–23; Küchler 1987, 240–41.
10 There are cases of images that are thought to *represent* several different (fictional) objects at once; see p. 146 below.

Was this an image of an actual flesh and blood horse, which was known to the artist's clan (maybe they sacrificed it)?[11] Or was it perhaps a horse that only existed in some story? Was the horse given a name? Or was it 'just a horse', perhaps an image made in response to the request: "paint a horse (some horse, any horse)". Whichever scenario is accepted, these meanings will correspond to Panofsky's 'iconography' (in the narrow sense). In what follows we will be using the word 'representation' to describe this iconographic level of meaning; we will say that the image reproduced in fig. 2.2 represents a named horse, or represents a specified horse or represents a generic horse. So it might be that the painting in Lascaux:

resembles a horse, a spirit, a fetish, a totem and more
depicts a horse
represents the horse we sacrificed yesterday to the spirits of the underworld

Note how resemblance underdetermines depiction, and depiction underdetermines representation.[12] We cannot tell, purely from looking at the resemblance of an image, what it depicts, and we cannot deduce, purely from an awareness of the depiction of an image, what it represents. You may think of this image as depicting a horse, and a contemporary of the Lascaux artist might have agreed with you about that, but that will not tell you what the people of the Palaeolithic thought the image represented. To understand what an image depicts or represents we must rely on information that lies outside the image itself.

Conceptual depiction

The people of Lascaux may have thought of the image in fig. 2.2 as a depiction of a horse, but of course that is, at one level, impossible, because they did not speak English, and so did not share the word 'horse'. It may be thought that this is hardly an objection, since they probably had a word in their language with which they could indicate a horse. Maybe they did – but then again, perhaps they had a word that referred to large quadrupeds with furry pelts, like deer, horses and bison, which they did not differentiate verbally.

We do not need to get involved with this issue now (we will return to it at the end of Chapter 6). Let us consider instead if the people of Lascaux thought the image in fig. 2.2 depicted a mammal. All horses are mammals, and so, we might think, the painting on the wall of Lascaux depicts a mammal. Of course, the people who lived when this image was made did not have the concept of 'mammal', which only entered the world's languages in the eighteenth century. We might then feel confident that, for them, the image did not depict a mammal. But what about for us? When we look at the painting from Lascaux, do we see a mammal? If we do, then we need to accept a situation of depictive relativism, in which anyone who does not have the concept of 'mammal' will not see a painting of a horse as depicting a mammal, and anyone who does have the concept will see it as depicting a mammal.

---

11 See Chapter 3, ftn. 31.

12 The reader might ask why the image could not *depict* the horse we sacrificed yesterday. The answer is that it could, as will become clear once we have distinguished conceptual and indexical depiction in the next two sections.

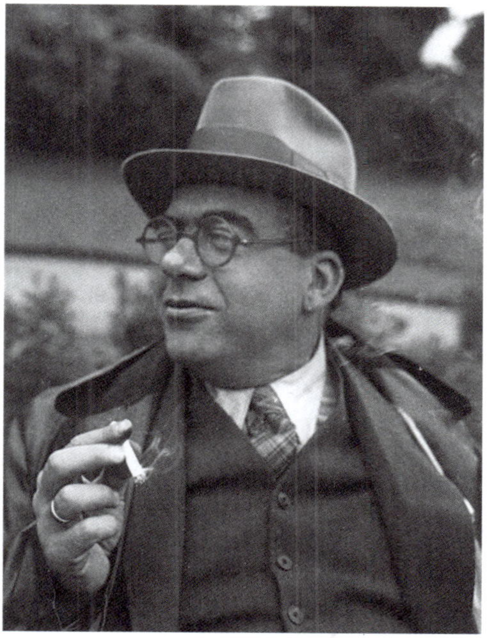

2.3 | Photograph of Erwin Panofsky, 1927

In fact, the situation is more complex than this. For what do we think when we look at the photograph of the horse we encountered in the Introduction (fig. 0.1)? Does this image depict a mammal (for those who have the concept 'mammal')? Perhaps you will reply 'yes'. But then what do you think when looking at fig. 2.3 instead? This is a photograph of Erwin Panofsky, and Panofsky was a mammal too. So does this photograph depict a mammal? You might be tempted to think that it does, but you may also feel, as I do, and as everyone whose opinion I have canvassed on the issue does, that to call this a depiction of a mammal feels rather strange. It would of course be preferable to do more than just ask some friends, and instead construct a well-designed experiment, in order to find out if there is much variety (perhaps cross-cultural) in people's intuitions on this matter. Unfortunately, experimental iconography requires a larger research budget than I can muster; but maybe its day will come.[13]

For now, let us consider the sense of unease of the non-random sample of people with whom I have discussed this question. When we look at fig. 2.3 we might take it to represent Erwin Panofsky and to depict a human being, a man, a German, an art historian, a man enjoying a cigarette, a man in a hat in a garden, a scholar at a conference in Göttingen in 1927 (if we happened to know that) and so forth; but perhaps we would not take it to depict a mammal, a vertebrate, a bilaterian, a multicellular eukaryote, a mass of atoms, an entity at the coordinates 51°32′02″N 09°56′08″E, a speaker of several Indo-European languages and so forth, even though Erwin Panofsky was, in fact, all those things at the time. One

13 Experimental approaches have begun to play a part in the philosophy of language: see Machery et al. 2004; McGinnis 2017; Islam and Baggio 2020.

can imagine contexts where the photograph might come to be given senses of these latter kinds – if it was used as an illustration in a biology textbook, for example (we shall return to this thought) – but in most contexts (e.g. in Panofsky's wife's wallet, in a biography of Panofsky, in the pages of this book) it could seem odd to call it a depiction of a eukaryote, even though Panofsky was a eukaryote, like almost all living beings.[14]

If this line of argument has any merit, then depiction would seem to be a form of meaning. We might say that fig. 2.3 is an assertion that certain properties co-exist – hat, cigarette, man etc. – but that it is not asserting the co-existence of all the properties of the depicted subject – mammal, vertebrate, eukaryote etc. If this is right, images do not function in the same way as names or singular terms. A name refers to an individual and can be used to say everything that there is to be said about that individual. Since images depict individuals, and we can see the individual right there in front of us, it is tempting to suppose that, semantically, images operate according to the same logic.[15] But it is not at all clear that people think about images as working like this. Instead, some of us – perhaps many of us – are happy to allow seemingly invalid syllogisms like the following:

This photograph depicts Erwin Panofsky.
Erwin Panofsky is a vertebrate.
This photograph does not depict a vertebrate.

Indexical depiction

Before we travel further down this route, we should pause, since it may seem that I have just been inconsistent with my own jargon. I wrote that fig. 2.3 depicts Erwin Panofsky, and yet I have said that depiction corresponds to (part of) Panofsky's concept of pre-iconography, and that it is representation that corresponds to his concept of iconography. The iconography of this photograph is surely Erwin Panofsky (or a portrait of Panofsky, or Panofsky at a conference in Göttingen in 1927, or Panofsky enjoying a cigarette, but Panofsky anyway), so should I not have written 'this photograph represents Erwin Panofsky'? Yes and no; it does represent Erwin Panofsky (although, as we will see, it does not have to) but it also depicts him. Here I need to introduce the notion of 'indexical depiction'.[16] A photograph can resemble its object by virtue of

14 Eukaryotes are organisms with membrane-bound nuclei. When I write "almost all living beings" I am referring to types, not tokens: there are a lot of primitive microorganisms. On types and tokens see Chapter 1, ftn. 5.

15 Kulvicki 2020, 56–58, 83–86 thinks of certain pictures as 'singling out' or 'delivering' individuals.

16 The concept of 'indexical' is of course inspired by the terminology of C.S. Peirce, who divided signs into three broad classes: icons, indices and symbols. He defined these words at differing lengths and in various ways in the course of his career; here is one of his briefer, simpler definitions from the last years of his life: "the most frequently useful division of signs is by trichotomy into firstly Likenesses, or, as I prefer to say, *Icons*, which serve to represent their objects only in so far as they resemble them in themselves; secondly, *Indices*, which represent their objects independently of any resemblance to them, only by virtue of real connections with them; and thirdly *Symbols*, which represent their objects, independently alike of any resemblance or any real connection, because dispositions or factitious habits of their interpreters insure their being so understood"; Peirce [1909] 1998, 460–61, quoted in Bergman and Paavola 2014, s.v. 'Icon'; see also ibid. 'Index' and 'Symbol'. For a brief discussion of Peirce's concept of 'index' see Lyons 1977, 105–06; for a fuller analysis, see Atkin 2005. For a round-table discussion of the concept from different disciplinary perspectives, see Nakassis et al. 2020.

having been in physical connection with it; that is, the photo can be created by light streaming from the object into the camera and forming an image on the photographic plate. There is something out there in the real world that causes the image to come into existence; the image is an index of that something.

One might think, then, that the photograph must be 'of' the object that gave it birth.[17] As the philosopher Gareth Evans (1982, 78) put it, "we speak of a photograph's being a photograph of one object rather than another solely on the basis of which object was related in the appropriate way to its production". It seems to me that this is not always the case if we are thinking about an image's representation (the photograph of Panofsky, as we will see in a moment, could be presented as a generic image), and it is not the case either if we are thinking about an image's conceptual depiction (if, as I have been suggesting, conceptual depiction does not deliver the whole object in the way that a name does); but it may be half true if we think in terms of the 'indexical depiction' of the image. A photograph produced by aiming the camera at a person is an indexical depiction of that person, a photograph produced by aiming the camera at a building is an indexical depiction of that building, and so on. This does not necessarily mean that the photograph represents either the person or the building. A photograph of someone called George Holt does not have to represent him as George Holt; he might be represented as the anonymous model in a sunglasses advert, or a man standing in the background when the king visits Liverpool. To say that a photograph is 'of' one object rather than another is ambiguous; it might be 'of' the object at the (indexically) depictive level but not at the representational level; or it might be 'of' the object at both levels.

Clearly, not every image can be said to have an indexical depiction. Photographs can, but very many paintings cannot. Leonardo did not construct a room like the one in the Last Supper (fig. 1.1) and carefully paint what he saw; in all likelihood he just invented everything in it, the table, the food, and all thirteen men (although he may have used sketches from the life as part of the process). The same can probably be said for the works by Caucig (fig. 1.6), Delacroix (fig. 1.2), Bellini (fig. 1.3) and the Moche potter of the cassava deity (fig. 1.9), as well most probably of the Moche cassava itself (fig. 1.8). Albert Eckhout and Francisco Goya, on the other hand, were both carefully trying to capture the appearances of what they saw in front of them, and we can think of their works (figs. 1.10 and 2.1) as depicting indexically a cassava root and the Duke of Wellington respectively. The painting by Cezanne (fig. 1.7) is less clear cut. Cezanne painted in front of the motif, but comparisons between his canvases and photographs of the motifs he was depicting generally show that, while the motifs are recognizably the same as those in the paintings, he distorted what he saw for artistic ends (Loran 1970). Deciding what is and what is not an indexical depiction will not always be a straightforward choice.

I shall take even inaccurate depictions to be indexical so long as they are attempts to depict a specific individual in the real world. A two-year-old girl asked to draw her mother may produce an oval with four circles inside it and some scribbles on either side (Golomb 1992, 28), but I shall still call it an indexical depiction. However, if the same

17 There is a recent theoretical stance that argues against the indexicality of photographs; see Geimer 2007. The distinctions put forward here between indexical depiction, conceptual depiction and representation may be found useful by those on both sides of this debate.

child were asked to make an image of 'a woman' (any woman, some woman), then I would not take the result to be an indexical depiction.

On this definition there will be a very large number of borderline cases between indexical depictions and non-indexical depictions, but this should not worry us unduly, so long as there are abundant unambiguous cases on either side of the border, and there are. The vast majority of traditional African, Oceanic and pre-Columbian images depict non-indexically, and the vast majority of modern Western images depict indexically, a contrast that, in itself, makes the distinction worth drawing. It is true of world art in general that there has been a great increase in indexical depiction over the past 500 years, and a small relative decline in indexical depiction in recent decades, as digital technologies have enabled the creation of artificial images that mimic photographs. If we do not have 'indexical depiction' in our conceptual toolkit, we may not notice these global trends.

Not every image depicts indexically, but every image depicts conceptually. When an image depicts both indexically *and* conceptually, then we should not expect its beholders to think that every property of the indexically depicted object is depicted conceptually. The conceptual depiction is the assemblage of properties that beholders take the image to depict, and they will not take the image to depict all of the indexically depicted subject's properties. The portrait of Erwin Panofsky (fig. 2.3) can be thought of as an indexical depiction of a mammal, since Erwin Panofsky was a mammal, but that does not entail that the photograph depicts a mammal conceptually. Conceptual depiction, so to speak, overlays and filters indexical depiction. Just because Panofsky was a mammal and a eukaryote, that does not mean that we must think of a photograph of him as a depiction of a mammal and a eukaryote. Indexical depiction refers to the object that has caused the image, but no more than that; the way that the object is understood is expressed by the conceptual depiction.

If an image designates an individual indexically then it does so no matter what anyone in the world thinks about it. The photographer who took our portrait of Panofsky may have thought, wrongly, that they were taking a photograph of Panofsky's art historical friend Kurt Badt, and may have kept the photograph in their studio with the caption 'Kurt Badt' on the frame, and could even have sold it to publications who wanted a portrait of Badt and used it as such. But none of this would matter; the photograph would continue to be an indexical depiction of Panofsky, just as the name 'Erwin Panofsky' denotes Erwin Panofsky.[18]

With indexical depiction, we are thinking of images as picking out objects or persons in a way not dissimilar to that by which verbal descriptions denote people. This may be thought problematic, since images, of course, refer to things as entities in regions of space and moments of time, and they refer to them also from particular vantage points. Take the two photographs in figs. 2.4 and 2.5, which show the same statue from two different angles. The statue represents Prince Albert, the husband of Queen Victoria, and it forms the gigantic centrepiece of the Albert Memorial, the neo-Gothic monument bristling with allegorical figures, portraits, lions and angels that Victoria had built in Albert's memory. Although these two photographs have

18 For the idea that names are 'rigid designators', see Kripke 1981, 71–97. For discussion and criticism, Evans 1973; Dummett 1981, 143–51; Machery et al. 2004.

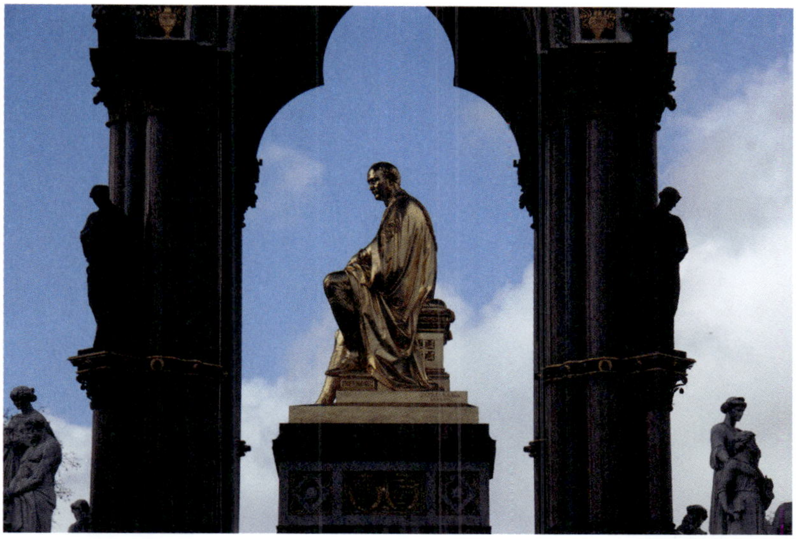

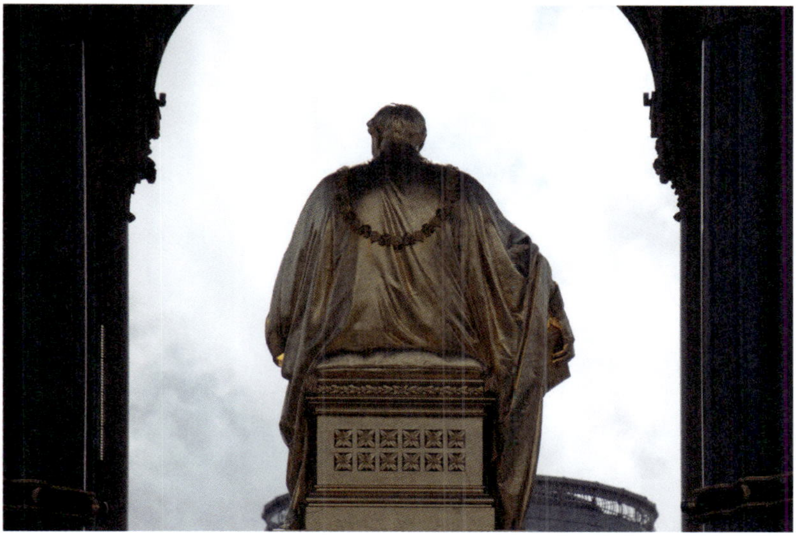

2.4, 2.5 | John Henry Foley and Thomas Brock, *Prince Albert* (from the east and from the north), 1876. Albert Memorial, Kensington Gardens, London

enough in common to allow their viewer to see that both images are of the same statue, they are nevertheless obviously different. Albert is seen from behind in fig. 2.5, so that someone who did not recognize the statue would not be able to tell that it depicted the prince. Both photographs indexically depict a statue, which in turn indexically depicts Prince Albert, but they do so from different viewpoints. We could also note that the statue indexically depicts Albert, but at a certain age, around 40, in the last years of his life. Statues that depict him as a child or a youth also indexically depict him, even though his appearance changed over time. And images of Albert, like images of other people, show him in different postures and with different facial expressions; they show different attitudes of the man. What is more, these two photographs do not only depict Albert's statue. Fig. 2.4 also depicts some of the allegorical personifications that adorn the memorial, and fig. 2.5 depicts part of the roof of the Albert Hall, and the clouds of a brewing storm.

Any image will represent its subject from a viewpoint and on an occasion, and most will also depict peripheral items. No doubt it would be possible to generate more categories to provide a more complex analysis, based on light, colour and so on. One could break down indexical depiction into sub-concepts that take these categories into account. However, indexical depiction remains constant across its sub-concepts: a photograph of a dirty statue in poor light seen from above is still a photograph of that statue, just as a photograph of Panofsky as a child, and a photograph of Panofsky as an old man, are both photographs of Panofsky.

There are certain affinities between the conceptual/indexical distinction and a well-worn distinction in the philosophy of meaning, that between 'sense' and 'reference'. The phrases 'the author of *Studies in Iconology*' and 'the father of Wolfgang K.H. Panofsky' both have the same referent, Erwin Panofsky. If someone told a friend of Wolfgang that the father of Wolfgang was the author of *Studies in Iconology*, then the friend could have learned something. But if we think that, with language, we are denoting objects in the real world and making assertions about how they relate to one another, then it seems that the friend has only been told that Erwin Panofsky was Erwin Panofsky, which is hardly informative. Gottlob Frege tried to solve this puzzle by distinguishing the sense and reference of a name or phrase: 'the father of Wolfgang Panofsky' and 'the author of *Studies in Iconology*' both refer to Erwin Panofsky, but they present their referent in different ways, or, as Frege put it, they express different senses (Frege [1892] 1977; cf. Dummett 1981; Salmon 1986).[19]

One can see how conceptual depiction might be taken to correspond to sense, and indexical depiction to reference. The fact that many images do not have an indexical depiction is not a problem, since many sentences do not have a reference; indeed, Frege thought that one of the advantages of his theory was that it could account for language describing fictional characters. In his view, a statement such as 'Odysseus was set ashore at Ithaca while sound asleep' has no referent, but it does have a sense. Referring expressions always have senses, but expressions with senses do not always have referents; a similar situation to ours, where indexical depictions always have conceptual depictions, but not vice versa.

However, if there are some general similarities between the two pairs of concepts, there are also important differences. One of these is that indexical depiction does not play the same semantic role in the image as reference plays in the verbal statement. An image, as we will see, can depict someone or something indexically without either depicting conceptually or representing that person or thing. And while sense and reference express the meaning and determine the truth value of the sentence, the same

19 On the application of these terms to pictures, see Hyman 2012. Hyman (137) suggests that two portraits of Tolstoy at different ages should be thought of as having different modes of presentation, or senses, but the same reference. Hyman's 'reference' corresponds to what we call 'indexical depiction'; his 'sense' has no exact equivalent in our discussion. As argued in the following section, a painting may resemble Tolstoy at certain periods of his life, and it may indexically depict him, but still not represent him.

is not the case for conceptual and indexical depiction. It is the representation, the iconography, that provides the content of the image.

Another point to note is that, as we are using the term, conceptual depiction (in this, like Panofsky's pre-iconography) is generic. It presents the kind of thing depicted in the image, but it does not individuate it. One can indexically depict an individual, but one cannot conceptually depict an individual.

Representation

Why do we need these different levels of interpretation when describing images? If our photograph of Panofsky indexically depicts him and conceptually depicts his status as a man smoking a cigarette, wearing a suit and a hat and so on, then have we not said everything that needs to be said about the relationship between the photograph and its object? No, because the two types of depiction do not tell us that this is a portrait of Panofsky, and it did not have to be: the same photograph could have had other iconographies (Gombrich 1949, 72). Perhaps the photographer was unacquainted with Panofsky and was not intending to make a portrait. He might have been an amateur photographer who was amused by Panofsky as a type; or he might have been a photographer working for a local newspaper in Göttingen, who wanted a shot of a professor to give an idea of the conference taking place at the university; or he might have been working for a tobacco company, and looking for a photograph he could work into an advertisement for a brand of cigarettes; or he might have been working for a stock photo company, and thought he could sell this photograph in future to anyone who wanted it for whatever reason, and so on. When people take photographs of individuals, often they are not interested in them as individuals, so much as in their generic appearance. Images that have indexical depictions, but generic representations, have become increasingly widespread with the growth of commercial imagery. Models in Western advertisements are often presented as anonymous, while the goods or services they are selling are named.[20]

If we think of Panofsky's photograph in these terms, then fig. 2.3

resembles Panofsky, a waxwork of Panofsky, a man who looks just like Panofsky, a powerful ancestor spirit and so on
conceptually depicts a man, a smoker, someone wearing a suit and spectacles, with an amused expression, and so on
indexically depicts Erwin Panofsky
represents e.g. a professor enjoying a break from this year's conference at Göttingen University (as a possible caption)

Over time, representations can change. That would be evident if our portrait were shot by a photographer from a stock photo company; they might rent it out to a cigarette manufacturer, then a milliner, then a medical company, then a local newspaper, and each time the caption and the representation would be different. Another possibility is that on its commercial travels a print fell into the hands of someone who was taught by Panofsky, who realised who was depicted and bought it off the stock company to keep

20 For more on this subject, see p. 202 below.

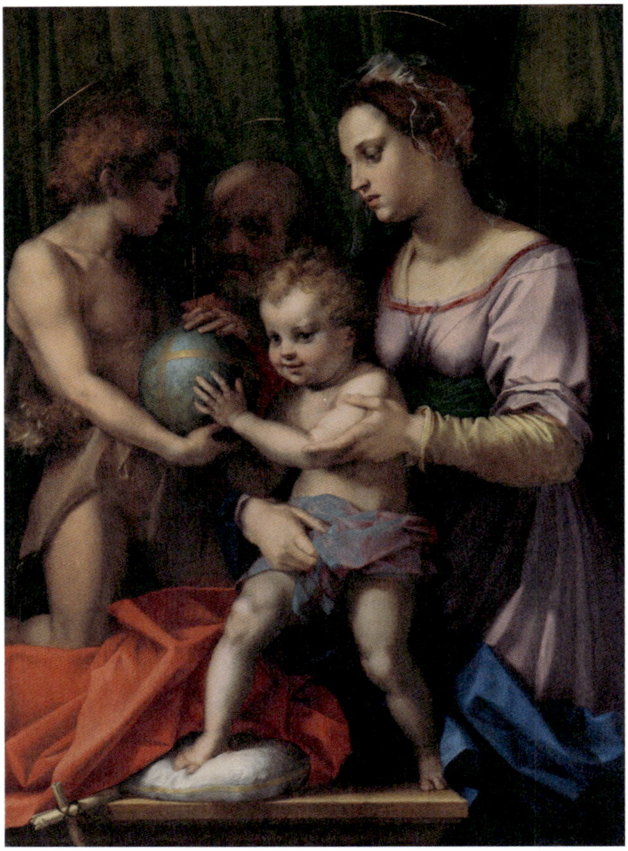

2.6 | Andrea del Sarto, Holy Family, c. 1528.
The Metropolitan Museum of Art, New York

as a memory of her professor. She then donated it to the Photographic Collection of the Warburg Institute, and so it was transformed from a generic image of an unknown man into a portrait of Erwin Panofsky.[21]

Note that the intentions of the photographer do not necessarily govern the representation. A photograph can be made by someone who does not know who Panofsky is, but it can then become a portrait of Panofsky. Indeed, this happens frequently in commercial photography; a wedding photographer will only know the names of a handful of people at the reception, but the resultant photographs will be kept as portraits of individuals.

So an indexical depiction can become a generic representation, and a generic representation can be transformed into a representation of the indexically depicted individual. But can an indexical depiction become a representation of an individual

21 I do not know how this photograph entered the Warburg, nor who took it.

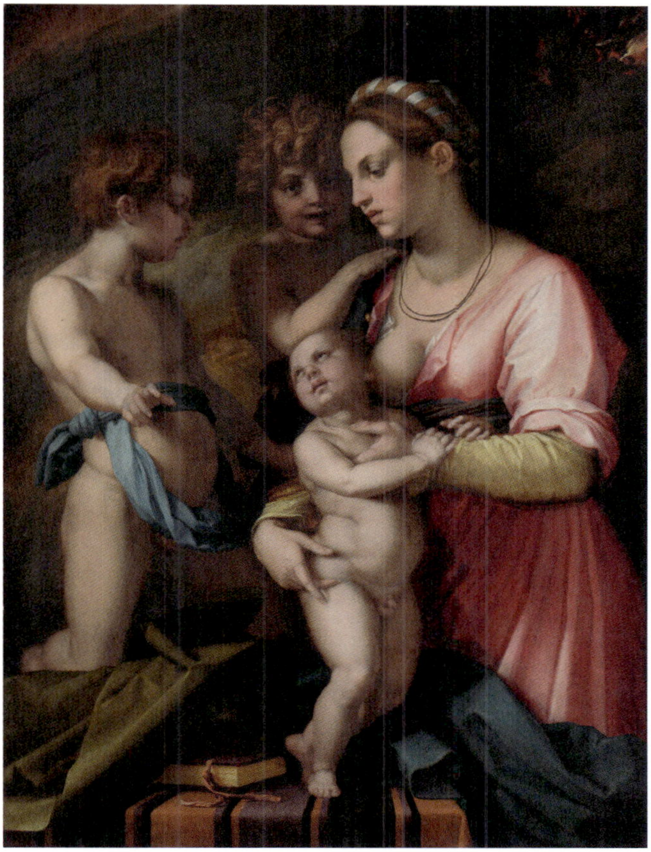

2.7 | Andrea dela Sarto, Personification of Charity, before 1530.
The Metropolitan Museum of Art, New York

other than the individual who is indexically depicted? In painting, this is certainly possible. For example, in Giorgio Vasari's *Lives* we are told that when Andrea del Sarto was painting women, he would use his own wife as a model (Vasari 1550, 750).[22] If this anecdote is true (certainly the women in Andrea's paintings look very similar to one another) then in this painting (fig. 2.6) the figure on the right indexically depicts Andrea's wife but represents the Virgin Mary, while in this painting (fig. 2.7) she represents the allegorical personification of Charity.

We are willing to accept a split between indexical depiction and individual representation in the manual arts, but can the same be said of photographs? In this still from the 1936 film *Rembrandt* (fig. 2.8) we see a photograph of Charles Laughton

22 The life of Andrea del Sarto may not have been written by Vasari himself; see Hope 2014. Hope, who is currently writing a book on the making of Vasari's *Lives*, believes that Bastiano da Sangallo is more likely to have been the author (pers. comm.).

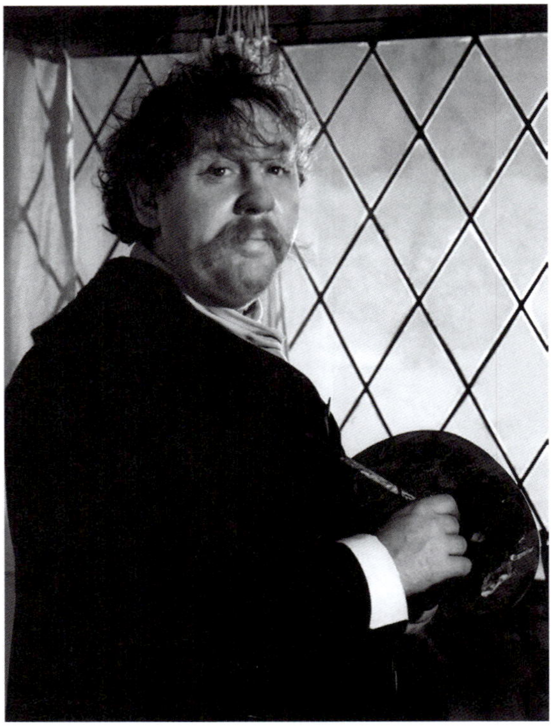

2.8 | Charles Laughton in the title role of the film *Rembrandt*, dir. Alexander Korda, 1936

mixing paint on his palette; he is obviously in character as Rembrandt van Rijn. Does the image *represent* Rembrandt, or does it represent Charles Laughton acting the part of Rembrandt? I imagine, although a social survey may prove me wrong, that most people would think of the image as a representation of Charles Laughton. And yet if an artist wanted to paint a posthumous portrait of Rembrandt, and, not having a living model to depict, asked Charles Laughton if he would sit for it, then, even if the result looked more like Laughton than Rembrandt, we might be willing to accept the portrait as a representation of Rembrandt.

To give a different example, this time using a fictional character, we may be happy to think of the standing figure at left in Delacroix's print (fig. 1.2) as representing Hamlet, even if we learned that Delacroix worked closely from the features of a particular actor who had recently played Hamlet on the Paris stage; but when we see a photograph of an actor as Hamlet (fig. 2.9) we tend, I think, to see the photograph as representing the actor, playing Hamlet. This is true both when the actor is someone very famous whose face we can recognize, and when the actor is someone whose face we do not recognize. A hundred years ago the face in this photograph would have been identified with ease by tens of thousands of people, since here in the role of Hamlet we see the great French actress Sarah Bernhardt; but now most readers of this book will I imagine just read the image as a photograph of an actor from the past. Bernhardt's Hamlet was famous in its day, and a poster for the production, designed by Alphonse Mucha (fig. 2.10), provides

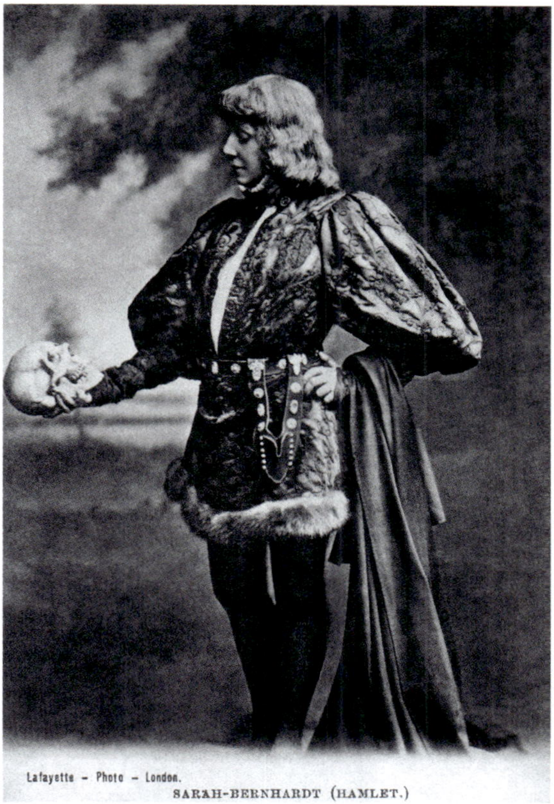

2.9 | Postcard of Sarah Bernhardt in the role of Hamlet, 1885–1910. Library of Congress, Washington, D.C.

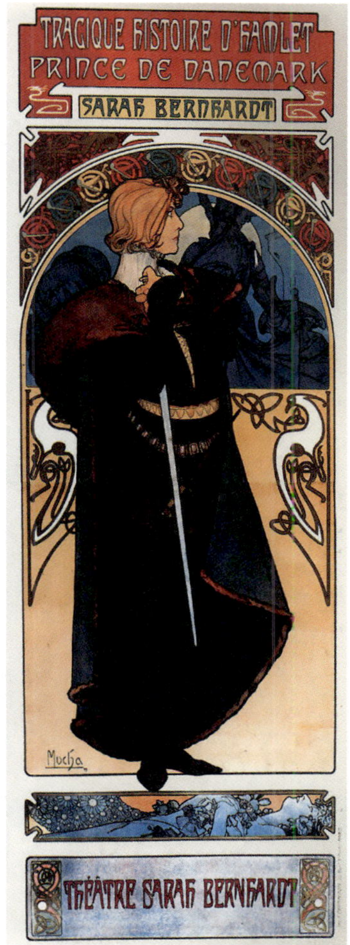

2.10 | Alphonse Mucha, Poster for *Hamlet*, with Sarah Bernhardt in the title role, 1899. Private Collection

a counterexample to the rule that in paintings representation overrides indexical depiction. This seems to me to be a painting of Sarah Bernhardt in role, although I find it hard to say quite why the face cannot be that of Hamlet.

A more extreme example of this identity-shifting phenomenon would be if we imagined someone looking at our photograph of Panofsky and – even though they knew it to be an indexical depiction of Panofsky – taking it to represent someone else entirely – Ernest Hemingway, say. This idea seems peculiar to us, but at other times and places it might have seemed less strange. Scholars in early modern Europe liked to own busts of their favourite Greek and Roman authors, so that they could contemplate them and be inspired by them. However, few of the ancient busts that claimed to be portraits of ancient poets or philosophers were actually taken from the life or resembled their sitters, and those who owned them were usually aware of this. In particular, everyone knew that Homer lived in such an early period that no portrait of him could claim to be accurate, but that did not mean that contemplating a bust of the greatest of Greek poets

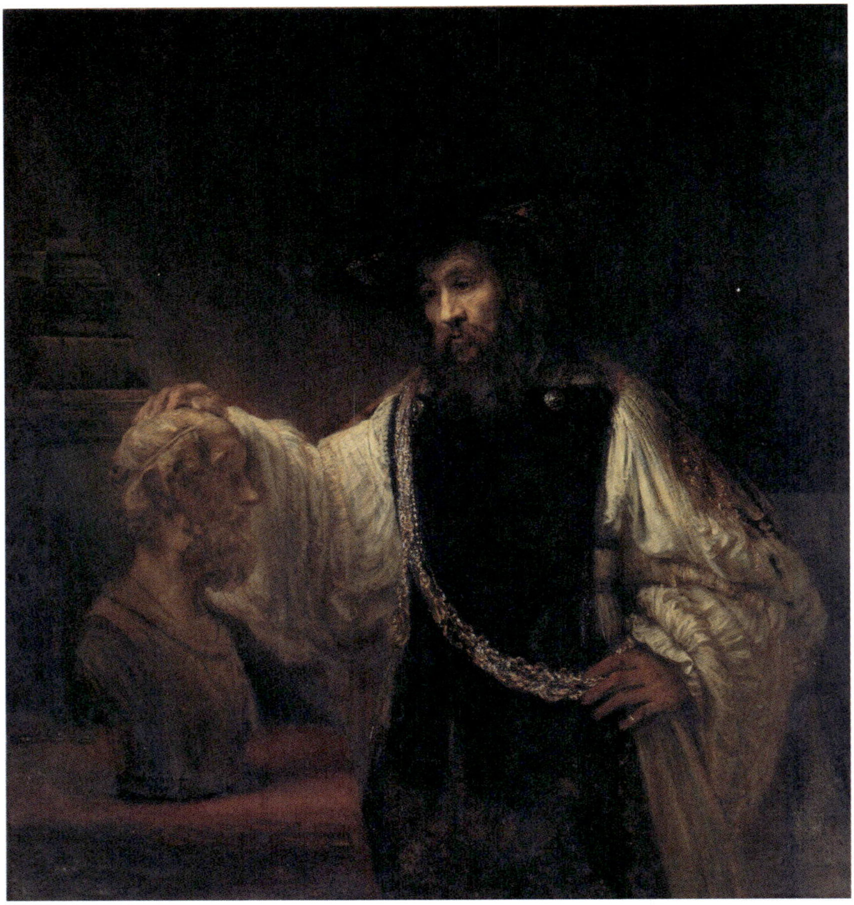

2.11 | Rembrandt, Aristotle with a Bust of Homer, 1653.
The Metropolitan Museum of Art, New York

might not be an enriching meditative activity, and so statues and paintings and prints of Homer were manufactured and sold to the literary-minded. In Rembrandt's painting of Aristotle contemplating a bust of Homer (fig. 2.11) we see this phenomenon in duplicate; an imaginary Aristotle contemplates a bust of an imaginary Homer. The figures are props in a game of make-believe,[23] but nevertheless the standing figure still represents Aristotle, just as the bust on which his hand is resting represents Homer.[24]

If figures in paintings can represent Homer or Aristotle without indexically depicting them or even resembling them very closely, can we imagine someone ordering a portrait representing Ernest Hemingway, even though it did not look very much like him? If we can, would there be any objection to using a photograph of Erwin

23 The terminology is from Walton 1990, although he does not discuss cases of this sort.

24 There have been debates over the identity of the figure with the hat; see p. 216 below.

Panofsky for that purpose? Try it yourself: stare fixedly at fig. 2.3 and imagine that it represents Hemingway. Read virility, toughness and a love of guns and bullfights into those features. What we are doing here is surely similar to what early modern scholars did when they looked at their fictive busts of Homer and thought of the *Iliad* and the *Odyssey*. It is make-believe, but it is make-believe that succeeds in referring to the world. The bust portrait really does represent Homer. It does not indexically depict him, but it represents him. The photograph of Panofsky really does represent Hemingway. It does not indexically depict him, but it represents him.

The reader may well feel uncomfortable about this. It is one thing to see a statue of a generic bearded man as Homer, another to see Panofsky as Hemingway. What is the difference? One difference is that we have a record of Hemingway's appearance, but we do not have a record of the appearance of Homer. Playing make-believe with the features of someone we have never seen is easier than playing make-believe with the features of someone we have seen. Another difference is that in the Panofsky/Hemingway case we are dealing with photographs, and we seem to have different semantic intuitions when it comes to photographs. When photographs represent individuals in the real world, we expect them to resemble their subjects accurately (cf. Walton 2008). This may be a passing cultural convention, or it may be due to some cognitive mechanism hard-wired into our brains: we can leave it to the neuroiconography of the future to settle the matter.

In this discussion, we have been thinking of depiction and representation as broadly comparable to the linguistic phenomena of sense and reference. Images represent individuals, things, places, and in a similar way nouns and names denote individuals, things and places. Should we go further, and suggest that images can also express propositions, and (be used to) make statements? There is a sizeable philosophical literature on this issue, and most philosophers deny that images express propositions.[25] Could we not say, however, that if an image represents Panofsky smoking, then it also expresses the proposition that Panofsky was a smoker? Of course, the image could not be taken to express this notion at the levels of depiction or resemblance, since it might not be used to represent Panofsky or indeed a cigarette; but within a context of representational meaning, could it not be taken to assert elements of its represented content? We do not need to take this thought further, but it brings home how images can be made to mean in contexts of what might be called 'iconographic utterance'.

Feedback revisited

In Chapter 1 we considered the phenomenon of iconographic feedback. At that time, we were still using Panofsky's concepts of pre-iconography, iconography and iconology, but now that we have taken pre-iconography and iconography and distributed them between resemblance, conceptual depiction, indexical depiction and representation, we can see that the situation is more complex than it seemed. Both resemblance and indexical depiction are outside the feedback loop. What an image can be taken to resemble is not governed by what it depicts or represents, even though the resemblances one tends to see may be suggested by what one expects from the representation

25 For a dissenting view with a summary of the literature, see Grzankowski 2015. See also Gombrich 1960, 59, 77.

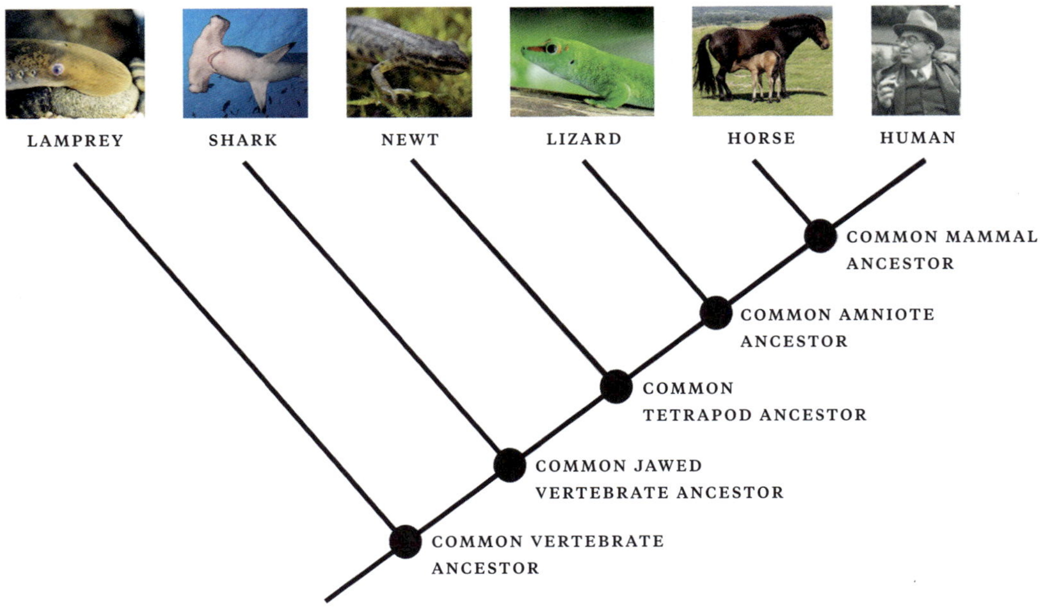

2.12 | Diagram showing the phylogeny of vertebrates

(Gombrich 1960, 170–244). But any image will always resemble more things than its representation prescribes.

With indexical depiction we have a simple historical fact that cannot be altered by the representation of the image; though it may not be possible for the historian to ascertain the fact. Did the Duke of Wellington sit for Goya (fig. 2.1), or did the artist base his portrait, not on a personal inspection of the duke's features, but on a print he encountered? A lot of hard historical labour may be needed to establish the truth of this. But whether we can discover the truth about the past does not affect the truth about the past; whatever happened cannot un-happen.

Iconographic feedback, then, is a relationship between conceptual depiction and representation (and iconology). The kinds of things we take the image to depict conceptually will suggest its specific representation, and its representation will lay down the properties of its conceptual depiction. Conceptual depiction always underdetermines representation, but representation determines conceptual depiction. A decision that a portrait represents Erwin Panofsky iconographically entails that it depicts a man. It also iconographically entails, it seems to me, that it does not depict a vertebrate, because it is a portrait of a specific human being, not of some vertebrate or other. If, however, we were to take fig. 2.3 and include it in a diagram showing the phylogeny of vertebrates (fig. 2.12), then the change of iconographic context would alter its conceptual depiction; now it would depict a vertebrate. Representation and conceptual depiction are both dependent on context, and thus they can change as the context changes.

Iconographic devices

Since conceptually depictive and representational meanings change according to context, they are not intrinsic to the image.[26] To find out what an image depicted or represented in any historical period, we need to understand both the general iconological background and the specific context of the image's use. But we also need, and this will be the task of most of the rest of this book, to understand the mechanism by which meaning is attached to the image – what we will be calling its 'iconographic device'.

The representations of images are established in various ways. Sometimes they are simply assigned by word of mouth; sometimes symbols within the image indicate intentionality; sometimes depicted events allow the viewer to identify the characters represented; sometimes resemblance to people or things helps us to establish identities. In the following four chapters I will be discussing these 'iconographic devices' – designation, attributes, narratives and likeness – in turn, exploring how they function and what differences their introduction has made to representation and depiction.

Iconographic devices do not always attach a meaning to an image; often they transmit meanings from image to image. For example, attributes can allow viewers to identify a particular figure, but only if they already know what figure the attribute signifies. You can look for as long as you like at a saint with an attribute, but that will not tell you who the saint is, you will need either to be told by someone who knows, or to see some text, a caption or an inscription. Once you have learned the connection between the attribute and the personage you will be able to recognize images of this specific saint whenever you encounter them, but the attribute alone does not give you this information; rather, it transmits the information. We can talk of 'identifier devices' and 'transmitter devices', and in what follows I will be arguing that only one iconographic device, designation, is an identifier device; all the others rely on transmission.

Although I shall be devoting chapters to four different iconographic devices, these are not the only types of iconographic device. Others will drift in and out of the discussion, and in Chapter 4 I shall pause to discuss three in particular: statistical reasoning, inscriptions and contextual deduction. If I do not give them separate treatment that is not because they are any less important, but because it is hard to deal with them separately; all three are important for many instances of designation, attributes, narrative and likeness.

Understanding the structure of iconographic devices will help us to get clearer about the nature of the meanings of images, but it will also provide us with conceptual tools that allow us to observe changes in meta-iconography over the millennia. Meta-iconography has a history, and my aim here is to trace its development and understand the reasons for its change. In Chapter 7 I shall deal with these questions directly.

---

26 This may run counter to a recent theory that images can be thought of as having desires and intentions. See e.g. Deleuze 1984, 83–103; Mitchell 1996, 71–82; Bredekamp 2010; Bredekamp 2014. It is certainly the case that images have sometimes been said, and possibly believed, to have desires and intentions, see pp. 141–43. Theorists of the 'image act' appear to be on the believers' side of this issue.

3. Designation

Children's drawings

When two- and three-year old children are asked to produce images of specific items, they will often represent things and people using slightly wobbly ovals. Humans, animals, trees, machines and buildings can all be given this oval treatment, and were it not for a parent or child psychologist carefully recording the representational meanings intended by the child, it would be quite impossible to know which oval depicts a baby, which a giraffe and which a car (Golomb 1992, 22–23; Stumpel 2014, 109). There is not much in this that is iconic, and despite the fact that the child has been asked to make an image of a baby, a giraffe etc. and seems to understand the instruction, we might think of these named shapes more as symbols than as images. They certainly cannot be said to resemble their objects in any but the most distant way, and we might also wonder if they can be said to depict anything. Can we say that an oval represents a giraffe, just because the child says that it does? We are dealing again with semantic intuitions. Personally, I would call this a representation, but would not be surprised if you disagreed.[1]

As they grow older, children begin to make drawings which resemble the world more, but there is still a massive underdetermination of depiction by resemblance. Take fig. 3.1 for example. We have no idea who is represented, or even what is depicted by the drawing in the child's hand. It might be an image of a god or a ghost or a goblin, or if it is a human, it could be a self-portrait, a portrait of one of the child's parents, a portrait of someone outside the child's family, or a portrait of some historical, mythical or literary figure. It could also be an indefinite representation, an image of 'a person', some person or other. We do not know if the child drew it, or whether he is holding up a drawing made by someone else – the artist, for example.[2] Let us assume, for the sake of argument, that the drawing is by the boy. Then, if he said 'That's me!', the drawing would be a drawing of him; if he said 'That's you!' addressing his father, then the drawing would be a drawing of his father. He might also have started out trying to make a self-portrait, looking at himself carefully in the mirror, and then decided when he had finished it that it was a portrait of his father. Children's drawings are not bound by the ordinary rules of indexical depiction.

1 This means that, in my view, resemblance (in any meaningful sense) is not necessary for representation, an issue I carefully avoided in the opening section of Chapter 2. On this I agree with Goodman 1976, 5.

2 We also do not know whether the child is a boy or a girl, nor if this is an indexical or conceptual depiction. Everyone who writes about the painting assumes that the figure is meant to be a boy; I am not sure why. Schnell 1989 provides discussion and further literature.

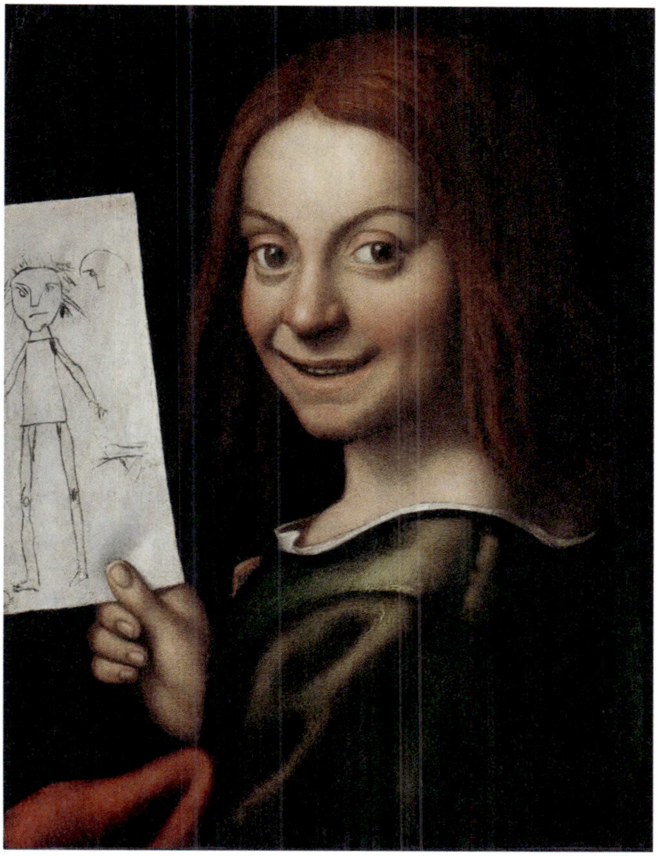

3.1 | Giovanni Francesco Caroto, Boy Holding a Child's Drawing, 1515–20. Museo di Castelvecchio, Verona

Children designate the referents of their own images. Nevertheless, there are some limits to this game of make-believe.[3] The boy's drawing does resemble a human being, and so also a statue, an angel, a god and so forth, and this narrows down the possibilities of depiction. If he told us that his drawing represented a herd of pigs, or a tree, we would think he was being silly and tell him it could not be. He is welcome to designate any individual within a broad class of humans, gods, statues and so forth as the subject of his drawing, or he can tell us that he has made an indefinite representation of *a* human, *a* god, *a* statue, but he does not have an entirely free hand.

Even when a child's drawing is so vague that it opens many more possibilities for representation, limitations are put on its depiction by certain social rules and expectations. The six-year-old boy who made the drawing in fig. 3.2 was trying to depict a tree from memory, but if he had said that he was trying to depict a herd of pigs or a

3 Surprisingly, there is no discussion of children's drawings in Walton 1990.

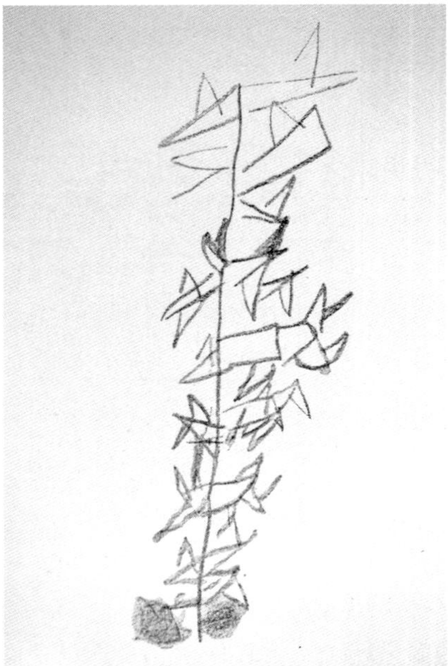

3.2 | Six-year-old boy, Drawing of a tree (Kerschensteiner 1905, p. 197)

firework display, he might have been believed. As it happens, the boy in question was told in school to draw a tree so that his efforts could form part of a study of children's drawings (Kerschensteiner 1905, 197). If he had seemed to understand the instruction, had spoken with his fellow children while they made their drawings of trees, had handed it in to his teacher in response to the question 'Have you finished your tree, Peter?', shouted 'Yes!' when the teacher asked the whole class if they had enjoyed the exercise of drawing a tree, and then told his parents afterwards that he had in fact drawn a herd of pigs, would they have believed him? Perhaps it would depend on how consistently and sympathetically he stuck to his story. But one could understand the teacher, if she or he refused to accept the boy's representational decision and insisted it was in fact a tree.

In a case like this, we are faced with a second limitation on the child's semantic prerogatives. We thought that the boy in fig. 3.1 could not have represented a herd of pigs because his drawing does not resemble a herd of pigs. In fig. 3.2 the drawing does resemble a herd of pigs, a bit, so this cannot be the teacher's reason for dismissing the child's opinion. Here, instead, the teacher might be thinking that if the child was trying throughout the exercise to draw a tree, then the result must be a tree. But we have seen that children are entitled to change their representational minds, and call what started out as a self-portrait a portrait of their father. So why is this right sometimes granted, sometimes denied? There is a battle of wills, and of social ranks, in deciding whether or not to grant powers of representational decision-making. A teacher who orders a child to do something will expect the child to comply. The parents may be more indulgent, but the teacher may want to stick to protocols.

Is anyone right in this disagreement? If the parents and the teacher disagree, is there any way to settle the dispute? If there is no way to settle the dispute, then is there any real disagreement in the first place? We are back with semantic intuitions, but while these are elastic, they do not stretch forever. If the child claimed a different subject for his drawing once every five minutes, then his parents would begin to fear for his sanity. But this too is perhaps a matter of cultural convention.

Children's drawings offer many more possibilities for representation than illusionistic art or photographs because they are so generic and ambiguous that they suggest many more possibilities for depiction. A six-year-old child's drawing can be taken to depict a tree, a herd of pigs or a firework display, and it is hard to imagine a photograph with similar powers of suggestion. If children's drawings are rarely taken to represent all those things at once, that is perhaps because they are produced under the supervision of adults (who provide the crayons and the paper) and the adults' assumptions and presuppositions lay down the rules for representation. Most grown-ups in Western societies are used to the idea of images with one referent, and children are indoctrinated in this view from the earliest of ages.

Representation in children's drawings is generally fixed by means of designation. A drawing that could equally represent most primates is said to represent 'Daddy'. Another drawing that does not resemble the first one at all closely is also said to represent 'Daddy'. The child may be behind these decisions and may have been making a sincere attempt to depict his father. But the representational decision has not of course been taken because these drawings resemble the child's father. An iconographic identity is designated to the image, and while the father may see the image as being in some way an image of himself, this is surely no more than a fond form of psychological projection. Children do not make images of individuals; they make generic images that are said to be images of individuals.

Ancestors

It is not only children's drawings that employ designation; in many societies where images are intentionally generic, similar mechanisms are applied.[4] Take, for example, the statues in figs. 3.3 and 3.4, which were carved in the Lebialem highlands in western Cameroon in the late nineteenth century by a sculptor called Ateu Atsa (Harter 1990; LaGamma 2007, 122–23). Both statues are ruler figures of the Bangwa, a Bamileke people.[5] They are about the same height as one another (86 cm), and, although they can easily be told apart, they have many features in common, such as pointed teeth, a very similar headdress, a staff (broken in fig. 3.2) and a drinking horn – an object kept as a relic of Bangwa rulers after their deaths and found on many such figures.

Any person familiar with Bangwa customs would immediately recognize that these statues were meant to depict rulers, but what would be more difficult to decide was with which rulers the figures were supposed to be associated. As it happens, we know the names of both individuals (just as we know the name of the artist) since the German businessman who acquired the sculptures at the end of the nineteenth century noted down their identities.[6] Fig. 3.3 is a figure of Fosia, and fig. 3.4 is a figure of Moawu.[7]

---

4 Gombrich argued that the generic nature of these images is unintentional. For a contrary view, see Taylor 2014.

5 The name 'Bangwa' was invented by the Germans, who were told by their Bali interpreters that the inhabitants of the Lebialem region were the *ba ngwa*, the people who spoke Ngwa, Ngwe or Nweh, a Bamileke language unique in Africa for its large number of vowel sounds; Webb and Kembo-Sure 2000, 141, 160; Ayotte and Ayotte 2002, 11–12. 'Bangwa' was used to describe all Nweh speakers by the British colonial government in 1921, even though these speakers were divided into nine autonomous states and did not think of themselves as forming one people; Brain and Pollock 1971, 5–6; Lockhart 1994, 6–8; Ndobegang and Bowie 2009, 96–97. Bangwa sculpture was only made in the more southerly states; there appears to have been very little sculpture produced in the northern Bangwa regions; Brain and Pollock 1971, 5.

6 He was Gustav Conrau, a German factory manager who was trying to lure Bangwa workers to his trading post near the coast. Unfortunately for Conrau, the Bangwa came to hear of the shocking working conditions at his factory. For Bangwa and German accounts of his violent death and the resultant war between the Bangwa and the Germans, see Dunstan 1965; Chilver 1967; Ndobegang and Bowie 2009.

7 Pierre Harter (1990, 73) believed that, due to their lack of patina, the statues given to Conrau were copies, and that the original figures were kept hidden. Bangwa history does not record information about Fosia or Moawu, but we will assume that the names are correct.

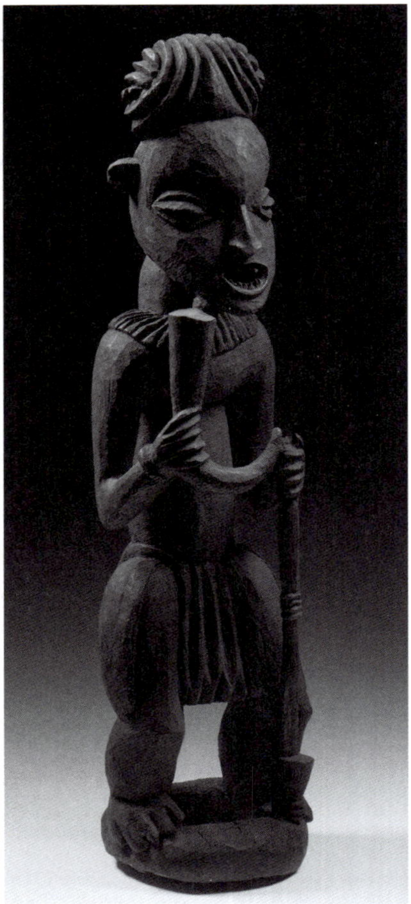
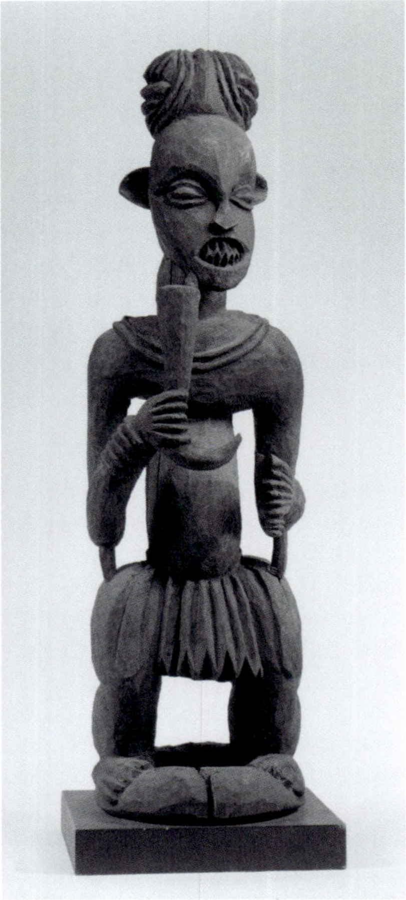

3.3, 3.4 | Ateu Atsa, Fosia and Moawu, before 1903. Ethnologisches Museum, Berlin

Figures of important Bangwa chiefs were made during their lifetimes and could act as a substitute for the chief at ceremonies when he could not be present. After his death they became commemorative figures, but this commemoration was rather different from that of a photo of a dead relative on a mantelpiece. For most of the time they were kept hidden, and they were only handled by special retainers, who were members of a powerful secret society called the *lefem*, after the sacred *lefem* copse where sacrifices were made to Bangwa ancestors. The statues themselves were also called *lefem* and could only be touched if their handlers had refrained from sex and prohibited foods beforehand. The statues were brought out on certain ritual occasions, when they were made the focus of incantations and animal sacrifices, and where they were said, for the duration of the rite, to contain the spirits of the dead chiefs.[8] They were treated with the

8 The chief's spirit was generally resident in his preserved skull.

same deference that the chiefs themselves received during their lifetimes; they were addressed by name and were each assumed to have the differing personalities of their prototypes. They were also credited with supernormal powers; they could fly through the air on special missions. It is said that one set of *lefems* managed to bring a German brass band by air for the funerary ceremony of a Bangwa princess (Brain and Pollock 1971, 57, 118–19; Harter 1990, 72–73).

It might not be wrong to say that the figures in figs. 3.3 and 3.4 are *of* Fosia and Moawu, but that is not to say that they are meant to be *portraits of* Fosia and Moawu. In the words of Pierre Harter, a scholar of Cameroonian art and both doctor and personal friend to a number of local chiefs:

> As is the case throughout traditional Africa, these images are stereotyped, bearing no resemblance to the individuals they represent; they are not really portraits in the Western sense. This avoidance of likeness – extending even to the faces – precludes the possibility of differentiating between the figures. ... Bamileke tradition ... held that 'portraits' should not bear any resemblance to their models, and should even tend to be repetitive.
> (Harter 1990, 70, 75)[9]

The appearance of these images is precise enough for the Bangwa viewer to be able to identify the rank of the figure, but not the individual identity of the chief in question. Since the faces of the statues look very little like Fosia or Moawu, it would not be possible even for someone who knew both men to work out, purely from an examination of the physical appearance of the statues, which was designated to which chief. The identities are given to the statues not on the basis of resemblance, but on the basis of designation, legitimated by incantation and the ritual application of appropriate substances.

Once an identity has been given to them, the statues differ among themselves sufficiently for the viewer who knows their names to be able to remember which name is designated to which statue. The statues are repetitive, but they are not identical. They need to be visually distinguishable, since in the royal skull house they are placed next to the skull of the relevant chief, but on certain occasions they are removed for celebrations and then returned to the house.[10] If they were indistinguishable then the wrong statue could end up next to the wrong skull.

These Bangwa statues are not unique; ancestor figures of not dissimilar kinds are found among many other peoples in Africa, as well as in Oceania (LaGamma 2007).[11]

---

9 See also Rudy 1972; Vansina 1972; Thompson 1973. However, Brain and Pollock (1971, 119) claim that these figures are "intended as realistic portraits". It seems to me that, even if they are meant as realistic portraits, they are, as Harter observes, stereotyped, so their identity must in practice have been fixed by a form of designation. Brain and Pollock add that "at great ceremonies *lefem* figures are borrowed from lesser nobles and, by a kind of subterfuge, converted into the appropriate ancestors" (118).

10 Harter 1990, 72; Brain and Pollock 1971, 2, 68, 85, 116, 118. Harter and Brain disagree about when the statues are resident in the skull house. For Brain they are usually there, and sometimes removed; for Harter they are usually removed, and sometimes there.

11 In Africa, ancestor worship is particularly prominent among peoples, like the Bangwa, who speak Bantu languages; see Evans-Pritchard 1956, 315. For warnings against the tendency to assume that African figures are always connected to the cult of the ancestors, see Siroto 1979; Roberts and Roberts 2007, 12.

In most cases their appearance is as generic as those of the Bangwa, if not more so.[12] In fig. 3.5, for example, we can see drawings of a selection of figures from the coast and offshore islands of the Cenderawasih (Geelvink) Bay area of northwest New Guinea. Some of the figures stand while others sit, and most of them have disproportionately large heads. A few figures of this kind contain skulls. Skulls of chiefs and of first-born children who had died young were taken from decomposed corpses after their deaths and placed inside one of these carved receptacles (De Clercq 1893, 185; Corbey 2019, 138–47; cf. Breckenridge 1968, 18–27). The majority of such figures, however, did not contain skulls, and many were too small to hold even the skull of a child. But whether they contained a skull or not, they were supposed to make a residence for the spirits of the dead.[13]

These figures are generally referred to in the scholarly literature as *korvar* (*korwar*, *karwar*), a word that in the Biak-Numfor language means either a corpse or a spirit (De Clercq 1893, 159–67; Corbey 2019, 26). They were kept in the homes of the bereaved and were offered small gifts such as tobacco and pieces of cloth (Van Baaren 1968, 30). On festive occasions they could be joked with in a playful way, having cigarettes placed behind their ears and plates of food set before them (De Clercq 1898, 158; Van Baaren 1968, 39). Gifts were given in the hope that the spirit resident in the *korvar* would reciprocate and protect the family from evil spirits, as well as bring success in gardening, love, hunting and warfare; and then, if the spirits obliged, their living descendants were required to give further offerings. The people who made *korvars* also made small talismans that they wore round their necks, which were sometimes surmounted by miniature images that closely resembled the domestic *korvar*, and which were also thought to be homes to ancestral spirits (De Clercq 1898, pl. xxxvii). These were taken as protection on raids and long journeys, but had other uses too; they were "tethered to objects to prevent theft, worn while receiving dowry gifts among relatives, attached to fishing nets, carried on the back by young men in order to attract girls, etc." (Corbey 2019, 249).

Like the *lefem* figures of the Bangwa, *korvars* are stereotyped in appearance, with their noses, in particular, carved in the same style on every piece as a flat, down-turned arrow. They do not and are not trying to look like the people whose spirits they contain, and they were also not taken to be images of the spirits themselves (Forge 2017c, 112). In Cenderawasih Bay, spirits of the dead were thought of as resembling the humans they had left, but to be white rather than brown in colour (Corbey 2019, 39; cf. Malinowski 1916, 368). *Korvars* can be recognized as *korvars* from their generic appearance, but in order to discover which *korvar* they are – whose spirit dwells in them – one has to ask someone acquainted with the departed.

The two kinds of ancestor figures that we have been considering relate to individuals, but sometimes a single ancestor figure can refer to more than one ancestor. Some peoples in equatorial Africa, such as the Kota (fig. 3.6) and the Fang (fig. 3.7), fill containers with relics of several ancestors, and then place one or two figures on top of them. Among the Kota, these figures, known as *boho-na-bwete* (Perrois 2012, 39), were given names, which were not the same as those of the people whose relics were kept in

12 There are exceptions to the rule, for instance Yoruba Àkó effigies; see Poynor 1987; Abíódún 2013.

13 I use the word 'spirit' as a shorthand for concepts of posthumous existence that varied among the peoples of the region. For concepts of the spirit elsewhere in Melanesia, see Malinowski 1916, 367–68; Gunn 1992, 116–18.

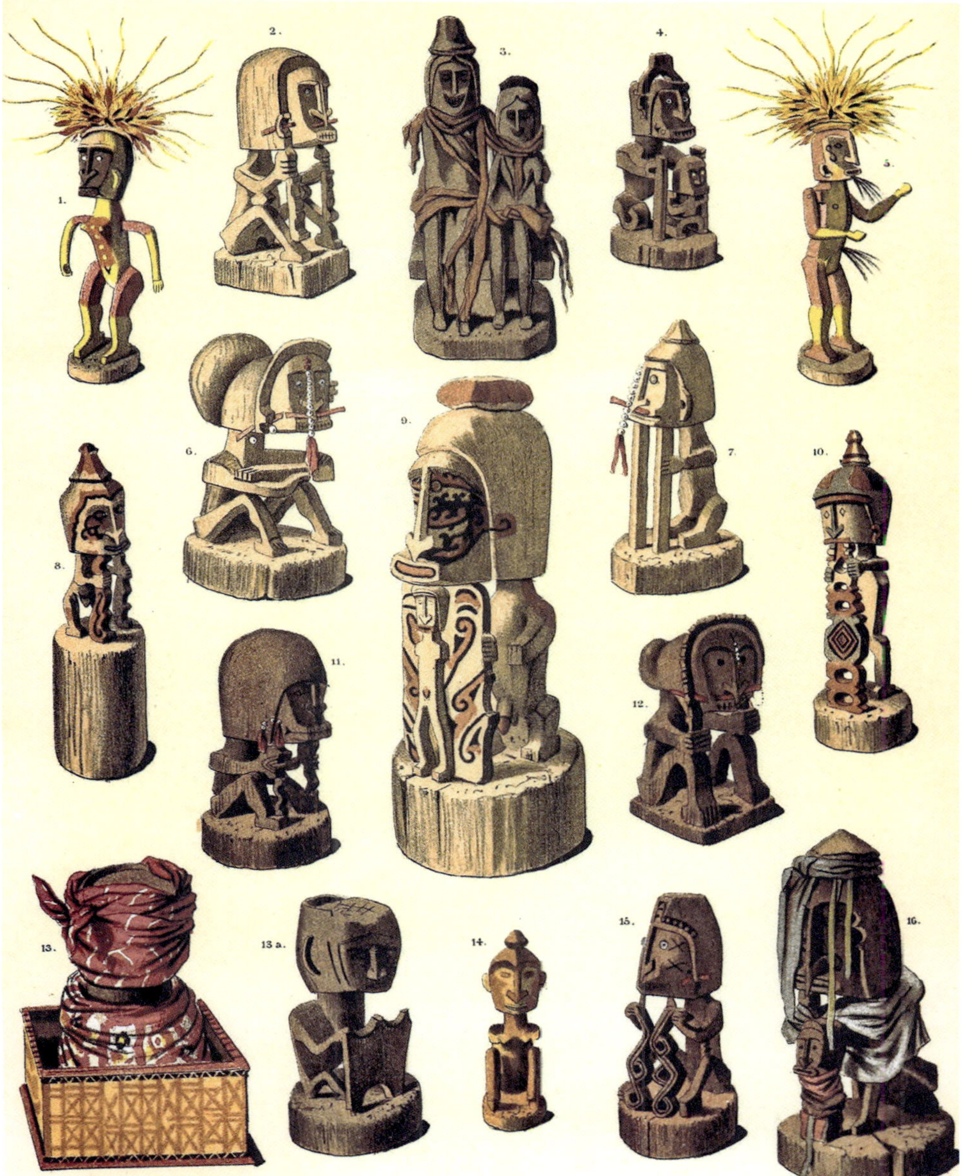

3.5 | Cenderawasih Bay *korvars* (De Clercq 1893, pl. xxxv)

the container below. The names were supposed to have power, which was needed, since the main purpose of the figure was to protect against hostile sorcerers who might try to drain the power of the relics. The figure also gave a face and identity to the reliquary, so that when people called on the relics for aid and protection, the face provided a focus for invocations. In certain regions of Kota territory, the figures were sometimes taken out of the reliquaries and held aloft in ritual dances (Siroto 1968, 27, 86, 88).

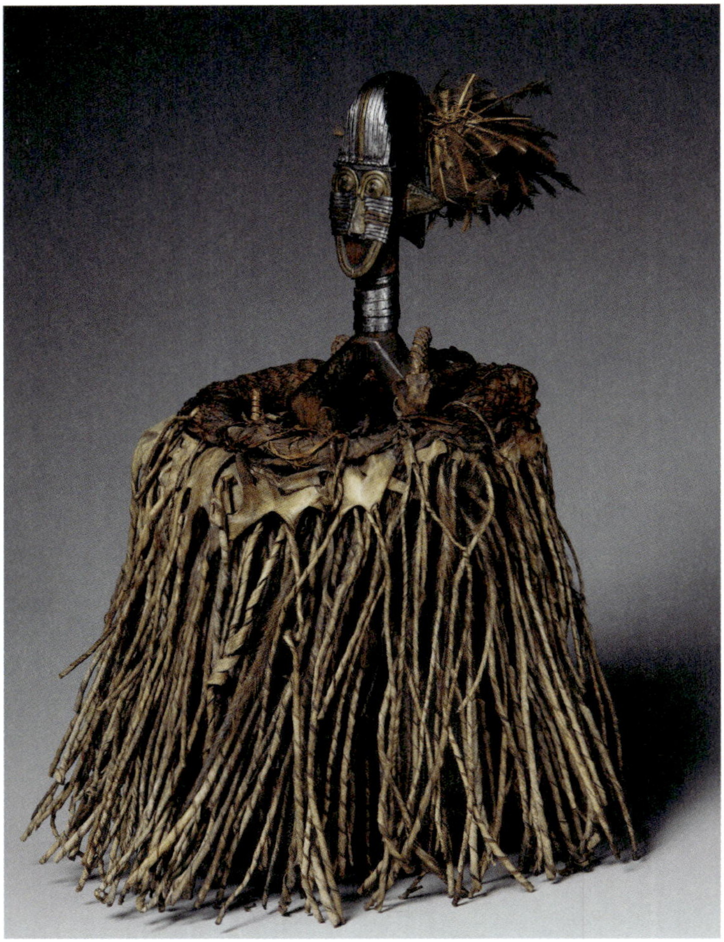

3.6 | Kota reliquary with basket, before 1897. Musée du Quai Branly, Paris

The Fang and the Kota are neighbours, and their reliquary figures seem to have had not dissimilar purposes, as protectors of, and faces for, the relics. The latter function has been described by Essona Ekwaga, a Fang from Gabon:

> The figure represents no ancestor. There are many skulls in the reliquary. Who should we choose to represent? And who would be satisfied with the choice if his own grandfather should be ignored? The figures were made to warn others that this was 'the box of skulls' and they were made to represent all the ancestors within. What causes us satisfaction in seeing the *eyima* [statues] atop the *bieri* [relics] is that there we see disclosed our ancestors. Their faces are strong, quiet and reflective. They are thinking about our problems and how to help us. We see that they see.
> (Fernandez 1973, 205)

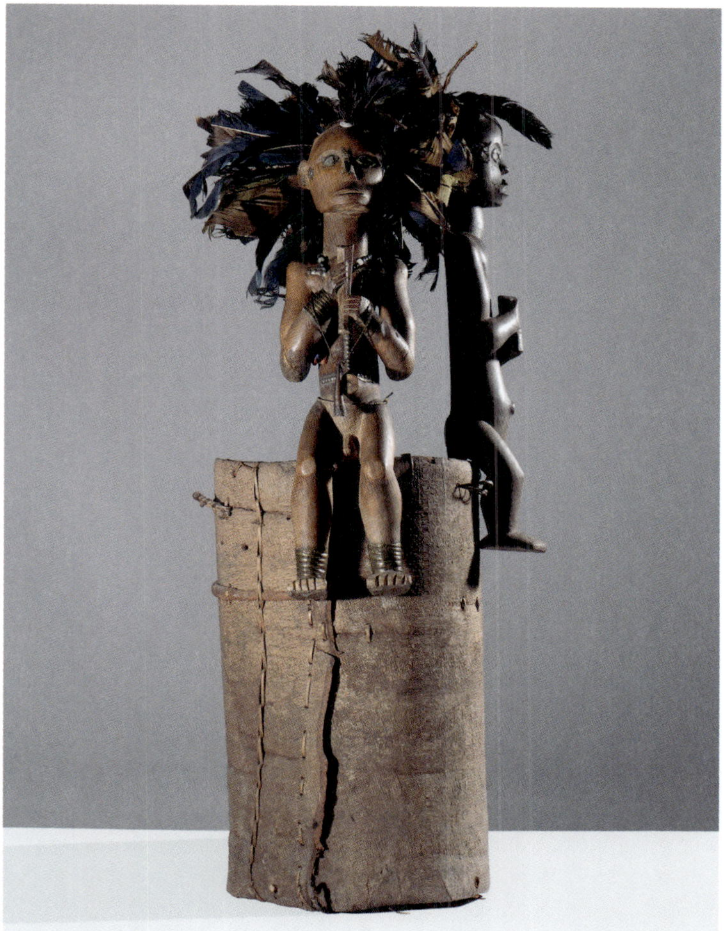

3.7 | Fang reliquary with basket, before 1897. Ethnologisches Museum, Berlin

Ekwaga, as a modern Fang, may not be speaking for his forebears in this matter, and it may be that there has always been a wide variety of opinion among the Fang about the meaning and function of their reliquary statues.[14] But we will assume for the sake of argument that Ekwaga's response is not uncommon.

In all of these examples the ancestor figure does not resemble the ancestor, and there is also no other iconographic device, no attribute, no pertinent narrative to help the viewer find out who the statue represents. In order to identify the ancestor, you have to be *linked* in some way to the original act of designation that gave the statue its identity; in this, the process is rather similar to the way we come to know a person's name (Kripke 1981, 91, 96). The examples we have considered, then, differ from ancestor figures in

14 On variability in belief within societies, see Malinowski 1916, 428–30; Humphrey and Laidlaw 1994.

some other cultures, which make use of likeness as a way of connecting the statue with the ancestor. We are told by Polybius that in ancient Rome

> After the burial and all the usual ceremonies have been performed, they place the likeness of the deceased in the most conspicuous spot in his house, surmounted by a wooden canopy or shrine. This likeness consists of a mask made to represent the deceased with extraordinary fidelity both in shape and colour. These likenesses they display at public sacrifices adorned with much care. And when any illustrious member of the family dies, they carry these masks to the funeral, putting them on men whom they think as like the originals as possible in height and other personal peculiarities. And these substitutes assume clothes according to the rank of the person represented.[15]
> (Polybius, *Histories*, 6.53)

That these two situations are not quite as different as they may seem, from a meta-iconographic point of view, will emerge when we come to discuss likeness in Chapter 6.

Pragmatics and semantics

In Chapter 2 I very briefly introduced the concept of pragmatics, defining it as the analysis of all those aspects of communication that are needed to bridge the gap between literal meaning and speaker's meaning. This is one definition of pragmatics, but there are a number of others. One thing they all have in common is that none satisfies everyone in the field (Levinson 1983, 5–34; Ariel 2010, 23–55; Ezcurdia and Stainton 2013). Nevertheless, thousands of books and articles are published every year with 'pragmatics' in the title, which confirms the idea that we sometimes use words we cannot define (Wittgenstein 1953, 31–35).

Students of pragmatics are at least agreed that certain topics are central to their research, such as 'deixis', 'implicature', 'presupposition', 'speech acts' and 'aspects of reference'. Of these topics deixis might be considered quintessentially pragmatic (Levinson 1983, 54). The term 'deixis' is derived from the ancient Greek verb for 'to show' or 'to point out', and it refers to those grammatical features that need the context of utterance in order to make the meanings of words and sentences explicit. We use deixis every day; when you say 'I'm just going out to the shops', you assume that the person you are talking to knows who 'I' refers to and which shops you mean. If you say 'He seems ill to me', then you might be referring to some person or animal in your vicinity, or perhaps to some person or animal you have just been discussing (this form of deixis, relying on an earlier referring expression, is known as anaphora). There are numerous words in every language that make contextual references of this sort. In English, besides the personal pronouns, we have demonstratives like 'this' or 'those', place and time adverbs like 'here' and 'now', and numerous generic expressions that need context in order to be fully understood (e.g. the woman at the table in the corner is my boss).

Researchers into pragmatics do not usually consider names to be deictic parts of speech, but those of us with common names might feel that they should (Macrae 2019, 42–43). The Paul Taylors of this world include a saxophonist, a comedian, a cricketer,

15 Cf. Breckenridge 1968, 146–51. I thank Ilaria Bernocchi for bringing these passages to my attention.

three footballers, a murderer, an ambassador and a professional wrestler, but none of them is the author of this book; anyone who says 'I know Paul Taylor' needs to be questioned further on which Paul Taylor they are talking about.

Pragmatics studies how language manages to refer to the world, but our problem is rather the opposite: to investigate how the world manages to be referred to by language. And yet the nature of the two problems is sometimes very similar. Just as you will not fully understand the statement 'Fosia is standing by the door to his house' if you do not know which of the houses in the village is his or what Fosia looks like, so too you will not know which of the many men standing by the doors of their houses is Fosia until you somehow acquire this piece of verbal information, by asking 'Where can I find Fosia?' or 'Are you Fosia?' The problems have the same structure; in the first the name 'Fosia' does not give us enough information to allow us to decide on the appearance of its bearer, and in the second the appearance of Fosia does not give us enough information to allow us to decide on his name. 'Fosia' could refer to any number of men, because it is a generic name; similarly, men have a generic appearance and could be referred to by any number of names.

For the iconographer there is a further level of complication. Suppose that you know what Fosia looked like but that he has died, and what you are looking for is not Fosia but a statue of Fosia, which you have been told is standing in the shrine where these statues reside. If Fosia came from a culture that made illusionistic ancestor figures then you might have been able to recognize the statue of Fosia by its resemblance to the man himself; but since his culture – the Bangwa – made generic ancestor figures that do not resemble specific people, then you are back to square one, and will need to ask, 'Which is the statue of Fosia?'

The iconographies of the Bangwa *lefems* – and the Cenderawasih Bay *korvars* – rely on pragmatics, while the Fang reliquary figures rely on semantics. If a member of the *lefem* society says to you, 'The *lefem* figure in the corner is Fosia', then you will be able to identify the iconography of that *lefem* figure (fig. 3.3). Even if you were familiar with Bangwa iconographic conventions and were aware that the figure in question was both a *lefem* figure and a depiction of a chief, you would not be able to identify it as Fosia without having that information provided. It is not possible even for a Bangwa, merely from looking at the statue, to ascertain its specific iconographic intentionality. The Fang reliquary figures, on the other hand, have no names (fig. 3.7). They are generic ancestor figures; if you have seen an ancestor figure on one Fang relic basket, you will be able to identify similar figures on any other Fang relic basket. They are not images of a particular person, and so, unlike the Bangwa figures, they do not take on the name of that particular person. They also do not have their own names, in the way that the Kota figures, the *boho-na-bwete*, do (fig. 3.6). Once you know the conventions of Fang reliquary carvings, then you are able to recognize the iconography of any Fang reliquary carving.

Of course, to identify the function of a Fang figure you will also need information that the figure does not provide; merely looking at one of these statues will not tell you what the image means. The difference is that, with the Fang figures, once you have learned the iconographic convention then you will be able to understand the iconography of other Fang reliquary figures you encounter in future; but the same is not true of the Bangwa *lefem* or the Cenderawasih Bay *korvar*. They are irreducibly pragmatic, and there will always be a gap between the depictive content of the figures and their iconographic meaning.

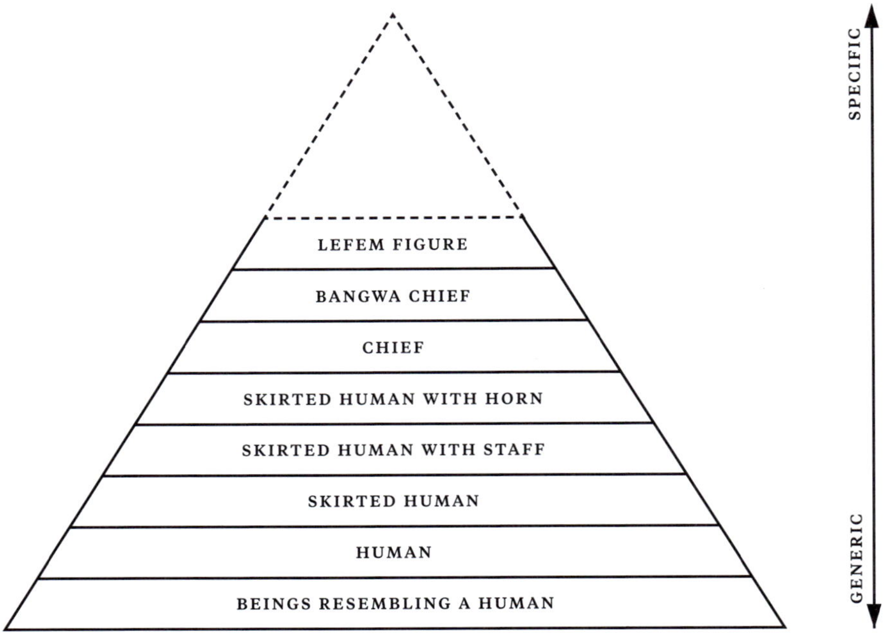

3.8 | Triangle of Content for a Bangwa *lefem* figure

To put this idea in diagrammatic form, we might say that images of this pragmatic kind have a truncated Triangle of Content (fig. 1.4), which never reaches its iconographic apex. In the empty summit of this diagram (fig. 3.8), the name 'Fosia' is absent.

Varieties of non-representation

In the last two sections, the word 'representation' has only appeared in other people's quotations. The reason is that, while all the figures I have been discussing can be said to have an iconography and to resemble, it is not clear that any of them can be taken to represent, or that all of them can be said to depict.

Pierre Harter argues that the Bangwa *lefem* figures (figs. 3.3 and 3.4) are not meant to be portraits of Fosia or Moawu, claiming that, if they had been, they would have broken the 'rule of nonresemblance' that holds in Bangwa and much of traditional African art (Harter 1990, 75, 77). The purpose of these sculptures is not to remind us of what Fosia or Moawu looked like – in fact, they go out of their way to make sure that they do not – but to provide a place where the spirits of the chiefs can reside.

The Cenderawasih Bay *korvars*, with their huge heads balanced on spindly bodies and their stereotypical features (fig. 3.5), are still less realistic than the *lefem* figures, and are clearly making no attempt to represent the people whose spirits are thought to reside within them. They were also not meant to represent the spirits of the dead themselves. Among the people of the Cenderawasih Bay region it was common to bury people in a seated position, and so seated *korvars* do resemble a generic buried corpse, or at least a generic buried corpse with an enormous head; but whether they were meant to depict a corpse in its grave is unclear, especially as some *korvars* were shown standing.

So, for both the *lefem* figures and the *korvars* we can say that they contain the individual spirits that inhabit them, but that they are not meant to be images of those spirits. It seems right to say that the *lefem* depicts, generically, a Bangwa chief, but does it represent its indwelling spirit? Perhaps it would be better to say that, if *lefems* contain the spirits that live within them, then they embody them, or even in a sense that they *are* those spirits, who are now alive in their enveloping form. It might be tempting to think of fig. 3.3 as 'representing' Fosia, but if we do, then we are saying that the *lefem* statue is iconographically analogous to the images of Herod (fig. 1.6), Christ (fig. 1.1) or Hamlet (fig. 1.2), and this surely is to fail to take account of fundamental differences. The works by Caucig, Leonardo and Delacroix are taken to be images of people or characters; they are not thought to be embodiments or incarnations of those people or characters. The figure of Fosia is not an image of Fosia. It is, perhaps, Fosia – or at least it is on those ritual occasions when his spirit is taken to enter the statue.

Using a similar argument, we might decide that the *korvar* does not represent the spirit that inhabits it. So what does it depict? If the *korvar* portrays anything at all, it is other *korvars*; the aim is to make its identity as a *korvar* clear. The shape of a *korvar* was also carved into talismans and the columns of buildings, and these too were thought to be the homes of ancestral spirits. Presumably, the traditional form of the *korvar* was thought to be a necessary precondition if the spirits of the dead were to agree to take up residence.[16] Should we then think of a *korvar* as a depiction of a *korvar*? Or is it itself a *korvar*? We might remember Nelson Goodman's remark that "none of the automobiles off an assembly line is a picture of any of the rest" (Goodman 1976, 4). Similarly, perhaps, no *korvar* depicts any other *korvar*. If the *korvar* does not depict or represent, should we think of it as an image at all? Perhaps we should not, and should think of it as being the kind of man-made visual sign that E.H. Gombrich discussed in one of his best-known essays, 'Meditations on a Hobby Horse':

> The idol takes the place of the god. The question whether it represents the 'external form' of the particular divinity or, for that matter, of a class of demons is quite inappropriate. The idol serves as the substitute of the god in worship and ritual – it is a man-made god in precisely the sense that the hobby-horse is a man-made horse; to question it further means to court deception.
> (Gombrich 1963, 3)

This formulation, however, does not quite capture the particular character of the *korvar*. The *korvar* is not a substitute for the spirit of the dead, it is the home of the spirit of the dead.

Since a *korvar* was a visual artefact with a clear semantic identity, and since its appearance was non-arbitrary – that is, one could not substitute a very different artefact in its place, in the way that one can συβστιτυτε letters without altering the meaning of a word – then we might conclude that it is not a symbol in the sense outlined by C.S. Peirce.[17] And even if it is not an image *of* anything, it might be considered to have an iconographic

16 On 'the sociological weight of tradition', see Malinowski 1922, 115. Cf. Hubert and Mauss 1902–03, 10–12, 20, 43, 53; Horton 1965, 28; Forge 2017a, 64; Forge 2017c, 118–19.

17 See Chapter 2, ftn. 16.

identity. If it is reasonable to think of abstract paintings as having an iconography, as we did in Chapter 1, then surely *korvars* can be thought of in the same terms.

The Fang reliquary figures (fig. 3.7) resemble humans more closely than the *korvars*, and, according to Essona Ekwaga (p. 68 above), they depict ancestors. It seems fair to say as well that they represent Fang ancestors in a generic sense. But we might want to make a distinction between two kinds of generic. These figures are not so much 'some Fang ancestor or other' as 'a Fang ancestor whose name is not known' – that is, Ekwaga thinks of the figures as having a certain individuality: they are approached with reverence, as if they were persons of power. They are in an interesting liminal position between the generic and the individual.

The Kota *boho-na-bwete* (fig. 3.6), despite their seeming closeness in function to the reliquary guardians of the Fang, operate in a different way from an iconographic point of view. In a similar way to the Fang figures, they do not depict or represent individual people or spirits, but it is not clear that they depict or represent generic people or spirits either. Rather, like the *korvars*, they seem to be not images of other beings so much as man-made artefacts, which have their own iconographic intentionality.

The relic cult for which the *boho-na-bwete* were made has been largely eradicated by a combination of Christianity and indigenous witch hunting movements (Siroto 1968; Perrois 2012, 9–10). As a result, ethnographic fine details of the cult have been lost, with modern Kota often unsure about the precise rationale behind the *bwete* figures. It is not recorded if the figures were themselves thought to be the homes of spirits, or whether they were thought to be no more than potent conduits between the relics in the baskets beneath and the people who came to consult those relics. The fact that they were given names, as we have seen, suggests a certain agency; and it is probably unwise to draw too crisp a distinction between images with and without indwelling spirits.

Fetishes

In eighteenth- and nineteenth-century anthropology the word 'fetish' – derived from *fetiçao*, the Portuguese word for a sorcerer's magical object or image (Pietz 1987, 36–38) – was used to describe certain kinds of artefacts and natural objects that were imbued with power, from human-like figures to bundles of potent materials to sticks and stones. There was also much talk of 'fetishism', taken to be "a stage of religious development associated with a low grade of consciousness and of civilisation" (Haddon 1921, 91). In the twentieth century there was repeated criticism of the term's vagueness (Rattray 1927; Pietz 1985; Pietz 1987; Ellen 1988; Pool 1990), but 'fetish' has not disappeared from the anthropological literature. Indeed, in recent years it has staged something of a comeback, in part because the alternatives with which people have tried to replace it, such as 'power figure' and 'power object', are also vague (Albert and Kedzierska-Manzon 2016, 16).[18]

---

18 If anyone feels reluctant to use the word 'fetish' because they think it is offensive, they might consider an anecdote told me by the anthropologist James Laidlaw. While he was engaged in fieldwork in India he mentioned to some Jain idol-worshippers that in Western academia the word 'idol' was considered disparaging, and that it was thought more acceptable to use the word 'image'. They replied that they were well aware of the fact that Westerners considered the word 'idol' disparaging, but that they did not, because they were idol-worshippers (cf. Humphrey and Laidlaw 1994, 57–58; Laidlaw 1995, 5). Cf. Douglas 1966, 74: "I suspect that our professional delicacy in avoiding the term 'Primitive' is the product of secret convictions of superiority".

It might be thought that the solution to the semantic nebulosity of 'fetish' would be to abandon it and use African terms instead. But that would not solve the problem, since African words referring to a similar range of objects can be just as nebulous. An African word that 'fetish' is often used to translate is *nkisi*, variants of which (*nkosi, nkishi;* pl. *minkisi, bankishi*) are employed by a number of peoples who live in the Congo basin. It can refer to nature spirits (Hersak 2010b, 618), to non-figurative charms which do not contain spirits (Lehuard and Lecomte 2010, 130–32, Bourgeois 2014, 20), to non-figurative charms which do contain spirits (MacGaffey 1994, 125), to figurative statues which do not contain spirits (Bourgeois 2014, 27), to figurative statues which contain non-ancestral spirits (Roberts and Roberts 2007, 50, Wastiau 2006, 21, MacGaffey 1990, 49) and to figurative statues that contain ancestral spirits (Hersak 2010a, 41). Italian Capuchin friars in the Congo region took the polysemy of the word and adapted it to Christian ends, calling the eucharist *nriwa a nkisi* (spiritual food; Hilton 1987, 304). This is a classic example of a 'cluster concept', where the sense of a word has spread by analogy and so acquired a range of referents that do not share a common property:

> And we extend our concept of *nkisi* as in spinning a thread we twist fibre on fibre. And the strength of the thread does not reside in the fact that some one fibre runs through its whole length, but in the overlapping of many fibres.[19]

In what follows I will continue to use the word 'fetish', since its very vagueness reflects the polysemy of indigenous terminology; we also need some term to refer to a range of objects that are used in similar ways in various African and non-African cultures but are described by different words in local languages.[20] Objects of these kind, as we will see, are unusual and interesting from a meta-iconographic perspective.

There is nothing that all fetishes have in common, so attempts to come up with a global definition of 'the fetish' are bound to fail. But it can be said that the objects or figures that have been called 'fetishes' have mostly been rendered powerful by the incantation of spells, often with the addition of potent materials or 'medicines', and that these rituals have been used to entice a spirit – usually a non-human and non-divine one – to reside in the object.[21] Sometimes these inspirited objects were used to protect their wearer or bearer against witchcraft or other misfortune (Ward 1956, 52–53), and sometimes their power was put to use by diviners (Bouttiaux 2016, 54); but they were frequently employed for more hostile purposes.

Fetishes of the aggressive kind could generate great fear in the communities where they appeared. E.E. Evans-Pritchard wrote that fetishes entered Nuer territory in South Sudan at the end of the nineteenth century and caused consternation on their arrival:

19 Wittgenstein 1953, 32, with '*nkisi*' substituted for 'number'.

20 Cf. Gunn 1992, 114: "I use the term 'totem' because I do not intend to add to the confusion created by anthropologists and others who use indigenous or other terms to individually label this widespread phenomenon".

21 I thank Adeyemi Akande for discussing this with me. I write 'usually' because the relationship of fetish spirits to divine spirit can be intricate; see Evans-Pritchard 1956, 112–13, 192–93.

> They are highly dangerous, not only to those who are at enmity with their owners, but also to their owners' families, kin and neighbours if they do not receive sufficient attention. When they seize people death follows rapidly on the first symptoms, which are said to be generally violent pains in the abdomen sometimes combined with blood in the faeces, unless steps are at once taken to appease them and, in the case of enemies, their owners also. Therefore a *gwan kulangni*, an owner of a fetish, whom I shall speak of as a wizard, is much feared by those with whom he disputes and by those around him.
> (Evans-Pritchard 1956, 101)[22]

The 'wizard' may use the fetish to achieve his own ends, or he may deploy it to act on behalf of others.[23] Those, for instance, whose cows have been stolen or whose spouse is being unfaithful or whose relatives have been killed in a feud may go to the wizard to ask him, in return for payment, to use the power of the fetish to obtain revenge. The fetish itself may also be given payment, in the form of food, alcoholic beverages or other gifts (Evans-Pritchard 1953, 212; Ward 1956, 57; Colleyn 2009, 39). The Yombe fetish in fig. 3.9 has received offerings of rope and (like the *korvars*) pieces of cloth. It has also been hit with nails to make it angry, so that its vengeance will be swifter and harsher (MacGaffey 1977, 174). That was not the only method of angering a fetish; other methods included "insulting it, exploding gunpowder next to it, banging on the ground in front of it, even making obscene references to its mother-in-law" (MacGaffey 2015, 154).

Because the spirits inside fetishes are usually anonymous, their identities can become merged with their containers more easily than the spirits of ancestors, which everyone knows are different entities from the figures in which they reside (Evans-Pritchard 1954). The cruel punishments doled out by vengeful fetishes are often reflected in the unsettling appearance of figurative examples (fig. 3.10), and so the statues themselves acquire a kind of personality and character. Early descriptions of fetishes assumed that, since there seemed to be no external god or ancestor to which the fetish could be taken to refer, those who revered them were praying to the material objects themselves; whereas it was (usually) the indwelling spirit that was important (Pietz 1988).[24] It was from this misconception of the fetish that the secondary meanings of the word, Marxist and erotic, were derived.

From an iconographic point of view, figurative fetishes are not easy to characterize (we will ignore non-figurative fetishes, since we are thinking about the meanings of images). As with the *korvars*, it is hard to decide what they might be thought to depict. The examples in figs. 3.9 and 3.10 resemble humans more than *korvars* do, but does it make sense to think of them as depicting humans? Or would it be better to think of them as not depicting at all, but rather as *being* fetishes? These are intricate questions that cannot be answered from the armchair; one would need to talk to fetish makers, owners and users to find out more about their thoughts and attitudes, and one might well find that they had differing intuitions on the matter. One might also decide that talk of

---

22 Cf. Evans-Pritchard 1940, 177. Nuer fetishes were not figurative, but consisted of bundles of wood, rather like the Asante fetish in fig. 5.9, discussed on p. 167. See Evans-Pritchard 1956, 137–38.

23 Sometimes fetishes are owned not by individuals but by associations; see Gagliardi 2015, 229–41.

24 For examples of fetishes that do not contain spirits but are *loci* for power, see Bourgeois 2014, 20, 27.

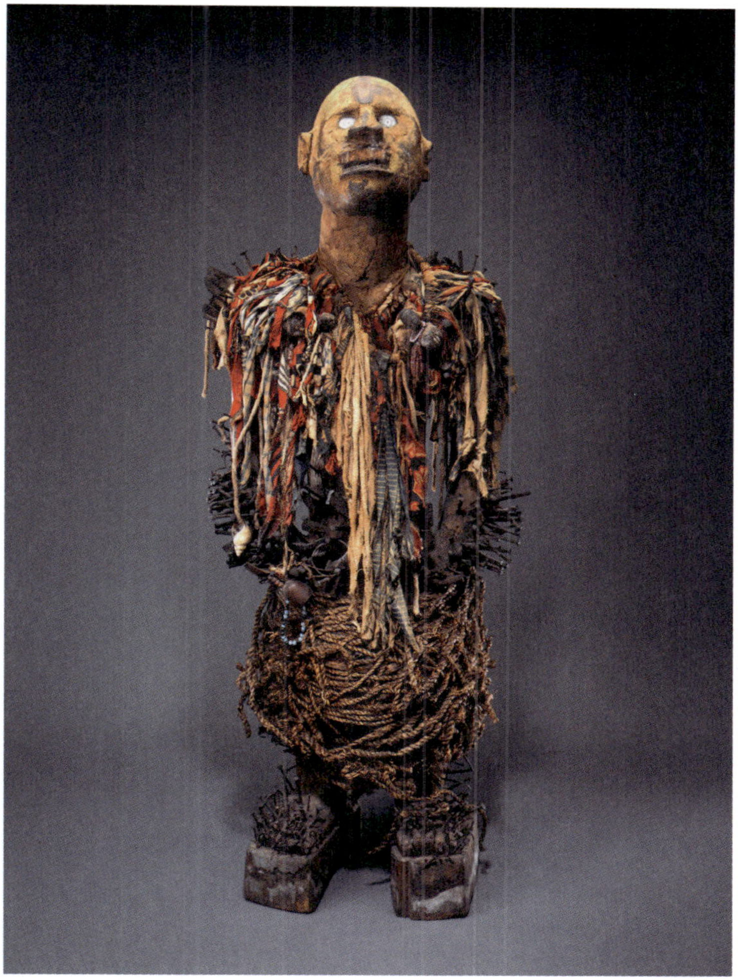

3.9 | Yombe *nkisi* fetish, 18th–19th century. Fowler Museum, UCLA

'depiction' misses the point in some way, and that in order to understand what is going on in these images one must use local concepts. "To understand a people's thought one has to think in their symbols", as Evans-Pritchard put it (1951, 79). This should not concern us; terminology should be jettisoned when it is no longer of use. To be told that 'depiction' is not the right word is information of value, helping us to close in on the right way of thinking about an image and its meaning.

Whatever we decide about 'depiction', 'representation' seems to be the wrong word when applied to fetishes. For what do fetishes represent? They cannot be taken to represent the spirit that resides within them. The wooden statue is, so to speak, the body of the fetish, and just as your body does not represent your mind, and does not represent anyone else's body, so the fetish's body should not be thought to represent its spirit. Like ancestor figures, one might wonder if fetishes should qualify as images at all.

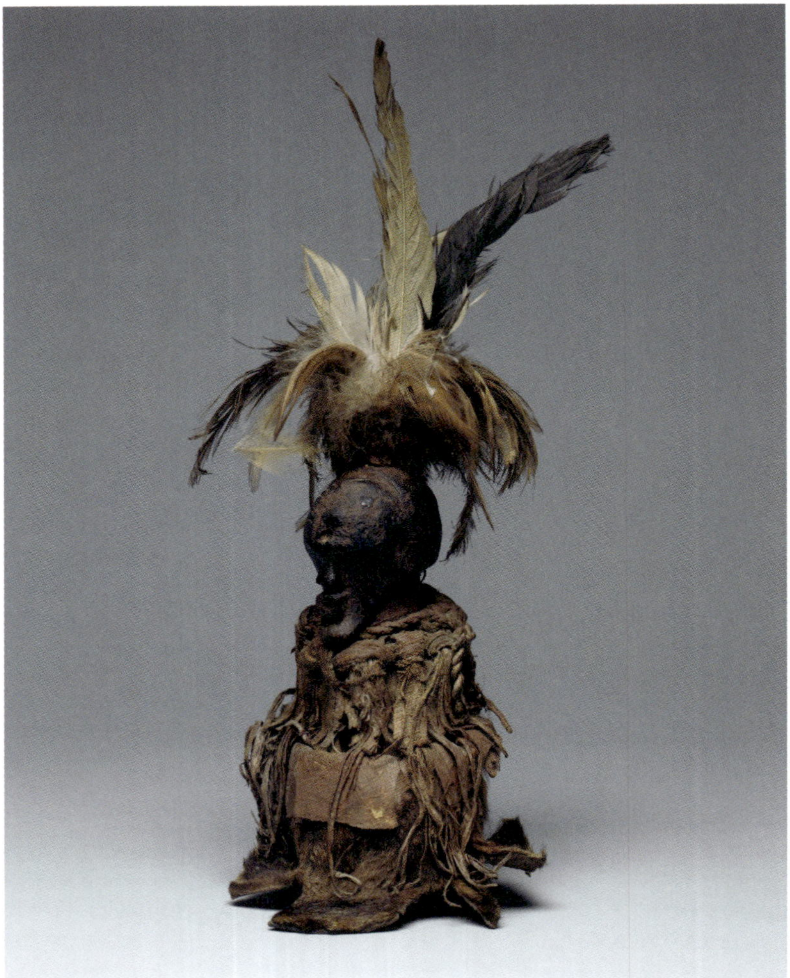

3.10 | Songye *nkishi* fetish, late 19th-early 20th century. Brooklyn Museum, New York

Although this depends on one's standpoint; for those outside that culture, it looks like an image of a human, but for those inside the culture of the fetish, it is not an image but a living being.

It might seem here as if we are moving towards some form of iconographic perspectivism, in which a fetish depicts and represents one thing to a person within a traditional culture, and something else to a person in a modern technological culture. But that may not be the right way to think about it. One does not have to believe in angels to use the word 'angel', and atheists and theists agree about a great deal of the word's meaning. To use the word 'angel' correctly, even in a non-religious context, one needs to know that the properties of angels include being able to fly from heaven to earth, etc. An angel is, from an atheist's point of view, non-existent, but it has a conceptual character, just as unicorns, legendary saints and cartoon characters have a conceptual character. If you want to use the word 'angel' correctly, then you need to use it, so to speak, on religious territory; it assumes religious concepts which you must take on board, if only in a make-believe fashion, in order to apply the concept yourself. Of course, you can say 'Angels do not exist', but if you are then asked, 'What does not exist?', you have to reply 'Creatures who can fly from heaven to earth, etc.'

Similarly, if you want to know what the word 'fetish' means (or its African equivalents, such as *suman, kungang, nkisi, kulangni*), you have to understand it on magico-medical territory. If you do not know that *suman* is a general word for a variety of objects with great powers, then you do not understand that Akan word. What looks like a broom to us is in fact a powerful *suman* called Kunkuma, which has been carefully medicated through sacrifices, imprecations and the attachment of potent materials, and is said to protect its possessors against misfortunes of all kinds: "the springs of the flint-lock gun bound upon its handle will prevent you being shot'"(Rattray 1927, 13). Presumably, the *suman* cannot actually do this,[25] but this does not detract from the fact that to know what *suman* means, you have to be aware of what a *suman* is said to be able to do. And just as the words *suman* and 'fetish' need to be understood on magico-medical territory, so too the objects themselves need to be understood in the same way. In order to understand the iconographies of figs. 3.9 and 3.10, to know what (or if) they depict and represent, you need to understand their function and something of the discursive system within which they were given meaning.

Singles and multiples

One thing that most of the examples we have been studying in this chapter have in common is that they are what I will be calling 'singles', a concept that makes best sense when compared with another new concept, 'multiples'. To give an idea of multiples, take figs. 3.11–3.13. They are all images of Laocoön, the priest killed with his sons by sea serpents after he had thrown his spear at the Trojan horse and urged his fellow citizens to reject this gift from the Greeks (Virgil, *Aeneid*, 2.199–249). Laocoön almost certainly never existed, but this does not matter; many of the people who represented him were probably not as sure as we are about his non-existence, and, in any case, non-existence is no bar to representation, as innumerable images of mythical and fictional entities show.

I have illustrated three Laocoöns, but might have illustrated hundreds more. We have one mythical entity and hundreds of images of that mythical entity. Each of these images I shall call a multiple. Most images these days are multiples or, if they are not, they are possible multiples. It may be that there is only one print of a distant relative

25 Those involved in the cult of the fetish, however, may not see it that way. Ward 1956, 59: "[The fetish owner] was not a hypocrite; he himself believed in his fetish – had it not cured him and set him on the road to prosperity?" Against this, see for example Evans-Pritchard 1937, 183ff., on scepticism among the Zande, and 229–39 on the trickery of their witch-doctors. See too Tuzin 1997, 1, who records that in 1984 the men of Ilahita, an Arapesh village on New Guinea, confessed in church that "contrary to what the women and their foremothers had been told for generations, the spirits of the Tambaran [the secret men's cult] did not materialize and sit with the men in their secret conclaves, did not eat their sacrificial feasts, did not sing in voices of another world. These were merely illusions, created by initiated men with the help of imaginative tricks, prodigious appetites, and clever man-made devices such as flutes, trumpets, whistles, gongs and bullroarers."

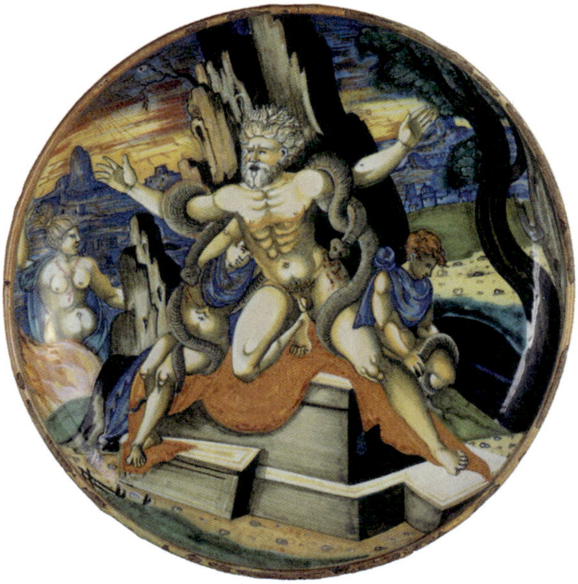

3.11 | Francesco Xanto Avelli, Maiolica shallow bowl with The Death of Laocoön and his Sons, 1539. National Gallery of Art, Washington, D.C.

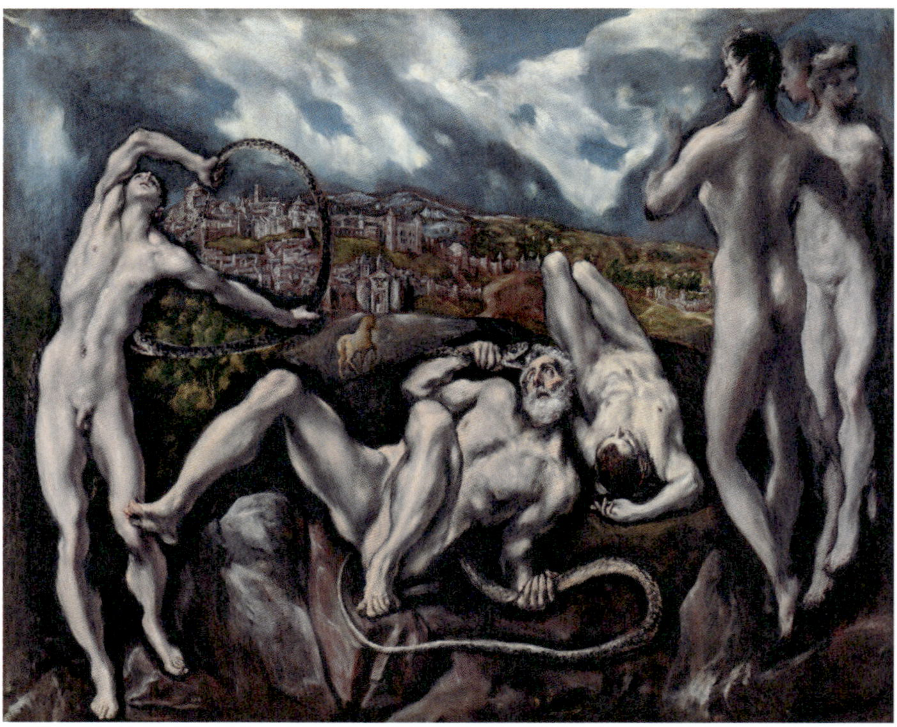

3.12 | El Greco, The Death of Laocoön and his Sons, c. 1610–14. National Gallery of Art, Washington, D.C.

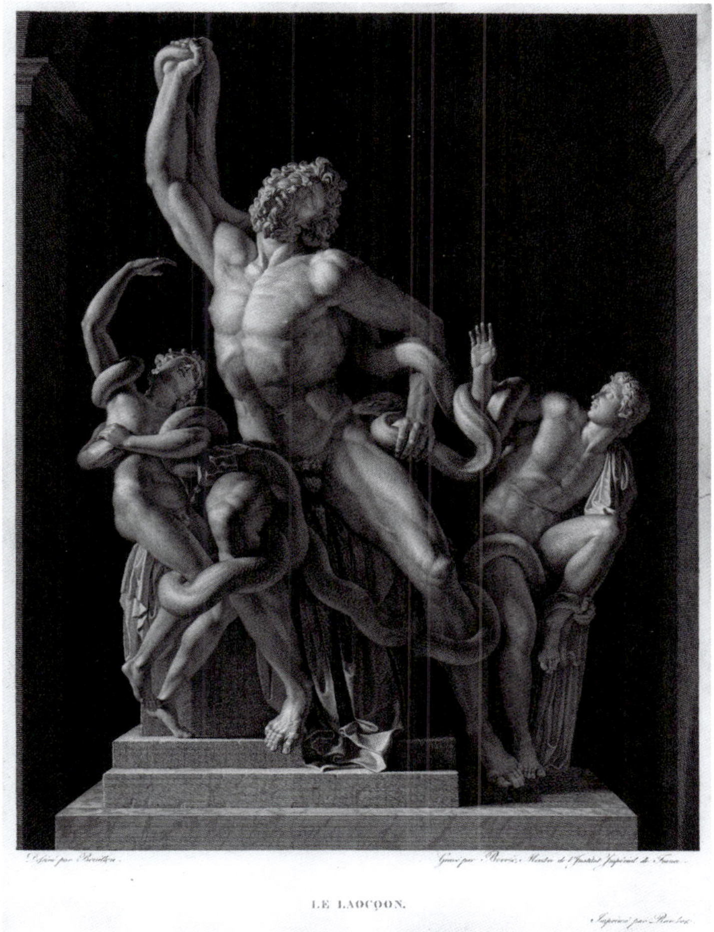

3.13 | Charles-Clément Bervic, after Pierre Bouillon, The Death of Laocoön and his Sons, engraving, c. 1809. Photographic Collection, Warburg Institute, London

in your family photo album, but when the original negative was made, an indefinite number of prints could have been manufactured from it. There is nothing to stop you scanning the print or photographing it and then reduplicating it in various digital media. Photographs made digitally can be posted online or sent to friends with the press of a button. The idea that photographs can be multiplied is an inherent feature of the medium.

There are two main kinds of multiplication. There is reproductive multiplication, when a print or photograph is reproduced a certain number of times by some technical process; and there is what we can call generative multiplication.[26] The images of

26 Walter Benjamin [1936] 1980 ignored this distinction, focusing on the difference between manual and technical reproduction. See also Taylor 2022a.

Laocoön reproduced in figs. 3.11, 3.12 and 3.13 are generative multiples: the artists have made original images of the narrative of Laocoön's death – they are not copies of one another, they are all independent representations of the mythical entity Laocoön.

Images can be both generative multiples and reproductive multiples at the same time. In fact, every reproductive multiple is a generative multiple (or at least a potential generative multiple); but not every generative multiple is a reproductive multiple. Take fig. 3.9 for example. This is a reproductive multiple, since it appears in every copy of this book and in any other book that uses this photograph from the Fowler Museum at UCLA. At the same time, it is a generative multiple, since it is only one of the possible photographs that can be taken of this particular Yombe statue; others have been taken from different angles, at different distances, in different lighting conditions and so on. Between them, visitors to the Fowler Museum will have hundreds or thousands of different photographs of this striking statue in their smartphones.

Not every generative multiple is a reproductive multiple, since one can make a generative multiple that is not reproduced; one might, for example, make a drawing of Laocoön and keep it at home. Before the birth of printmaking the majority of multiples were generative, not reproductive, though there are some early exceptions to the rule. Recently, a very unusual cache of small limestone figurines of fleshy women from the Gravettian period (c. 25,000 BC), mostly in fragments but some nearly whole, and all so alike that there seems to have been an attempt at multiple production, was discovered in north-east France (Paris et al. 2019). In European antiquity metal sculptures were recast and marbles were recarved, resulting in numerous near identical versions (Gazda 2002; Perry 2005; cf. Bagley 2009). In the Middle Ages, when manuscripts were copied, the illuminations were sometimes recreated in the style of the original, although the divergence between the original and the copy was often considerable (Noel 1995).

With the invention of printing techniques in the fifteenth century, reproductive multiples quickly began to grow in number. In fig. 3.13 we see an engraving of the famous Hellenistic sculpture of the Laocoön in the Vatican Museums. The sculpture itself is a generative multiple, since there are other images of the same fabulous event. It is also the original for reproductive multiples, since already in the sixteenth century, after its excavation in 1506, numerous marble, bronze and plaster copies were made, and it was drawn and engraved repeatedly (Bober and Rubinstein 1986, 151); today it has also been photographed millions of times. The Vatican marble is not itself a reproductive multiple; just as photographs of a celebrity are reproductive multiples, but the celebrity is not, so too images of an artefact are reproductive multiples, but the artefact is not.

An important difference between the images of Laocoön and the figure of Fosia (fig. 3.3) is that, in Bangwa culture, as in most cultures with ancestral statues, figures of recent ancestors are made just once. Since the figure of Fosia is meant to be the residence of his soul, during or after his life, there is no need for duplication. It is like a gravestone, which exists in one copy, because – assuming the parts of your body are buried in one place – there is no need to carve two. So Fosia's ancestor statue is unique; it is, for now, the only statue of Fosia in the world. In this it is unlike the many statues, plaster casts, prints, paintings, maiolica plates, photographs etc. of Laocoön. There are many photographs of this statue of Fosia – including all the illustrations in the different copies of this book – and they are both generative and reproductive multiples. But the statue of Fosia itself is not a multiple, neither generative nor reproductive.

Statues of recent ancestors make one class of what I will be calling singles. A related class consists of figures that are also the homes of spirits, but not ancestral spirits (though they may be closely related to, or work in company with, ancestral spirits). Examples would include figurines containing nature spirits, tutelary spirits or spirits employed in divination (Vogel 1973; Boyer 2008; Peek 2008; Bouttiaux 2016; Boyer 2019). Some of the most appealing of the figures in this class are the 'spirit spouses' of the Baule (fig. 3.14). The Baule believe that there are two worlds, our own and a parallel, spiritual world called the *blolo*.[27] When people die, their souls return to the spirit world; when babies are born, they come from the spirit world. There are close and constant relations between this world we know and the *blolo*. The inhabitants of the spirit world can have considerable influence over our lives, so we need to ensure that we do not anger them. In particular, we all have a spouse in the *blolo*, one to whom we are married and who expects our devotion. If we anger our spirit spouse, all kinds of sexual unhappiness can result – sterility, impotence, disease.

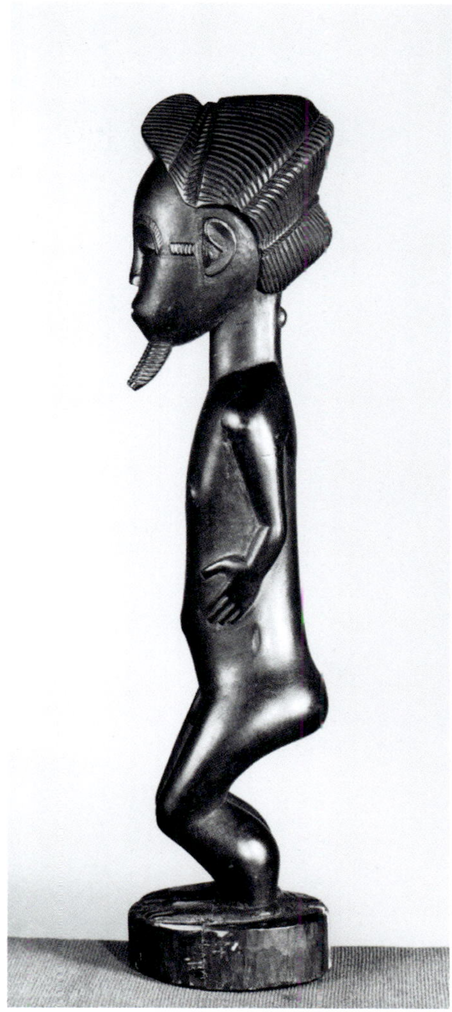

3.14 | Baule, *Blolo bian*, possibly early 20th century. Brooklyn Museum, New York

We need to keep our *blolo* spouse contented, and one way to do this is with a *blolo* figure. The spirit spouse can enter the figure, allowing you to show your devotion in a tangible way; you can caress it, feed it and keep it close by to show that you care about it. Since the *blolo* spirit is present in the figure, it knows how it is being treated, and can exact revenge if standards slip. The figure should be beautiful, because if it is ugly the spirit will be offended. However, no one supposes that the figure is a portrait of the spirit. Rather, the figure is, as with ancestor figures, a container for the spirit, and the container is its body on earth; it is treated with the respect shown to a real person.

It would be a bad idea to own two spirit spouses, since that would anger the spouse in the *blolo*. Thus, *blolo* figures are unique, there is only one earthly statuette per spirit spouse. This makes them, like figures of recent ancestors, singles. There is no need and no desire to make more than one (Ravenhill 1996; Boyer 2008).

27 The Baule split off from the Asante in the eighteenth century, and similar views are recorded among the latter, see Rattray 1927, 59: "When a child is born in this world, a ghost-mother mourns the loss of her child in the *samandow* (spirit-world)".

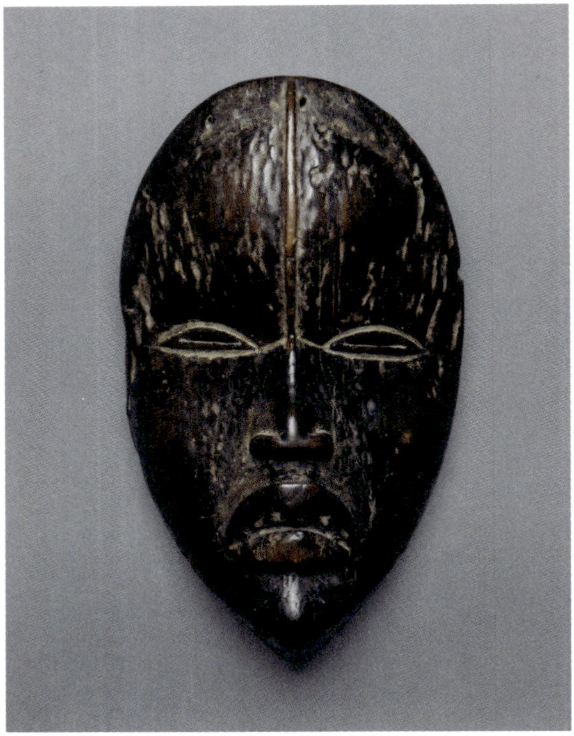

3.15 | Dan, Dean Gle mask, late 19th–early 20th century. Brooklyn Museum, New York

Certain masks can also be thought of as singles. The celebrated masks of the Dan people (fig. 3.15) are extremely numerous, and each one is thought to be a single. A forest spirit enters into a mask after appearing to its maker in a dream. It will then be given its own name, develop its own personality and even enter its own profession:

> there are masks which are debt collectors; others are messengers and town criers, military specialists and agricultural experts, while others work in the field of health and illness; many, probably most, are dancers, acrobats, mimics and general entertainers.
> (Jędrej 1986, 72)

Dan masks are unusual in being so numerous and singular, but they are less exceptional in being inhabited by spirits, which is commonly claimed as a feature of masks in Africa, Melanesia and the Americas (e.g. Horton 1965; Imperato 1970; Corbin and Fabricant 1979; Bastin 1984; Fienup-Riordan 1996; Adler 1998; MacDonald 1999; Merrill 2004; Denner 2008; Boyer 2008; Lawal 2012; Cole 2013; Roy 2015; etc.).[28] If the

28 On the extent to which masks are genuinely thought of as inhabited by spirits, and the extent to which the idea is a form of make-believe, see Ottenberg 1975, 11–12, 95, 129, 201.

spirit represented or embodied is not a generic type, this will usually result in the mask being a single. However, it is hard to make general rules; the ways that spirits can come to be connected to masks is very varied, and there does not have to be one spirit per mask. Certain murderous masks of the Arapesh, a people on New Guinea, were said to contain the spirits of their many victims:

> These *hangahiwa wandafunei* ... are universally feared, and nothing can vacate a hamlet so quickly as one of these spooks materializing out of the gloom of the surrounding jungle. The reason why even men flee before it is that the spirits of its victims have putatively impregnated the mask. Thus, when an ordinary man dons one of these costumes he feels the 'heaviness' of the mask, and the indwelling spirits transform him into a compulsive killer; his own child or brother would not be spared if he came upon them. To this extent, the men are not entirely deceiving the women when they tell them that the *hangahiwa* are spirits incarnate.
> (Tuzin 1980, 50–51)

In fact, these masks did not only contain the spirits of their victims, they were also decorated with their victims' bones, so that no one encountering such a mask could mistake it. As a recognizable mask type, we can think of *hangahiwa* as a multiple of a sort, and analogous to multiple fetishes, which we will encounter in the next section. We might also think of them as singles, in that each mask had its own gory history and victim list. But, unlike Bangwa or Kota ancestor figures, the masks seem not to have had their own personal names, and were considered as a generic class rather than as a group of items of which each had a specific identity.

The indwelling of a spirit or spirits is not a universal characteristic of masks. Indeed, no feature is a common characteristic of all masks, which form an exceptionally diffuse cluster concept.[29] The Mende think of their spirit masks as representations, not homes, of spirits, and although they say that their masks are not made but found underwater in lakes or rivers in the forest, they in fact buy copies of them from their neighbours (Jędrej 1986). These, then, can be thought of as multiples, not singles. The same can be said for certain masks of the Dogon in Mali, which represent specific personages, Dogon and non-Dogon, and are reproduced in different regions of Dogon territory (Griaule 1963, 510–87).

Some spirits have individual identities but they can also be anonymous and generic, and masks can represent them as such. The masks worn by Tlingit shamans in Alaska depict animals and humans, and represent spirit-helpers who can aid the shaman in his battle against evil spirits. The shaman dons them in sequence and, as he does so, he is possessed by the spirits they represent (Jonaitis 2006). The spirits, however, are types rather than individuals, and the masks are generic representations, which many different shamans own. Thus, they too are multiples.

Not all masks in traditional societies are the homes of spirits, and not all represent spirits. Some are thought of as little more than striking designs for entertainment dances (Himmelhener 1964; Denner 2006; Boyer 2008; Bouttiaux 2009; Roy 2015), while others,

---

29 For discussion of the idea that the concept of 'mask' is too extended to be useful, see Jędrej 1980; Picton 1990.

though they are conceived of as having a symbolic power that can intensify the mystery and effectiveness of festivals or rituals, owe this more to a combination of tradition and the expressive force of the mask than to any inherently potent nature (Perrois 2006; Strother 2008; Binkley and Darish 2009; Lawal 2012; Curtis 2018). Still others function like non-spiritual fetishes, or charms, which are given power by the ritual application of 'medicines' (Bourgeois 2014).

Non-transmissive multiples

Fetishes count as singles, though there are certain complexities. Kongo *minkisi* can be multiplied, but when they are multiplied they retain many of the characteristics of singles. A wizard (to continue using Evans-Pritchard's term) with a very powerful *nkisi* may allow an aspiring wizard, for a fee, to make a duplicate of his fetish, on condition that it operate in a different locale so that there will be no commercial competition. The duplicated fetish will advertise itself as another version of the original fetish, with all its powers, and will share its name. This may sound like a clear example of a reproductive multiple, but it is a peculiar reproductive multiple, since the second fetish is not an image of the original. It is, rather, another instance of the older fetish. In certain areas the new *minkisi* are called 'children' of their progenitor, but these are children with only one parent – a sort of iconographic parthenogenesis (MacGaffey 2015; Jędrej 1986).

Wyatt MacGaffey, the leading expert on Kongo *minkisi*, has analysed the appearance of different fetish types with the aim of producing a typology of 'children' groups. On the basis of this research, he argues that some *minkisi* can be identified by their attributes. This is not always possible; for example, *minkisi* that have come down to us with the name Mavungu do not seem to have anything in common with one another. The 'children' of Mabyala, on the other hand, show more consistency. Besides having a face with an open mouth and two mirror-faced containers for 'medicines', "all had among their attributes a knife, an occipital hole for 'medicines', a 'crown' of feathers surmounting the bald head, a ball of fibres, a bell on a chain and an apron in front of which hung an object that may have been a cup for administering the *nkasa* poison ordeal" (MacGaffey 2015, 150).

MacGaffey notes that many of these attributes do not appear on surviving Mabyalas, but he suggests that this is because they have gone missing. He also argues of a particular *nkisi* in the Pitt-Rivers Museum in Oxford that, since it possesses a significant number of the relevant Mabyala attributes, it should be thought of as a Mabyala – even though an early ethnographer, Richard Edward Dennett, who spent 23 years in the region where these fetishes were made, and also studied and collected them, said that it was called Mavungu (fig. 3.16) (Dennett 1902; Cadbury 2008; MacGaffey 2015).

Clearly MacGaffey is making an assumption: that Kongo fetish users were orderly and consistent iconographers. This may or may not be justified, but the fact that at least some Mabyalas can be recognized from their appearance marks them out as multiples, in one respect. As we saw earlier, it is not possible to identify the iconography of Bangwa ancestor figures from their appearance alone. One must be party to non-iconic information; they are, as we said, irreducibly pragmatic. We can now see why this is so; it is because Bangwa ancestor figures are singles. Because the Fosia statue is iconographically unique, we cannot use other examples of the same iconography as a

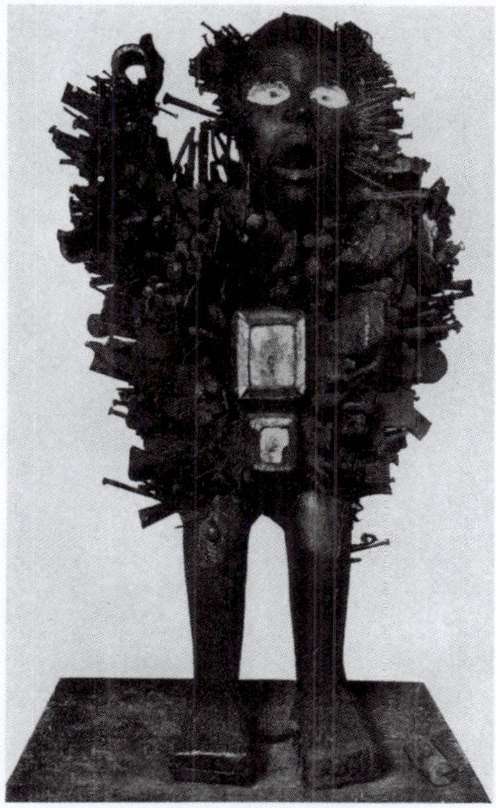

MAVUNGU. Fig. 1.

3.16 | Mavungu (or Mabyala?) *nkisi* in the Pitt-Rivers Museum, Oxford (from Dennett 1902)

comparison to identify it. Mabyala figures, on the contrary, are multiples, so identifying one Mabyala enables us to identify others.

If you and I can identify any Mabyala, it is only because information has been transmitted from a Kongo wizard through a chain of intermediaries to Wyatt MacGaffey, who has published an image of the fetish and told us its name. Nobody can identify a Mabyala purely by looking at it. The name is not part of the sculpture. To know what it is called one must acquire knowledge that is outside the fetish itself. It was in Kongo territory, where the fetish was made and used, that the name Mabyala was designated, so we have to rely on that name being "passed from link to link" (Kripke 1981, 91, 96) from the mouths of the Kongo down to us. Multiples make the recognition of iconographies possible, but only by means of *transmission*, and an act of linguistic designation is needed in order to initiate that process of transmission.

Some fetishes, then, are reproductive multiples, but they are multiples of an unusual sort. Most reproductive multiples are representations of some entity, real or fictional, that is not identical with the multiples themselves. There are many representations of Laocoön, or Mount Everest or Humphrey Bogart, and these representations are reproductive multiples; but Laocoön, Everest and Bogart are not. What makes Mabyala atypical is that the individual reproductive multiples are not representations of anything. They are not representations of the first Mabyala in the series, nor are they representations of the spirit of Mabyala. They work to some extent like individual photographs of Humphrey Bogart, which are all representations of Bogart but not of one another. Except that, in the case of the Mabyala fetishes, there is no Mabyala which they all represent. They simply *are* Mabyala.

We might say, then, that Mabyala *minkisi* are multiples, but not reproductive multiples, since they are not meant to be reproductions of anything. Nor are they generative multiples, since there can be no alternative representations if an act of representation is not taking place. But they are multiples in the sense that they allow iconographic identities to be transmitted. We can call them transmissive multiples. As we can see from this example, not all transmissive multiples are reproductive or generative.

In fact, if MacGaffey's assumption that Kongo fetish users were orderly and consistent is wrong, and if the fetish in fig. 3.16 was indeed known to its users as Mavungu, then the Mabyala fetishes would also not be transmissive, or at least, not fully transmissive. It may be that four or five Mabyalas look the same, but if it is possible for a sixth *nkisi* that looks like a Mabyala to be a Mavungu, and if the only way of establishing for sure that a Mabyala-style *nkisi* is indeed a Mabyala is by patient research into its individual historical identity, then Mabyalas would only be, at best, semi-transmissive.

There are other non-transmissive multiples. The children's drawings we considered at the beginning of this chapter would count as examples. A child may make three drawings of Mummy and two drawings of Auntie on a sheet of paper, and it may be impossible for anyone to know which is Mummy or which is Auntie, or even if they are meant to be Mummy or Auntie at all. It is only by asking the child to designate the subjects of the drawings that their identities can become clear. The drawings are multiples in the sense that they provide more than one image of Mummy and Auntie, but they are non-transmissive since they do not allow iconographic identities to be established between samples. Once the child has said that the drawing in the top left-hand corner is Auntie, the identities of the others will still be left begging, and each of the other drawings will need to be designated one by one.

Non-transmissive multiples also exist in Eurasian art. Jain, Buddhist and Christian saints are often impossible to identify at the representational level. However, we will leave a discussion of these until the next chapter, on attributes.

The Gravettian figurines mentioned earlier are the oldest examples of reproductive imagery presently known. Quite what or how they were supposed to mean is impossible to reconstruct in the absence of any verbal information. They might have been intended as images of some Mother Goddess, as certain iconographers of prehistoric art used to claim (James 1959); but we cannot be sure that they were images of a goddess at all. Perhaps they functioned more like charms or fetishes and multiplied by 'iconographic parthenogenesis'; or perhaps they were meant as votive images, which I shall discuss further in the next section.

Multivalence and polysemy

I have been describing the designation of singles' identities as a pragmatic process, but a student of pragmatics would probably object that none of the examples given so far is fully deictic. The designations that we have been discussing are similar to deixis only in the sense that identities have to be established through context. Ordinary deictic words, however, are not merely used to designate, they are used to designate over and over again with different referents. In a sentence like 'You, you, you and you, come with me', 'you' is referring to four different people. In the examples we have been discussing, on the other hand, identities are designated through context, but they are then fixed, rather like the naming of a baby. Once an image's representation has been decided, it usually does not change, and it does not constantly shift reference in the way that deictic terms do.

There are a handful of images that form exceptions to this general rule, but very few of them are as adaptable or unambiguous as deictic words. Recently invented images that come close to linguistic deixis are certain emojis (Grosz, Kaiser and Pierini 2021). They do not refer to people in the same way that the word 'I' refers to the speaker, but a laughing emoji in a message from me will mean that I find something funny, and in an email from you that you find it funny, and so on. There are a number of other, simple, expressive emojis that work in similar ways (tears, frowns, laughs, winks, kisses etc.). Since they are identified with the person who uses them in a message, they can be said to form an example of what linguists call 'person deixis' (Levinson 1983, 68–73).

There are other images that, like the expressive emojis, alter their representational meaning depending on context, but none of them have the same degree of rapid deictic interchangeability. An example from European religious iconography is the votive offering, or ex-voto (fig. 3.17): images can be used as testimony of favours received from deities or saints by those who have had their prayers answered. Those afflicted with pain in their arm or leg or eyes or breasts and whose sufferings have been allayed through prayer to a certain saint, for instance, will hang up an image of an arm, a leg, eyes or breasts in the saint's chapel. The votive image will be a witness to the saint's power and will also typically be the fulfilment of a vow made to the saint while the devotee was still afflicted by the ailment – 'If you cure my leg pain, then I hereby pledge to hang an ex-voto of a leg at your shrine' would be a typical form of vow (Van der Velden 2000; Wood 2011).[30] The objects themselves are generic depictions, made by specialists and bought by devotees, and are given their representational meaning by designation – 'this is my leg'. Of course, very few people besides the devotee (and, in theory, the saint) would ever know which limb belonged to which person.

Anatomical votives of limbs and body parts were also used in ancient Crete, Mycenae, Greece and Rome (Scopacasa 2015; Lawton 2017). There are many other forms of votive image and offering, of which the most interesting for this discussion are images of generic animals and people. Thousands of small bronze and terracotta figurines of cattle and horses have been retrieved from one cult centre in ancient Greece, the Pelopion at Olympia. Here there is a black layer of earth, made up of ash, charcoal, bones and votive offerings, which was once a place for fiery sacrifice. This sacrifice may have been to the shade of Pelops, but was more probably to Zeus, who was the main divinity

30 On votive images from different parts of the world, see Osborne 2004. For a suggestion that some Paleolithic images in caves may have been meant as ex-votos, see Bahn 2008.

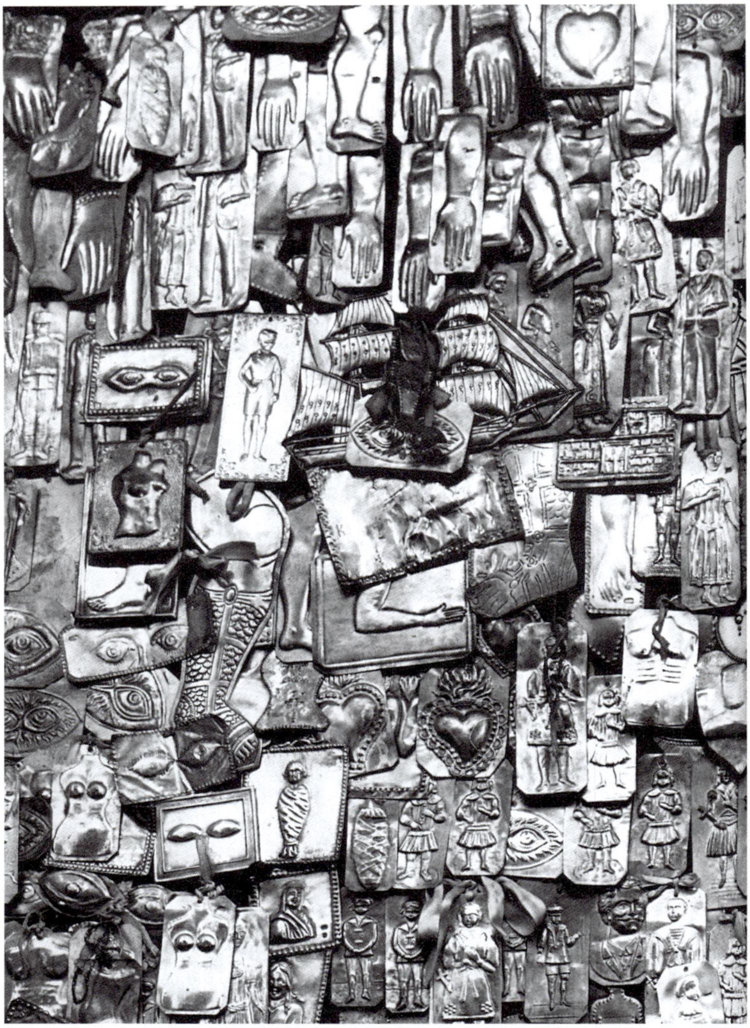

3.17 | Ex-votos. Hagios Georgios, Santorini, 1967

of the site (Bocher 2006–07; Ekroth 2012). The depictive meaning of these animal figurines is clear enough, but quite what they were supposed to represent is harder to gauge. Were they meant to function like anatomical votives, were they gifts to thank Zeus for preserving the health of an expensive animal? Probably not, because there were also many charred animal bones at the site. It seems more likely that the figurines were meant as the sacrificial offerings of the poor.[31] If this is so, then we might think of

31 Another possibility is that the figurines were mementoes of animals that had been sacrificed elsewhere. Pausanias tells us that there was a votive image at Delphi of a bull that had been sacrificed to Poseidon on Corfu; Pausanias, *Description of Greece*, 10.9.3–10.9.4.

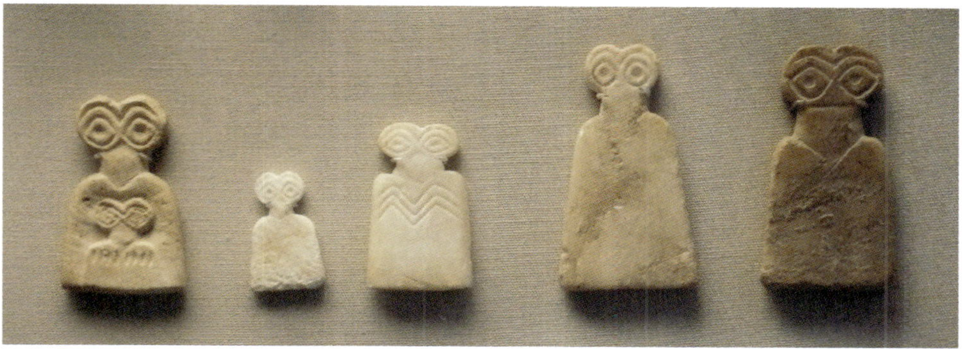

3.18 | Tell Brak (Syria), Eye-idols, 3300–3000 BC. The British Museum, London

them as representing non-existent animals, or perhaps simply as *being* votive offerings, which, since they cost a certain amount to purchase, showed the worshipper's readiness to give to the deity (and since travelling to Olympia to cast the image into the fire would also have been an expense, this could be added to the devotional sum) (Van der Velden 2000, 211–12). Votives (especially bronze votives) were presumably made by specialists and bought by devotees, who then privately designated the identity of the animal they had bought. The votive images went from being a generic animal to being the animal offered by the donor.

The votive images we have discussed up till now have meaning given to them by designation, but they are not fully deictic since, once they are offered up to the saint or deity, their meanings are fixed and do not change again. A group of mysterious stone objects from the late fourth millennium BC,[32] found in great numbers in a swathe of territory from Anatolia to Iran, may have been more flexible in their meanings (fig. 3.18). These are usually called 'eye-idols' after they were so christened by the archaeologist Max Mallowan during the excavations he led at Tell Brak in Syria, where 20,000 examples, whole or in fragments, were discovered in what seemed to be a cult context (Mallowan 1947).

Eye-idols vary greatly in size, from 3 to 30 cm, and since Mallowan's day they have turned up in all kinds of archaeological contexts, some of them cultic and some domestic. There is still no uniformly accepted explanation of their function or meaning. It has been argued, on the basis of contemporaneous visual evidence from cylinder seals, that some eye-idols, which have pierced eyes, were used as weights for twining thread. Only those with pierced eyes can have fulfilled this purpose, however, and only if they were the right size – 3 cm is too small, 30 cm is too big – so we need other explanations for the rest (Breniquet 1996; Caubet 2006).

If, as Mallowan himself thought, eye-idols were images of a god, then they would be early and striking examples of multiples. If they were anatomical votives, they functioned in the same way as the other examples we have seen. But a third possibility is that they were stylized images of devotees. In the third millennium BC votive images

32 In this book I use BC/AD rather that BCE/CE because we do not live in a Common Era – different peoples mark time in different ways. Imposing Western dates on the rest of the world is calendrical neo-colonialism.

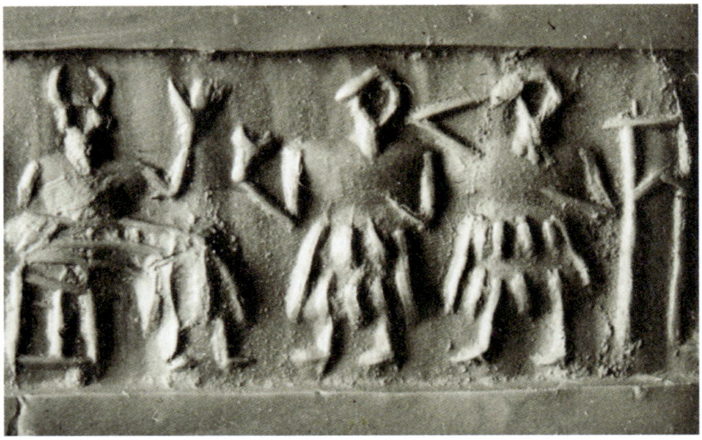

3.19 | Tell Asmar (Iraq), Cylinder seal impression with presentation scene, Early Dynastic III (2600–2300 BC) from the Iraq Museum, Baghdad (Frankfort 1955, 511)

of worshippers with wide-open eyes were placed in Mesopotamian temples gazing at idols of deities, as constant memorials of their devotion (Frankfort 1954, 45–46; Jacobsen 1989). Eye-idols may have had a similar function, and this would explain why they appear both in temples and in domestic contexts, where they could have been placed before a domestic shrine to gods or ancestors. Of course, we do not know if they were meant to represent individual worshippers, but if they were then they could have been bequeathed, or gifted in some other way, and have changed representational identity as they did so.

Eye-idols are from the Archaic period of Mesopotamian history, for which we have very little literary evidence. In later periods writing emerged, helping us to understand the meanings and functions of images. Our richest source of iconography in ancient Iraq is that provided by cylinder seals, of which around 35,000 have come down to us (Collon 1987). These objects were small (c. 2–3 cm long) cylinders of incised stone, which when rolled across clay left an image, and often some text, in relief. They were kept about the person and applied to all kinds of sealing requirements, from documents to door sealings to vase tops; they also functioned as amulets. A type of seal common between around 2200 and 1500 BC is called by modern art historians the 'presentation scene', in which a worshipper, who may be bearing an offering, is introduced to a deity or (deified) king by a minor deity. The (major) deity or king may be recognizable through attributes or an inscription, and the worshipper too is often identifiable via a cuneiform text that gives his name (Winter 1986; Collon 1987; Felli 2006). The more deictic seals, however, are those that provide less information (fig. 3.19); sometimes the worshipper is unidentified and/or the deity has no individuating attributes. These figures needed to have their identities designated by the owner of the seal, who would of course identify the worshipper as him or herself. If the seal came to be owned by someone else, through inheritance or some other means of acquisition, then the identities could be changed. In fact, changes could also take place on seals with text that identified the owner; there are surviving examples where the inscription has been filed off (Collon 1987, 120–22; Lambert 1997, 4).

Changes in representational use occur more frequently with various forms of the mask. Masks in Africa and Melanesia, as we have seen, tend to have fixed, specific meanings, but there are exceptions to the rule. Among some peoples in the south-western region of the Ivory Coast there are examples of masks shifting in meaning from one context to another. The Yaure (fig. 3.20) will take a mask that is normally used in one ceremony and redeploy it in another, if the need arises; and visually similar masks have different identities in different villages (Boyer 2016, 166–69). Guro masks can change function from year to year, and indistinguishable masks can have different meanings, depending on the context in which they are used (Bouttiaux 2016, 15, 19–21). Dan masks that look very similar can have different, indeed antithetical, functions depending on the designations given them by their owners, and for the same reason they can change their functions over time, as the mask passes from owner to owner. One might think that the spirit living inside the mask would have its say, but in practice this is not so (Boyer 2016, 169). The Wè are more radical; for them the mask itself has no particular meaning (or at least none that elders of the villages can agree upon). It is the costume that goes with the mask, and the use to which it is put, that is significant, and the mask itself can have different senses, depending on what it is sewn on to it and how it is danced (Boyer 2019, 31–32).

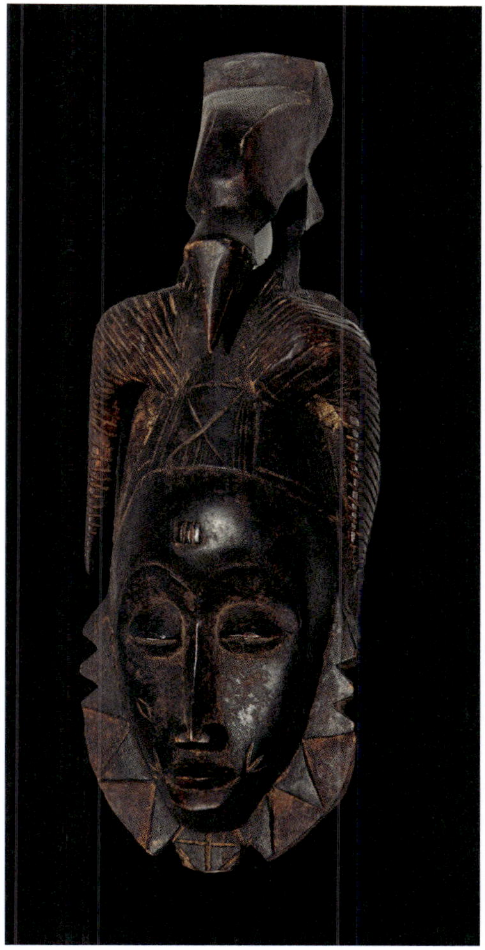

3.20 | Yaure mask, 20th century. Private collection

In the traditions of Noh theatre in Japan, masks depict different ages, personalities and expressions: a cheerful boy, a jealous woman, a melancholic old man. They can mostly be used in more than one play, to represent different parts with suitable characters, although a small number of masks are associated with one character only (Ishii 1994, 57; Kadowaki 2014, 108). The masks of ancient Greek theatre were fewer in number and more stereotypical, but they too could be used in more than one play, to represent different roles (Webster 1965; Marshall 1999). Indeed, masks of the same type could be used for different characters in the same play (Dearden 1975, 77).

The examples I have given so far in this section can be thought of as examples of polysemy, but polysemy can be both contemporaneous and non-contemporaneous (Lyons 1997, 550–69). A word may have a number of different meanings in current parlance (e.g. 'mouth': 'orifice for eating', 'place where a river meets the sea', 'opening to a jar', etc.), but other words are, so to speak, historically polysemous. 'Imminent'

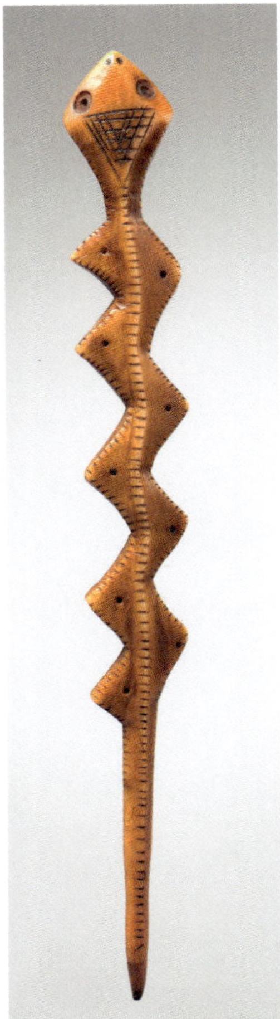

3.21 | Lega, Snake, 19th–20th century. Fowler Museum, UCLA

today means 'impending', but in the past it also meant 'intent' and 'overhanging'. In order to point to this difference without wasting too many words we can use the word 'polysemy' for contemporaneous polysemy, and 'multivalence' for historical polysemy. A number of the images considered in this section are multivalent, since they only have one representation at a time – the votive images, the cylinder seals and probably the eye-idols too.[33] The expressive emojis and most of the masks are polysemous, although the Dan masks, which change their meanings when they pass from person to person, are multivalent, since their significance changes over time.

In our discussion of polysemy and multivalence we have been focusing on images that are representationally polysemous and multivalent. There are also some images, although they are rare, that might be considered depictively polysemous. Certain Dogon rock paintings are given different interpretations by different Dogon interviewees – one and the same image can be said to be a snake, a lizard, a bird – and while that may be due to cultural oblivion (of which more in a moment) it has been suggested that the cause may be more complex.

> Such interpretations, apparently contradictory (at least to our eyes), have been explained by the fact that increasingly subtle interpretations of the same symbols are given to the initiates as their initiation progresses. So it should not be surprising if people who have attained different degrees of knowledge have made comments about the images that corresponded to their own level of initiation ...
> (Le Quellec 2004, 63–64)

Similar considerations come into play in another example of depictive polysemy. The Lega, who live in the east of the Congo basin, use figurines in elaborate and sophisticated ways as part of the initiation rituals into their communal association, the *bwami* (Biebuyck 1973; Cameron 2001). The initiate is shown natural objects, artefacts and figurines, and is expected to associate them with moral aphorisms. So a figurine of a snake (fig. 3.21) might be associated with the following aphorisms: 'The little child plays in the wading place: *ngimbi* [a poisonous serpent] is death' (a warning against those who mock the *bwami*); 'I have been bitten by *ngimbi*, therefore I shall not die because of a *mulinde* [a non-venomous snake]' (an expression of confidence after the successful passing of an initiation level); 'Snake has bitten me at night; I do not know its name' (with

33 On this definition there will be words that are both polysemous and multivalent; e.g. 'silly', which has a number of obsolete meanings ('pious', 'fortunate', 'feeble', 'lowly') and a number of current ones ('foolish', 'uncomplicated', 'in cricket: designating a fielding position very close to the batsman facing the bowler'). I thank Anthony Ossa-Richardson for the example. There may also be images that are both polysemous and multivalent; some of the Ivory Coast masks may count.

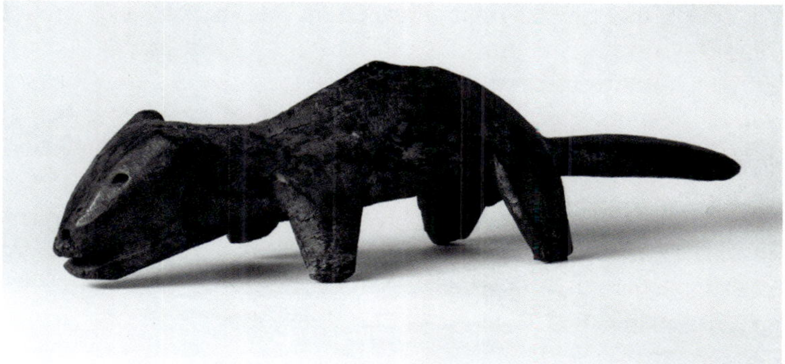

3.22 | Lega, *Mugugundu*, 20th century. Royal Museum for Central Africa, Tervuren

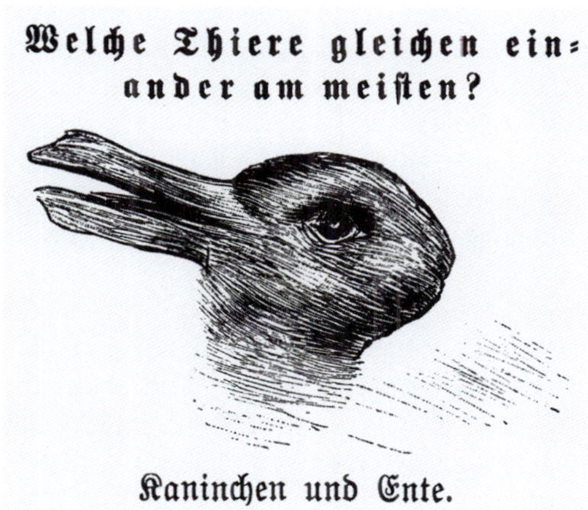

3.23 | Duck-Rabbit (*Fliegende Blätter*, 23 October 1892)

which a confident initiate encourages his preceptors to continue with the initiation proceedings), and so on (Biebuyck 1973, 224–25). So for this figurine there is considerable polysemy at the metaphorical level, and some at the representational level (we may be looking at a *ngimbi* snake, a *mulinde* snake or a snake with no name). Whether it should be thought of as polysemous at the depictive level is harder to judge; should we imagine the object as shifting depictive meanings from *ngimbi* to *mulinde* to nameless snake, or does the object simply depict a (generic) snake?[34]

Other Lega objects emphasize this dilemma, because the object itself is generic at a higher level of abstraction and as such is given its own name. In fig. 3.22 we see

34 Biebuyck 1977, 65, writes that "any object can express more than one meaning, mainly because of differences in the contexts of usage"; he is presumably thinking of the aphoristic level of meaning.

a generic quadruped that the Lega call *mugugundu*. This can be used to represent different animals depending on the aphoristic context: "a hunting dog, a pangolin, an aardvark, a turtle or some other animal" (Biebuyck 1973, 164, 222–24). It can also switch representational meaning from species to species in succession – it is one of the most deictic of images. Should we apply the principle of iconographic feedback and say that it also switches its depictive meaning? One could argue that when it is being used to mean a pangolin it depicts a pangolin, and represents the pangolin as described in the relevant aphorism: Kilinkumbi (drum-name for the giant pangolin), Ikaga (real name for the giant pangolin), Ikaga Kalubuta (the pangolin who has rolled himself up in anger), and so on (Biebuyck 1973, 224). But this, it might be thought, is to put too many words into Lega mouths.

We can compare the *mugugundu* to examples of visual ambiguity that are familiar in the West, such as the 'duck-rabbit' (fig. 3.23) (Wittgenstein 1953, 194–96, 199, 205–06; Gombrich 1960, 4–5; Mitchell 1994, 45–57). Unlike the *mugugundu*, the duck-rabbit looks like a duck, and then a rabbit, and then a duck; the *mugugundu* does not look much like any real quadruped, and the decision to call it a dog, a pangolin, an aardvark etc. is a matter of designatory choice. The *mugugundu* is polysemous, the duck-rabbit is ambiguous (Ossa-Richardson 2019, 14). We can say that the duck-rabbit shifts representation depending on how we attend to it; one moment it represents a duck, the next a rabbit. But what should we take it to depict? Given that it has been carefully composed to look like a duck *and* a rabbit, we might say that it depicts a duck-rabbit. And, if so, perhaps the *mugugundu* always depicts a *mugugundu*.

Oblivion

The examples we have been considering so far are all deliberate, but multivalence can also occur due to a kind of cultural accident, a failure of communal memory. An example of this phenomenon from Africa is the fate of crucifixes in the Congo region. After a 350-year attempt at evangelization that was never more than partially successful, Catholic missions withdrew from the Congo basin in the 1830s (Hilton 1987). Fifty years later British Baptist missionaries arrived to resume the work of Christian conversion, and they were surprised to see crucifixes being put to unfamiliar purposes:

> A flat wooden cross, about 2 feet long, 4 inches broad, is the common fetish which confers skill in hunting. It is called *santu* (*santa cruz*, 'holy cross'), and whenever the possessor of a *santu* kills an animal its blood is daubed on the *santu*. It is said that a *santu* loses its power if the possessor is guilty of any immorality; in such case a fine has to be paid and a ceremony gone through before its power can be restored by a doctor of *santu*.
> (Bentley 1900, 1:36)

Numerous crucifixes by the Kongo people have survived (fig. 3.24). It does not seem probable that they were all used as hunting fetishes; there were some Kongo who revered the Catholic devotional objects they had acquired (Monteiro 1875, 219; Bentley 1900, 1:35). Nevertheless, there is testimony from a variety of European sources that at the end of the nineteenth century crucifixes were being used as *minkisi* in different contexts, not only as hunting charms but also as guardians of burial places, and as emblems of chiefly power (Massing 2007; Mello e Souza 2007). A number of sources also claim that some of those who used the crucifixes in these ways had no idea what they originally signified (Massing 2007, 88).[35]

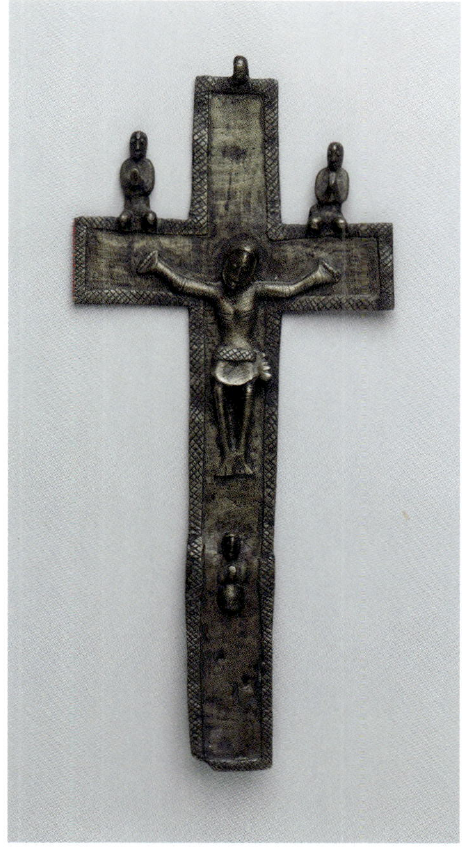

3.24 | Kongo crucifix (*Nkangi Kiditu*), early 17th century. Brooklyn Museum, New York

With the multivalence of crucifixes in the Congo we see a foreign iconography being forgotten and merged with a local iconography, but it can also happen that a culture forgets its indigenous iconography. Indeed, we can see this from the history of iconography itself. As noted in Chapter 1, the subject of iconography owes its origins to the tendency of Europeans to forget the meanings of their own imagery. An inscription above the interior entrance of the Warburg Institute reads ΜΝΗΜΟΣΥΝΗ – Mnemosyne, or Memory, the mother of the Muses. The institute does what it can to combat cultural oblivion.[36]

Europeans have the advantage of a vast written record of their cultural activity, so that when an iconography has been forgotten it can usually be retrieved; but for cultures that have no written record, the meanings of their images, once forgotten, cannot be recovered. At the same time, where there is no long-term memory there can also be no knowledge of what has faded into oblivion; societies can think they have remembered their own iconographies when in fact those iconographies have changed. Or, alternatively, it can seem they have forgotten their iconographies, when there was no consistent iconography to forget in the first place.

Forms are often more secure than meanings; in this, imagery is not unlike ritual. The anthropologists Caroline Humphrey and James Laidlaw asked Jain worshippers in Jaipur why they gave offerings of flowers to their holy idols, the Jinas. The answers they received were all different, and some were inconsistent with others (Humphrey and Laidlaw 1994, 34–35). But although the meaning of the gesture was understood in different ways by different people, the ritual action was performed in the same manner by each worshipper.

Rituals are visible and public and so can be imitated, but interpretations of those rituals must be shared by word of mouth, and, as anyone who has played Chinese whispers (the 'telephone game' in the US) knows, oral transmission of ideas is not at all failsafe. It is only when interpretations are written down, widely shared and preferably

35 Verses from the Qu'ran were incorporated in fetishes by the non-Muslim Asante; Rattray 1927, 20–21.
36 On the meanings of 'Mnemosyne' for Aby Warburg, see Mazzucco 2011, 147–52.

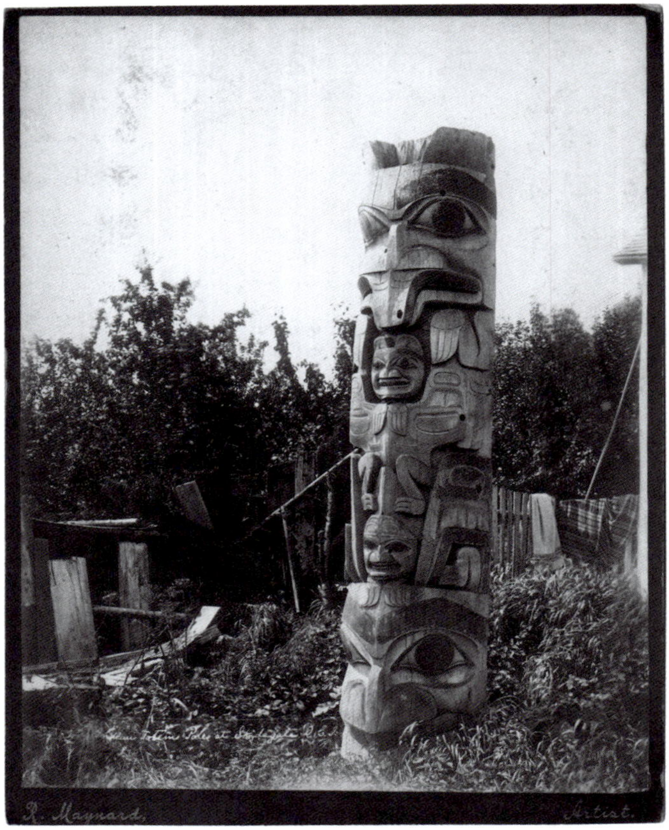

3.25 | Richard Maynard, Photograph of Haida totem pole at Skidegate, Queen Charlotte Islands, 1888. City of Victoria Archives

3.26 | Abelam men's house, 20th century. Museum der Kulturen, Basel

backed up with a system of political enforcement that ritual actions are likely to be interpreted in a consistent manner. However, even when ritual interpretations are policed there can be room for broad disagreement, as the history of the Eucharist in the Christian churches shows. Between the Catholic, Orthodox and numerous Protestant churches there are varying views as to what occurs when the wafer is taken in Holy Communion. This disagreement is between the official written doctrines of the churches; if anthropologists were to ask members of congregations what they thought was happening at communion, then the doctrinal differences would probably be broader still. Although the theological opinions are various, however, the act of taking the communion wafer is very similar in all Christian churches, so that someone raised as a Protestant can take communion in a Catholic church without being noticed.

Iconography, like ritual, has the advantage of publicity, so that its external features can be copied; but interpretations of it in an oral culture can be susceptible to semantic dispersal. The highly complex iconography of Haida art, on the west coast of what is now

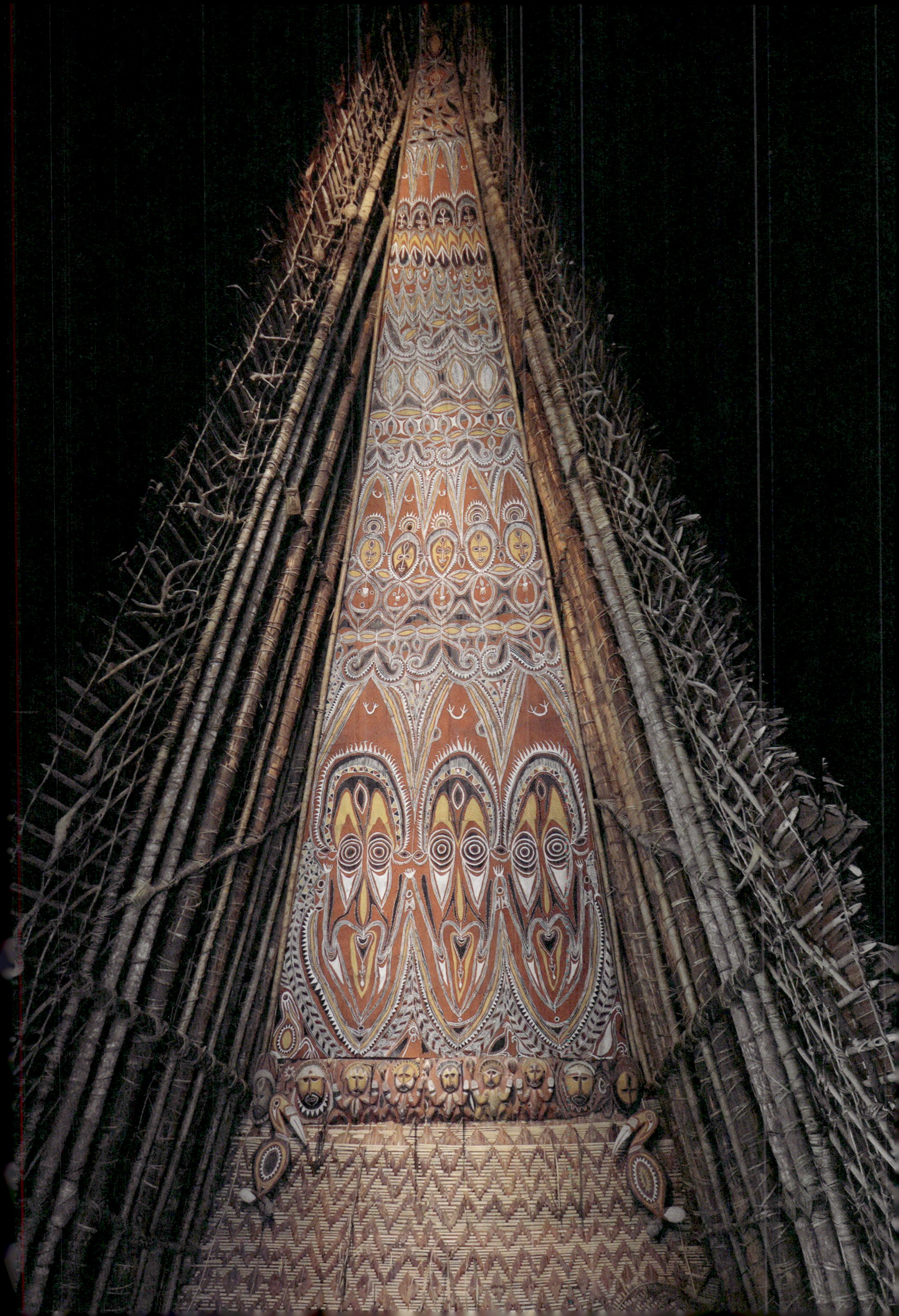

Canada, was already causing confusion and disagreement among the Haida themselves at the turn of the twentieth century. According to the anthropologist John Swanton:

> At the top of this pole [fig. 3.25] is an eagle, crest of the Eagle clan; but my informants differed regarding the rest of the design. Amos Russ explained it as a representation of Gunanasîmgît's wife being carried off by the killer-whale, the woman's face showing just below the eagle's beak, and the whale's blow-hole being represented by a small face above the face of the killer-whale. Tom Stevens, however, explained the large figure at the bottom as that of a grizzly bear, presumably meaning thereby the sea grizzly bear; and the small figure over it as the sea-ghost ... which usually rides upon its back. The woman's face he left unexplained; and I am inclined to think that he is in error, and that Amos Russ's explanation is the correct one. The killer-whale (or sea grizzly bear) may have been a crest of the house-owner's wife.
> (Swanton 1905, 129)

Can Tom Stevens, 'chief of Those-Born-at-Rose-Spit' (Swanton 1905, 128), be in error, if his interpretation is sincerely believed? What counts as truth in these matters? Whether or not we think he can be in error, the disagreement between Swanton's informants, both Haida chiefs, shows the real possibility of iconographic oblivion – at both the representational and depictive levels – in an oral culture with an allusive and ambiguous visual language.

For the anthropologist Anthony Forge, who was trying to decode the iconography of a most impressive series of paintings, those on the façades of Abelam men's houses on the island of New Guinea (fig. 3.26), the inconsistencies in the responses he received were exasperating, so that the temptation to fill in the gaps with speculation became hard to resist – witness the use of 'I would suggest' twice in the following quotation:

> There is, however, no secure iconography; the design elements and their combinations are essentially ambiguous, in the sense that translation from the language of flat painting to the language of words is not a matter of simple one-to-one correspondence. Interpretation of elements and whole compositions often varies according to the artistic and social contexts and according to the informant. ... the Abelam do not ask what a painting means. The design elements all have names and they are assembled into harmonious compositions, which appear to act directly on the beholder without having to be named. Abelam art is about relationships, not about things. One of its functions is to relate and unite disparate things in terms of their place in the ritual and cosmological order. It does this, I would suggest, directly and not as an illustration to some text based in another symbolic system such as language. One of the main functions of the initiation system with its repetitive exposure of initiates to quantities of art is, I would suggest, to teach the young men to see the art, not so that he may consciously interpret it but so that he is directly affected by it.
> (Forge 2017d, 135)

Forge's colleague Donald Tuzin was working nearby in a village of the Arapesh, who made men's houses with very similar designs to those of their neighbours the Abelam. He was more willing to accept the ambiguities:

> Even the most knowledgeable informants were vague and inconsistent on the subject of what these rows of figures are all about. Some claimed that the figures in the lowest, most representational row were ancestor spirits; the next highest were *nggwal* spirits, after which came 'more important' *nggwal* spirits, and so forth. Others maintained that they were *all nggwal* spirits, ranked according to relative importance. The problem was that no agreement could be elicited as to which *nggwals* occupied a given row; each informant was inclined to regard *his nggwal* as among the more important ones.
> (Tuzin 1980, 183–86)

Tuzin went on to observe that there is a doubt whether the paintings depicted *nggwal* spirits at all. In cases like these it is tempting to think that there was originally an agreed meaning that was later forgotten, and this may be the case. But another possibility is that there never was a consensus of interpretation. This is the more likely among the Arapesh, who took many of their iconographic elements from the Abelam, "without", according to Tuzin, "understanding what they mean, even at the most superficial level" (Tuzin 1980, 172). However, even the Abelam may have generated their iconography in a communal manner, in which the images were made by artists who did more painting than talking. In a scenario like this, images could be made and standardized without acquiring a universally accepted meaning. And in any case, the iconography is unlikely to have been invented in one go; it is more likely that it evolved slowly over generations.

One of the most complex cases of iconographic oblivion can be found on New Ireland, in the Bismarck Archipelago to the northeast of New Guinea. The carvings made on this island have fascinated art historians, curators and collectors for 150 years (figs. 3.27 and 3.28). But although there has been a constant stream of research publications on New Ireland and its imagery since the 1870s, and although anthropologists have been interviewing New Irelanders about their artworks since the turn of the twentieth century, the iconography remains elusive.[37]

The most impressive of New Ireland artworks are known as *malagan* images (or *malangan* or *malanggan*). These are assemblages of carvings that are set up during ceremonial festivals involving rites, masquerades and much feasting, which usually honour the memory of the dead.[38] The carvings themselves are often so intricate that it takes a while to understand what it is that one is looking at. They are carved by specialist sculptors who need time to complete them, and so *malagan* festivals can take place months or years after the death of the person being mourned. After the rituals are over, the *malagan* images are generally burned, left to rot or sold to collectors (Küchler 2002, 168–70, 175–76).[39]

It is considered honourable to hold a *malagan* festival after the death of a relative, and shameful not to, and the social implications of the event are of more importance to the participants than the iconography of the carvings. In the words of the ethnographer Hortense Powdermaker:

---

37 For a survey of the ethnographical literature on *malagan*, see Gunn 1992, 6–13.

38 *Malagan* ceremonies can also be held to coincide with circumcision rituals, or to settle a quarrel between siblings, or to celebrate a miraculous rescue at sea, or just because the village decided to hold one, for no particular reason. See Powdermaker 1971, 315; Heintze 1987, 42; Gunn 1992, 304.

39 In some areas *malagan* images are kept and reused, see Billings 2007, 282.

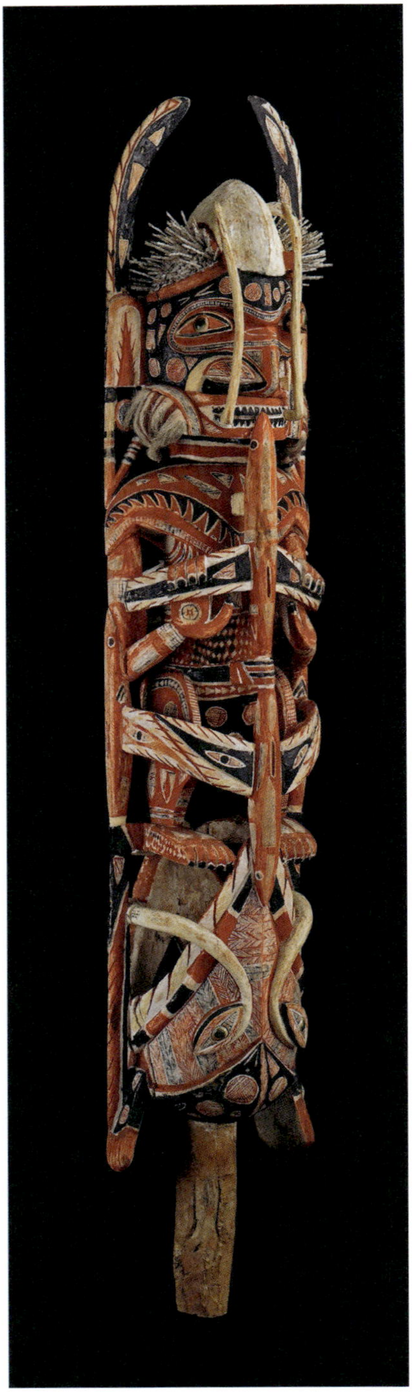

3.27 | New Ireland, *Malagan totok* figure, 19th century. The British Museum, London

> The identification of the carvings with wealth came out in many ways: if a man did not make a *malanggan*, it was scornfully said by everyone in the community that he did not have any wealth; in the speeches at the *malanggan* rites, stressing the wealth which had gone into their making; in an incident which occurred shortly before my departure, when some old men were watching my servants pack a few *malanggans* I was taking back with me. I had explained that they would be carefully housed (in a museum) and that 'my people', who had never seen such *malanggans*, would then know about them. After my explanation the old men very seriously urged me to tell these people who would look at the *malanggans* that they were not just carved, painted pieces of wood, but that I must make the people understand all the work and wealth that had gone into the making of them – the large taro crops, the many pigs, all the *tsera* [shell money], the cooking for the feast, and other essentials of the rites. These, said the old men of Lesu, are the important things to remember about *malanggans*. (Powdermaker 1971, 318–19)

Malagans consume and display wealth, and their use is governed by a complex set of regulations, which resemble those of the laws of copyright. Individuals and their kinship groups are considered to have the right to a particular *malagan*, and this right can be bequeathed, bought or sold. However, since *malagans* are mostly destroyed or disposed of after the ceremonies in which they feature, what is being transferred is not the ownership of a particular sculpture, but the right to ask a carver to execute a particular *malagan* design from memory.

Under the circumstances, it is unsurprising that the forms of *malagans* have altered with the years. While *malagan* ceremonies persist, the extraordinary intricacy of the sculptures illustrated here (figs. 3.27 and 3.28) is now a thing of the past. The *malagans* one sees in books (like this one) were made in the late nineteenth or early twentieth century, but those made in recent decades are simpler and cruder in style (Lewis 1969, 146–68; Heintze 1987; Gunn 1992, 2; Billings 2007).

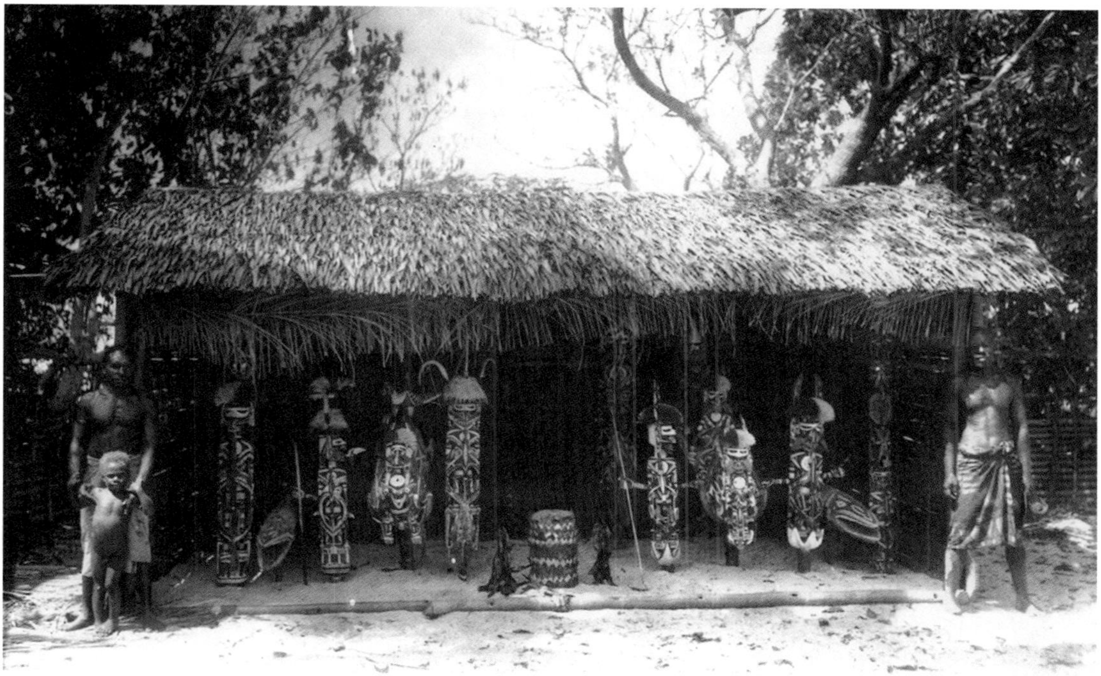

3.28 | Felix Speiser, *Malagan* house in Medina, New Ireland, 1930. Museum der Kulturen, Basel

Although we know a great deal about the production and social context of the *malagan* images, their iconography has always been less clear. Early anthropologists in the region voiced their irritation at the responses they received from New Irelanders. The priest and linguist Gerhard Peekel wrote in the 1920s:

> Everything that the natives, including the artists, are able to say about their sculptures can be boiled down to two sentences: 'That is time-honoured tradition!' and 'That is a snake, that is a bird and that is a fish!' What goes beyond this is of no interest to them, so that it is pointless to bother them with questions.
> (Peekel 1927, 32)

Thirty years later the anthropologist Phillip Lewis met with a similar response, but described the problem in Panofskian terms:

> One of the art objects I saw in the field was the *Malanggatsak malanggan*. From informants one got little beyond Panofsky's lowest level, that of pre-iconographical description. A naïve beholder could infer that the figure represented was human in form and was depicted wearing a towering headdress, some elements of which were feathers and birds. This indeed was what informants were able to tell, and nothing more.
> (Lewis 1969, 18)

Lewis dealt with the issue by concluding that there was no point in investigating *malagans* at the level of iconography (22), and in this he was partly right, since, for New Irelanders themselves, the iconography of *malagans* is of little interest. This was brought home to the anthropologist Michael Gunn when he travelled to the island of Tabar, 25 km north of New Ireland, which is traditionally considered the home of *malagan*:

> My initial inquiries were directed toward eliciting information which could be used for a structural analysis of *malagan* symbolism, but the local people dismissed my questions as irrelevant, the product of a Western mind following Western interests. *Malagan* owners kept insisting to me that the 'meaning' of *malagan* was not to be found in an explication of the iconography of the various elements, but instead emphasised that the 'meaning' of any particular *malagan* was "that this particular man, as leader of his lineage, owns this particular *malagan*".
> (Gunn 1992, 1)[40]

Gunn allowed the people of Tabar to guide his research, and found himself swamped with information about the names, ownerships, affiliations and interconnections of *malagans*. Some of this was of an iconographic character; he was told, for example, that the human figures in *malagan* sculptures are supposed to be representations of the spirits of clan totems, rather than embodiments of the spirits of dead ancestors, as other researchers had been told (Lewis 1969; Küchler 1988; Küchler 2002; Gell 1988; Derlon 1990/1991).[41] Here 'representations' is the right word, since Gunn's informants, or most of them, were insistent that there were no spirits present in *malagan* images:

> *Malagan* sculptures are understood by the people of Tabar to be merely wooden pictures and are not conceived to be 'active' in any way. All of the sculptors and most of the *malagan* owners of Tabar were emphatic that *malagan* sculptures are merely pieces of carved wood and that the power associated or attributed to them comes from men. In this view, a *malagan* sculpture is not a 'spirit image' in the sense of being a wooden image which somehow contains a 'spirit'. Nor is a *malagan* an 'ancestor figure' in the sense of representing and maintaining a link with some primal ancestor, human or otherwise.
> (Gunn 1992, 116)

Gunn caustically refers to "a major problem that seems to arise in a number of New Ireland ethnographies, the one that stems from thinking that New Irelanders believe in fairies" (Gunn 1992, 13). However, it is not clear that the people of Tabar are as robustly positivist as this makes them sound. Gunn describes certain *malagans*, known as *vavara*, which, even in the 1980s, were considered potent and dangerous, and which

---

40 For a comparable system of image ownership in Australia, see Morphy 1991, 57–74.

41 The differences between the information gathered by Gunn (on Tabar), Lewis (in Kavieng, on the northern tip of New Ireland) and Küchler (in Panangai, on the southern side of New Ireland) may reflect different local understandings of the *malagan* cult. Billings 2007, 258, concurred with Gunn, but she was working in Mangai, in northeastern New Ireland, on the same side of the island as Tabar. Parkinson 1907, 649, wrote that the totemic sign of the dead person was always present on their *malagan* statues; see too Derlon 1994, 41.

were constructed close to a corpse, so that the spirit of the dead would be captured. Those whose job it was to make these *malagans* ran the risk of having their own spirits and those of their clans enmeshed with the spirits of the dead (Gunn 1992, 103 and 263).

Gunn's indigenous informants were mostly churchgoers, and some were doctors or schoolteachers, and one might wonder if their understanding of Tabar's traditional culture had not passed through the filter of their education. Did Tabarans in the nineteenth century also think of *malagans* as 'wooden pictures'? There is no evidence with which to settle the issue. Anthropologists who have studied *malagan* rituals in other parts of New Ireland report that the human figures in *malagans* function in much the same way as Bangwa ancestor statues, with the spirits of the dead making the carvings their homes for the duration of the funerary rites; but reports from other areas align with the Tabaran view that the *malagan* statues are 'pictures'.[42] Is this Tabaran view a continuation of earlier views, or a break with them? Again, we cannot know, but we do know that the people of Tabar are losing contact with their past. Much of the linguistic vocabulary involved in *malagan* rituals was already unintelligible to them forty years ago, and, when shown photographs of late nineteenth- and early twentieth-century *malagans* in museums they were unable to interpret the iconography, other than at the most generic levels (horizontal or upright, with or without human figures) (Gunn 1992, 129, 294–95; cf. Küchler 2002, 120–21). Their understanding of art from their own past is, as Phillip Lewis noted in the 1950s, pre-iconographic in nature.

42 See previous note.

4. Attributes

Transmitting multiples

In the last chapter we dealt for the most part with the iconographic practices of small-scale groups, and we saw how such groups make use of direct, word-of-mouth designation as their principal iconographic device. In this chapter we will turn our attention to larger societies, inhabiting cities, regions, states and empires. As societies expand in size, both demographically and geographically, they find themselves in need of new kinds of imagery, for which new iconographic devices must be introduced. Peoples spreading over large swathes of territory will break up into smaller centres of power or be governed at a distance by hierarchies above them. In either case there can still be a great deal of local imagery, the meanings of which will be assigned by designation – such as fetishes, masks or images of the village chief's immediate ancestors. But if a people is to preserve some cultural unity across a sizeable region, it will find itself in need of common legendary or mythical figures, such as distant ancestors or deities, and also common images of those beings. In fact, to return to the distinction made in the last chapter, it will need multiples, rather than singles. If a large number of villages and towns are all to worship the same deity or primordial ancestor, they will want their own versions of images that represent, or embody, this shared figure.

To give an example of this process, consider the Chokwe, a cluster of peoples who speak a dialect group that covers a large territory in what is now northeast Angola, the southern Democratic Republic of the Congo and northwest Zambia. There are over two million Chokwe speakers today; that compares with around 80–90,000 speakers of Nweh, the language of the Bangwa (C.I.A. 2023; Ayotte and Ayotte 2002).[1] The fact that these millions of people are closely related linguistically suggests a common origin, and Chokwe historians believe that they expanded southwards from the Congo basin in the seventeenth century, at a time when they were ruled by a dynasty said to be descended from a Luba king called Chibinda Ilunga (Wastiau 2006, 7–11 and 138–39). The political unity they seem to have displayed in the seventeenth century has since dispersed into a network of local chiefdoms, but their shared past is shown not only in their language but also in common styles and themes in Chokwe carving.

Chibinda Ilunga, their supposed Luba ancestor, is still revered across Chokwe territory, and is thought to be represented by seven or eight surviving statues

1 In 1922 the Bangwa population was said to be 13,961 and "unusually thickly populated" (Cadman 1922).

(fig. 4.1).[2] We do not know anything about how these statues were used, since they were carved in the eighteenth and nineteenth centuries and left Chokwe territory for Western collections at an early date, but they appear to form a multiple, and so made available an image of a revered cultural figure across a broad territory. The Chokwe still make use of many singles, in the forms of masks and fetishes, at local levels in their chiefdoms (Bastin 1984; Wastiau 2006, 15–22), but the shared multiple of Chibinda Ilunga unites a cultural zone so large that most of its members, before the rise of mass media, cannot have been aware of its extent.

In theory, these multiples did not have to be similar in appearance. Each regional area of the Chokwe territory could have developed its own iconography of Chibinda Ilunga, and their images of the hero king might have had very little in common with one another in terms of appearance. In practice, however, multiples usually are similar, so that those visiting a distant village or town, in a region that forms some kind of iconographic unity, are able to identify figures in the cult places of strangers. In the case of Chibinda Ilunga, the large headdress with its front brim bent back and two lateral wings, together with the posture and the outsized hands and feet holding a staff, a horn or a rifle, are the common elements that allow his statues to be recognized as representations of him.[3] Once the viewer has learned how to identify one Chibinda Ilunga, and has accepted the principle that images might be found in more than one place, then representations of other images of the hero can be identified without prompting. They are transmissive, to use the term introduced in the previous chapter.

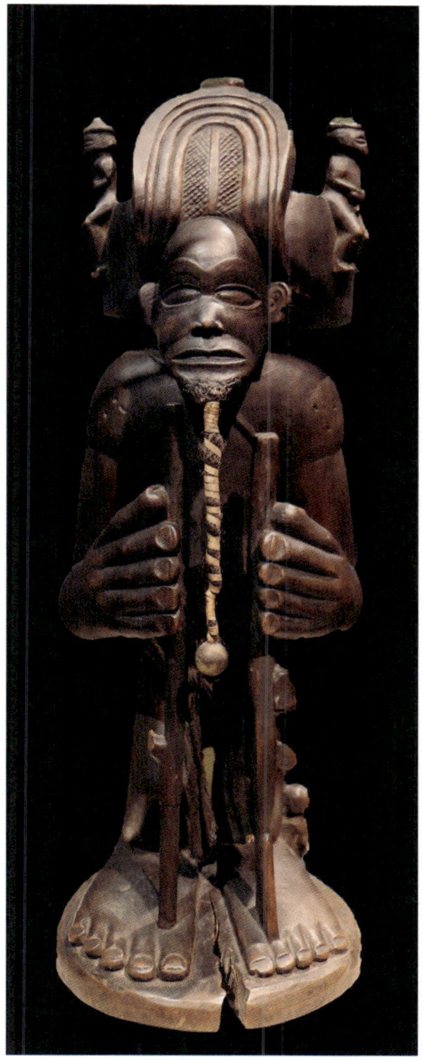

4.1 | Chokwe, Chibinda Ilunga, 19th century. Ethnologisches Museum, Berlin

2 The identification of these figures as Chibinda Ilunga is based on the identification of one of them made to Marie-Louise Bastin by a Chokwe diviner in 1956 from a photograph of a statue, and on extrapolation from that example. The claim is widely accepted in the literature, but is impossible to confirm, given that the statues were carved in the eighteenth and nineteenth centuries. See Bastin 1976; Wastiau 2006, 27–28. It has also been suggested that these statues should be thought of not as multiples of Chibinda Ilunga but as images of Chokwe chiefs impersonating Chibinda Ilunga: LaGamma 2011, 195, 197–99, 221. Given the uncertainties surrounding the images, the argument I am trying to weave round them may be a just-so story, but perhaps it is an illuminating just-so story. On just-so stories in anthropology, see Evans-Pritchard 1965, 24–26.

3 This argument is circular, as those who have read ftn. 2 will realise; more on this later in this chapter.

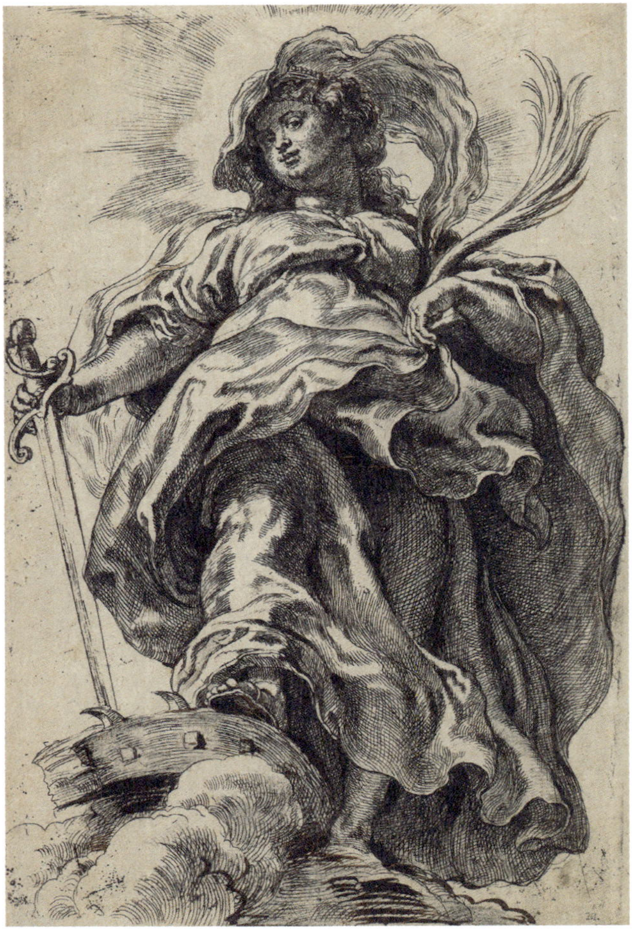

4.2 | Peter Paul Rubens, St Catherine of Alexandria, c. 1620. The Metropolitan Museum of Art, New York

Attributes and properties

Transmission is achieved by means of shared attributes or properties (Wentzel 1937; Braun 1943, 803–32; Volp and Kaute 1968; Hermeren 1969, 99–101; Kulvicki 2020, 79–86), although deciding what is a property and what is an attribute, as we will see in this section, is not an easy business. Some figures in world art have accessories that seem so unusual we assume they are symbols meant to have conventional meanings. Why would a well-dressed woman with a crown be shown accompanied by a broken piece of toothed wheel (fig. 4.2), if it did not have some significance? Why would a four-armed male hold a rosary, a mace, a wheel and a conch (fig. 4.3), if they were not trying to convey a meaning? These conspicuously out-of-place accessories that have a symbolic purpose have been called 'attributes' by art historians since around the beginning of the eighteenth century (Addison 1718, 243, 264; but cf. Valeriano 1556, 358r; Samperi 1645, §6v; Du Fresnoy 1668, 79).

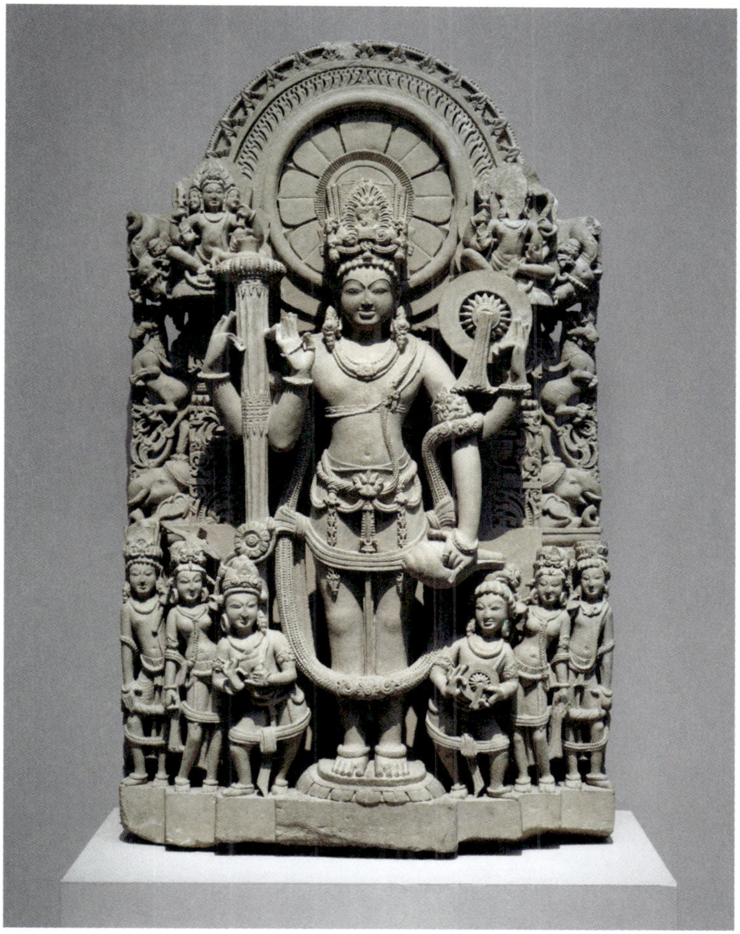

4.3 | Punjabi, Vishnu, 10th–11th century. The Metropolitan Museum of Art, New York

Attributes can be divided into generic and specific. The broken piece of toothed wheel is a specific attribute of St Catherine of Alexandria, since it identifies her as a particular personage; a toothed wheel was set up to torture her but was destroyed by angels; she was eventually beheaded with a sword. Catherine also has certain generic attributes; a halo tells us that she is a saint, and a palm in her hand that she is a martyr. And she has properties; she is young and beautiful. While these properties in no way individuate her, they are necessary to her identity; a picture of an old woman with crown and wheel and sword would not be Catherine, since it is part of her legend that she was a beautiful princess who died young. One can make an image of Catherine without her attributes, but not without her properties; properties are necessary, attributes are not, and neither are sufficient.[4]

4 On 'necessary' and 'sufficient', see Chapter 2, ftn. 2.

Vishnu has specific attributes in his four hands, and he also has generic attributes, such as his halo; perhaps his multiple arms might themselves be considered generic attributes of deity, rather than properties. His youth and beauty, as well as his bejewelled costume, are fitting to his divine nature and can be considered properties like those of Catherine; although Vishnu, who has the power to transform himself into other creatures, does not always need his properties (Blurton 1992, 111–53). Nevertheless, a wizened old man with four arms, holding the attributes of Vishnu, could hardly be considered an image of Vishnu.

Recognizing Vishnu's attributes is in part a result of recognizing Vishnu. His mace in fig. 4.3 could be mistaken for a torch and looks very little like the maces he holds in many other images; his wheel or disc, unlike here, is often shown rotating around his forefinger. Iconographic feedback thus applies here, as it must do for all attributes, which can always be taken to depict something else; we assume that St Catherine's sword is made of steel, not wood, that the object in her left hand is a palm, not a frayed piece of rope, and that the object on which her right foot rests is a broken part of a wheel of torture, rather than a piece of some machine (fig. 4.2).

Deciding what is an attribute and what is a property is a vague and uncertain business. We can perhaps agree that someone's bodily appearance is in most cases a property, not an attribute, although there will be a few counterexamples (e.g. Shiva's third eye, Francis of Assisi's stigmata). Perhaps clothes are properties rather than attributes, although there are bound to be exceptions (Hercules's lion skin, Coatlicue's snaky skirt). If a Christian saint holds a sword, that may be because he was a soldier who used it for work. One could call a sword worn in a professional capacity a generic attribute, since it narrows down the range of possibilities for the saint's identity, but one could also call it a property. However, some soldier saints – Gereon, for example – were beheaded; does this turn their sword into an attribute? When St Catherine has a sword, it is a reference to the fact that she was beheaded, and everyone is agreed that it is one of her attributes, together with the wheel (fig. 4.2). In fact, hundreds of saints were said to have been beheaded, so swords are very commonly held by martyrs and, as a result, they are of limited use when trying to establish a sword-holder's identity. Swords do not often serve as specific attributes, and when they do they require a great deal of contextual assistance. St Paul is often shown with a sword because he was beheaded; since he also has a fairly consistent appearance in Christian art, with a serious expression, a long face, thinning hair and a beard, the sword and the face reinforce one another, although here too context helps, especially if he is shown with his fellow apostle, St Peter (fig. 4.4).

St Paul has what might be called 'make-believe features', and so do a number of other personages in traditional art forms around the world. We do not know what St Paul looked like, but artists have settled on a particular way of representing him, so that he can usually be recognized in art. Tradition also allows us to recognize the features of Christ in religious images, even though the long-haired, bearded figure that is so familiar to us (fig. 1.1) is not likely to be a very accurate portrayal of the historical Jesus.[5] In Hindu imagery Lord Krishna has the iconographic advantage of being blue, and besides having four arms he has many attributes and distinctive scenes, but he also has

5 Taylor 2018 argues that Christ was likely of undistinguished appearance and middling height, with cropped woolly hair and a short beard.

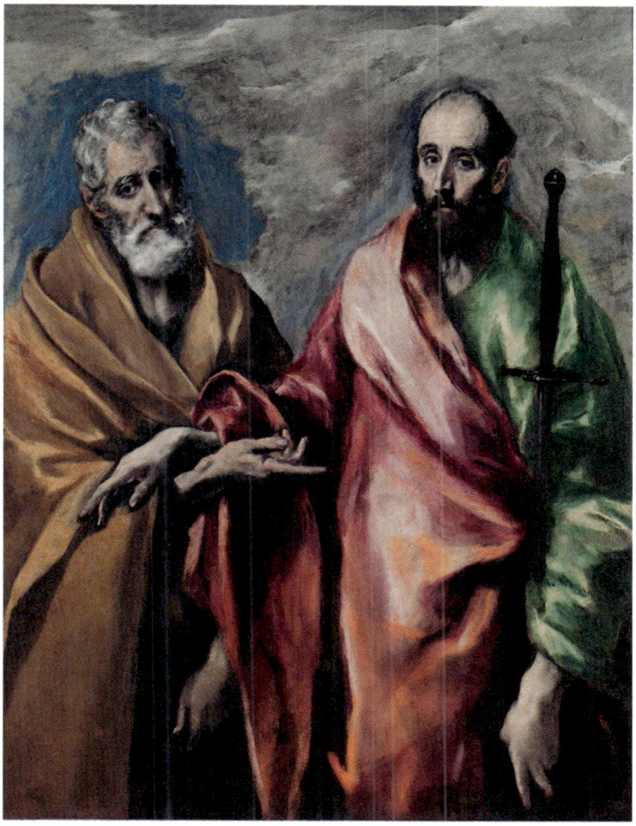

4.4 | El Greco, St Peter and St Paul, 1590s.
Museu Nacional d'Art de Catalunya, Barcelona

a beautiful broad face with big almond eyes that aid his recognition. Tlaloc, the Central Mexican rain deity, besides having a mouthful of large fangs, also has peculiar discs round his eyes, like goggles. Chibinda Ilunga, too, has make-believe features, with very large eyes, high brows and a broad mouth. All these physical features surely count as properties rather than attributes, and yet they function like specific attributes in the sense that they help us to identify individuals.

Semantics and pragmatics

The Chokwe live across a region that is larger than that of ancient Mesopotamia and ancient Egypt combined, but in terms of population these two early civilizations were much denser (Snape 2014, 37–39; Tenney 2017, 775–76), and this is reflected in their iconography. Apart from Chibinda Ilunga, the Chokwe make little use of multiples, but from Mesopotamia and Egypt tens of thousands of multiple images have come down to us, representing thousands of deities. Some of these deities can be recognized because they have attributes that identify them, while others are depicted in too generic a way to permit identification and must have been identified at the time by means of designation.

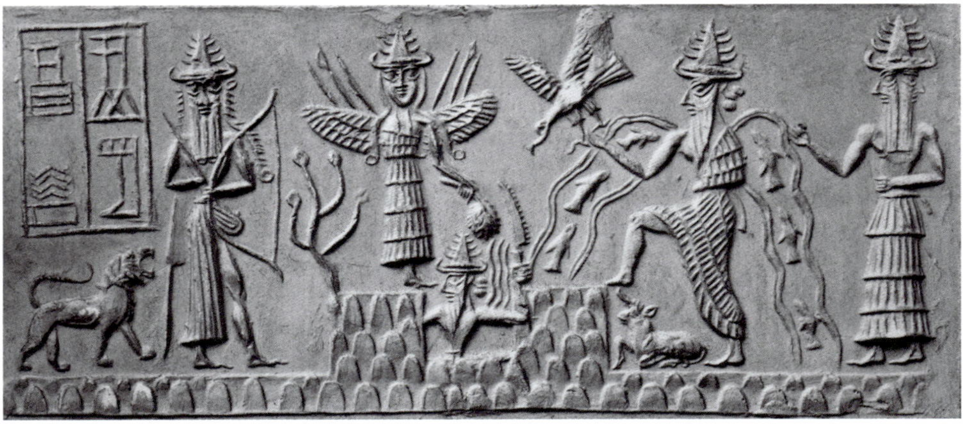

4.5 | Akkadian, Adda Seal, c. 2300 BC. The British Museum, London

In fig. 4.5 we see an impression of a Mesopotamian cylinder seal datable to around 2300 BC and known as the Seal of Adda after the scribe whose name is carved on it (Collon 1982, 92). It shows us five deities, four of whom we can name. We know that they are deities because they have horns on their heads and hats bristling with further horns. Horns are generic attributes of deity in ancient Iraqi iconography, just as the halo is a generic attribute of sanctity in Christian, Hindu and Buddhist imagery.[6] Besides these generic attributes, three of the deities also have individuating attributes. The winged female figure with weapons fanning out from her shoulders is Ishtar, the goddess associated with sex, warfare and the planet we call Venus. Next to her feet we see her twin brother, the sun god Shamash, rising between the mountains in the east (Black and Green 1992, 108, 184). Behind his back there are lines depicting solar rays, which form one attribute, and in his hand there is a toothed saw, another attribute.[7] To the right of the mountains we see a god who has fish swimming between rivulets up to his shoulders. This is one of the standard attributes of Ea, god of the subterranean waters (Black and Green 1992, 75). Behind Ea there is a two-faced god, and cuneiform texts tell us that Ea had a two-faced attendant, called Usmu.[8] The fifth god, however, we cannot at present name. With his long hair, bare leg, roaring lion and conspicuous bow he has ample individual traits, but whether these are generic or individuating attributes is hard to say.

We can give these deities names because on some seals there are cuneiform inscriptions referring to them, which allow us to link names with attributes. It is only because of these texts that we can name the deities. Without them we might be able to

6 And elsewhere. For a rare example of global iconographic history which traces the halo across four continents, see Collinet-Guérin 1961.

7 It is often claimed that ancient Iraqis thought Shamash used the saw to cut his way through the mountains in the morning (Van Dijk 1957, 538; Collon 1987, 165; Herles 2006, 260). That may well be right, but there is no textual support for the idea, and we do not actually see him cutting rock in Mesopotamian imagery. Rather, he emerges over the mountains and brandishes his saw, as here.

8 I have given the Akkadian names of the gods. They also had Sumerian names: Inana, Utu, Enki and Isimud, respectively. See Black and Green 1992.

group together images of gods with saws, and of gods with fish swimming up to their shoulders, but we would not know that they were called Shamash and Ea. Attributes *transmit* identities, but they do not *assign* identities. You might deduce from looking at ten cylinder seals depicting a rayed god holding a saw that the same god was represented on each seal, but without the assistance of texts, no matter how long you gazed at the collection, you could not discover the name of the god – nor that they were the same god, a point to which we will return. The name is attached to the attribute by a similar method to the one the Bangwa use to give names to their ancestor figures, by designation. Of course, in a small-scale group, designation can be a simple process involving no more than a handful of people, much like the naming ceremony for a child. In a complex society, the connection of attribute and name may well be the result of an evolutionary process, involving different stages and different agents – but the attribute needs a meaning, and the connection of the two must involve the ascription of sense. Without that initial designation, or process of designation, a group of figures with attributes would be no more than a set of images resembling one another in a certain regard.

Despite the power of specific attributes to convey identities, very few Mesopotamian deities have individuating attributes. There are over three thousand divine names in the religious literature of Mesopotamia, but the number of deities we can recognize by means of specific attributes is probably no more than fifty (Black and Green 1992, 147; Taylor 2006b, 15). That does not mean that the thousands of gods without attributes were not represented in Mesopotamian art: they were, but with generic attributes only. What this meant is that they needed to be given their specific identities by designation. As we have already seen, on certain cylinder seals the figures are depicted so simply that it is not possible to identify them through specific attributes, so the owner of the seal must have designated the identity of each figure, just like the ancestor figures of the Bangwa.

To put it in different terms: the vast majority of Mesopotamian deities were given their identities pragmatically, rather than semantically. Note that the figures are nevertheless multiples, or possible multiples; a god may be represented on many seals, or may have many idols dedicated to him in temples, and yet be referred to by the designatory method. This may be either because he does not have a very stable and consistent iconography, or because his attributes are not considered necessary in a particular context. A ziggurat with a shrine to a large idol of a certain god hardly needs to make a special effort to delineate his attributes; the people in the neighbourhood will know the temple's purpose. In fig. 4.6 we see a scene of worshippers before an idol of Shamash. The idol is holding a rod and ring, a generic symbol of divinity held by a number of different high-ranking deities.[9] It is not holding the sun god's specific attribute of the saw, but it does not need to, since it is the main idol in a Shamash temple; and besides, it has a large solar disc in front of it (though scholars disagree as to whether this is being installed or removed).[10]

9 Black and Green 1992, 156. Some scholars believe that the rod and ring is a specific attribute of Shamash, but, as noted by Black and Green, it is also held by Ishtar, Marduk, Asshur, Enlil or Sin, Nabu and Adad.

10 Woods 2004, 50–53. The text on this tablet tells us that the idol of the god disappeared during attacks on his temple, and that for over a century the devotees of Shamash made offerings to a sun disc instead. Then a clay model of the idol was 'found' and a copy of it was made for the temple. We see the new idol being installed; some think the sun disc is being removed. Woods makes a good case that it was instead placed in front of the idol.

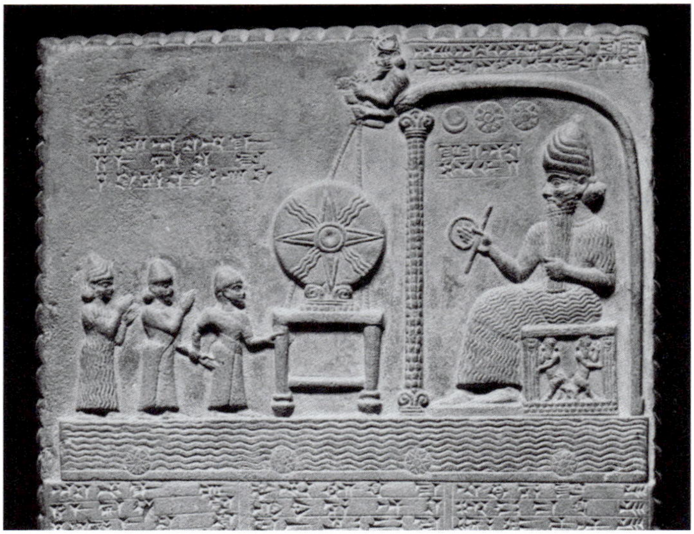

4.6 | Babylonian, Tablet of Shamash, 860–850 BC. The British Museum, London

A god may have clear attributes, but not in every context. Shamash is sometimes recognizable by his saw, but that does not mean that he cannot also be recognized by the method of designation; so a cylinder seal of a god with no specific attributes could nevertheless be taken by its owner to represent Shamash. Deities in house shrines might also dispense with their attributes, since they could rely on the pragmatic context of the family worshipping them.

If designation can be used for multiples, so too attributes can be used for singles. Attributes help viewers reidentify multiples, but they can also allow the viewer to distinguish different figures placed together, and this can be an advantage for assemblies of singles. When ancestor figures have been made in the same style, their visual differences may not be strikingly evident (fig. 4.7), so adding an attribute can assist the task of identification. This is, however, an addition that is rarely made by those who create singles. An exception to prove the rule is that of *ndop* figures, portraits of the kings of the Kuba, who live in the south of the Congo rainforest (fig. 4.8) (Vansina 1964, 1972, 1978; Binkley and Darish 2009; LaGamma 2011). These functioned in a similar way to ancestor figures among the Bangwa, except that, it appears, the Kuba did not practise ancestor worship:

> After the various rites of investiture were completed and he had been crowned in his new capital, the king ordered a sculptor to carve his *ndop* and his drum of office. Only one *ndop* could be made for a king .... During the king's life the *ndop* was ... supposed to house his double, the counterpart of his soul .... While the king was still alive, his statue was kept in his women's quarters. Some of the general powers of fertility clustered in Kuba kingship were believed to adhere to the image itself; for when a woman of the harem was about to give birth, the statue was placed near her to insure a safe delivery. It was also a substitute for the king himself to his

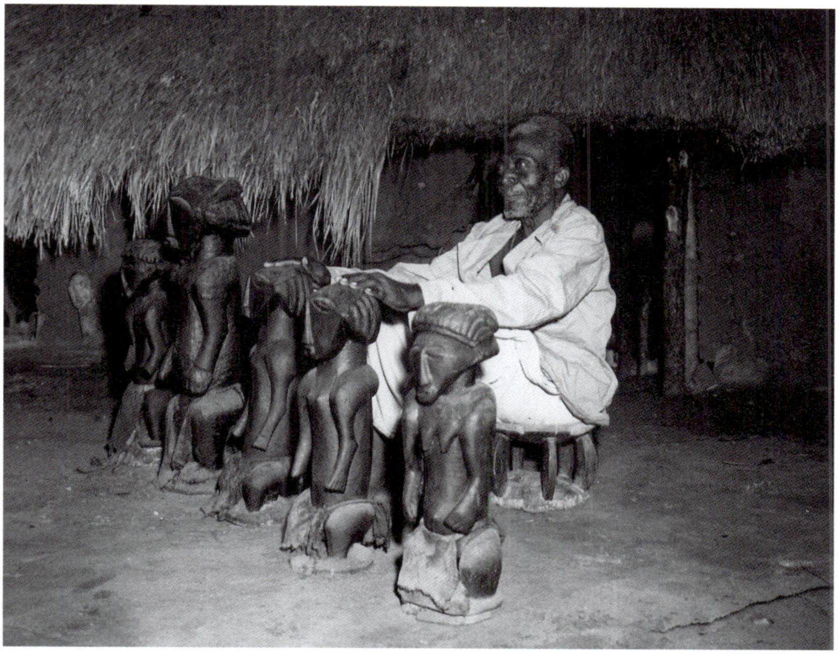

4.7 | Ancestral figures from the shrine of the Basiatshiwa-Mwamuwa (Bahutshwe-Boyo), Chief Kimano II. Kabambare territory, Maniema (D. R. Congo)

womenfolk, who would anoint, stroke and fondle it in their husband's absence. After death, Kuba kings were believed to become nature spirits (*ngesh*), ancestor worship being unknown among the Kuba. Then the *ndop* became a commemorative object and was removed along with the royal drum to a storage room, sometimes near the grave of the deceased. But even these *ndop* were exhibited on certain important occasions.
(Vansina 1972, 44–45)

The *ndop*, then, were singles (although since the early twentieth century, when Europeans began to express great admiration for these sculptures as works of art, many copies have been made). Nevertheless, each one had its own emblem, an object placed in front of the seated figure of the king – in the example in fig. 4.8, a drum marked with a hand. This object helped the Kuba to tell which statue represented which king, since in other regards the *ndop* were stylized, idealized portraits which, like the Bangwa ancestor figures (figs. 3.3 and 3.4), did not resemble their prototypes (Vansina 1972, 43).[11]

Very few cultures that make singles have emulated this Kuba practice of attaching emblems to their images. In order to distinguish portraits from one another, most

11 Vansina suggested that the statue illustrated here may have alluded to the corpulence of king Mbó Mbóosh. The argument is speculative, since we do not know if this statue represents Mbó Mbóosh, and any evidence that he was corpulent is based on a 300-year-old oral tradition.

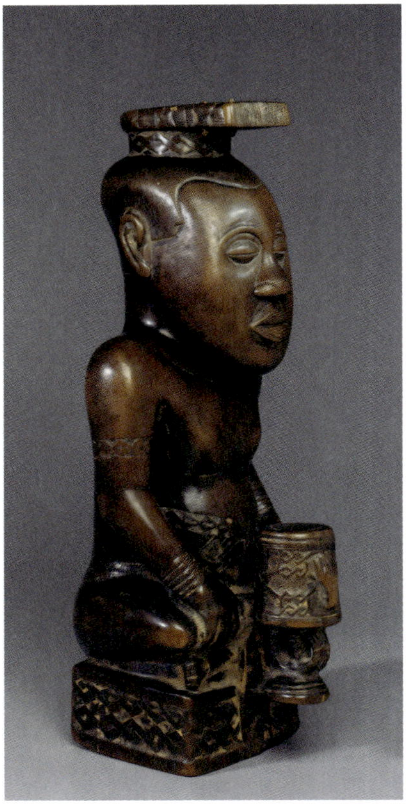

4.8 | Kuba (Bushoong subgroup), *Ndop* figure depicting Nyim Mbó Mbóosh (r. c. 1650), Nyim Mishé miShyááng máMbúl (r. c. 1710), or Nyim Kot áNée (r. c. 1740), c. 1760–80. Brooklyn Museum, New York

have relied on designation and linkage, based on differences of scale, style and technique (fig. 4.7) (on 'linkage', a term we will be using frequently in what follows, see the discussion on pp. 69 and 87 above). When one has only five or six statues to tell apart – and in Africa, where termites take a heavy toll on wooden sculpture (Van Huis 2017), preserving large numbers of royal effigies is a challenge – it is not difficult to individuate statues in this way.

Problems arise as the statues that need differentiation increase in number. Take the Jains in India. They worship holy figures, the Jinas or 'conquerors', saintly ascetics who have managed, like the Buddhas, to transcend the cycle of death and rebirth (Laidlaw 1995; Pal 1994a). There have been 24 Jinas in our own period of history, but the Jains believe our period is only one of many, and periods in the past and future have had and will have their Jinas (Babb 1988; Cort 1995). In the copper alloy piece in fig. 4.9 there are 78 Jinas (Pal 1994b). It is, however, only the 24 Jinas of our own period that are actively worshipped in temples. Observant Jains visit idols of these Jinas each day and take part in the rite known in this and other Indian religions as *puja*: the statues are bathed, dabbed with sandalwood paste, presented with flowers, offered gifts of food and money, prayed to and so forth (Babb 1998, 69–72; Humphrey and Laidlaw 1994, 21–31; Cort 1994).[12] These Jinas look almost identical to one another. In theory, all the Jinas are of equal merit and spiritual importance, and so there is no reason for them to differ. Jain deities, of which there are many, display the same variety as deities in other polytheistic religions, but the Jinas are strikingly uniform. Only one, the 23rd Jina, Parshvanatha, can usually be distinguished from the rest by his appearance, since he has a canopy of seven serpents over his head (fig. 4.9). Sometimes too the seventh Jina, Suparshvanatha, is shown with a canopy of five serpents, but this is much rarer. In some images, the first Jina, Rishabhanatha, can be identified by his long hair, and the nineteenth Jina, Mallinatha, is considered by one of the two Jain sects to have been a woman – although there is only one surviving image of a female Mallinatha (Gorakshakar 1994). For the rest, the only way that idols of the Jinas can be told apart is by their attributes, which are not held, but (when they appear at all) carved discreetly into the marble at the base of each statue. In paintings, colour can also play a part. Most Jinas are golden, but some are red, white, blue or green – though since the temple idols are usually white, this indicator is rarely of use to a *puja*-goer.

12 On the use of the word 'idol', see Chapter 3, ftn. 18.

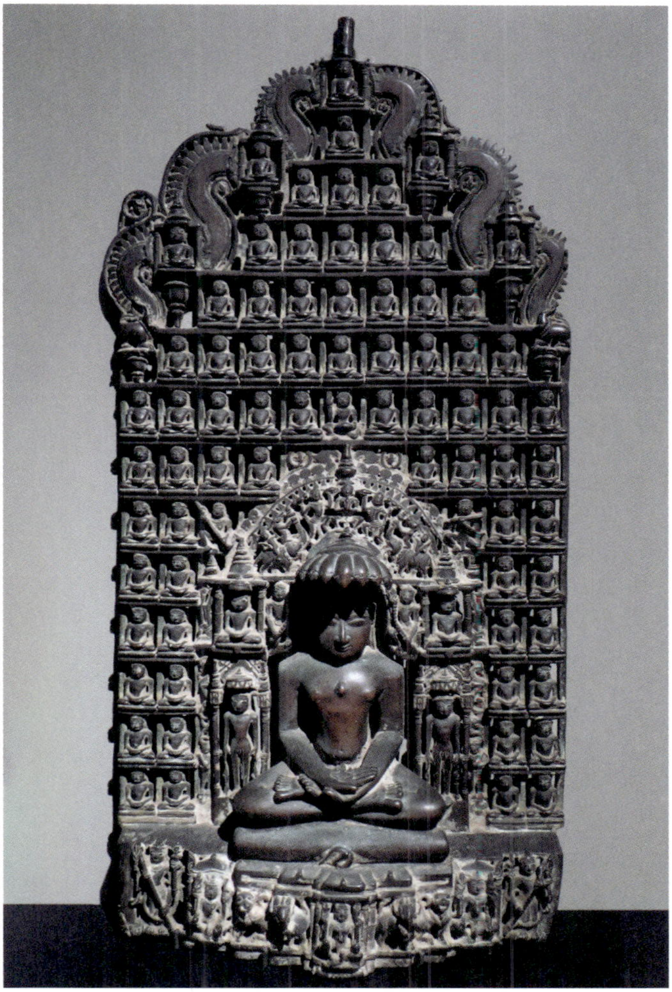

4.9 | Rajasthani/Gujarati, Altarpiece with multiple Jinas, c. 1500. Norton Simon Museum, Pasadena

When the Jains began to make idols of their Jinas, between the second century BC and the third century AD, they did not distinguish their statues using emblems (Pal 1994a, 25); the only way to know their identities was to remember which was which and where they were located. While this can be done when it is a matter of a handful of ancestor figures (fig. 4.7), with 24 Jinas it would have taxed the memory. The introduction of emblems must have greatly helped devotees identify Jinas.

Early Jain idol-worshippers were dealing with a group of figures which may have been hard to identify without the help of attributes, but it was very small compared to the image populations found in other traditions. From the fifth century AD onwards, with the rise of the Mahayana movement, the Buddhist pantheon grew rapidly, leading to the worship of thousands of different Buddhas, bodhisattvas and their divine emanations, as well as deities of the directions, of doors, of light, of virtues, of spiritual disciplines and more (Nukariya 1913; Bhattacharyya 1958; Clark 1965). At the same time, a language of attributes of exceptional complexity was invented, so that, in theory at least, each divine being could be recognized from the objects held in its hands. Since many of these beings have multiple pairs of hands, and each hand can hold its own attribute, the possibilities for semantic individuation become very extensive. Indeed, the actual number of attributes does not need to be very large, since identities can be assigned by placing the attribute into individual hands and specifying exactly which hand holds what. It would take a huge effort of memory to recall the details of such a system, but happily the iconographic code was recorded in manuscripts such as the *Sadhanamala*, a Sanskrit text compiled not later than the twelfth century. This was written for devotees who wished to meditate on mental images of deities, but it is also one of our prime sources for Buddhist iconography.

According to the *Sadhanamala*, Vidyujjvalakarali, an emanation of the Buddha Akshobhya, besides having twelve faces, also has 24 hands, and holds the following attribute in each:

> ... in her twelve right hands, 1. the sword, 2. the thunderbolt, 3. the discus, 4. the jewel, 5. the elephant-goad, 6. the arrow, 7. the dart, 8. the hammer, 9. the pestle, 10. the saw, 11. the drum and 12. the rosary; and in her twelve left hands she has 1. the bow, 2. the noose, 3. the raised index finger, 4. the flag, 5. the mace, 6. the trident, 7. the wineglass, 8. the blue lotus, 9. the bell, 10. the axe, 11. the severed head of Brahma, and 12. the skull.
> (Bhattacharyya 1958, 195)

These attributes can also be found in the hands of other sacred beings. The *Sadhanamala* tells us that Mayajalakrama, a fierce form of the bodhisattva Avalokiteshvara, has five faces and half as many arms as Vidyujjvalakarali, but carries a very similar selection of attributes:

> He carries in his right hands 1. Damaru [the drum], 2. the Khatvanga [club], 3. the goad, 4, the noose, 5. the Vajra [thunderbolt] and 6. the arrow, and in his left hands 1. the raised index finger, 2. the Kapala [skull cup], 3. the red lotus, 4. the jewel, 5. the discus, and 6. the bow.
> (Bhattacharyya 1958, 139)

The semantic variety that this hand-placing system generates means that a core of less than fifty attributes can be used repeatedly to denote thousands of identities. However, if the system is to allow transmission between locations, it needs to be consistent, and that is not always the case. The same Buddhist deity can hold different assortments of attributes in different images. On an image of Mayajalakrama that is part of a cycle of the forms of Avalokiteshvara in the Machhindra Bahal temple in Kathmandu (fig. 4.10),

> The six right hands carry the Tridandi [trident], the Khatvanga [club], the jewel, the Khadga [sword], the Vajra [thunderbolt] and the rosary, and the six left show the noose, the Kapala [skull cup], the Utpala [blue lotus], the fruit, the Cakra [discus] and the lotus.
> (Bhattacharyya 1958, 394)

This clearly differs from the arrangement of attributes described in the *Sadhanamala*, with only four of the twelve hand attributes being the same between the two images. Other features of the imagery are the same – the number of arms, the number of faces and the pose (Bhattacharyya 1958, 86, 394) – but a visitor to the temple might find it difficult to be sure if the image in fig. 4.10 represented Mayajalakrama, without looking at the inscription that names him.

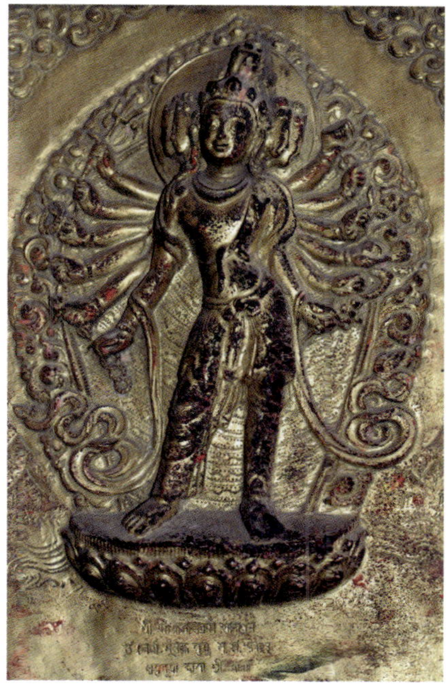

4.10 | *Mayajalakrama*, 16th–18th century. Temple of Machhindra Bahal, Kathmandu

Similar inconsistencies of attributes can be found in the iconographies of Hindu deities such as Vishnu. I introduced the sculpture in fig. 4.3 as if it were a typical image of Vishnu, but the first attribute I mentioned, the rosary, is an anomaly. Hindu children learn that the attributes of Vishnu are the mace, the lotus, the conch and the disc: here the lotus is missing. In theory, the four attributes of Vishnu should be held in different permutations in different hands, depending on which of the 24 main forms of Vishnu is being depicted. However, this systematic arrangement is not laid down consistently; four authoritative texts, the *Agnipurana*, the *Padmapurana*, the *Rupamandana* and *Chaturvarga Chintamani* of Hemadri, give different orders of attributes for over half the forms of Vishnu (Bidyabinod [1920] 1998, 25; Daniélou 1964, 154). As we can see in fig. 4.3, inconsistencies are also to be found in the statues, which fail to follow the prescriptions of the (inconsistent) texts. In the end, the precise sense of almost any idol of Vishnu must be settled by linkage to the original act of designation.

It might be thought that this does not matter, since, in the age before tourism, images were not made for travellers. Those who worshipped Vishnu or Avalokiteshvara in towns many miles apart were unlikely ever to notice discrepancies between the attributes on different idols and, in any case, what was important to Buddhists and Hindus was that they should be able to identify the deities in their local temples; if other worshippers in distant towns codified the distinctions in different ways, that would not interfere with anyone's devotion.

A religion with even more holy figures than those of Hinduism and Buddhism, Christianity, dealt with the problem of attributes and identification in a less systematic way, closer to that of ancient Mesopotamia. In standard hagiographical dictionaries there are over 15,000 Christian saints, but probably fewer than one in twenty of these have specific attributes. These saints are, however, the most popular and widespread saints, so that while fewer than one in twenty saint-types have attributes, the great majority of saint-tokens have attributes.

This may seem slightly paradoxical; the famous saints who are widely known have attributes to identify them, while the obscure saints who are little known do not have the attributes they need. However, the widely known saints are also those who can be found in many different churches across Christendom, and whose specific identifiers allow them to be recognized between locations. At the same time, obscure saints are generally obscure because they have few images made of them, and the rarer they are the easier it is to remember their identities by the method of designation and linkage.

Identities

'Ideally', writes John Kulvicki, 'attributes are unique to iconographic subjects, lest we wind up with ambiguous icons' (Kulvicki 2020, 79). This would indeed be the ideal, but in practice things are not always as clear as we might like. It is not just that some attributes are inconsistent between images of the same personage, as with the examples of Vishnu and Mayajalakrama; sometimes we have different figures with the same attributes. This is true of some of the forms of Vishnu. Despite the fact that his multiple hands would allow 256 different permutations of his four attributes, amongst the 24 forms of the deity there can be duplications; according to the *Agnipurana*, Vishnu Madhava and Vishnu Pradyumna have their attributes in the same order, as do Vishnu Padmanabha and Vishnu Hari (Bidyabinod [1920] 1998, 25).[13]

Unsurprisingly, repetition can also be found among Christian saints. Erasmus, Bishop of Formia, is one of the most distinctive of martyrs, since he is shown carrying a windlass which has his own guts wrapped round it (fig. 4.11). The story is that he was tortured by having his intestines drawn out of his stomach. According to the most widely read medieval compilation of saints' lives, the *Golden Legend*, Erasmus survived this and several other cruel ordeals, and died peacefully some days later, while being addressed by an angel. However, although the attributes of Erasmus are certainly distinctive, they are not unique. St Thiemo, Archbishop of Salzburg (fig. 4.12), a much less famous figure who is only revered in a region of about 150 km around Salzburg, is also shown holding a windlass bearing his intestines. We are told that he joined the First Crusade and was subjected to the same torture, which in his case had the more foreseeable outcome of killing him (Böhm 1976).[14]

In both fig. 4.11 and 4.12 inscriptions tell us which saint is which; without them the figures would be iconographically indistinguishable. There may well be figures of Erasmus or Thiemo that were initially designated as Thiemo or Erasmus, but have changed identities due to an understandable confusion by subsequent generations of devotees. For all we know, the inscription beneath St Thiemo in fig. 4.12 may be a later addition, and the statue may once have been meant to represent St Erasmus.

A third example of the phenomenon is less clear-cut, since it stems from a culture with a sparser literary record, making it harder to be sure about identities. In early Buddhist sculpture, before the development of the highly complex system of significance based on multiple hand-held attributes, there are many figures of bodhisattvas but few specific attributes. One exception is a water flask, held in the left hand of a number of the statues of bodhisattvas in fig. 4.13, which were all excavated in the late nineteenth century in the Swat Valley in northwest Pakistan, a region that once formed part of the kingdom of Gandhara. It is widely supposed that this water flask

---

13 Other arrangements of the attributes of Vishnu are more careful to avoid duplication, but systematically disagree with one another; see Daniélou 1968, 154.

14 I thank Berthold Kress for bringing Saint Thiemo to my attention.

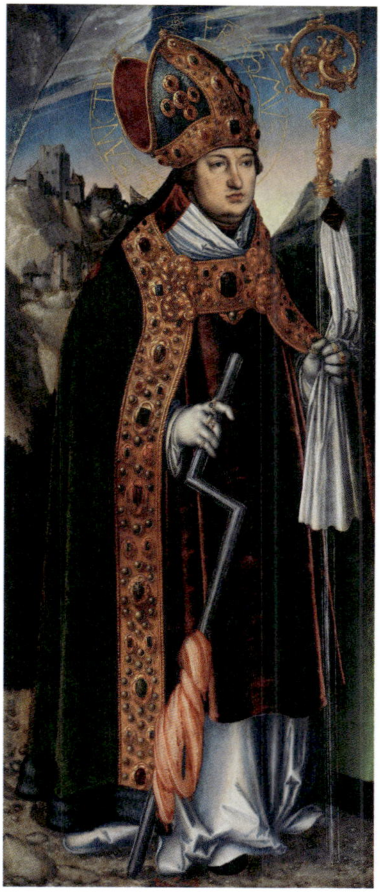

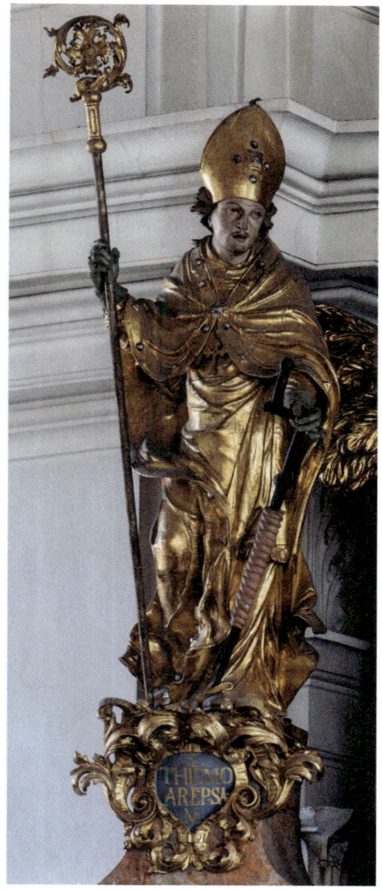

4.11 | Workshop of Lucas Cranach the Elder, St Erasmus, 1524–26, from the Pfirtsch Altar. Staatsgalerie im Schloss Johannisburg, Aschaffenburg (Germany)

4.12 | Bavarian, St Thiemo, 18th century. Abbey of Sts Mauritius and Nicholas, Niederaltaich (Germany)

is an attribute of Maitreya, the future Buddha; but it is not entirely clear that it is an identifying attribute at all.

In Gandharan art bodhisattvas are depicted with a tight cluster of generic attributes and properties, which usually include a halo, earrings, bracelets, armlets, necklaces, moustaches and long hair. A cord or chain over one shoulder will have a row of charm boxes attached to it. Bodhisattvas are depicted with bare chests and stomachs, and wear sandals on their feet. The dress and hairstyle are those of an Indian prince, and some elements of this attire are meant to refer to the bodhisattva's human, not divine nature – deities are not shown wearing shoes, and do not have the need for charm boxes (Pal 2006). Only the halo is a reference to the bodhisattva's cosmic destiny as one who will attain *nirvana* and become a Buddha, and yet haloes are not essential attributes of depicted bodhisattvas. As can be seen in fig. 4.13, some of the bodhisattva images have haloes, others do not.

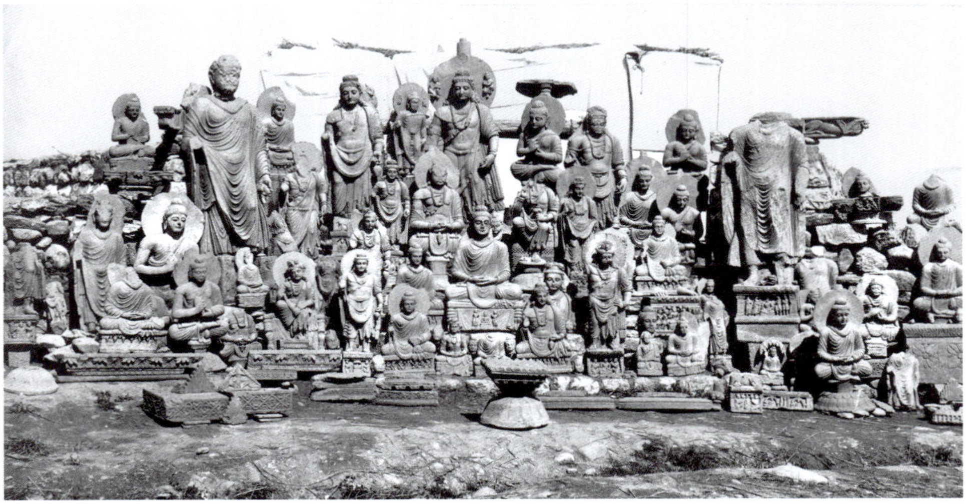

4.13 | Gandharan, Buddhas and Bodhisattvas from Lorian Tangai, 1st–3rd century AD

The water flask is generally considered Maitreya's specific attribute (Foucher 1922, 217–28; Luczanits 2005), but it is possible that there are more Maitreyas in Gandharan statuary than there are flask-holding bodhisattvas. Many bodhisattvas from this period do not hold any specific attributes (fig. 4.14).[15] They must have been identified by means of designation and linkage, and some of these anonymous bodhisattvas may have been designated as Maitreya: we have no way of telling. Flask-holding Maitreyas are (or may be) a subset of Maitreyas.

In fact, it may also be that not all flask-holding bodhisattvas were meant to be Maitreya. The argument that all bodhisattvas holding the flask must be Maitreya is based partly on surviving inscriptions, partly on a specific iconography in which Maitreya features and partly on a detail of Buddhist theology. An inscription on a statue of a bodhisattva holding a water flask (which is not from Gandhara) identifies him as Maitreya, and there are also some Gandharan coins on which a bodhisattva who is probably holding a flask is identified as 'Metrago' (Luczanits 2005, 181; Boucher 2008). The iconography of the Eight Buddhas shows the seven who have already attained *nirvana* and the one (Maitreya) who is to come. In these carved reliefs, all but one of the Buddhas have turbans, but one has his hair in a loose topknot; this unturbaned Buddha is placed at the end of the row and holds a water flask. Although these reliefs do not bear inscriptions, it is assumed that the flask-holding figure must be Maitreya (Boucher 2008, 317). A prophecy from early Buddhist scriptures relates that the next Buddha will be from the priestly Indian caste, the Brahmins. The god Brahma is sometimes depicted in early Buddhist art with long hair and a loose topknot, holding a flask (Dobbins 1968). Therefore, so historians of Gandharan art have argued, Maitreya too is depicted with

15 The scene beneath the Bodhisattava's throne does not appear to identify him. Kurt Behrendt (pers. comm.) tells me that bodhisattvas with no attributes have in the past been identified as Siddhartha, but that this, in his view, is an interpretation for which there is no substantive evidence.

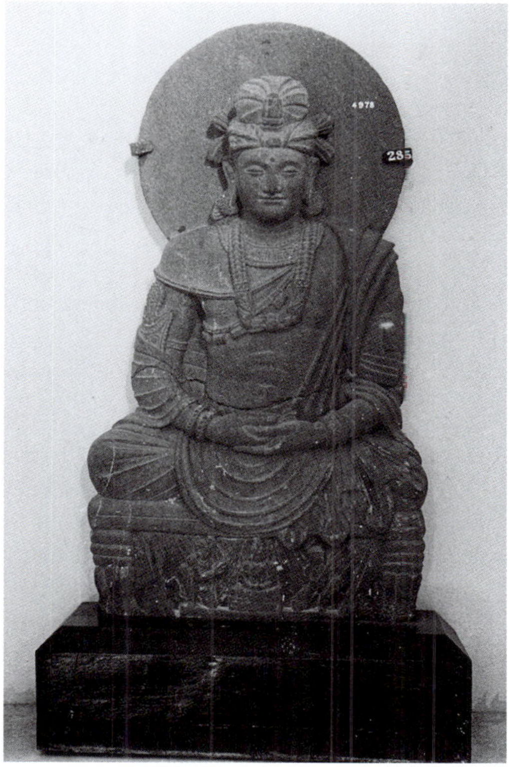

4.14 Gandharan, Bodhisattva, 1st–3rd century AD.
Indian Museum, Kolkata

long hair and a loose topknot, holding a flask (Foucher 1922, 218–26; Luczanits 2005, 182; Pal 2006, 105; Miyaji, 131, 145).

These arguments have convinced most students of Gandharan art that the flask is Maitreya's attribute. However, while they prove that the flask-holding bodhisattva is *sometimes* Maitreya, they have not shown that *every* flask-holding bodhisattva is Maitreya; and there is evidence that other bodhisattvas sometimes hold water flasks. In fig. 4.15 we see Indra and Brahma urging the bodhisattva Siddhartha to pursue his destiny as the Buddha, an event known as the *samcodana* (Zwalf 1996, 1:163–64).[16] In this image, Brahma does not hold a water flask, but Siddhartha does.[17] There are other examples of the same phenomenon, in which a bodhisattva holds a flask in a narrative scene that is normally associated with Siddhartha, not Maitreya (Luczanits 2005).

16 There is some disagreement among scholars as to where and when this event is supposed to have occurred, with some saying that it happened in the Tushita heaven before the bodhisattva's birth, and others placing it during his last earthly life, just before he was about to be crowned king.

17 He also has (fairly) long hair and a (fairly) loose topknot, making his figure indistinguishable from a Maitreya.

We seem then to have a situation in which two bodhisattvas with a water flask have different identities. There are various ways of solving this conundrum. One solution is to deny that the narrative scenes represent Siddhartha. Buddhism maintains that all of the Buddhas go through very similar life events, and so it may be that the Buddha in fig. 4.15 is not Siddhartha, but is instead Maitreya (Luczanits 2005, 185–86). Another way of dealing with the issue would be to argue that some, or perhaps many, bodhisattva statues that historians of Gandharan art identify as Maitreya may in fact be images of other bodhisattvas. Or we can just suppose that flask-holding does not confer identity; that different bodhisattvas can carry flasks (Boucher 2008; Fussman 2012). In fact, perhaps our mistake is to suppose that the flask is meant as an attribute; it may act more as a property than an attribute, and may be meant, as Alfred Foucher suggested, to be "the characteristic emblem of someone who has embraced the contemplative life" (Foucher 1922, 218).[18] In which case any bodhisattva could hold the water flask.

Whether or not this was the case in Gandhara, in later periods the flask did not have an exclusive association with Maitreya. Although in post-Gandharan art Maitreya had a water flask as one of his attributes, usually balanced on top of a flower (Getty 1914, 21–22), over twenty other bodhisattvas and deities included a flask among their attributes (Getty 1914; Bhattacharyya 1958). Perhaps in Gandharan times bodhisattvas holding the flask were given various identities by designation. In fact, even if we think that every flask-holding bodhisattva is Maitreya, we are still committed to a designatory scenario; for if the scene of the *samcodana* is identical in the future life of Maitreya and the past life of Siddhartha, then the only way to choose between the two is by designation and linkage.

With Gandharan iconography we have inscriptions that identify Maitreya, and we also have a body of early scriptures that recount the Buddhas' lives and previous lives, foretelling events in the world to come. Even with this precious information, our theories about the bodhisattvas' attributes remain less conclusive than we might like. When dealing with other societies, which have left us no texts at all, we must rely purely on appearances, and need to proceed with caution.

The vase in fig. 4.16, for example, was made on the north coast of Peru between 200 and 800 AD. The people who made this dish did not have a writing system, and, as a result, we do not know their name(s); they are known to modern archaeologists as the Moche, after the river in the Moche Valley, where archaeologists first found remains of their culture. To what extent they formed a state or empire, or whether they were instead a cluster of people who shared a culture, or a cluster of peoples who shared (superficially) related cultures, is still being debated by scholars of Peruvian archaeology (Quilter and Koons 2012). They left behind buildings bedecked with wall paintings (Trever et al. 2017), tombs filled with gold, silver and turquoise jewellery (Alva and Donnan 1993), and most of all a mass of representational ceramics, some moulded and painted (figs. 1.8 and 1.9) and some just painted (fig. 4.16), which probably show a greater variety of motifs than that found on the artefacts of any other preliterate people (Donnan 1978; Donnan 2004; Donnan and McClelland 1999). The great majority of these ceramics are bottles with distinctive 'stirrup-shaped' spouts (fig. 1.8), which seem from Moche imagery to have been carried with straps passed through the stirrup-shape and over the shoulder (Donnan and McClelland 1999, 21).

18 Foucher did, however, think of the water flask as Maitreya's attribute; see Foucher 1922, 232.

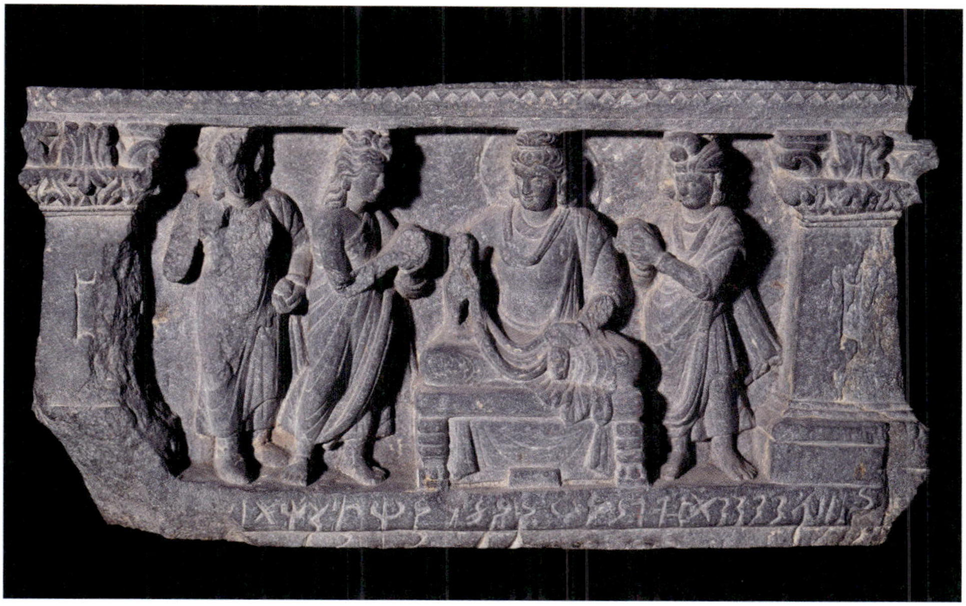

4.15 Gandhara school, Hashtnagar Pedestal, dated year 384 of an unknown era, 1st–3rd century AD. The British Museum, London

Quite how great a variety of iconographic motifs is depicted on Moche ceramics is not entirely clear. On Moche bottles and, to some extent, on other Moche media one finds much similarity of motif. The supernatural cassava we met in Chapter 1 (fig. 1.9) is far from unique; there are many cassavas (and indeed other vegetables) with fanged heads in Moche ceramics. The question then becomes: are they all multiples of one cassava being or deity, or are they representations of various cassava beings or deities?

We can ask the same question when looking at the vase in fig. 4.16. Its rim is decorated with a number of humanoid figures with large fangs, and some of them seem to be wearing belts with two serpentine tassels. Do these serpent belt-wearers form a multiple, representing a unique personage? Many have thought that they do, and that what we are looking at here is a mythological cycle of the Moche deity, Ai Apaec; indeed, this is how the vase is currently catalogued at the Museo Larco in Lima.

Given that the Moche were a preliterate people, it might be wondered how we can know the name of one of their deities. Ai Apaec's name is regularly used in popular journals, on the internet and even in academic publications to refer to a god of the Moche, since local indigenous peoples speak of an important god with this name. However, scholars have noted that his name was a generic word for 'maker' in later languages of the Moche valley, and was used by Catholic missionaries who were trying to convert the locals; we do not know if the ancient Moche used it (Makowski 2005; Prządka-Giersz 2015). A number of scholars who refrain from using the name Ai Apaec since they think it is a later invention nevertheless believe that many of the figures on Moche ceramics represent one deity, whom they call by names such as Wrinkle Face, or God F, or the acronym PACS (*Personaje antropomórfica con cinturones de serpientes* – Anthropomorphic personage with serpent belts).

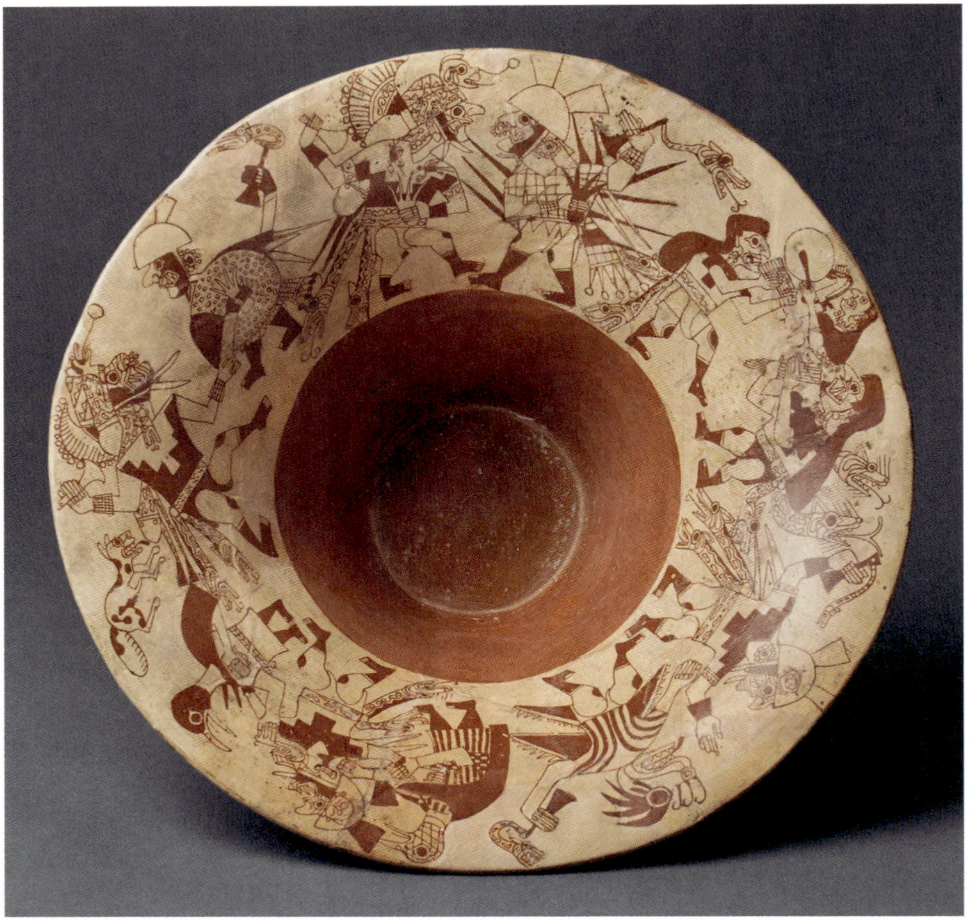

4.16 | Moche vase with the battles of Ai Apaec (?), Auge Period (1–800 AD). Museo Larco, Lima

Our vase, then, is thought by many to be a cycle of representations of one supernatural individual, engaged in battle with a number of monsters. Similar scenes, with similar supernatural beings and similar monsters, can be found on Moche stirrup-spout bottles and on wall paintings (Trever et al. 2017, 301–06). The idea that we are here witnessing a Moche myth, 'the Battles of Wrinkle Face' – the visual counterpart, perhaps, to some narrative that all Moche learned from childhood – is very tempting. It may also be correct. However, each of the serpent belt-wearers is different in numerous respects from the others, and even if they were not, how could we be sure that they were not meant to be a group of individuals with generic properties, like Gandharan bodhisattvas, or with duplicate attributes, like Erasmus and Thiemo? And this is to suppose that we are on the right track in thinking of Moche art as illustrating divine myths at all. Perhaps, instead, they were meant to represent the relations between the spirits of clans, or combats between actual clans, and so on (cf. Gombrich 1972a, 4). We have to hope that our researches are not "the product of a Western mind following

Western interests", as the people of Tabar put it to Michael Gunn (Gunn 1992, 1; p. 104 above). After all, any attempt to reconstruct the iconography of New Ireland *malagan* by means of simple visual comparison would be hopelessly wide of the mark (cf. Bagley 1993; Bagley 2008).

Returning to the anthropomorphic cassava in fig. 1.9: should we think of every stirrup bottle that depicts a cassava with a fanged head as being a multiple of a cassava god? Perhaps, but the relationship between the image on the bottle and what it represents may be more complex than that. We are told by Spanish sources that the Inca made offerings of food and maize beer to idols carved in many different shapes, as humans, animals, fish, birds and vegetables (Cobo [1653] 1990, 45–46). Moche ceramics include bottles shaped in all these forms too, and it is possible, though not provable, that they were used to pour out libations to the idols they represented (Taylor 2008b). If that were right, would the bottle be a representation of the idol or the deity, or would it be an embodiment of the deity, and how many bottles would be used per idol, and how many idols would there be? And were the idols themselves representations of a deity (perhaps multiple representations) or were they considered to be (like fetishes) single containers for spirits?

The only access we have to Moche thought comes from much later periods, either from the ethnographic research of sixteenth- and seventeenth-century Spanish missionaries, or from the descendants of those people today, twelve centuries after the dissolution of Moche culture. These sources may give important insights, and there is no reason not to investigate them. But we cannot be certain that later opinions will be accurate reflections of Moche realities – after all, the people of Tabar are unable to interpret art produced on their island a century ago (p. 105 above). And, even if we guess correctly, we have no means of knowing that we have done so without Moche texts to confirm our hypotheses.

These objections also apply to the images of Chibinda Ilunga discussed earlier in this chapter. Although I presented the argument in the text (but not the footnotes) as if the iconography of these figures were unproblematic, many of the objections that apply to Ai Apaec can also be levelled against the Chokwe ancestor. We have a group of statues made over a century ago that resemble one another to some degree. One of these statues was identified by a Chokwe diviner, from a photograph, as an image of Chibinda Ilunga.[19] This diviner gave his judgment in 1956, decades after such statues had left Chokwe territory for Western collections; so while his identification may be correct, it is not based on the sort of immediate cultural experience that might be decisive. The other images of Chibinda Ilunga have been identified on the basis of their resemblance to the statue identified by the diviner, but, as we have seen, a number of figures that resemble one another do not necessarily have to represent the same personage. The iconographic argument may be correct, but we have no secure way of confirming it.

19 See ftn. 2 above.

Further devices: statistics, texts and contexts

That a group of images share attributes and properties does not guarantee that they have the same iconography. In practice, the attribute as an iconographic device has to rely not only on properties but on a number of further devices in order to assign representation (cf. Müller 2015).

Statistics. In order to know what an attribute signifies, one must also know what it does not signify; before one decides that an image represents St Catherine (fig. 4.2), one has to be sure that there is no other saintly princess with the wheel of torture as an attribute. This involves reasoning by statistical assumption. There may be some saint you have never heard of who was a princess and who could be shown with a toothed wheel of torture. As it happens, a martyr called Euphemia is said, amongst other tortures, to have been subjected to the wheel. She is not often painted in western Europe outside Italy, and she is not usually shown with the wheel as her attribute; but she is sometimes shown with a crown, even though she was not a princess. The print in fig. 4.2 *might* represent Euphemia, although it would probably not occur to any art historian to make the identification. Why not? Because Catherine is usually shown with her wheel of torture, or part of it, and she was far more widely represented than Euphemia in Rubens's Flanders. The chance that Rubens would have decided to make an image of St Euphemia at all is much less probable than that he would have chosen to represent the popular St Catherine. This, then, is a statistical assumption.

Statistical arguments are usually regional. We have a lot of evidence that Thiemo was worshipped in the Salzburg region, and very little evidence that he was worshipped anywhere else. This obviously will support us in thinking that an image of a bishop with intestines on a windlass from the Salzburg region may originally have been considered a Thiemo, but that a saint with a similar accessory from any other part of Europe is more likely to have been Erasmus.

Of course, we only know that outside the Salzburg area Erasmus was popular and Thiemo was not because we have a large amount of textual evidence to support the claim. There are many written lives of Erasmus, many churches, chapels and altars dedicated to him, many paintings and prints with his name inscribed on them, and the converse is true of Thiemo. If we had none of these texts, if early modern Europe had been preliterate, we would have been left wondering if all the bishops with guts on windlasses in European art were the same person, several different people or a class of people, and we would have had no way of knowing for sure. Images in themselves can settle nothing; it is only when they are connected to a verbal and iconological context that we can think to distinguish their iconographies.

Texts. A direct way to connect an iconography to a verbal context is with an inscription, and it is perhaps surprising that inscriptions are not used more often in the iconography of peoples who have developed writing systems. Attributes emerged in the ancient Near East at around the same time as writing, and, as we have observed, it is through the inscriptions on some images that we are able to interpret the attributes at all. Given that the attributes are reliant on the inscriptions, why, we might ask, did people need the attributes?

One answer to this might be that the attributes are there for the majority of the population, who could not read. This sounds like a plausible line of reasoning, but in Mesopotamia the illiterate majority seems to have been happy to do without attributes for all but a few of their deities, as we observed earlier. Designation was apparently considered a satisfactory method of assigning identities, and so the need for attributes can again be questioned.

What is more, certain cultures that were far from fully literate have used textual inscriptions a great deal to assign the identities of their deities. Roman coins frequently have allegorical personifications – worshipped as deities in the Greco-Roman world – on their reverses. These personifications hold attributes, but for anyone who could not read the inscriptions that almost invariably appear on these coins – and it has been suggested that 90–95 % of ancient Romans were illiterate (Harris 1989; Curchin 1995; Woolf 2015) – it would not have been easy to work out which personification was represented, even if they had been told the meaning of similar personifications on other coins. Personifications frequently held different attributes on different coins, and most of these attributes were shared with other personifications. Pax (Peace), for example (fig. 4.17), could be depicted with a torch (applied to armour), a column topped by Minerva, an olive branch, a palm branch, a cornucopia, a caduceus, a sceptre, a poppy, ears of corn, a tripod, or a patera. She shared all but the first two with other personifications and deities: the olive branch was held by Concordia, Germania and Hispania; the palm branch by Judaea, Phanebal (a war-deity) and Victoria; the cornucopia by Aequitas, Africa, Annona, Concordia, Felicitas, Fides, Fortuna, Genius, Honos, Justitia and Liberalitas; the caduceus by Felicitas, Fides, Mercury and Nemesis; the sceptre by Aequitas, Ceres, Genius, Hera, Hestia, Juno, Jupiter, Libertas, Pietas, Providentia, Roma, Salus and Tranquillitas; the poppy by Bonus Eventus, Ceres, Fides, Hispania and Salus; ears of corn by Abundantia, Annona, Bonus Eventus, Hispania and Salus; the tripod was found with Africa, Concordia and the Emperor; and the patera was used to pour libations by Bonus Eventus, Concordia, the Emperor, Fides, Genius, Jupiter, Pietas and Salus. The torching of weapons and the column topped by Minerva were exclusively associated with Pax, and yet for some reason they were among her rarer attributes. Of the over 2,200 Roman imperial coins in the British Museum that show Pax, only 30 depict her setting fire to arms, and only two represent the column with Minerva. It is hard to think of an attribute given to a figure inscribed as Pax that would be so incongruous that we would assume the inscription was an error; it is the inscription that gives the meaning to the personification.

Another literate civilization with high levels of illiteracy (Houston 1994), the Maya, also made widespread use of inscriptions. All the major Maya deities have their own personal glyph, and without these glyphs it would often be impossible to identify them, since their visual appearance can vary considerably. In fig. 4.18, for example, we see a humanoid face emerging from the mouth of what Mayanists call 'a vision serpent', which has risen in clouds of smoke from a brazier. What is happening is described in the adjoining inscription: "On 4 Kawak 12 Sip [24 March 755 AD], the Waterlily Serpent is conjured. He is the *way* [the animal transformation] of K'awiil."[20] Without the text we

20 Corpus of Maya Hieroglyphic Inscriptions, Peabody Museum of Archaeology and Ethnology, https://www.peabody.harvard.edu/cmhi/detail.php?num=15&site=Yaxchilan&type=Lintel (accessed 12/2/2021). On the Maya concept of 'way', see Kerr and Kerr 2005.

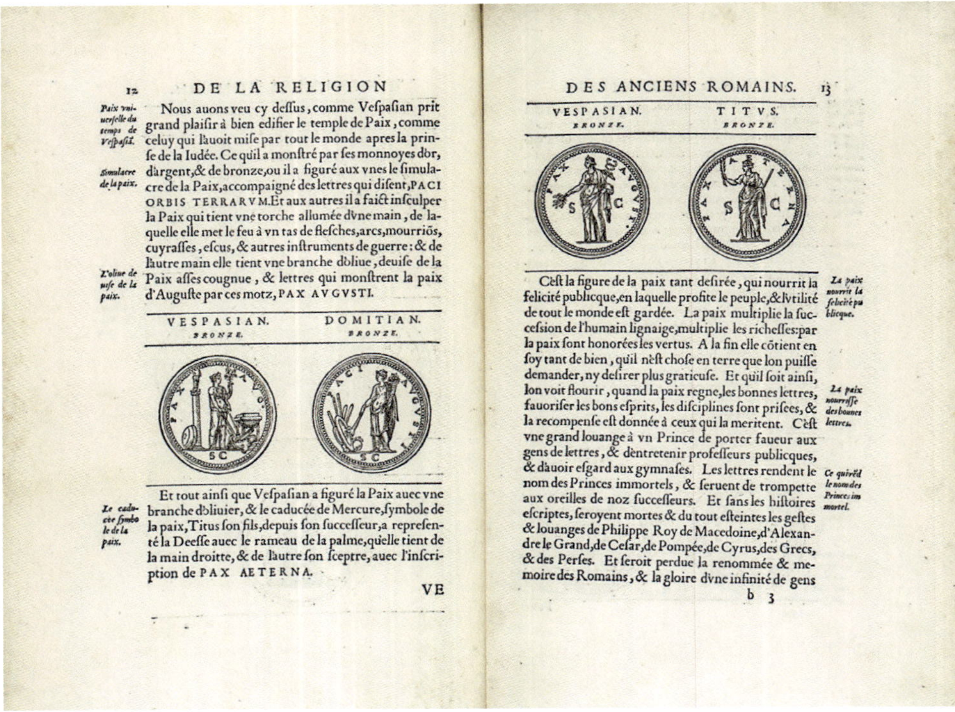

12 DE LA RELIGION

Paix vniuerſelle du temps de Veſpaſiā. Nous auons veu cy deſſus, comme Veſpaſian prit grand plaiſir à bien edifier le temple de Paix, comme celuy qui l'auoit miſe par tout le monde apres la prinſe de la Iudée. Ce qu'il a monſtré par ſes monnoyes d'or, d'argent, & de bronze, ou il a figuré aux vnes le *Simulacre de la paix.* ſimulacre de la Paix, accompaigné des lettres qui diſent, PACI ORBIS TERRARVM. Et aux autres il a faict inſculper la Paix qui tient vne torche allumée d'vne main, de laquelle elle met le feu à vn tas de fleſches, arcs, mourriōs, cuyraſſes, eſcus, & autres inſtruments de guerre: & de l'autre main elle tient vne branche d'oliue, deuiſe de la *L'oliue deuiſe de la paix.* Paix aſſes cougnue, & lettres qui monſtrent la paix d'Auguſte par ces motz, PAX AVGVSTI.

VESPASIAN. BRONZE. DOMITIAN. BRONZE.

Et tout ainſi que Veſpaſian a figuré la Paix auec vne *Le caducée ſymbole de la paix.* branche d'oliuier, & le caducée de Mercure, ſymbole de la paix, Titus ſon fils, depuis ſon ſucceſſeur, a repreſenté la Deeſſe auec le rameau de la palme, qu'elle tient de la main droitte, & de l'autre ſon ſceptre, auec l'inſcription de PAX AETERNA.

VE

DES ANCIENS ROMAINS. 13

VESPASIAN. BRONZE. TITVS. BRONZE.

C'eſt la figure de la paix tant deſirée, qui nourrit la *La paix nourrit la felicité publicque.* felicité publicque, en laquelle profite le peuple, & l'vtilité de tout le monde eſt gardée. La paix multiplie la ſucceſsion de l'humain lignaige, multiplie les richeſſes: par la paix ſont honorées les vertus. A la fin elle cōtient en ſoy tant de bien, qu'il n'eſt choſe en terre que lon puiſſe demander, ny deſirer plus graticuſe. Et qu'il ſoit ainſi, lon voit flourir, quand la paix regne, les bonnes lettres, *La paix nourriſſe des bonnes lettres.* fauoriſer les bons eſprits, les diſciplines ſont priſees, & la recompenſe eſt donnée à ceux qui la meritent. C'eſt vne grand louange à vn Prince de porter faueur aux gens de lettres, & d'entretenir profeſſeurs publicques, & d'auoir eſgard aux gymnaſes. Les lettres rendent le *Ce qui rēd le nom des Princes immortel.* nom des Princes immortels, & ſeruent de trompette aux oreilles de noz ſucceſſeurs. Et ſans les hiſtoires eſcriptes, ſeroyent mortes & du tout eſteintes les geſtes & louanges de Philippe Roy de Macedoine, d'Alexandre le Grand, de Ceſar, de Pompée, de Cyrus, des Grecs, & des Perſes. Et ſeroit perdue la renommée & memoire des Romains, & la gloire d'vne infinité de gens

b 3

4.17 | Guillaume du Choul, *Discours de la religion des anciens Romains*, Lyon 1556, 12–13

would not know the name of the serpent, nor that the face was that of K'awiil, since this deity is usually thought to be recognizable by a conspicuous, ornamentally upturned snout (fig. 4.19).[21]

Even in Buddhist art, which in theory has a complete system of identifying attributes, inscriptions are used as a kind of semantic safety net. In fig. 4.10 we can see an inscription, मायाजालक्रम, Mayajalakrama, for anyone who is unable to interpret the multiple heads, the twelve attributes and the pose; and given the variability of Buddhist iconography, the inscription is welcome.

In all these cases inscriptions are used alongside attributes and properties. From the point of view of representation, the attributes are unnecessary, but they are nevertheless there; which perhaps suggests that it was not their main purpose to communicate iconographic identities. We will return to this thought later in the chapter.

21 K'awiil (or Kauil) has also been known as God K. Iconographers of Maya art assume that every god with an upturned ornamental nose is K'awiil/God K, which may be right. Some are identified by glyphs, but others are not. See Taube 1992, 69–79. In general, Mayanists make the assumption that it is reasonable to deduce identity of representation from identity of attributes, and they also assume identity between Maya deities and central Mexican deities who are not of course identified by means of Maya glyphs: see e.g. Taube 1992, 103–05. For an optimistic take on the possibilities of decoding Maya representations from the period before the emergence of glyphs, see Houston and Taube 2008.

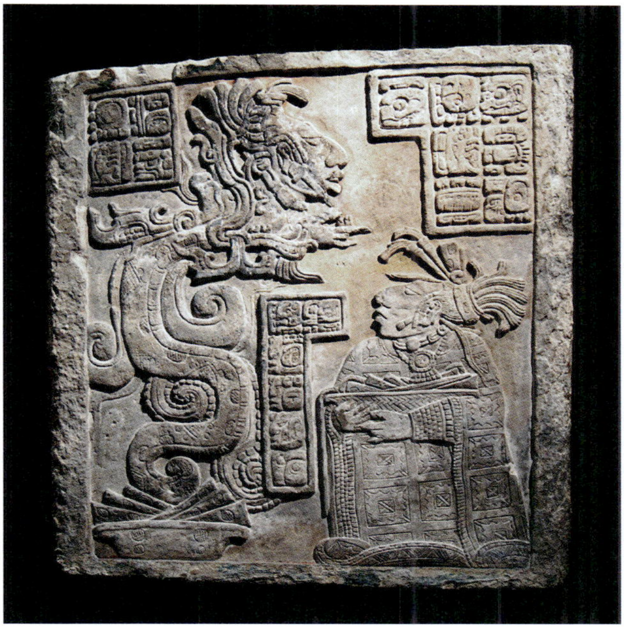

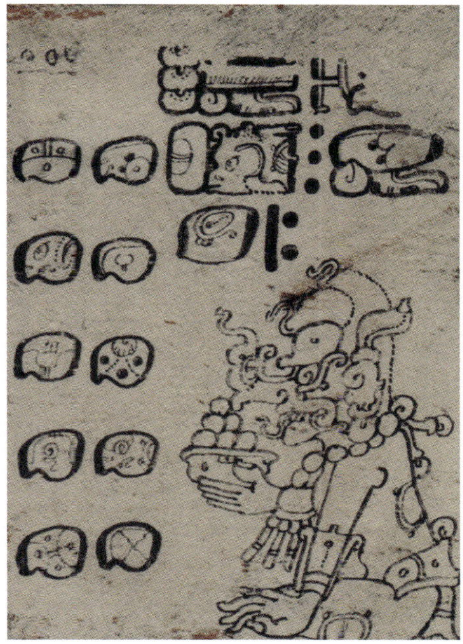

4.18 | Mayan, Yaxchilan lintel 15, 770 AD. The British Museum, London

4.19 | Mayan, K'awiil, detail from image 12 of the Dresden Codex, 1200–50. SLUB, Dresden

Some societies have been willing to use inscriptions not only in conjunction with but also instead of attributes. Eastern Orthodox imagery has travelled further down this path than most iconographic cultures: that this man (fig. 4.20) is a saint would be easy to tell from his halo and cross, but which saint he is would be impossible to know without the inscription, Ὁ ΓΕΟΡΓΙΟΣ, George.

Contexts. Using inscriptions is an ideal method for settling iconographic identities, but in Western Christianity, for some reason, it is less common than in the East. For the most part either attributes are used, or people rely on linkage and designation, sometimes combined with what we can call 'contextual deduction'. Andrea Mantegna's St Luke Polyptych of 1453 (fig. 4.21) provides a good example of the use of contexts. Now in the Pinacoteca di Brera in Milan, the altarpiece was originally located in the chapel of St Luke in the Benedictine abbey of St Justina in Padua. Relics of St Luke the Evangelist were kept in the abbey, and they were preserved in a large fourteenth-century reliquary, next to the altar on which Mantegna's polyptych was once mounted.[22] The reliquary is decorated with carvings of St Luke, angels and Luke's attribute of the winged ox, and it is perhaps because the Lukan context was so obvious to all those in the abbey that Mantegna did not add the ox to his own painting. The evangelist, in the centre, writing

22 The chapel of St Luke was originally in a different part of the abbey complex from its current location in the left transept of the basilica.

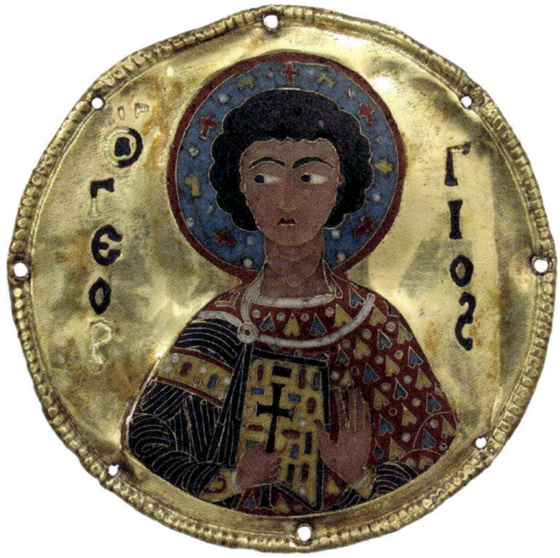

4.20 | Byzantine, Medallion with St George from an icon frame, c. 1100. The Metropolitan Museum of Art, New York

at his desk, has only generic attributes: a halo, a pen and clothing that looks antique rather than medieval; he could be any evangelist, any apostle, any early theologian. His identity is fixed by designation, although it is a designation with a certain contextual logic to it. Anyone visiting the chapel could either ask a monk or sacristan to name the saint, or they could assume it from the proximity of the reliquary.

The same faculty of contextual deduction is needed for other figures on the altarpiece. At bottom right we see a young woman with a sword in her chest and holding a palm branch, which is often a generic symbol of martyrdom. Presumably, she is one of those saints who died by the sword, but there are so many such martyrs that this does not fix her identity. Again, we can use contextual deduction; since we are in the abbey of St Justina, surely she is the early martyr Justina. The bishop who is standing second from left holds a water jug, and St Prosdocimus was supposed to be a bishop who baptized Justina. What is more, his relics are kept in the basilica of St Justina, and he is much venerated in the Padua region. He usually holds the attribute of a jug, so his identity would be plain to any local Catholic. And since the abbey is a Benedictine abbey, it seems likely that the man in a black habit standing to Justina's right is Benedict. In fact, he also holds a scourge, which was sometimes used as his specific attribute. If he did not have the scourge – and about 80% of the time he is painted without the scourge, but with the generic attributes of his habit and possibly a staff or crozier and/or a book – then we could assume that he was Benedict purely from the context. There is also the statistical assumption that any saint in a Benedictine habit is more likely to be Benedict than anyone else. While this is probably true, there are over 500 Benedictine saints, and so it is quite probable that a number of the saints identified by art historians as St Benedict were originally meant to be someone else.

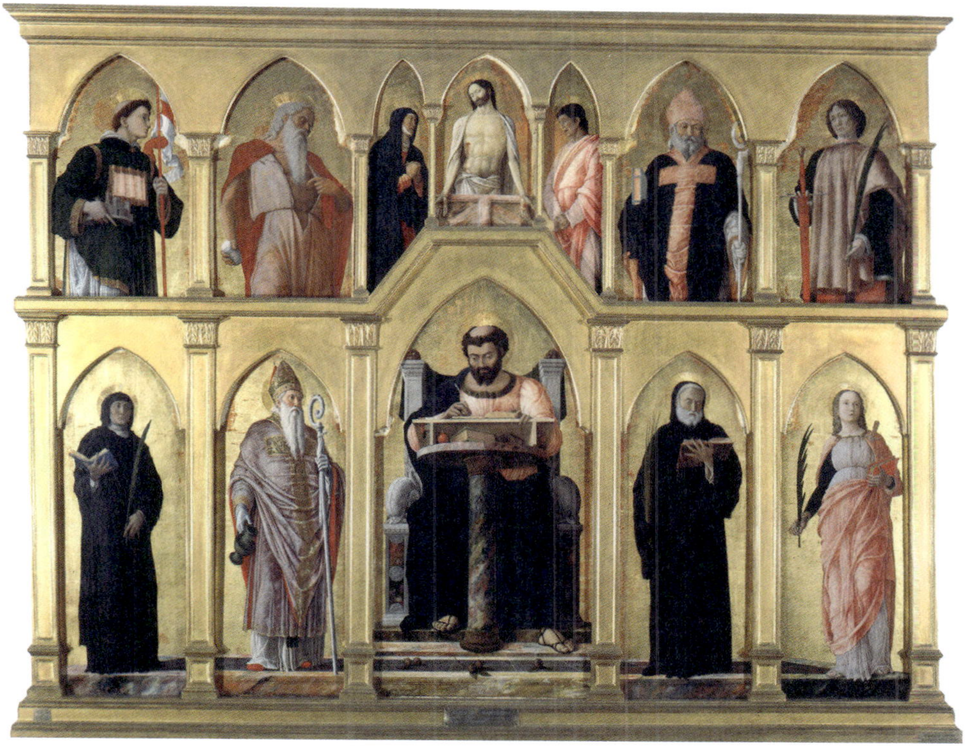

4.21 | Andrea Mantegna, St Luke Polyptych, 1453. Pinacoteca di Brera, Milan

The woman at the far left is also dressed in black, in the costume of a Benedictine nun. Since Benedict's twin sister, Scholastica, was a Benedictine nun, it has often been supposed that this figure must represent her. However, since the relics of the Benedictine St Felicity of Padua are kept in the same abbey, it is perhaps more likely that this figure is Felicity.

We have managed to identify the figures on the bottom row using contextual deduction, and the process continues to be of use when we examine the top row. Some of the figures are easy to recognize for anyone who knows some Catholic iconography – Christ, the Virgin Mary, St John, St Jerome – and the figure at the far left, a deacon holding a town, is likely to be another figure from the Justina story, Daniel, the deacon of Prosdocimus. But the figures on the right, a bishop and a martyr with the ubiquitous sword, are not so easy to interpret. They could be almost any bishop saint or beheaded martyr, but since the relics of St Maximus and St Julian are also preserved in the abbey of St Justina, it seems probable enough that they should appear in the polyptych (Salmazo 2000). If the altarpiece had been dismantled and the original context of the panels had been lost, however, we would have been quite unable to identify them.

Figures and narratives

Attributes are most often held by a particular class of traditional representations, which we can call 'figures'.[23] Figures are usually depicted on their own, or in situations where they are not interacting with other figures around them. Cult images of deities, saints, bodhisattvas and ancestors may all act as figures, and fetishes and personifications can be similar in function. Since figures have no immediate narrative context, they are reliant on other iconographic devices to specify their representation.

Take for example the fifteenth-century German altarpiece in fig. 4.22. Here we see a row of saints who are all carrying attributes of varying degrees of specificity. St Lawrence's gridiron and St Apollonia's tooth held in a pair of pliers are unique identifiers, but the saints at either end of the altarpiece, St Jodocus and St Maurice, are dressed generically as a pilgrim and a soldier, and, given that there are so many pilgrim and soldier saints, they would not be securely identifiable without the inscriptions beneath them. Without attribute or inscription none of the saints would be recognizable, precisely because they are doing nothing except standing next to one another in a nondescript way.

That a lack of narrative makes it difficult to tell the saints apart is acknowledged by the attributes they carry, since most of them refer to distinctive events in the saints' lives; Apollonia had her teeth pulled out, Lawrence was roasted on a gridiron, Sebastian was shot full of arrows and so on. In some Italian altarpieces the missing action is provided by a narrative painting beneath the saints' feet, and sometimes this replaces the attributes. Fig. 4.23 shows four figures in the main panel, and four narratives below, in what is called the predella. The narratives are all connected to the saints above them; St Mammas is thrown to the lions, St James is beheaded, St Zeno exorcizes a woman and St Jerome removes the thorn from a lion's paw. In the main panel, only Mammas has a specific attribute, a group of lions; the others are depicted generically as a pilgrim, a bishop and a cardinal. As it happens, the main panel was painted by one artist, Francesco Pesellino, and the predella was painted by another, Filippo Lippi. Pesellino may have planned the predella in advance and felt that he could dispense with attributes, but he died before he could paint it.

The distinction between figures and narratives was recognized in Christian culture at the time. Those who commissioned altarpieces would frequently ask for 'figures' or 'images' of the saints and might add a request for 'stories' (Hope 1990). The image/story distinction can be found in various European languages of the period (*ymago/ystoria*, *imagine/storia*, *imagen/istória*, *image/histoire*, *beeld/historie*, *Bild/Historie*) (Hope 2007).[24] This distinction was not merely semantic; figures/images were made as the focus for devotion to the saint they represented, and some of them were said to work miracles, but this was not true of stories. One often hears of miraculous images, but rarely if ever of miraculous stories.

Collections of figures could be assembled in an arbitrary way, reflecting the devotional preferences of the people who commissioned them. The altarpiece in

23 As we will see in a moment, the term 'image' was rather more common than 'figure', but I have chosen 'figure' since 'image' is used so often elsewhere in this text.

24 Other scholars have used other terms: Kaftal 1952 writes of 'images' and 'scenes', Winter 1985 writes of 'iconic' and 'narrative' modes.

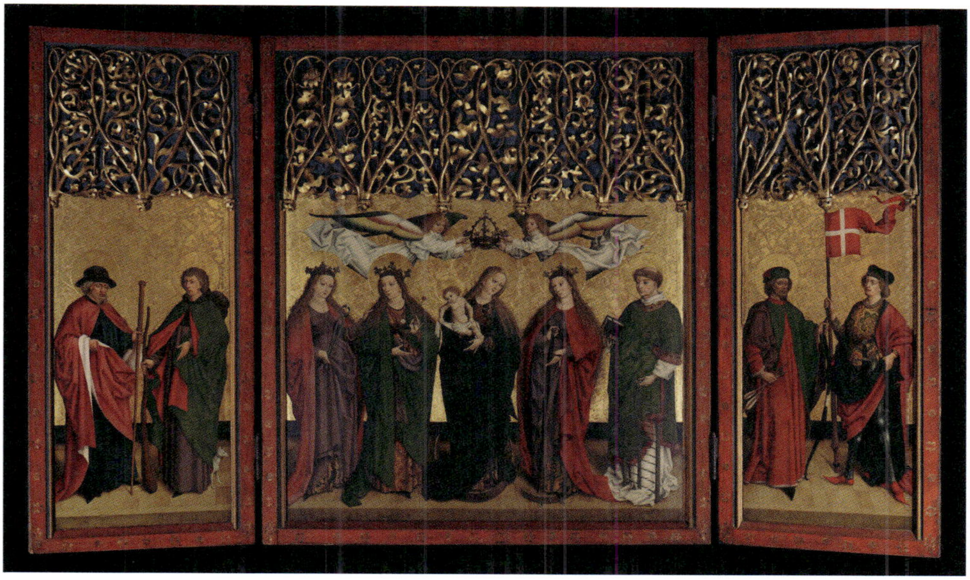

4.22 | German (Master of the Burg Weiler Altarpiece), Burg Weiler Altarpiece, c. 1470. The Metropolitan Museum of Art, New York

fig. 4.23, now in the National Gallery in London but commissioned by the Company of the Trinity for their church of the Holy Trinity in Pistoia in 1455, provides a good example of how this process could take place. We happen to know the motives for the choices of saints with fair accuracy because, unusually, a document has survived that records the deliberations of the committee responsible for deciding who should be represented (Bacci 1904).

In the centre we see the Holy Trinity, which obviously fits with the name and allegiance of the commissioning Company. St James the Great and St Zeno, on either side of the Trinity, are two saints of whom important relics were preserved in Pistoia, and who were said in the committee's document to be 'advocates for' the city and its clergy. These three decisions make contextual sense, but the two other choices are less obvious. St Jerome, on the right, has no particular connection to Pistoia. His name is also much less closely connected to the Trinity than that of his fellow Father of the Church, St Augustine, who from a purely theological point of view would have made a more suitable choice. It is true that at around this time a spurious text was circulating that claimed that Jerome had enjoyed a vision of the Trinity, and perhaps this lay behind the decision to include him here (Ainsworth 2007). We do not know, because the document that tells us why the saints were chosen gives no reason for the inclusion of Jerome.

That the decision to include him may have been arbitrary is suggested by the account explaining the inclusion of St Mammas, a late-Roman shepherd who became a martyr:

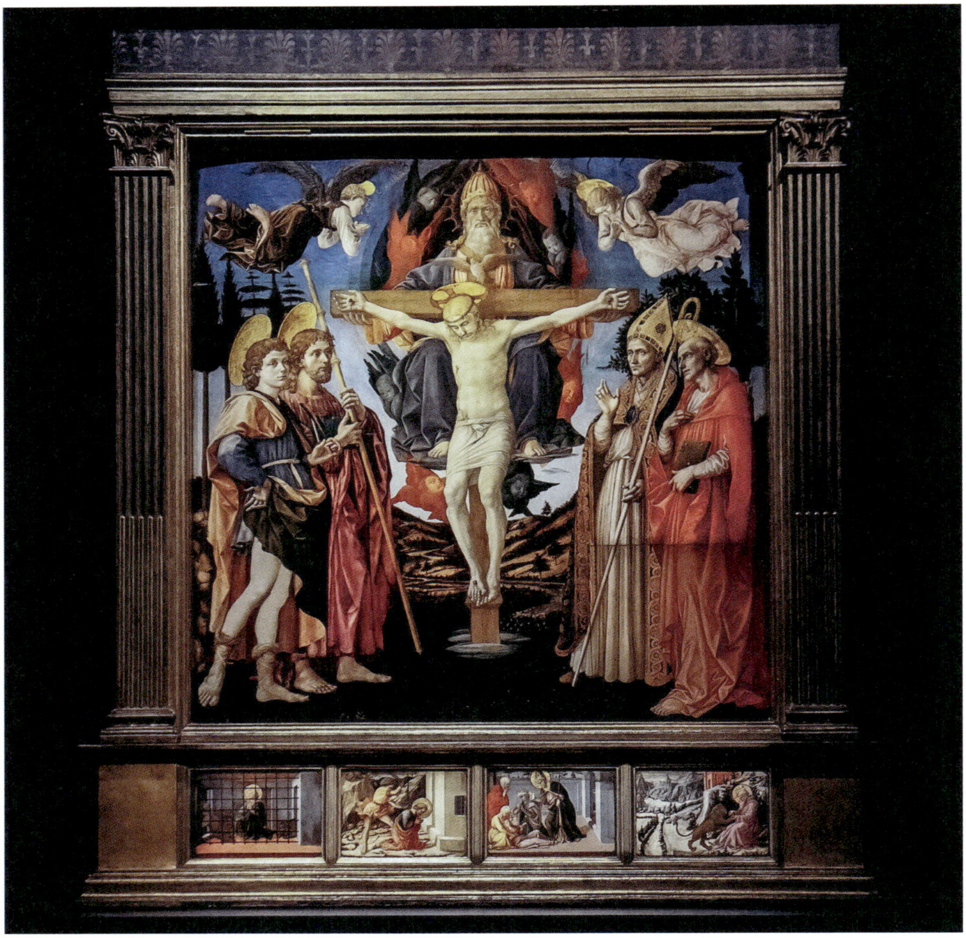

4.23 | Francesco Pesellino and Fra Filippo Lippi, Pistoia Santa Trinità Altarpiece, 1455–60. The National Gallery, London

> Because the fourth saint was lacking, I the priest Pero Ser Landi humbly beseeched the Company, seeing as I am exceptionally devoted to the glorious saint and martyr St Mammas, that if it pleased them, his figure should be painted, [and] I would resolve to make every year his feast within the Company and bequeath for this feast in perpetuity six *omine* of grain as payment ....
> (Bacci 1904, 164–45)

If the document written by Pero Ser Landi had not survived we would never have known why St Mammas appears on the altarpiece, and indeed we would not have known for sure that the young martyr with the lion was Mammas; there are a number of other young male martyrs who are said to have been thrown to the lions (e.g. Abdon, Agapius, Felicianus, Germanicus, Pantaleon, Primus, Sennen, Vitus) so the visual information

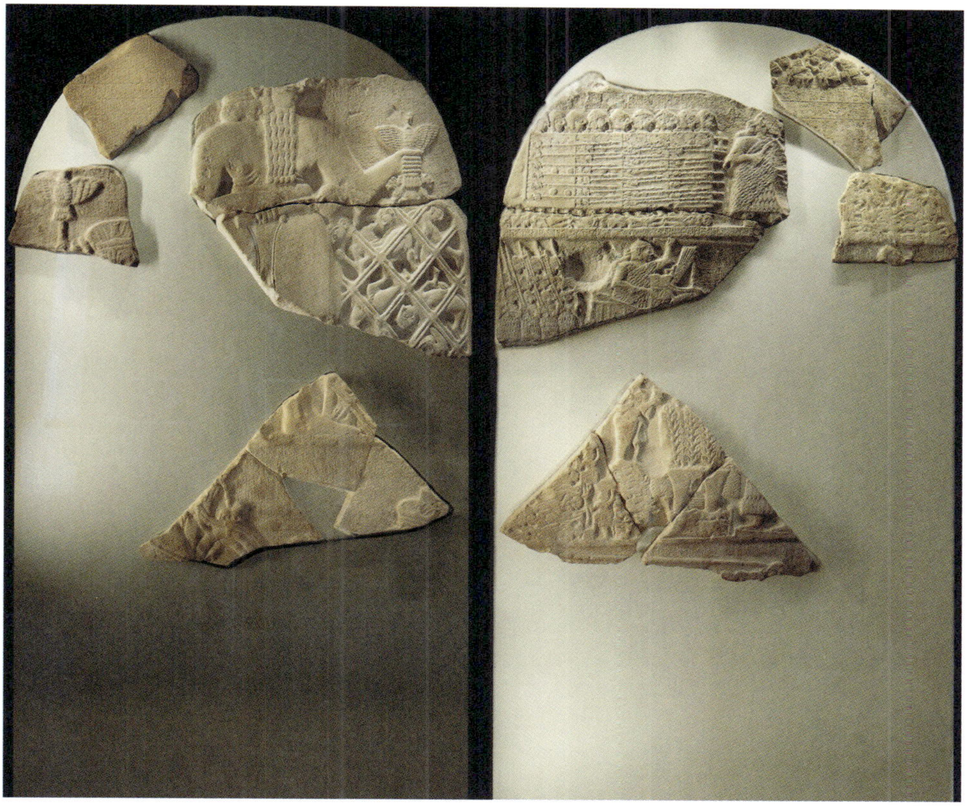

4.24 | Sumerian, Stele of the Vultures, 2450–2425 BC. Musée du Louvre, Paris

we are given is not enough to settle his identity. This is another way in which texts can be used to identify iconographies: when they constitute archival records of acts of designation.

The fact that Mammas is there for no reason to do with Pistoia or the Trinity, but simply because Pero Ser Landi was devoted to him, strongly suggests that there is no overarching theological or intellectual theme to hold the saints in this altarpiece together. In this, our example is not unusual among altarpieces, which tend to be assemblages of saints who are only loosely related and who have been collected because the patrons wanted them to be there (Hope 1990).[25]

Distinctions between figures and narratives can be documented in some detail in Europe, but a similar division of religious function can also be found in other parts of the world. An early example from ancient Sumer, dating to around 2,500 BC, is the so-called Stele of the Vultures (fig. 4.24). This is now in a very fragmentary state, but originally it had divine figures on one side and a battle narrative on the other (Winter

25 There is more to say about this; see below, pp. 164 and 170.

1985). According to the lengthy text inscribed on the monument, Eannatum, King of Lagash, repelled the invasion of the ruler of Umma, who had encroached on land that was thought to be owned by the god Ningirsu. The victory and the stele were dedicated to Ningirsu, and on one side we see the figure of the god, holding a net full of captives, while on the other we see the events of the battle itself. The stele may have been set up to allow devotion to Ningirsu on one side and to show the narrative of his victory on the other. We cannot be sure of this, given the scant historical evidence; it may be that this particular figure of the god was not thought to be an idol. Still, in Mesopotamia figures received devotion or sacrifice depending on where they were situated; in fig. 4.6 worshippers approach a huge idol of Shamash, while on the cylinder seal in fig. 4.5 we see Shamash emerging from the mountains of the east. Adda, the owner of the seal, was no doubt a devotee of Shamash, but there is no reason to think that he made offerings to the deity on his seal, in the way that he would have made offerings to the idol of Shamash in a temple.

Another example of a difference between figures and stories can be seen in the early Buddhist sculpture of Gandhara. Figures of Gautama Buddha, of the Buddhas who preceded him in earlier aeons and of the bodhisattvas, the Buddhas of the future, are very frequent in Gandharan art (fig. 4.13), and so too are narrative scenes (figs. 4.15 and 4.25), mostly telling the life of Gautama Buddha and his previous lives. Many of these narratives functioned as stair-risers or as bands of relief on stupas, the domed shrines within which relics of the Buddha were preserved. The stupas were the prime focus of devotion in Gandharan Buddhism; figures like those in fig. 4.13 were distributed in side chapels around a courtyard that centred on a stupa (Rhi 2005). One might think, then, that the narratives, since they were closer to the sacred remains of the Buddha, were treated with more veneration than the figures. But this does not seem to have been the case; the figures (but not the narratives) were made to share in the power of the relics, by having small relics inserted into them. Indeed it appears that, with time, the figures became more attractive than the stupas themselves, since they provided a face for the sacred beings with whom worshippers wished to communicate (Rhi 2005, 203).

Multiple idols

In Chapter 3 I devoted two sections to images that, it was argued, did not represent, because there was nothing out there in the world, not even a mythical entity, that they were meant to denote.[26] Many ancestor figures do not represent the ancestor they commemorate, since they are the containers for the ancestor's spirit; and fetishes too are containers for, not images of, the spirits that dwell in them.

Multiples, in theory, represent entities that do not simply reside in an image but have an independent existence in another location. There are many images of Shamash who, as the Mesopotamian sun god, travelled through the heavens each day, but who (like Apollo) also appears in myth as a divine person who interacts with deities and humans. An idol of Shamash (fig. 4.6) is not a container of Shamash in the way that an ancestor figure can be the sole container for the spirit of a dead chief. The many idols of Shamash all represent a deity who we can see moving across the sky between dawn and dusk. This

26 On fictional and mythical entities, see above, p. 79, and below, p. 185.

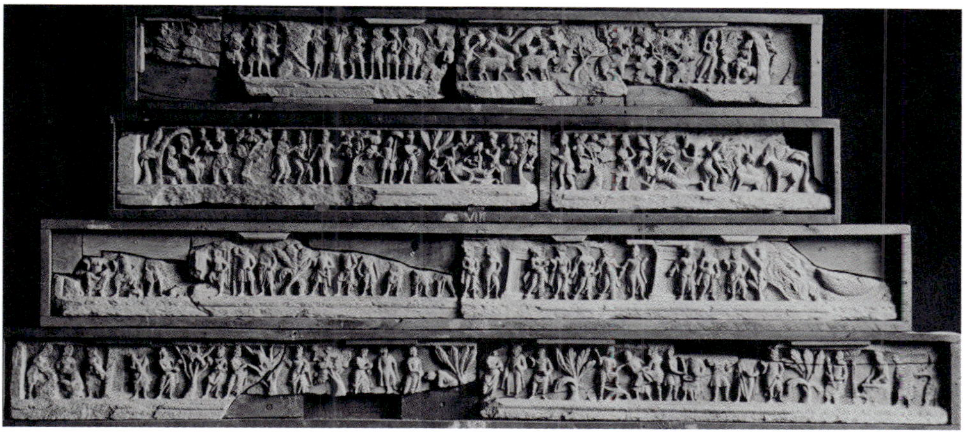

4.25 | Gandharan, Stair-risers with narrative scenes, 1st–3rd century AD. Lahore Museum

is in theory – but in practice, idols and other kinds of figures have often been considered in ways that are rather like that of non-representational singles. In ancient Mesopotamia the mouths of idols were ritually opened and washed so that they could be fed, with food either burnt in front of the statue or consumed by priests, to preserve the illusion that the idol had eaten the meal itself. Idols even appeared as witnesses in legal cases. They were treated not as substitutes for deities, but as actual deities, living and present among the faithful (Berlejung 1997; Walker and Dick 2001; Giovino 2006; Pongratz-Leisten 2015). According to the cuneiform text on the tablet in fig. 4.6, the idol of the sun-god we can see on its throne had just been made. Everyone knew that it had been made, but that did not detract from anyone's devotion. The idol, even though it was not the sun, was now the sun-god, and it was treated with the reverence that deities deserve.

Similar attitudes can be found in the two drawings in the so-called Florentine Codex (fig. 4.26), which depict another sun-god being made, over two thousand years later, on the other side of the world. In this before-and-after scene we see a statue of Huitzilopochtli, the Aztec god of war, blood and the sun, being assembled and then worshipped. The event was recounted by Aztec scribes as follows:

> On the evening before the fiesta of Toxcatl, the celebrants began to model a statue of Huitzilopochtli. They gave it such a human appearance that it seemed the body of a living man. Yet they made the statue with nothing but a paste made of the ground seeds of the chicalote, which they shaped over an armature of sticks .... Early the next morning, the statue's face was uncovered by those who had been chosen for that ceremony. They gathered in front of the idol in single file and offered it gifts of food, such as round seedcakes or perhaps human flesh. But they did not carry it up to its temple on the top of the pyramid.
> (Leon-Portilla 1992, 72–73)

This statue was made to act as the focus for ritual dancing in the courtyard before the Great Temple in Tenochtitlán (Mexico City). At the top of the pyramid there were

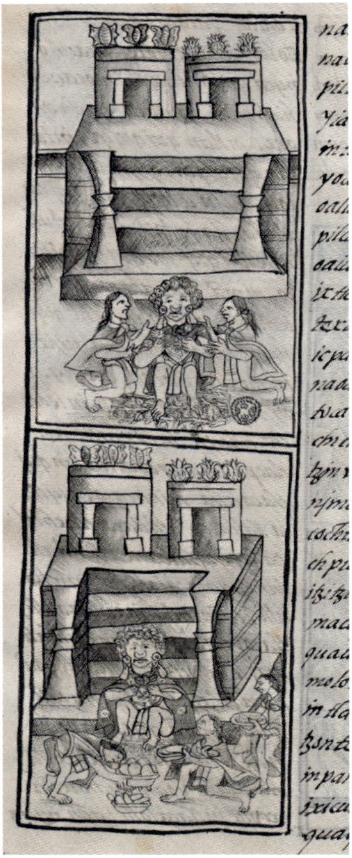

4.26 | The statue of Huitzilopochtli, from Bernardino de Sahagún, *Historia general de las Cosas de Nueva España*, 16th century. Biblioteca Medicea Laurenziana, Florence, MS Florentine Codex, 3:fol. 437v

shrines to Huitzilopochtli and Tlaloc, and in the shrines there were idols to those gods; Huitzilopochtli, therefore, was at the top of the steps and at the foot of the steps, but he was a god in both places. Some of the dancers had been fasting for a year before this festival and were treated with special veneration; they were known as the Brothers of Huitzilopochtli. Shortly after the dancing began, Spanish soldiers attacked the unarmed dancers, this being the opening event in their armed conflict with the Aztecs. One of their first outrages, as recorded by a Mexican scribe, was to hit the idol in the face (Leon-Portilla 1992, 80–81).

The idol of Huitzilopochtli at the top of the pyramid was the principal recipient of human sacrifices in the Aztec empire, and some of the Spanish soldiers who had desecrated the god's festival would later be sacrificed to this idol. According to the Spanish *conquistador* Bernal Díaz del Castillo,

> We saw that, with blows and punches and beatings they were forcing our companions who they had taken in the defeat they had inflicted on Cortés, and that they were forcing them upwards to sacrifice them, and when they had arrived at a small place in the shrine where their accursed idols were, we saw that they put feathers on the heads of many of them, and with pitchforks made them dance in front of Huitzilopochtli; and after they had danced, they placed them on their backs on top of some stones that they had made for sacrifices, and with flint knives they sawed through their chests and pulled out their beating hearts and offered them to the idols that were present there, and taking the bodies by the feet they threw them down the steps.
> (Díaz del Castillo [1568] 1870, ch. 152)

Whether or not Bernal Díaz (who was writing these recollections many years later) remembered all the details correctly, there is abundant evidence, from both Aztec and Spanish sources, that Mexican idols were fed hearts in this way.

The idol is then both an image of a god and a living god who can consume offerings. Although people behaved towards it in ways that are not entirely dissimilar to the ways in which people behave towards certain ancestors or fetishes, there are fundamental differences. Here we can talk of 'single idols' and 'multiple idols'. Ancestor figures, fetishes and spirit spouses can be thought of as single idols; they exist in one example, and they contain one spirit, which they do not represent. Multiple idols exist in numerous examples and are treated as if they too contained the spirit of the deity, which they also represent; and yet the deity is thought to reside elsewhere, in some heaven or other divine location. One can see straight away that multiple idols – but not single idols – face a certain logical objection; the god is both in the idol and not in the idol at the same time.

Most of the cultures that have worshipped multiple idols have been entirely unconcerned by this problem: the Egyptians, Mesopotamians, Greeks, Romans, Hindus, Buddhists, Jains, Island Southeast Asians, Mesoamericans and Peruvians seem to have assumed that deities can be in as many places as they like. It was the monotheistic cultures, Judaism, Islam and Christianity, that found themselves worrying about the embodiment of the deity. The apparent contradictions of multiple idol-worship do not seem to have troubled unapologetic polytheists, but offered monotheists a useful stick with which to beat them.

Judaism and Islam dealt with the 'problem' of idol-worship in a consistent manner and banned figures of the deity. Some Christian denominations, however, took a more complicated course, which led to much conflict. On the one hand they agreed that, if a spiritual being resides in heaven, then it cannot reside in an idol. But rather than banning idols, they kept them; or rather, they kept figures of saints, which have often been treated as if they were the saints themselves.

Veneration towards figures is always scrupulously distinguished from idolatry by the largest of the figure-venerating denominations, the Catholic Church. Catholic theologians hold that (in the words of the Council of Trent)

> the honour which is shown [the images of Christ, of the Virgin Mother of God, and of the other saints] is referred to the prototypes which those images represent; in such wise that by the images which we kiss, and before which we uncover the head, and prostrate ourselves, we adore Christ; and we venerate the saints, whose similitude they bear.
> (Waterworth 1848, 235)

In practice, however, Catholic and other figure-venerating Christians often behave towards their images as if they were rather more than plain representations. Many images have been considered to have miraculous healing powers, and while theologians can provide non-idolatrous explanations for this phenomenon (Molanus 1618, 2:xxxvi), there are many tales suggesting that venerators sometimes blur the distinction between figure and prototype. Consider for example this account of figures of saints being subjected to punishment for failing to produce rain, in a drought in Sicily in 1893:

> At Palermo they dumped St Joseph in a garden to see the state of things for himself, and they swore to leave him there in the sun till rain fell. Other saints were turned, like naughty children, with their faces to the wall. Others again, stripped of their beautiful robes, were exiled far from their parishes, threatened, grossly insulted, ducked in horse-ponds. At Caltanisetta the golden wings of St Michael the Archangel were torn from his shoulders and replaced with wings of pasteboard; his purple mantle was taken away and a clout wrapt about him instead. At Licata the patron saint, St Angelo, fared even worse, for he was left without any garments at all; he was reviled, he was put in irons, he was threatened with drowning or hanging. "Rain or the rope!" roared the angry people at him, as they shook their fists in his face.
> (Frazer 1912, 1:300)

Whether or not these Sicilian acts were entirely serious, there are numerous historical examples of Christians behaving towards their figures as if they believed the

Virgin or the saint was present within them (Freedberg 1989; Maniura and Shepherd 2006; Van Eck 2015). For other Christians, these behaviours were profoundly troubling, since they seemed to revive attitudes towards idols that were sharply condemned in the Old Testament, and which had also been rejected by early Christians, who had refused to obey the commands of the Roman authorities that they worship idols of Greco-Roman gods, and sometimes paid for it with their lives. At various times these concerns about idolatry erupted in iconoclasm, during which figures of the saints were destroyed – in particular in eighth-century Byzantium and sixteenth-century Switzerland and the Low Countries.

We do not need to go into these events, the complexities of which have been discussed in detail in recent scholarship (Freedberg 1986; Eire 1986; Freedberg 1989; Belting 1994; Dupeux et al. 2001; Wirth 2011). With our meta-iconographic outlook, the point of interest is that, if some of the single idols we discussed in the last chapter were embodiments of an indwelling spirit but not representations of that spirit, multiple idols can be considered both embodiments and representations at the same time. This makes images of idols particularly complex; the representation of the idol of Shamash in fig. 4.6 is both an image of an image of a god and an image of a god. Indeed, it is also possible to take photographs that have similar layers of complexity. A photograph of an idol may seem to a Westerner to be a photograph of so much stone or painted wood, and yet to a devout polytheist it may be the image of an actual god.

This can also be true when we are dealing with photographs of people, who can be given religious identities. Take for example the event we see in fig. 4.27. This photograph was taken at a Hindu festival in the sacred town of Varanasi on the Ganges. The festival is known as Nag Nathaiya, and it celebrates the occasion, recounted in the *Bhagavata Purana*, when Krishna subdued and banished the poisonous water serpent Kaliya. Having seen how birds fell dead when they crossed the river Yamuna in which Kaliya was living and how all plant and animal life in its vicinity died because of the snake's poisonous breath, Krishna decided to purify the waters of their contamination. He climbed a *kadam* tree and plunged into the river. After wrestling beneath the surface with the snake he subdued it by climbing on to its 101 heads and began to dance. Unable to support the pain of this divine trampling, Kaliya prayed for forgiveness and worshipped Krishna, who commanded him to leave the Yamuna and swim out to sea (*Bhagavata Purana*, 10.16).

The festival retells this narrative; an artificial *kadam* tree is built by the shore and a youth dressed as Krishna jumps into the river. There an artificial water serpent is waiting for him. The youth climbs on to the serpent's head and strikes a dancing pose, while swimmers in the water make the snake circle round before the devotees of Krishna watching from the bank or nearby boats (Pintchman 2005, 69–70).

This performance is considered by devout Hindus to be more than a piece of religious theatre. The youth who plays Krishna is not thought to be playing Krishna; he is thought to *be* Krishna for the duration of the performance. He is the embodied form – the term in Hindi is *svarup* – of the god (Arney 2007).[27] The photograph in fig. 4.27, therefore, does not represent a youth playing Krishna; it represents Krishna. There is, however, a deeper complexity, because while we can all agree that, for Hindus,

27 *Svarup* is applied not only to actors becoming gods, but also to idols of gods.

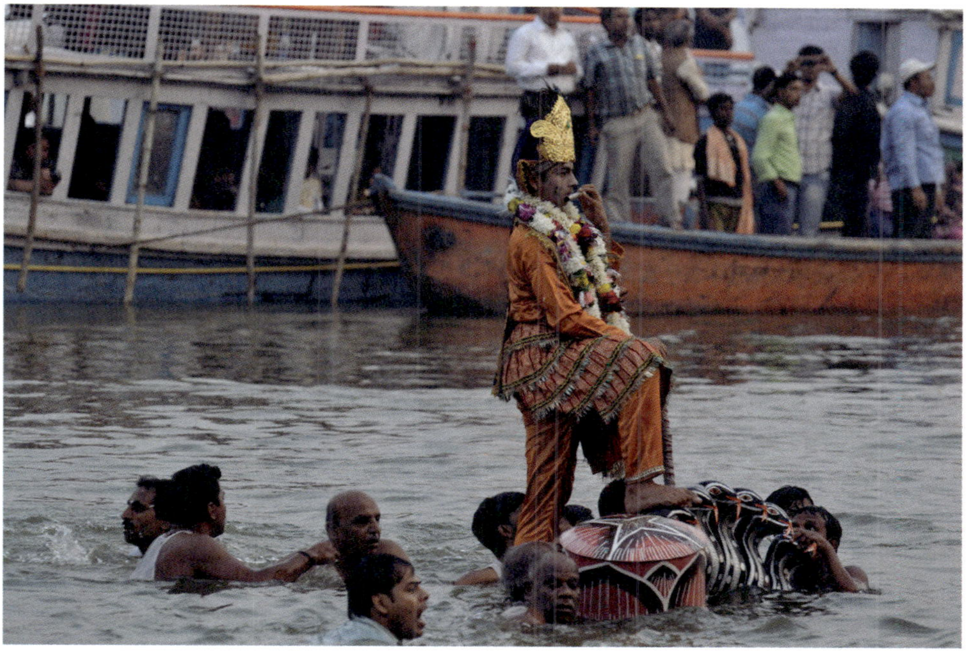

4.27 | Nag Nathaiya festival in Varanasi, India

fig. 4.27 represents Krishna and conceptually depicts a god, what do non-Hindus think is depicted indexically? The answer of a Hindu will surely be 'Krishna', the answer of a non-Hindu will be 'a certain youth from Varanasi'. Does this count as relativism? Not really: it is more a disagreement. Non-Hindus and Hindus might agree that there is a truth to the matter, it is just that they cannot (or will not) agree on what the truth might be. We do not have to think of it as 'our truth' and 'their truth': someone can be wrong.

Personification and ambiguity

In most of the examples considered so far in this chapter we have been dealing with religious images, but another large family of figures that uses attributes as an iconographic device is that of allegorical personifications. A personification is a non-human entity of some kind – a place, an object, an emotion, a science, a season, a virtue, an attitude – that has been represented as if it had human form. The idea of doing this goes back at least as far as Ancient Egypt. In fig. 4.28 we see a depiction of a woman with a basket full of butchered meat on her head and a live duck in her hand, and from similar figures in tomb reliefs, identified through inscriptions, we can feel sure that the figure represents an agricultural estate that is bringing food for a dead soul to consume in the afterlife (Harpur 1986).

Personifications were common in ancient Greece and Rome, in literature and art (Stafford and Herrin 2005), and they can also be found in Hindu iconography (Gopinatha Rao 1914–16, 2:287–96; Sivaramamurti 1955). They were used in Europe throughout the Middle Ages (Mâle 1898; Mâle 1908), and enjoyed a florescence between the sixteenth and eighteenth centuries (Giehlow 1915; Gombrich 1971; Gombrich 1972b;

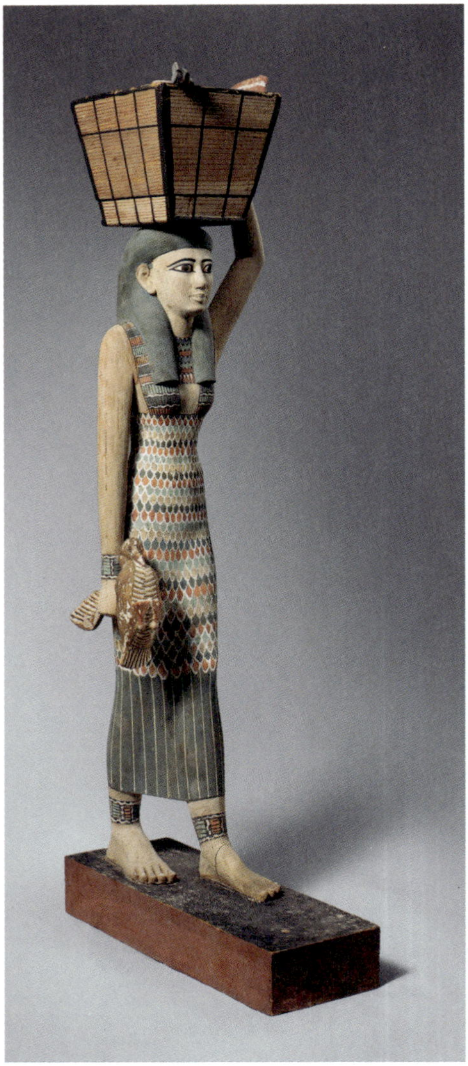

4.28 | Egyptian, Estate Figure, Middle Kingdom (1981–1975 BC). The Metropolitan Museum of Art, New York

Gabriele et al. 2013). Today they are much less common, but there are still some that are widely recognized, such as the Statue of Liberty (fig. 4.29) and Justice. The great majority of European allegorical personifications are female, since they tend to follow the gender of the noun they personify, and in the languages of the regions that spawned these allegorical personifications – Greece and Italy – abstract nouns are mostly feminine (Warner 1985).[28]

From a meta-iconographic viewpoint, allegorical personifications operate in a way that is akin to saints, bodhisattvas and deities. The attributes they carry, or stand next to, transmit identities that have been designated. Although their attributes are generally meant to be rich with significance, they inevitably underdetermine any possible meaning they might be given (Gombrich 1972a, 11–13; but cf. Gombrich 1965). Liberty in New York harbour holds a lit torch and a book, has a spiky crown that is supposed to resemble the sun and tramples a broken chain. These attributes could have had many other meanings. In Cesare Ripa's *Iconologia*, the widely used allegorical encyclopaedia of seventeenth- and eighteenth-century Europe, a lit torch was given as an attribute to Calumny, Cognition, Equality, Fury, Natural Day,[29] Patience and Wisdom (or Knowledge – Sapienza). Ripa did not give the torch to Liberty, which had since antiquity been symbolized by a cap, since slaves in ancient Rome who were freed were given a working man's cap, a *pileus*, as part of the manumission ceremony (Korshak 1987). Ripa also gave Liberty a sceptre, to show that she ruled herself freely, and added what may have been his own idea, a cat, since cats are great lovers of freedom (fig. 4.30). As with most personifications in

28 For examples where male personifications are used for female nouns, see Ripa 1593: *Consuetudine, Fuoco, Fama chiara, Forza d'amore, Gioventù, Giurisditione, Ignoranza, Industria, Opera vana, Pazzia, Perseveranza, Pieta dei figliuoli, Pueritia, Sapienza humana* and *Virtù heroica*. There are also male nouns with female personification, see ibidem: *lo Stige, Inganno, Piacere honesto, Pianto, Poema lirico, Gusto, Tatto, Silentio, Spavento, Autunno*.

29 Natural Day is the period of 24 hours that it takes the sun to rotate around the earth (in Ripa's geocentric conception); Artificial Day is the period between the rising and the setting of the sun.

the *Iconologia*, Ripa provided alternative possibilities. Although all three of his suggestions for a personification of Liberty hold caps, one of them is also given a Herculean club, and another holds a broken yoke. For the Statue of Liberty to mean liberty, then, her attributes on their own are insufficient, and there must have been an original act of designation, of which people became aware through a process of linkage.

If the choice of attributes for bodhisattvas is relaxed, with personifications it is very relaxed; as we have already seen when discussing Roman personifications of Pax/Peace (p. 129 above), different attributes can be used for the same personification, or swapped between personifications. As a result, it can be impossible to know which personification you are looking at without an accompanying explanatory text. In the second half of the eighteenth century critics began to complain about this (e.g. Diderot [1767] 1963, 287–90), and allegorical imagery, which had been a major genre of European art for 2,000 years, slowly decreased in popularity. Ripa's *Iconologia* went from being a European bestseller to almost complete obscurity; when it was rediscovered by Émile Mâle in the twentieth century he presented it as a forgotten work (Mâle 1927).[30]

The disappearance of Ripa in the nineteenth century did not stop artists from painting personifications, but it did make their interpretation more difficult, since the widespread use of his text in the two previous centuries had imposed a certain allegorical consistency that enabled representational transmission. In the nineteenth century artists increasingly invented their own attributes, and relied on texts – on the frame, in wall panels or in accompanying literature – to explain what those attributes meant – a literate form of designation, in short. If Ripa, like Panofsky's Australian, had been transported to New York harbour and asked to identify the meaning of

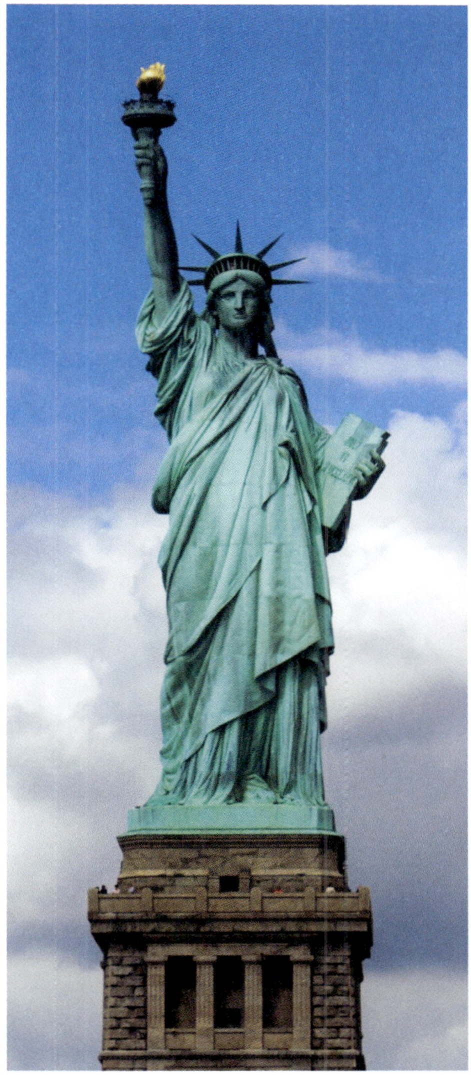

4.29 | Frédéric Auguste Bartholdi, *Liberty Enlightening the World*, 1880. Liberty Island, New York Harbor

30 Ripa's book was not as entirely unknown as Mâle thought; it was mentioned in a study that was well-known in its day, Barbier de Montault 1898, 1:297.

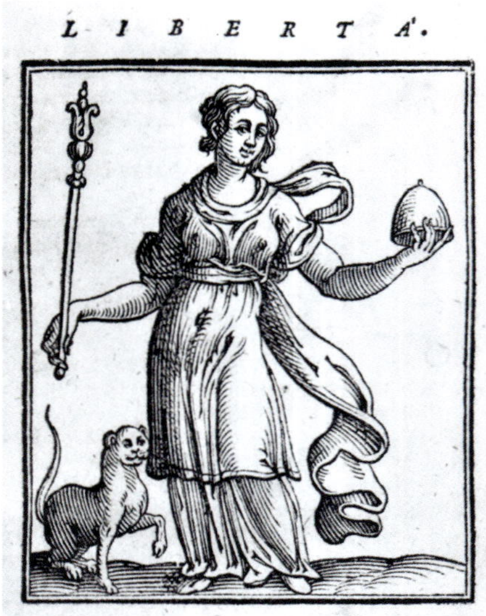

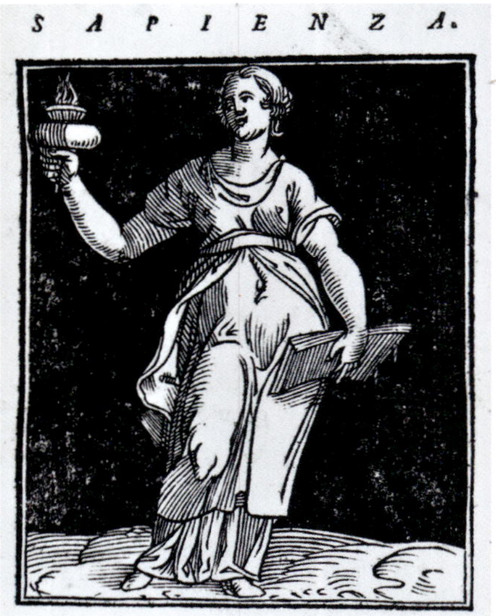

4.30, 4.31 | From Cesare Ripa, *Iconologia*, 1645: *Libertà* (p. 375) and *Sapienza* (p. 545)

the Statue of Liberty, he would probably have guessed that she represents Wisdom. She holds a lit torch and a book, and so too does one of the personifications of Wisdom/ Knowledge in the *Iconologia* (fig. 4.31). The broken chain, which of all the statue's attributes has the closest conceptual link with liberty, he could have read in various ways. A golden chain is one of the attributes of Avarice in the *Iconologia*, since "it shows us that riches, and great power, to whomever considers them rightly, are a very cumbersome weight, and a tiresome burden" (Ripa 1645, 51). In another place he takes the chain to show that "Avarice is the slave not only of wealth, but also of devils, witness St Paul writing to the Ephesians ch. 5 and the Colossians ch. 3, 'Covetousness is the service of idols'" (Ripa 1645, 53). It would not have been very difficult for him to work the broken chain into his interpretation of the Statue of Wisdom, and to read it as freedom from ignorance, or vice.

Another possibility, however, is that he would have taken the statue to be polysemous. We have some evidence that beholders of allegory in the seventeenth century were sometimes willing to allow plural readings of personifications. A figure holding a torch (or lamp) and a book also appears on one of the most impressive allegorical ceilings of the period, painted by Pietro da Cortona for the Palazzo Barberini in Rome (fig. 4.32). We have three separate written accounts of the iconography of this ceiling by contemporaries, and they variously refer to this figure as Spiritual and Ecclesiastical Government, Wisdom (Sophia, Sapientia) and Knowledge (Scienza).[31]

31 The situation is a little more complex, however, since one of the authors, Francesco Bracciolini, was writing before the ceiling was completed, and the figure in question, although it did hold a torch and a book and was surrounded by personifications similar to those that are there now, was at that time seated on a throne; see Frangenberg 2003, 291, 294.

Different readings of the fresco were not only permitted, but encouraged. So long as the exegeses were appropriate to the work, they could be developed at will (Frangenberg 2003, 291).

Playful inventiveness of a different kind was to be found in the Jesuit parlour game of 'enigmas' in seventeenth-century France. In this game, concepts were suggested by paintings with straightforward iconographies, so that an image of the Resurrection of Christ could lead one to think of an exploding mine, or the Assumption of the Virgin might suggest cirrus clouds (Montagu 1968). But from the meta-iconographic angle, the exegetes of the Barberini ceiling went further, in that they did not merely suggest strained allegorical similes, they changed the representation of the image as they reinterpreted it.

However, if some artists and interpreters were willing to allow polysemy, others were not. Peter Paul Rubens, who used a great deal of allegory in his work, appears to have intended that his personifications should have unique, fixed meanings; he did not encourage viewers to read them any way they chose (Fracassi 2024). This will not have prevented some of his viewers doing exactly that, but it suggests that in some quarters there were expectations of monosemy.

The point of attributes

Attributes are convenient symbols that, with sufficient contextual and textual support, can transmit designated iconographic identities over distances of space and time. But it is not clear that this has always been their main purpose.

The *ndop* figures of the Kuba kings (fig. 4.8) hold objects that art historians call attributes, but in their original context these 'attributes' were not meant as iconographic devices. The objects held by the *ndop* figures were images of the royal emblem, known to the Kuba as the *ibol*, that was chosen by the king on his accession to the throne (Vansina 1972). That it could be used to identify the king's statue might have been a useful side product, but it was not an important advantage, given that the main function of the *ndop* was to provide a substitute for the king during his lifetime. The statue, as noted earlier, was kept in the women's quarters of the royal palace, and "when a woman of the harem was about to give birth, the statue was placed near her to insure a safe delivery. It was also a substitute for the king himself to his womenfolk, who would anoint, stroke and fondle it in their husband's absence." The women in the palace quarters where the *ndop* was kept did not need an attribute, since they would of course have known who the statue represented. After the king's death the figure was moved to a storage room, where it and its *ibol* would not have been seen, except on certain occasions when it was brought out for public view with similar figures. At this point the 'attribute' became of genuine utility from an iconographic point of view; but presumably the *ibol* was not added to the figure at the outset with the sole purpose of permitting identification at these rare posthumous appearances. The purpose of the attribute representing the *ibol*, surely, was to intensify the spiritual power of the *ndop*, to link the soul of the king with his statue, so that his spiritual powers could be transmitted from the statue when, for example, it was assisting in childbirth.

We can tell a similar story about the statues of Chibinda Ilunga (fig. 4.1). The fact that Chibinda Ilunga's consistent appearance allows him to be recognized in different places (if it does) does not necessarily mean that this consistency was intended from the beginning to permit reidentification. After all, if a copy was made of one of his

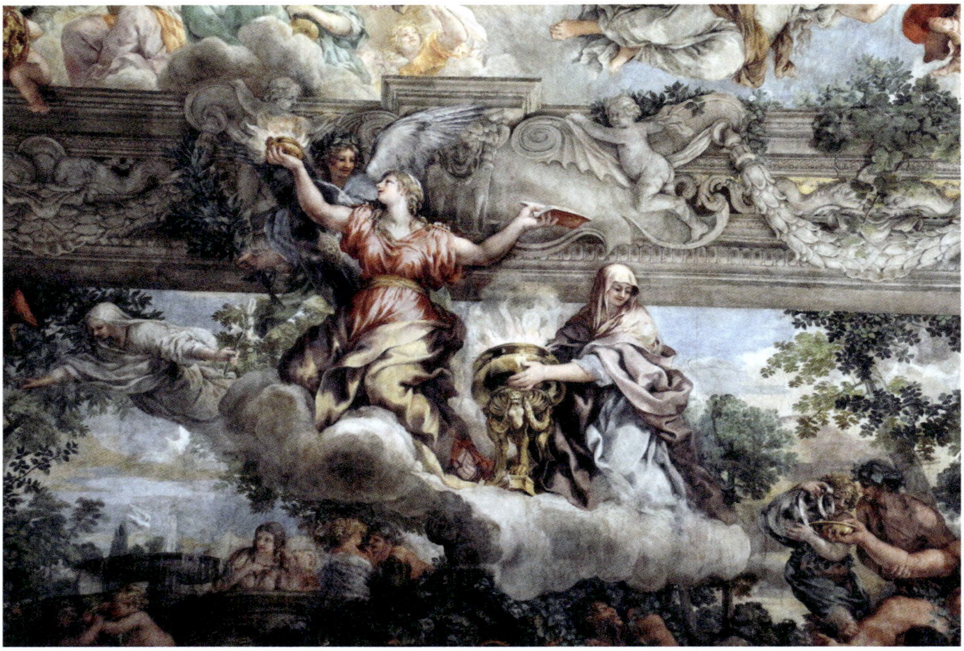

4.32 | Pietro da Cortona, Allegory of Divine Providence, 1633–39. Palazzo Barberini, Rome

statues, it might be taken to a distant place where it would not be seen by anyone from the village where the original stood. Being able to identify a statue of Chibinda Ilunga in a distant shrine would be little advantage in a society where travel was uncommon. The appearance of the statues may have been copied closely for another reason. In the previous chapter we noted that fetishes are sometimes copied, but that the aim of this copying is not to assert the identity of a multiple; each copy is in fact meant to operate in a different region, where it will not conflict with the business generated by the original. If the two fetishes look alike that is because they are supposed to have the same powers, and identity of appearance with an effective fetish will confer power on its copy. A similar story may also be the case with the multiples of Chibinda Ilunga; the aim may be to entice the spirit of Chibinda Ilunga into the copy, or in other ways to transmit the power of these images from original to copy.

The Kuba and the Chokwe were preliterate societies, for whom attributes might conceivably have served some real purpose, but most of the societies that have used attributes have been literate, and could just as easily have identified their gods and holy figures with the help of inscriptions (fig. 4.20). Even inscriptions are unnecessary in small temples and chapels, or on personal seals and amulets, where the designation and linkage method can be employed, as indeed it frequently has been. Attributes are of most use for those who do not worship figures and idols; if I am devoted to Vishnu or St Catherine then I will know which figure in my local church or temple represents them, since I will regularly return to it to pray. Tourists and art historians (art history is the handmaid of tourism) find attributes useful, since they want to identify figures based on scant knowledge; it is satisfying to walk round a church you have never visited before and will never visit again and find that you can give names to half the saints on the basis of their attributes. However, the worshippers who have been praying in that church since childhood will know the figures already.

So what is the point of attributes? There are no doubt different answers to this, just as there were different answers when Caroline Humphrey and James Laidlaw asked the Jains about their motives for offering flowers during *puja* (p. 97 above). One answer might be that attributes are meant to encourage meditation on the powers and virtues of the represented individual; many Christian saints' attributes point to their martyrdom, or to miracles they brought about, and the attributes of Vishnu are taken to refer to triumphs over demons, or to his virtues. Another answer might be that they make the figure more individual, more present; as we observed earlier, the *Sadhanamala* was originally written for Buddhist devotees who wished to meditate on figures of the Buddhas and bodhisattvas, and knowing that a figure really is an image of Mayajalakrama, and not some other bodhisattva, might strengthen one's devotion. Perhaps too there was, so to speak, a contractual element; when patrons ordered an image of St Catherine, they wanted to make sure that the artist had indeed given them a St Catherine, not a St Agnes or a St Barbara. These and other motives for painting attributes might turn into a social practice that – like the offering of flowers – could become a ritualized action that people obeyed because people obeyed it, and no one knew the reasons for the practice.

Attributes, orality and literacy

In the last chapter we noted that, when representational identity is given to an image by designation, then if that identity is forgotten it cannot be recovered. This, however, is not a feature of designation as such, but of orality. The same is true for attributes if they are assigned within an oral culture. As we saw in the case of the Moche vase (fig. 4.16), if the various figures with the serpent belt all represent the same personage then we cannot name that personage, because the linkage between the Moche period and our own time has been broken.[32] But we face a deeper problem than that: we cannot be sure that all the figures represent the same personage. There could be generic personages in Moche iconography who wear a serpent belt, just as there are generic personages in Christian iconography – Franciscan friars – who wear knotted rope belts, and generic personages in early Buddhist iconography – bodhisattvas – who wear charm boxes on a cord. And there could be different personages with the same specific attributes, like Erasmus and Thiemo, or Siddhartha and Maitreya.

Attributes cannot inform us of identities, and they also cannot transmit identities securely without other contextual information. In fact, there is a sense in which it is true to say that each time attributes are used, they are designated afresh. The priest who decides to commission a statue of St Erasmus in the nave of his church has an image made of a bishop with a windlass, but the same image could be used to represent St Thiemo, or some other legendary personage invented at the whim of the artist or the priest. If this is St Erasmus, that is because the priest has designated it as St Erasmus.

32 Some scholars have argued that early colonial texts preserve the linkage, although many additional assumptions need to be made; see Prządka-Giersz 2015.

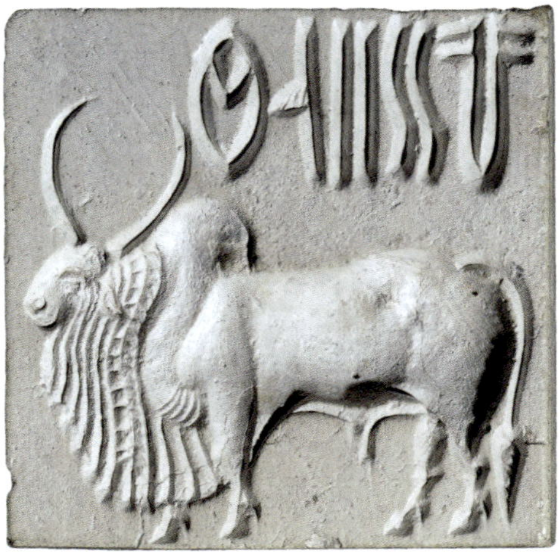

4.33 | Mold of a seal from the Indus Valley civilization, 2600–1900 BC. The British Museum, London

Suppose that the inscription 'St Erasmus' is written underneath the figure. This surely settles the intentionality. However, one can imagine a situation in which a priest decides to install a statue of St Thiemo in his church, and in order to deflect any confusion among his congregation, calls in a sign painter to inscribe Thiemo's name under the figure. The sign painter gets confused and writes 'St Erasmus' instead. By the time his mistake has been discovered the scaffolding has been taken down and he has travelled away to another job. The priest makes a point of telling his congregation that the statue really represents St Thiemo, that the inscription is incorrect. But with the passage of time this information is forgotten, and everyone takes the statue to represent St Erasmus; the statue has been redesignated.

For a figure with attributes to represent an individual, (a) the socially accepted symbols must be used, and (b) it must be acknowledged by all involved that these symbols have been used, and this latter is in effect a form of the designation and linkage system we studied in the last chapter.

In practice, statistical and contextual assumptions underpin the reading of attributes. We assume that the number of cases of iconographic indistinguishability is very small, and that we are justified in supposing that identity of attributes denotes identity of representation. In societies with large amounts of textual information to help us interpret iconographies, we can be sure that this is the case; the Erasmus/Thiemo problem is very rare. Another assumption that we make is that artists and patrons respect social norms; that they do not, as we imagined Leonardo da Vinci doing (p. 30 above), invent bizarre stories which when depicted might happen to look exactly like a socially sanctioned iconography. Just as we assume that the people talking to us are using the commonly accepted meanings of the words they are speaking, rather than meanings they themselves have invented, so too we assume that if an iconography looks like a figure or narrative we know, then it must have been meant to represent that figure or narrative.

With these assumptions in place, we can use attributes to identify further examples of iconographies that we have already identified. Where texts can be used to name different instances of the represented figure, then information about the figure's identity can spread like a plant with propagative roots, which sends out suckers that replant themselves. Each time someone who can read comes across an inscribed image of a deity, they can learn its intentionality without needing to be told in person by someone linked to the original designatory context. This system can also be proof against complete breakages in that communicative chain on which oral societies are reliant. For 2,000 years the iconographic identities of the Mesopotamian gods were forgotten, but many were rediscovered by scholars in the nineteenth century when cuneiform text was decoded. For 100 years most European allegorical personifications were unidentifiable, until the text which had been used to select them – Cesare Ripa's *Iconologia* – re-emerged. But these advantages of survival are only outcomes of literacy,[33] and of course of literacy featuring languages that can still be understood. In this seal from the Indus Valley civilization (fig. 4.33) the inscription may have told the seal's original users the name of the bovine creature (if it had a name) and have given some sense of its nature (is it a deity, or a deity's attribute?). Unfortunately, we do not know if it did either of these things, since we cannot read the script; and given the small number of surviving inscriptions, it may be that we will never do so (Parpola 1994, 278; Robinson 2009, 295).

33 Curiously, this fundamental difference between orality and literacy is not discussed in Ong 1982.

5. Narratives

Narratives and events

In the two previous chapters we have dealt with figures, rather than narratives, and our main concern has been with how figures are made to connect with their originals. As we move over to a discussion of narratives, we find that the problem becomes more complex, because, besides the issue of how depicted entities link to their representations, we also need to establish how the narrative of which they form part is identified. In fact, the problem has more layers than that, because in a narrative image there are three levels to consider: the referent, the narrative and the event, and sometimes images of events do not represent narratives.

Take a simple image like the one we see in fig. 5.1, taken from a website. This photograph depicts an old man walking up a steep hill.[1] It also resembles an old man standing stationary on one leg on a hill, an old man walking backwards down a hill, an old man walking on a flat surface with a film set built on a slant to create the illusion of houses on a hill, a younger man made up to look like an old man and so on. If we discount these alternative interpretations of the image and assume that it depicts an old man walking up a hill, that is partly due to statistical assumptions – the scenarios suggested are very unusual – and partly because the photographer who took the photo, Andy Neale, has provided a caption at his website that assures us that this is what is happening. Why should we disbelieve the caption? It is so unlikely to be incorrect. We do not even stop to question our initial interpretation that this photograph depicts a senior citizen ascending an incline. But that does not mean that the picture is visually unambiguous.

We assume that the photograph depicts an old man walking up a hill, but what is the broader narrative of which this event forms part? Presumably he is engaged in everyday activities, perhaps running errands, visiting a café or meeting friends. That is a statistical assumption, because most older pedestrians are involved in activities of this sort. Nevertheless, we cannot know for sure what has just happened and what will happen next. Perhaps the man has murdered a policeman or is heading out to rob a bank. The narrative might be more exciting than it appears.

Whatever the true story behind this photograph, we might say that it depicts an event, of an old man walking up a hill, and that it represents a narrative, of an old man going to the café, or fleeing a murder, or whatever the truth may be. But there is a sense

1 Cf. Wittgenstein 1953, 54.

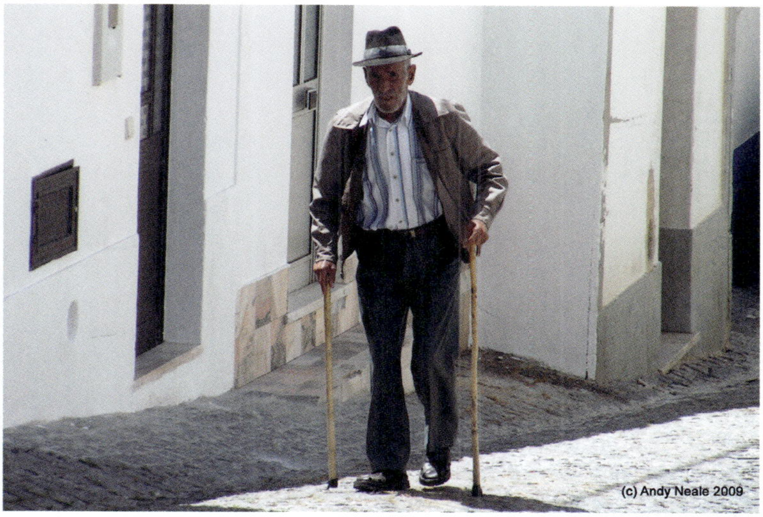

5.1 | Andy Neale, *Aljezur, Portugal 2008: Old man walking up a hill*

in which we might say that it does not represent whichever narrative is in fact the case. The photograph is presented with a caption that tells us it is of an old man walking up a hill. The man is not given a name, which suggests that Andy Neale and his subject were strangers to one another. Precisely what will happen next in his life is not relevant to the subject of the photo, which makes no claim about the future or the past. It is simply a photo of an anonymous man walking up a hill in (the caption tells us) the town of Aljezur in Portugal. We might say, then, that as well as depicting an event, the photo also represents an event. All Neale knew for sure about this old man was that one day he walked up that hill.

If, later or earlier in the day, some dramatic happening occurred in the man's life that gave this photograph some historical significance, then the image might have been lifted from Neale's website in order to appear in a Portuguese newspaper, where its narrative significance might have been spelled out in the course of a long article. Even if this were the case, however, Neale was clearly unaware of it, and presents the photograph on his website as no more than an image of an everyday event. The people who browse the images on his website, deprived of the local information, will also assume a mundane reading. Within the circle of information comprising the photographer and his public, the photograph is an unexceptional scene of everyday life and makes no narrative claims beyond the moment depicted.

So we might say that the photograph indexically depicts a particular man (to make it easier to refer to him we will give him an invented name, of Rodrigo Sousa) walking up a specific, named hill in Aljezur, that it conceptually depicts an old man walking up a hill, and that it represents some old man walking up some hill in Aljezur. But what if Rodrigo Sousa did appear in the newspaper, what if there were some striking narrative behind this photograph, a narrative of which Neale was unaware? Or what if the narrative was not newsworthy, but nevertheless one which the Sousa family remembered whenever they saw the photo (e.g., Rodrigo had berated Neale for taking his picture)? In the context of presentation, we are only offered one narrative interpretation, but that does not mean that there are not others to be had.

Up to now we have had to make do with two levels of depiction, the conceptual and the indexical. While that distinction has been sufficient when dealing with figures, the further complexity of narrative images seems to call for further conceptual differentiations, between the indexical depiction of a person, the indexical depiction of an event and the indexical depiction of a narrative. We might say that this photograph:

resembles Rodrigo Sousa walking up a hill, an old man walking up a hill, an old man walking on the flat with houses in forced perspective, an old man standing on one foot on a hill, and so on (event); also, an old man heading to rob a bank, an old man who has just won the lottery, an old man walking to the café, and so on (narrative)

conceptually depicts an old man walking up a hill, an old man in a striped shirt and a hat walking up a hill, and so on

indexically depicts Rodrigo Sousa

indexically depicts the event of Rodrigo Sousa walking up a certain street in Aljezur in 2009

indexically depicts the narrative of[2] Rodrigo Sousa walking to the café to meet some friends

represents an old man walking up a hill in Aljezur

I introduced the idea of indexical depiction in Chapter 2 while discussing a photograph of Panofsky enjoying a cigarette break at a conference in Göttingen (fig. 2.3). At that time only one form of indexical depiction seemed to be needed. However, could we not also have said that the photograph in fig. 2.3 depicted an event, of Panofsky smoking a cigarette, and a narrative, of his visit to the 1929 conference in Göttingen? One can see how we might have done. At the same time, Panofsky is the focus of fig. 2.3 in a way that Rodrigo Sousa is not the focus of fig. 5.1. While fig. 2.3 is a portrait of Panofsky, fig. 5.1 is not a portrait of Sousa. It is presented as an image of an old man walking up a hill, whereas the photograph of Panofsky is presented as a portrait of Panofsky. Sousa has quite as much individuality as Panofsky, but he is not being represented as an individual in the way that Panofsky is. The photograph of Sousa is captioned as the image of an event involving an anonymous old man, the sort of event that art historians sometimes call a genre scene. 'Genre' is the right word, since genre paintings involve anonymous types of subjects, rather than named specific subjects.

None of this means that our three levels of indexicality could never be applied to the photograph of Panofsky; that would depend on how the photograph was being used. The aim is simply to point to the social conventions of different kinds of imagery. Whether an image of an event is construed as an event or as part of a narrative will depend on the iconographic context.

---

2 This should really read 'indexically depicts a moment from the narrative of'; see the remarks at the beginning of the next section.

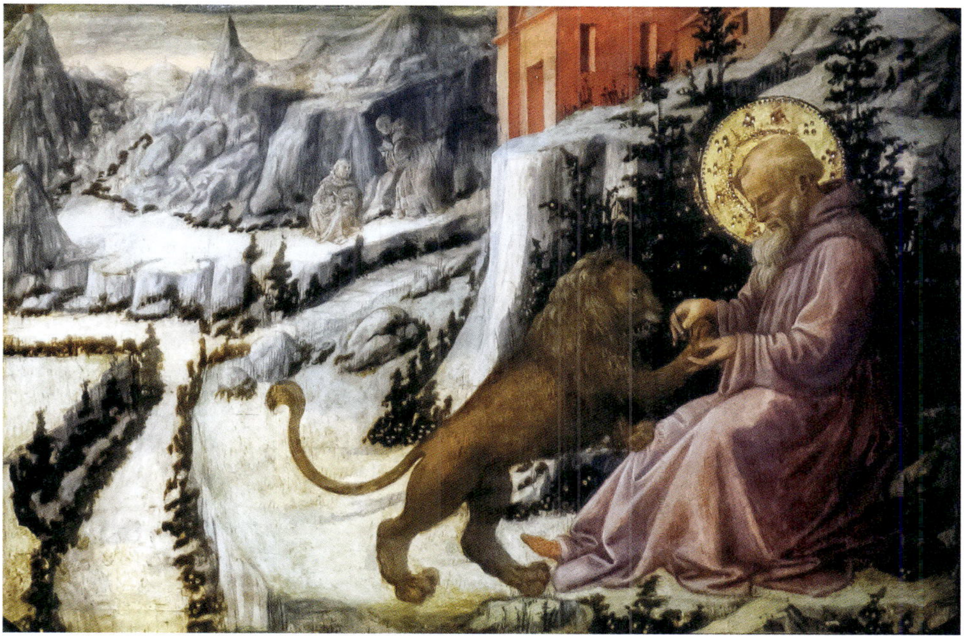

5.2 | Fra Filippo Lippi and workshop, St Jerome with the Lion, scene from the predella of the Pistoia Santa Trinità Altarpiece, 1455–60. The National Gallery, London

From event to narrative

Images can represent narratives, and they can indexically depict a moment from a narrative, but they cannot conceptually depict narratives. Narratives are made up of sequences of events, and single images can only depict events. One can show many images, each of which depicts one event in a narrative sequence, as in a pictorial cycle, a comic strip, or a film; or one can make a composite image, depicting several events: but the individual events will not depict narratives. When we say that an image represents a narrative, what we are claiming is that it depicts an event (or events) from a narrative in which we can identify what has just happened and what will happen next.

What happened to Rodrigo Sousa before and after the event depicted in fig. 5.1 we do not know, but it is clear that a great number of different events could have occurred to him; so fig. 5.1 could be taken to represent an indefinite number of narratives. Any event can be made to fit more than one story. The simpler the story, and the more common the action, the more probable it is that the event depicted can form part of more than one narrative. In the predella of the altarpiece in fig. 4.23 we see a scene of a man who is about to have his head cut off, a relatively uncommon event, but far from unique. Beheading was often the fate of early Christian martyrs, according to legend; it was the last resort of Roman executioners when other torments had failed. If this panel of the predella had become totally dissociated from the altar of which it forms part, then we could not have known which martyr was represented. It is only because this scene is placed directly beneath a figure who can be identified as St James that we can deduce the identity of the kneeling saint.

Another one of the saints in the predella of fig. 4.23, the old man in the last scene to the right, is engaged in a much less common event. A creature that looks like a lion (though it is little larger than a poodle) is holding a paw towards the saint (fig. 5.2). A number of different events could be depicted here; the saint could be performing surgery on the paw, or perhaps putting the final touches to a wooden statue of a lion. We cannot know, purely by looking, what is depicted or what happens next in the story; from the normal behaviour of lions (assuming it is a lion) one might expect the animal to walk off majestically after whatever is occurring has occurred, or to eat the saint.

Sometimes even one and the same narrative image can tell stories that feature different protagonists who have different histories. A good example of this phenomenon, since both protagonists are clearly identified, is the print by Hans Burgkmair in fig. 5.3. The story being told, as recounted in the text around the print, is that a fiddler played so beautifully before a figure in a church that the figure let its golden shoe slip off in gratitude, as a gift. The fiddler accepted the gift and left, but was arrested for stealing the shoe, and condemned to be hanged. He returned to the church with his accusers, put the shoe back on to the figure, played once more, and again the figure let its shoe slip off; so he was allowed to go free.

Of course, the event shown could, again, be made to fit many other narratives; but even if it is taken to represent the same story, involving the fiddler, the shoe, the arrest and the return to the church, different figures can be represented, and in this case they are. In the caption within the print the figure is identified as "the figure at Lucca". This is a reference to the Volto Santo, an eighth- to ninth-century statue in Lucca Cathedral of the crucified Christ wearing a long gown, a statue that was famous internationally due to its many copies. The text block at left, however, recounts the tale of the fiddler as part of the story of St Kümmernis, a princess who prayed that she be given the appearance of Christ so that she would be unattractive to every man except Christ, and who was crucified by her heathen father (Schnürer and Ritz 1934, Friesen 2001). Images of Kümmernis are often indistinguishable iconographically from images of the Volto Santo; she wears the same gown, has the same crown, the same beard and is nailed to a cross decorated in the same way. It is generally assumed that the cult of St Kümmernis grew from a misunderstanding of the Volto Santo; that the faithful took the unfamiliar long gown of Christ to be a dress and assumed that the bearded figure must be a woman. Presumably Hans Burgkmair was aware of the connections between the two legends (Taylor 2008a). Whatever the truth of the matter, both Kümmernis and the Volto Santo are shown giving a golden shoe to a fiddler, so that if one encounters an image of this event, such as fig. 5.4, which gives no textual indication of which figure is offering the shoe, it is hard to know whether Kümmernis or the statue of Christ is represented.

This example shows that any represented personage can in theory have a doppelganger, and that, even if it does not, the appearance of the personage and its narrative role are not enough in themselves to decide its intentionality. There must be some act (or process) of designation to settle the reference.

What of multiple images, such as pictorial cycles or films? When we have thousands of screenshots all carefully filmed and selected to tell a particular story, would it be possible to think of them as telling a different story? Could we take a film, redub it and use it to recount another narrative? This can happen with short clips of newsreel – for example in 2011 a film depicting an Indian political rally found itself used on British TV news as a representation of Libyans celebrating the overthrow of Muammar Gaddafi

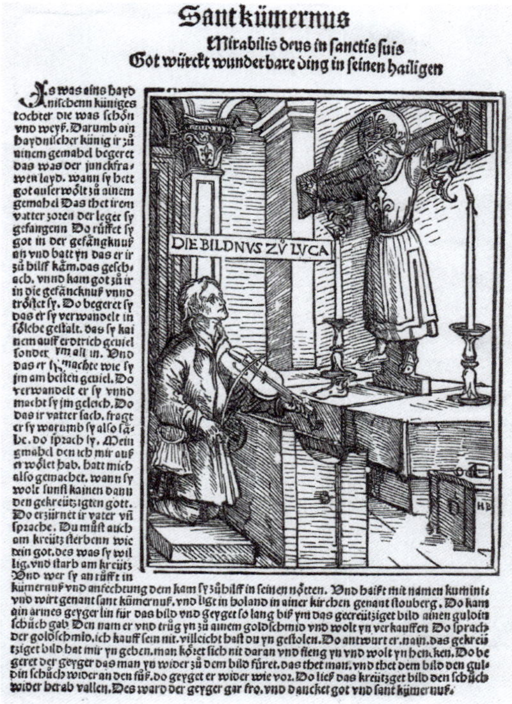

5.3 | Hans Burgkmair, Kümmernis/Volto Santo and the Fiddler, c. 1507. The British Museum, London

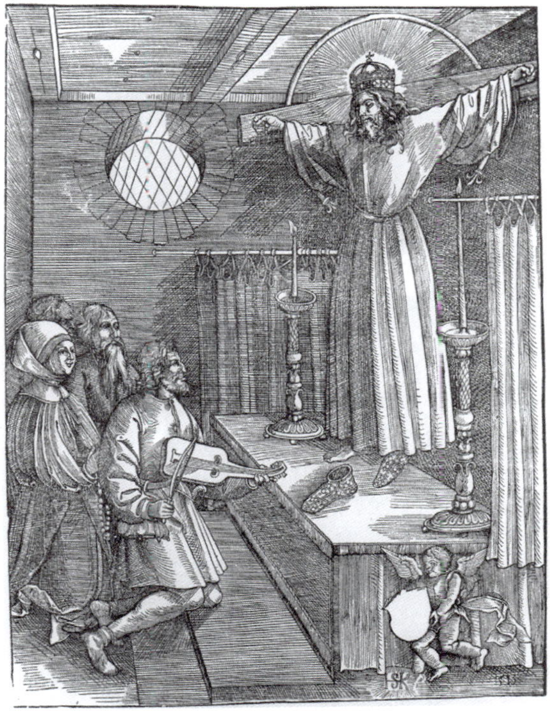

5.4 | Hans Springinklee, Kümmernis/Volto Santo and the Fiddler, 1513. The British Museum, London

(O'Byrne 2017; cf. Leonard 2013) – and there is no reason why it could not happen for long feature films. It is not merely that a plot could be changed by altering the dialogue, thus renaming all the characters and giving them different histories. Even without changing any dialogue at all, a plot can be reinterpreted by feeding in different assumptions. In any plot you are told about what has happened, but there will inevitably be large gaps in the story, and a great deal might also have happened that you have not been told about.

The ambiguity of plots is a theme of one of the most admired novels written in Dutch in the twentieth century [N.B. plot spoiler alert]. Willem Frederik Hermans's *De donkere kamer van Damokles* (Hermans 1958), which means both 'the [photographic] darkroom of Damocles' and 'the dark room of Damocles', starts off as a conventional, if well told, Second World War novel. Henri Osewoudt, who leads a dull life as a shopkeeper in The Hague, witnesses the Germans invading Holland. He is recruited to join the Dutch Resistance and engages in numerous dangerous exploits with glamorous new friends. Halfway through the book the war ends, and Osewoudt imagines that he will be acclaimed as a hero. Instead, he is arrested by the British, who accuse him of being a German spy. The rest of the book is devoted to an interrogation, during which he tries to defend his innocence. His Resistance colleagues have disappeared – the British claim they never existed – and thus he has no one to vouch for him. As you read this you start to feel a mounting confusion. The interrogators are so convincing, and Osewoudt's arguments in response are so weak, that you begin to wonder if what apparently happened to him really happened. You flick back to the first part of the book to see if you had interpreted it correctly, and you begin to doubt your own ability to read a story and understand the plot. Maybe Osewoudt was a German spy. Or maybe he was not. The book, in the end, only gives you the version of events you choose to take away from it.

If you were to take your favourite war film and feed into it the assumption that the hero was in fact a German spy, then its entire significance could change. You think that, at the end of *Casablanca*, Ilse Lund and Viktor Laszlo are flying to freedom in Lisbon, but perhaps they are being flown to Germany, because Rick Blaine has betrayed them. Any plot can have a different ending from the one you are shown.

Stories do not tell themselves. Just as paintings need the beholder's share in order to be interpreted one way or another (Gombrich 1960, 154–244; Gombrich 1982b, 145), so too plots need the reader's or the viewer's share; and the reader or the viewer is often making assumptions about the plot based on the supposed intentions of the teller. It is all very well for intellectual Dutch novelists to make ambiguous narratives, but we do not expect Hollywood to do the same; nobody imagines that Humphrey Bogart might play a German spy, and our interpretation of the plot is based on that assumption.

Those who have been taught to avoid the intentional fallacy (p. 43 above) may think I am here committing an expanded version of this error, but I believe I am innocent. I am happy to allow the possibilities of multivalence and polysemy: the meanings of images can be redesignated, and they can be designated to have more than one sense at any one time. The point is that the image itself does not have a fixed representation – nor indeed a fixed depiction – and so must rely on designations of sense by external agents.

Recognizing narratives

In the photograph of Rodrigo Sousa (fig. 5.1) we have no means of knowing the narrative in which he is involved. His doings that day are known to a tiny circle of people, possibly only to Sousa himself, and may in fact have been forgotten; in any case, viewers of Andy Neale's photo are most unlikely to be connected by linkage to Sousa's acquaintances, and so they cannot find out why he was walking up that hill in Aljezur. Many photographs, and realistic artificial images, are similarly impossible to interpret at the narrative level, and as a result many of them, like our photograph of Sousa, are presented as events, not narratives.

At the same time, traditional images that depicted events were not normally meant to depict events and nothing but. Most pre-photographic depictions of events were also meant to be representations of narratives. From a meta-iconographic point of view, the question is this: how did the maker of the image convey to the viewer the identity of the narrative of which the event formed part? Since an event can form part of any number of narratives, how is one narrative suggested and selected based on a polyvalent event? Image-makers use several meta-iconographic devices to convey their intentions to their audience.

First of these is designation and linkage. An artist can depict an event from a narrative that is not known to many, or perhaps to anyone beyond the artist himself or herself, by the simple method of telling those around him or her what the story is. Any example of a narrative single will need to be explained in this way; and a narrative image can be a single in at least two ways. It can be the only visualization of a story, or it can be a visualization of a story that has only been told once. If, for example, a child starts inventing private stories and illustrates a scene from one of them, then the resultant image will be a single in both senses. If she or he then draws other events from the same narrative, then they will be singles at the level of event but multiples at the level of narrative, though the narrative itself will remain a single.

In images made by adults, narrative singles are a rare phenomenon: for the most part, narrative images are multiples. Even when one thinks one has found a narrative single, one cannot be sure that another image of the same story is not lurking round the corner – rather like those Australian black swans that are used as examples in the philosophy of science (Bamford 1993). I had a black swan experience while writing this book: I thought that a Yoruba helmet mask in the British Museum might be a narrative single, only to come across a very similar Yoruba helmet mask, also in the British Museum; and, in any case, it is not certain that either piece is meant to be a narrative, as I will explain later in this chapter. Looking for actual examples of narrative singles, then, seems hazardous (without drawing one oneself), but it is possible to imagine what would be entailed.

No narratives are known to everybody in the world, and for any narrative the question will arise as to how large a circle of people is aware of it. With a narrative single, the circle of those who know its depicted narrative and who can recognize what is going on in the image will be very restricted indeed. The narrative of the guwak and the possums in fig. 1.5 also had a very narrow circle of acquaintance before anthropologists began to recount the tale, because the Manggalili clan consists of around fifty individuals, and aspects of the story were only known to older males in the clan (Morphy 1999). The story of the guwak and the possums is not a single – the artist Narritjin Maymuru has returned to it more than once, making creative multiples that treat the story in a variety of ways – but it is a very scant multiple (Morphy 1991).

A narrative single will be given its representation only by means of designation and linkage, while in the Manggalili case a visual narrative can make use of familiarity with a pre-existing verbal narrative, known to some of the painting's viewers. This second device is a widespread method of linking a story to an image, but, for it to work, it must rely on knowledge of the context. Merely because an image depicts an event that can also be found in a narrative, it does not follow that it represents that narrative.

How we read the narrative of an image will depend on what we know about the availability of that narrative to the makers and consumers of images in the period when it was made. The image by Delacroix in fig. 1.2 looks like the gravedigger scene from Shakespeare's *Hamlet*, but if this print had been made by a seventeenth-century, rather than a nineteenth-century, French artist we would resist the temptation to identify it as such, since the work of Shakespeare was barely known in France at that time. Instead, it would almost certainly be identified as a *vanitas*, a painting meant to encourage the viewer to contemplate the brevity of life. In the mid-nineteenth century, on the other hand, Shakespeare was famous throughout Europe, and we know from Delacroix's own *Journal* that he gave the playwright's works a great deal of thought. He also represented numerous scenes from *Hamlet*, and painted a self-portrait dressed in the role of Hamlet.[3] Even without the inscription, we would feel confident that the gravedigger scene from *Hamlet* was the narrative that Delacroix intended to represent.

3 1821, Musée national Eugène Delacroix, Paris.

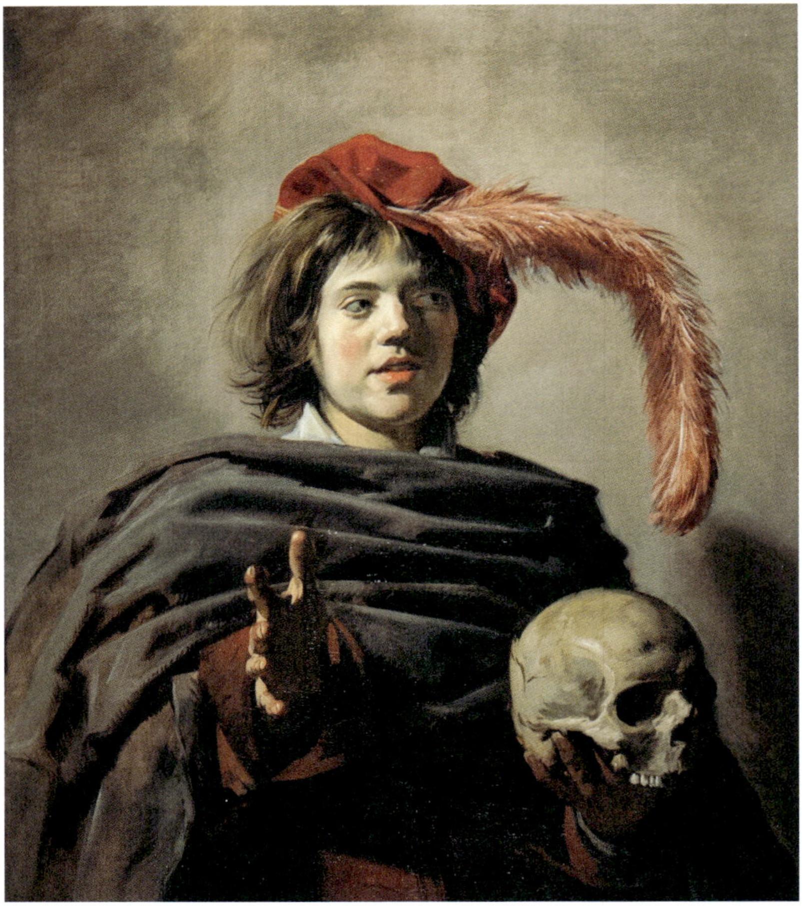

5.5 | Frans Hals, Young Man Holding a Skull, 1626–28. The National Gallery, London

Conversely, there is a painting by Frans Hals in the National Gallery in London of a young man in rather theatrical costume who is holding a skull, a painting that was in the past identified as Hamlet (fig. 5.5). This is now said to be a *vanitas*, since in the 1620s, when it was painted, Shakespeare was little known outside London (Slive 1989, 208–11, 387). If, however, the painting was discovered to contain pigments that could not have been known before the nineteenth century, then it would become more probable that the subject was originally Hamlet, since *vanitas* representations of boys holding skulls had long fallen out of fashion by the 1800s, when literary Europe was obsessed with Shakespeare.

A depiction of an event can be taken to represent a scene from many different narratives, but there are only so many widely known narratives available in any period. In the literature, ancient and modern, available to Franz Caucig in early nineteenth-century Europe there are hardly any stories containing events that feature Greco-Roman costume, camels, palm trees, an overturned waggon, an injured passenger, a distant army and a man brandishing a sword. In Flavius Josephus, however, there is an event that ticks all these boxes, and the text in question is very likely to have been known to Caucig. So we assume that it was this narrative from which Caucig took the event which he depicted in his drawing (fig. 1.6).

Here we are making further assumptions – perfectly reasonable assumptions, but assumptions all the same. We assume that Caucig did not find a story in a book unknown to us, a story containing an event that, by pure chance, looked just like the story in Josephus but had different agents and a different scenario. In this we are arguing from statistics; for what is the likelihood that two stories, independently invented, would look so similar? The same line of reasoning seems to make unlikely the idea that Caucig invented the story himself and had not read Josephus at all. Another assumption we make is that Caucig did not read the story in Josephus, and then, inspired by what he had read, deliberately invent a different, fictional scenario, in which some character killed his wife on the road. We discount this because it seems such a pointless thing to do; why represent a narrative that others would assume was a different narrative? It seems out of character for an artist of the period; a modern conceptual artist might do something like this, but not a Neoclassicist.

In the fifteenth century in Italy several stories were circulating that concerned a man who pulled a thorn from a lion's foot, thus earning its friendship. One might have thought that an event of this kind would be unique, but in literature it is told more than once. Given the popularity of the story, it becomes statistically probable that what is depicted in fig. 5.2 is a thorn being removed. In the *Attic Nights* of Aulus Gellius we hear about one Androcles performing this service for a lion, and the same scenario turns up in Aelian, Aesop and the *Gesta Romanorum*. Since none of the men in these stories were saints, they cannot be represented here. The thorn story also occurs in the legends of two saints, Jerome, and Gerasimos of the Jordan. However Gerasimos was not a cardinal, and yet we assume from the overall context that the predella painting is meant to represent the same person as the man in cardinal's dress who stands above it in the main panel of the altar (fig. 4.23). The one individual who fulfils all the desiderata is Jerome. We can express these classifications as a Venn diagram, which brings out the structure of the argument (fig. 5.6).

So in order to identify a narrative we cannot merely identify what is going on; we have to identify the agents acting in the events, and in order to do that, we need to make assumptions about the likely motives of those who made the image, or told the image maker what to do. The image in itself does not tell a story, it must rely on suppositions about which story was originally designated as its meaning. Of course, we live in a free world, and anyone who wishes can tell themselves a different story to the one originally intended; or can assume that an image which, in its cultural context, was taken to represent St Jerome removing a thorn from a lion's paw would better be redesignated as a representation of an old man painting a wooden lion. Radical redesignation like this has never become very fashionable, even in an academic age that prizes 'writerliness' (Barthes 1970). But whether we wish to engage in rewriting the stories in pictures, there will remain questions about which narratives were ascribed to images in the past, and these questions, if we care to answer them, will have to be approached via research into historic attitudes towards iconography, attitudes that, since they are fixed in the amber of time, can no longer be altered.

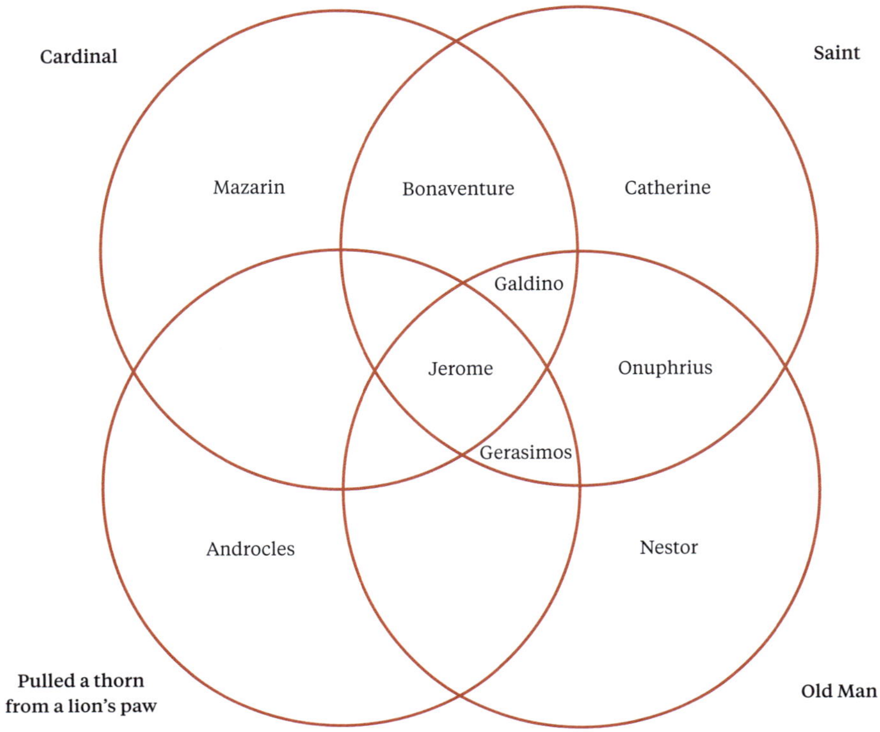

5.6 | Venn diagram of St Jerome's properties

Narratives or figures?

It is not only that a narrative needs the aid of designation and subsidiary devices to settle issues of intentionality, both of the personages and the actions involved; it is also not always clear that a depicted event is intended to represent an event. An image of Hamlet, on his own, holding a skull might be taken in certain contexts to represent the gravedigger scene, but it could also be taken simply to represent Hamlet, with the skull as his attribute. Here we are back with figures and narratives, which we encountered in the previous chapter. As noted there, the figure/narrative distinction is a pervasive one in both European and non-European art.

Take, for example, the Venetian altarpiece in fig. 5.7. This certainly looks like an event, in that it shows an interaction between two people, with a figure we can identify as St John the Baptist pouring water on to the head of a figure we can identify as Jesus Christ, while angels and cherubs and the dove of the Holy Spirit look on. However, the painting was made for the high altar of a church, San Giovanni in Bragora, of which John was the patron saint, and, in the words of Charles Hope, it "is essentially equivalent to a representation of a saint with his attribute, in this case the act of baptizing Christ" (Hope 1990, 549). Contracts for paintings could make this iconographic function explicit; an artist might be asked to produce a figure "of St John when he baptized Christ" (Hope 1990, 569, ftn. 38). The aim then was to provide a figure of St John the Baptist to which the devout could direct their prayers, in the guise of an event that would identify him; the event functions as an attribute.

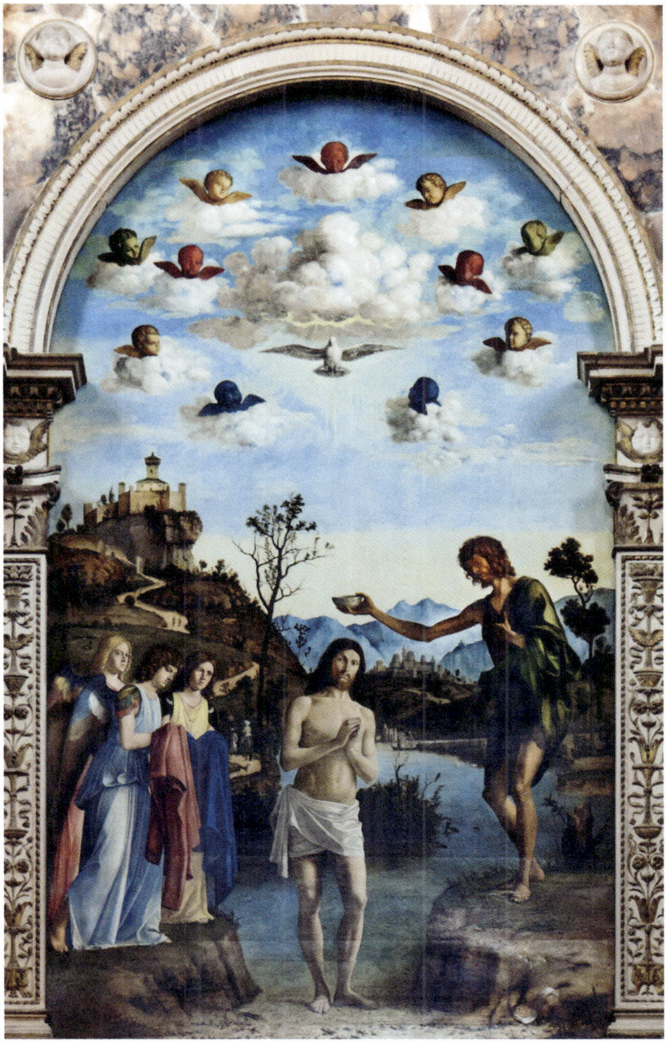

5.7 | Cima da Conegliano, St John Baptizing Christ, 1492.
San Giovanni in Bragora, Venice

Other Christian themes lent themselves to similar treatment, especially when representing the Virgin Mary. The cult of the Virgin is exceptionally complex, with figures made not only as representations of Mary but also as representations of particular aspects of Mary – her freedom from sin (immaculacy), her sufferings, her reign as queen of heaven and so on; in this regard her cult resembles the complex cult of Avalokiteshvara (pp. 118–119 above). Some of these aspects can be depicted as events: the Virgin receiving the annunciation of Christ's conception from the archangel Gabriel, the Nativity of Christ, or the Assumption of the Virgin. These look very much like narratives, with people interacting with one another, but they can also be considered figures of the Virgin as the Annunciate (Annunziata), or as the mother who has just given birth

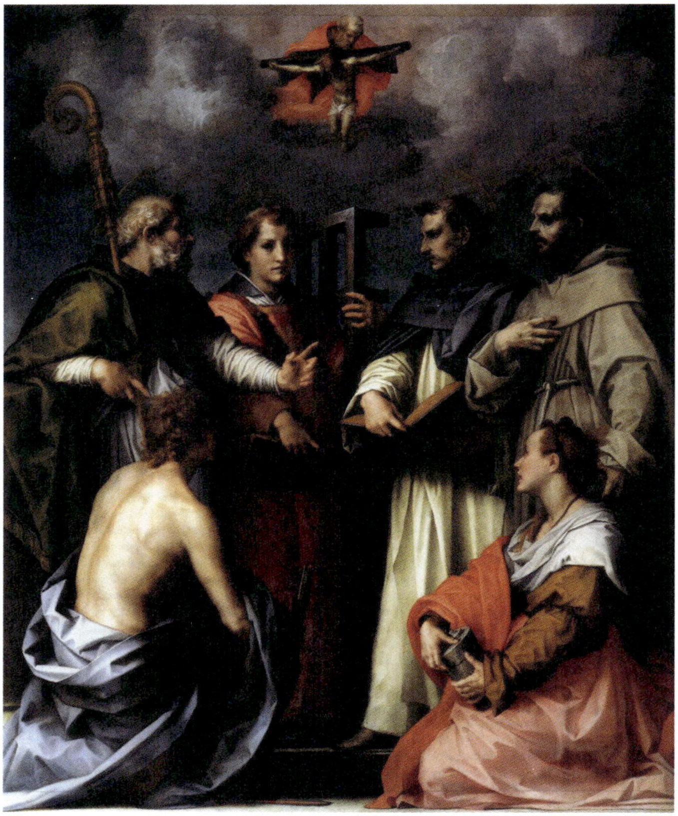

5.8 | Andrea del Sarto, The Disputation on the Trinity (?), 1517.
Galleria Palatina, Florence

(Puerpera) or as she who has just been taken up bodily into heaven (Assunta). Whether they are thought of as figures or as narratives depends on the context; on an altarpiece they might be figures, while in a cycle of the Life of the Virgin they will usually function as narratives (Hope 1990, 556–60). There are no hard and fast rules; in the end, whether these events are thought of as figures or as narratives depends on designation.

Since images depicting events can function either as narratives or as figures, viewers who are not connected by linkage to the designatory context can find it difficult to know what the original iconographic intention was. This is not merely a problem for modern art historians trying to reconstruct historical attitudes across the centuries. We can trace confusion about narratives and figures back to the sixteenth century, a confusion that came about in part due to changes in the pictorial traditions for painting figures. Between the fifteenth and the sixteenth centuries the Italian altarpiece evolved from a collection of framed windows in which individual saints were situated (fig. 4.21), to a scene in which the saints appeared to be talking to one another (fig. 5.8). This new kind of image came to be known as the *santa* or *sacra conversazione*, although the phrase was not contemporary, but entered the language of art at the end of the eighteenth century (Goffen 1979).

The *sacra conversazione* by Andrea del Sarto illustrated in fig. 5.8 shows a miscellany of saints who, on the face of it, have very little in common with one another (Stumpel 1990, 53–55). In the foreground at the right is St Mary Magdalene, identifiable by her attribute of an ointment jar. Kneeling before her is St Sebastian, holding his arrows, and standing second from left in the second row is another late Roman martyr saint, St Lawrence, with his attribute of the gridiron on which he was roasted. Standing to Lawrence's right is a bishop or abbot saint without specific attributes, but who is identified in Giorgio Vasari's *Lives* as St Augustine.[4] The other two saints can be identified by specific 'body attributes', and are both saints from the high Middle Ages; St Francis of Assisi, with a stigmatum on one of his hands, and St Peter Martyr, with a gash on his head, the legacy of his assassination by the heretics whom he, as an Inquisitor, was trying to exterminate.[5]

It has been suggested that this altarpiece represents a random group of saints who just happen to have earned the devotion of a family called Peri (Natali and Cecchi 1989, 76). If this is so, we must assume that the saints were not originally understood as holding a conversation together. However, that is not what is claimed in the pages of Vasari. In the life of Andrea del Sarto of 1550 we read that the saints were having a debate about the Trinity:

> [Andrea] made four figures standing, in dispute over the Trinity. Which are these: St Augustine, with an African air, dressed in the habit of a bishop, who moves vehemently towards a St Peter Martyr, who is holding an open book, with a proud and formidable air. His head and figure is much praised. Next to him is a St Francis, who holds a book in one hand and places the other on his breast, and expresses with an open mouth a certain warmth of fervour that makes it seem as if he is struggling with some line of reasoning; there is a St Lawrence who is listening, and as a young man seems to yield to the authority of the others. He made two figures kneeling: one is Mary Magdalene with beautiful draperies .... The other figure was a St Sebastian, nude, showing his back, who seemed not painted, but like the most living flesh. (Vasari 1550, 749–50)

As Jeroen Stumpel (1990, 55) has observed, "it would seem a very unlikely and rather blasphemous idea that such venerable Church Fathers and Saints from diverse centuries would be inclined to start a noisy row about the true meaning of the Trinity". Of these saints only Augustine had written on the Trinity, and he did so with such theological thoroughness that once he had finished there was very little for later theologians to argue about (Natali and Cecchi 1989, 72). Neither Peter Martyr nor Francis would have felt qualified to disagree with Augustine on the matter, and it would have been hard for them to do so without lapsing into heresy, since the Catholic doctrine of the Trinity is founded on Augustine's thought. And Mary Magdalene, Lawrence and Sebastian were

4 The author of this life may not have been Vasari himself: see Chapter 2, n. 22. Another reason for thinking that this saint represents Augustine is that the altarpiece was painted for an Augustinian church.

5 Shearman 1965, 241–42, identified this saint as Dominic or Thomas Aquinas since 'iconographically ... [they] make better sense'. I agree with Jeroen Stumpel that the altar makes no iconographic sense as a dispute over the Trinity, so there is no point in looking for saints with Trinitarian connections; and the scar on his head cannot I think be read as 'an unusually emphatic seam' on 'a scholar's cap'.

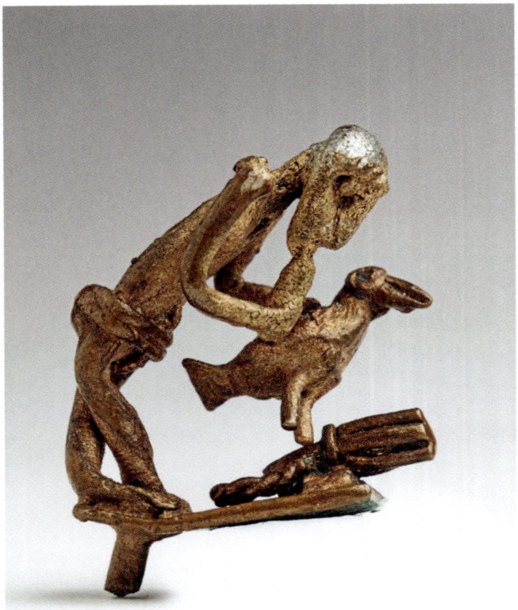

5.9 | Asante, Goldweight with *nkabere* ritual, 1700–1955. The British Museum, London

all early saints with no recorded theological opinions at all.

In short, the interpretation of the scene in Vasari is not at all plausible. Nevertheless, Vasari wrote these lines.[6] He probably knew very little about Trinitarian theology and was just trying to make sense of what he saw. After all, the Trinity is floating in the sky in the painting. Whether this is because the painting was destined for a chapel of the Trinity, or because Andrea wanted to give the idea that the saints were in heaven, or perhaps because Andrea – also no theologian – wanted to give the idea they were disputing about the Trinity, is unknown (Natali and Cecchi 1989, 72). But even if Andrea did want to paint a conversation in progress, a Trinitarian dispute between Augustine and miscellaneous other saints, he clearly did not choose the other saints with that in mind, since they are so clearly unqualified for the task. The saints were chosen because the patron was devoted to them.

This example shows that what looks like a narrative may just be an assemblage of largely unrelated figures, and that the simple appearance of the image needs to be understood within a pragmatic context. Whether or not the interpretation in Vasari's *Lives* reflected the original intentions of the patron or the artist, the narrative reading and the figure reading of the painting are both possible, given the appearance of the picture. Deciding whether something is a narrative is an interpretative decision, rather than an outcome of the structure of the image.

'Narrative figures' like these have been researched in Europe, where we have a relative abundance of archival and literary evidence with which to interpret historical images. Whether images on the cusp of figure and narrative also exist in other iconographic traditions is harder to say, in the absence of precise records as to how they were used. One iconographic type that seems as if it might be a possible instance of this phenomenon is the Asante goldweight in fig. 5.9. There are numerous other examples of the same representational theme, which is not easy to read and makes a striking example of iconographic feedback. The early scholar of Asante goldweights, Rudolf Zeller, described a piece in the Berne Museum, very similar in appearance to this, as follows: "An Ashanti man standing on crossed legs, takes a bird from a trap and seems at the same time to be eating something (a banana?)" (Zeller 1912, 43). From a purely visual point of view this is a plausible interpretation of what is taking place, but as the anthropologist R.S. Rattray observed:

6 Or possibly Bastiano da Sangallo: see Chapter 2, n. 22.

> It is instructive to see how wide of the mark Zeller is in some of his attempted explanations of these, and it seems a pity that he guessed at what he could not possibly have known, for as he himself says, "the meaning of many of the representations which we see in the weights can only be properly understood by making inquiries on the spot and of the natives".
> (Rattray 1923, 309)

Rattray had seen a performance of the ritual that is depicted here, and gave a lengthy description of it. The object that Zeller read as a trap was in fact three sticks bound together with string, which formed a charm or fetish (*suman* in Asante) known as *nkabere*.

> From time to time a fowl will be offered to this *suman*. The medicine man or priest will advance upon it with crossed legs and hands held behind the back and perhaps with a whistle in his mouth, to call up the spirits, and will stand over the charm with legs crossed. He then holds the fowl by the neck and blows the whistle. This is what is shown in the weight.
> (Rattray 1923, 311)

Here the most important part of the image is not the medicine man or the fowl but the *nkabere*; it is the fetish that has the power. We might then think, to adapt the remark of Charles Hope quoted earlier, that the goldweight 'is essentially equivalent to a representation of a fetish with its attribute, in this case the act of offering a fowl'. The purpose of the *nkabere* was to gain power over others, and Asante goldweights were used to weigh out gold dust. One can understand how representing the *nkabere* on a goldweight might seem an effective way of ensuring that the dust was weighed fairly.

This scenario is of course a speculation. We do not know enough about the *nkabere* weights to be sure that this was how the Asante thought of them. Nevertheless, it may be useful to keep this iconographic structure in mind as we investigate apparently narrative images from societies around the world.

Images that appear to depict events but are not representations of narratives do not of course have to be figures. Take the Yoruba helmet mask in fig. 5.10. We see an exciting scene taking place on top. Some creature that resembles a big cat is standing on a humanoid figure who is grasping two horns, while another humanoid figure is holding on to the same horns further up. On the back of the mask a female figure stands upright, facing away from the cat-like creature and reaching back to hold on to the horns. It is not difficult to think up possible stories that might fit with this scenario; the problem is to know which of them was meant by the artist, or how it was interpreted by those who saw it being danced. Some Yoruba masks of this type illustrate stories or concepts that are found in proverbs, songs or fables (Lawal 1996), but the British Museum, where this mask is stored, does not record the fable, song or proverb that might be illustrated here. And it is possible that no story is being told. The presence of a big cat in these iconographic contexts could signify the presence of witchcraft, and this helmet mask may simply be a warning of the evils of witchcraft and the need to flee it.[7]

7 I thank Adeyemi Akande for this suggestion. There is another helmet mask in the British Museum with a very similar iconography, inv. Af1909,-.118.

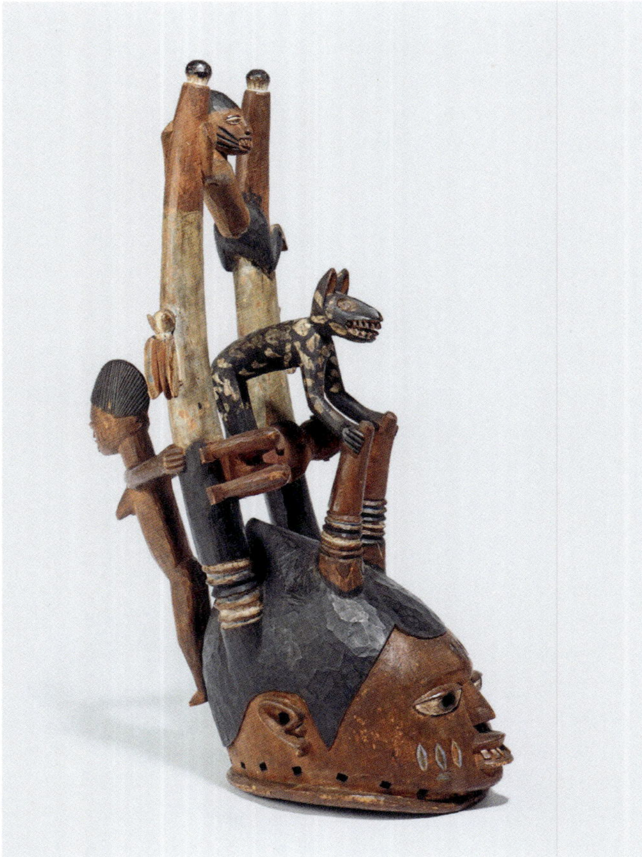

5.10 | Yoruba Gelede mask, before 1924. The British Museum, London

We have seen a number of examples of images that look like narratives, but are, or may be, functioning as figures. Of equal interest are images that look like figures but were treated as if they were narratives. An example of this phenomenon is the mosaic of the Virgin and Child in the apse of Hagia Sophia in Istanbul (fig. 5.11), which is not on the face of it a narrative, but which was discussed in a homily by Photios, Patriarch of Constantinople, in terms that went beyond the actual visual information presented in the image:

> A virgin mother carrying in her pure arms, for the common salvation of our kind, the common Creator reclining as an infant ... with the love from her womb, she turns her eyes on the begotten child with feeling, yet assumes the expression of a detached and imperturbable mood at the passionless and wondrous nature of her offspring, and composes her gaze accordingly.
> (Photius, Homily 7, trans. James and Webb 1991)

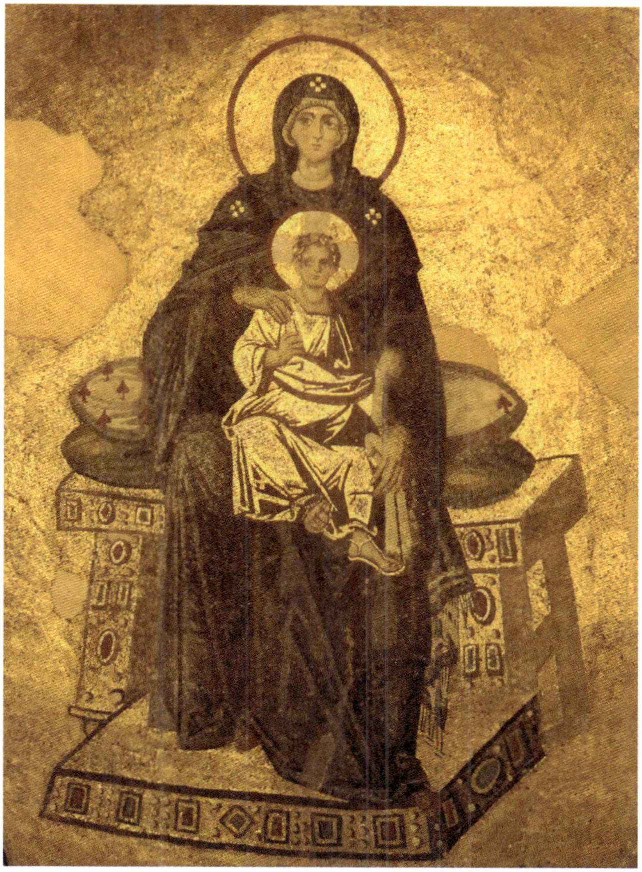

5.11 | Byzantine, Mosaic with the Virgin and Child, 9th century. Apse of Hagia Sophia, Istanbul

In the mosaic itself the Child is not reclining and is not being held in the Virgin's arms, and she is not looking at him, let alone turning her eyes on him with feeling. It would be easy to dismiss Photios's homily as a mere rhetorical exercise that was making no effort to be accurate. But Liz James and Ruth Webb (1991) have suggested that rhetorical exercises like these give us a real insight into how people in Byzantium thought about pictures: they were interested not in the static appearance of the image, but in the narrative it represented. This narrative could then be retold in vivid terms, bringing out its spiritual significance.

Whether or not this is an accurate summary of Byzantine attitudes towards images (the only examples given are from texts by highly sophisticated authors, which may not reflect the attitudes of less literate viewers), the principle that James and Webb put forward – that an image can be used as the starting point for a verbal narrative, and that viewers' responses need not confine themselves to what is actually before their eyes – is one that occurs in other societies. We have already encountered an example of this phenomenon in Chapter 1. For the Manggalili clan in northern Australia, images of the guwak and the two possums (fig. 1.5) stand in for a whole narrative of the mythical creation of their land, and the connotations of such images can be developed still further, referring to features of the local topography. The mere appearance of the image is only the starting point for an explication of clan mythology (Morphy 1991, 281–44; cf. Munn 1986).

Scholars of Oceanic art have remarked on the absence of narrative imagery in Melanesia and Polynesia (Forge 2017c, 112; Küchler 1988, 632; Gell 1998, 212), but the examples we have just considered make it clear that this is a difficult claim to support or refute, since deciding what is and what is not a narrative image is not easy. An ancestor figure may be the focus for stories, a collection of figures interacting may be an assemblage of mythical heroes and heroines, and a traditional iconographic type may receive different responses over time. Perhaps it is possible to distinguish between the *depiction* of an event and the *depiction* of a figure; but we will not know to which narrative the event belongs without understanding more of the pragmatic context than we can generally recover. It may then be true to say that in Melanesia and Polynesia there are fewer depictions of events than there are in Australia or Europe or Mesoamerica.

Quite why that should be so is hard to say. The answer might simply be that people in Oceania feel no need to depict events or narratives. Any attempt to explain this with an argument based on the alleged characteristics of 'primitive' image-making, of the kind that scholars such as Boas, Loewy and Gombrich found attractive in the past (Taylor 2014), is going to founder on the fact that there are numerous examples of 'primitive' artists who have depicted narratives. Besides the examples from Australia, there are also many rock paintings in Africa depicting hunting scenes and myths (Garlake 1995; Le Quellec 2004), there are complex African masks representing tales (Lawal 1996) and there are masks that, while not apparently narrative in themselves, are used in narrative dances (Roberts and Roberts 2007; Colleyn 2009; Cole 2013). Clearly, people in Melanesia and Polynesia could also have made narrative depictions if they had wanted to.

Communicating narratives

For a viewer to identify a narrative in an image, they must already know the narrative. One may, with some luck, be able to guess which event is depicted in an image, but to guess the narrative one must know not only the event shown, but events preceding and succeeding it, as well as the identities of the people represented; and it would be impossible to achieve so much by mere guesswork. How, then, are stories communicated by single images? For a narrative single, the necessary iconographic information can be imparted by simple, word-of-mouth designation and linkage; but for stories that are recognized over large regions, or even continents, oral linkage is unlikely to be an effective method.

As we noted above, even in a small society, images can be recognized by viewers without their being told by anyone what the image means. This could be the case in the story of the guwak and the possums (fig. 1.5) if the narrative in question is known beforehand. The same kind of pre-knowledge allows those who know stories such as Laocoön (figs 3.11, 3.12, 3.13) and St Jerome and the lion (fig. 5.2) to recognize images of these narratives.

In the case of the guwak and the possum, the story itself will have been communicated orally, since the Manggalili clan is small, and their narratives were not written down before the arrival of anthropologists. In the cases of Laocoön and Jerome, however, the spread of the story from one viewer to another will have been based for the most part on texts in which the story is told. Viewers read a story, remember it, and then can recognize it when they see it – bearing in mind the remarks made earlier (p. 158) about the need to use context and statistics to decide between different readings of the narrative. Some people may hear the story orally, but if they do, this will probably be, directly or indirectly, from someone who has read it. Narratives in literate societies spread through the media of writing and print, and since books can find their way into hands separated by broad swathes of territory, so certain narratives can be recognized by viewers living thousands of miles apart.

Images are parasitic on language, and representations of a narrative will rarely spread outside regions where the verbal narrative is unknown. In areas where many languages are spoken within a small region, as in much of Africa, narrative iconographies (and indeed other iconographies) did little travelling. However, when a language has spread across a continent, the image can follow in its footsteps. Before the modern era, iconographies were most widespread in regions where one language, such as Latin or Sanskrit or Chinese, was understood over a large territory.

I wrote above that for a viewer to identify a narrative in an image, they must already know the narrative. This seems true, but sometimes the narrative is conveyed while the image is being viewed, for example when an image is explained to the viewer by a companion, or a priest, or an elder. A young person from the Manggalili tribe could learn to recognize stories of the guwak and the possum in this way. You almost certainly learned to recognize those stories in an analogous fashion, the literate version of the same process; you read the narrative while you looked at the illustration in this book (fig. 1.5).

Texts that recount narratives can accompany images in different ways. They can appear in manuscripts (fig. 4.26), on prints (figs. 1.2 and 5.3) or with inscriptions (fig. 5.16), and they can give us either full descriptions of a story or hints to jog our memory. In Hans Burgkmair's print of the fiddler and the golden shoe (fig. 5.3) we are told the entire story, but in Delacroix's print of Hamlet and the gravediggers (fig. 1.2) we are given two lines from Shakespeare's play ("This same skull, sir, was Yorick's skull, the King's jester ... Alas, poor Yorick!"). To anyone who does not already know these lines from *Hamlet*, the inscription will leave them little the wiser.

In modern imagery language is rarely far away, in the form of captions, or text panels or soundtracks. A particularly complex form of interaction between text and image is found in comic strips. These differ from traditional manuscripts in the way they tell a story through images, with the help of text. In manuscripts and illustrated books images were usually illustrations of scattered events in the narrative, which was being told verbally in the surrounding text (fig. 4.26). Early narrative illustration, that is, consisted of episodes that could be widely separated in narrative time, whereas in the comic strip, illustrations often represent events only seconds apart in the story (Kunzle 1973). The narrative strategies of comic strips have been analysed in detail by linguists, semioticians and theoretically minded comic artists (McCloud 1993; Bateman 2014; Cohn 2016). A key concept in much of their work is 'multimodality', the idea that image and text combine to produce meaning, with each casting light on the other. Whereas a traditional, unillustrated manuscript will tell its story as effectively as one that is illustrated, in a comic strip the imagery cannot be removed without disrupting the reader's comprehension of the narrative; a comic book consisting only of speech bubbles would be less easy to follow than the combined artefact. At the same time, the text of a comic book, especially if it has many text panels explaining the background to the action, can be written out as a play, a piece of drama; and while certain stage directions will be absent, since they are provided by the image (e.g. *He points a gun at them*), it will usually be possible to follow the story. On the other hand, a comic book in which all the speech bubbles have been erased is harder to follow. It is not only that the characters cannot be named, the details of the plot become confusing. It is like trying to follow a film with the sound turned down; one can understand many of the events, but the pattern of the plot is obscure. Such, at least, is my personal impression, but experimental iconographers of the future might test our abilities to read the plots in multimodal contexts without either text or image.

It may be true that comic strips with no speech bubbles are harder to understand than comic books with no images, but that does not mean that books consisting only of images are unintelligible. There are, after all, novels without words, of which those by Frans Masereel were influential pioneers. The most admired of Masereel's picture novels, *Mon livre d'heures* (*My Book of Hours*; 1919), tells a story that seems, for the most part, to make sense. A man comes into a city by train. He seems astonished by all he sees, so presumably has not been in a city before. He meets a woman in the street, and follows her to her home where he makes love to her, an experience that so enraptures him that he is filled with love for all creatures, and embraces horses, gives alms to beggars, plays with children and so on. After several scenes of his joyful life in the city we see him working in the countryside; then he returns to the city and apparently becomes involved in politics. Once again, he meets a woman in the street (the same woman?). He proposes marriage to her (fig. 5.12), but she leaves him for a man wearing a top hat (fig. 5.13). He is in despair, and sleeps with a prostitute; but he has his purse stolen and is kicked out of the brothel. He goes to pray in a church. He sees a young girl being beaten and saves her; they have happy times together. She seems to grow into a young woman and stands nude before him (fig. 5.14). Then she is once again a child, who dies in bed (this section is rather confusing).[8] In his bereavement he takes long solitary walks in the countryside, after which he embarks on a liner for Africa, where he talks to natives and observes monkeys (fig. 5.15). When he returns to the city, he begins living a life of luxury (it is never clear how he pays for any of this), while insulting the rich. Then he heads back into the countryside, where he apparently dies in a forest, although these final scenes, in which he has the head of a skull and stamps on a heart, are presumably allegorical.

There are 165 woodcuts in Masereel's novel, so details are lost in this brief transcription of the plot. When summarized in this way it may not sound like a very good plot, and indeed, if the novel had been written in words, it might have been ridiculous.[9] However, from a meta-iconographic perspective, it is interesting that a plot of any kind can be extracted from a wordless novel. Many assumptions are built into our

---

8 Thomas Mann, however, found the story less problematic; in his introduction to the German edition of *Mon livre d'heures* (Masereel 1926, 38) he wrote: "Follow the wonderful Novella in eleven pictures, in which our hero takes in the mistreated young girl and is happy with her, only to see his beloved waste away and die". The problem is that, when he meets her, the girl is a small child; she has a doll, and he carries her on his shoulders. By the time of the scene in fig. 5.14 she is presumably a young adult. The eleven pictures seem to cover at least ten years.

9 Max Beckmann dismissed Masereel's work as "really nice for 14-year olds". On his disagreement with Thomas Mann concerning Masereel's value, see Schwarz 1988.

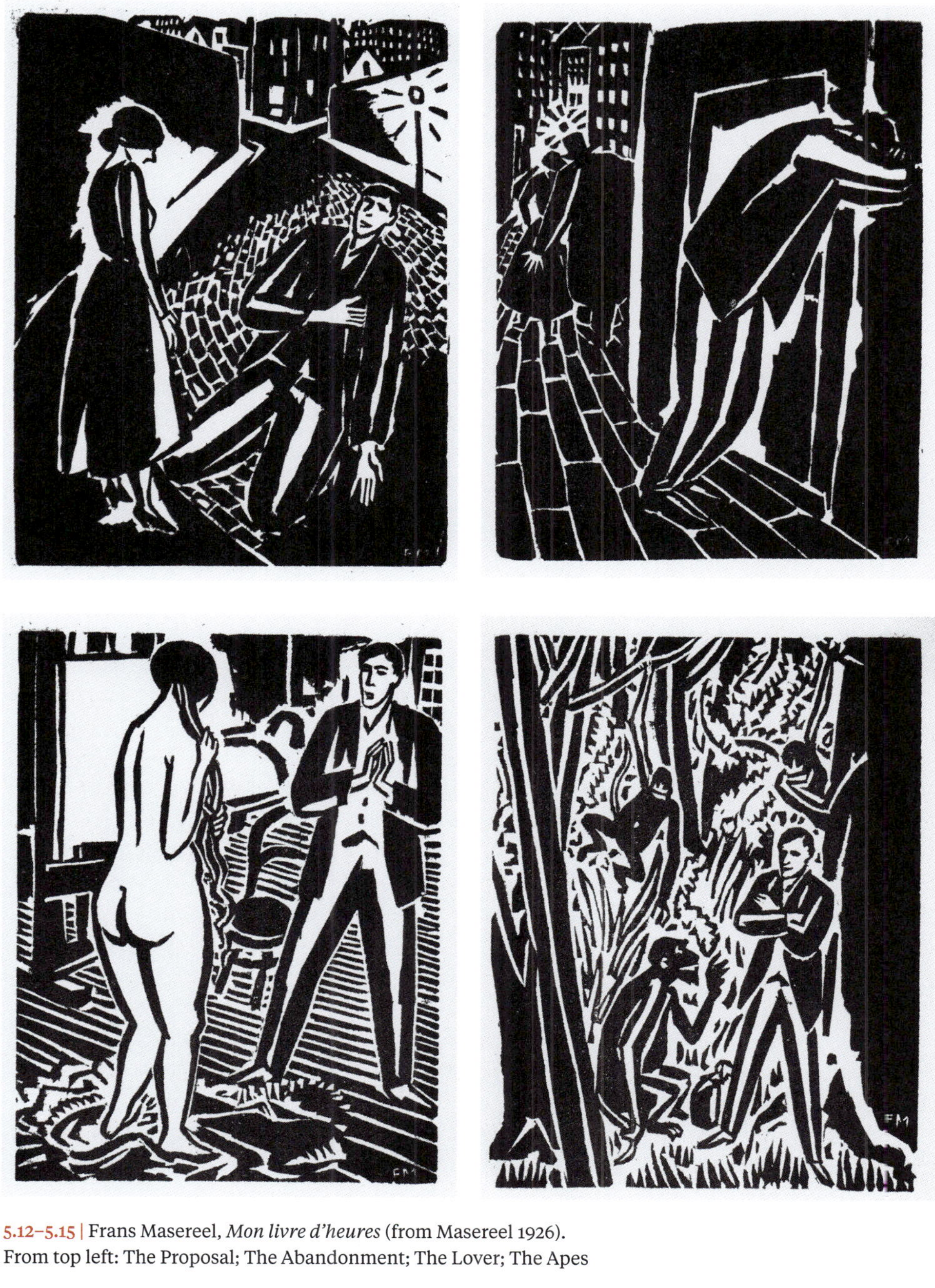

5.12–5.15 | Frans Masereel, *Mon livre d'heures* (from Masereel 1926).
From top left: The Proposal; The Abandonment; The Lover; The Apes

reading of Masereel's plot, though they are so immediate that we might not notice they are there. We assume, for example, that it is an original story, which has been created by the author; we do not go looking for the literary original of *Mon livre d'heures*. As a result, we think of the characters as nameless, rather than named. It seems possible that the hero of the novel is meant to be identified in some way with Frans Masereel (*Mon livre d'heures*), although if the story is based on the author's life, it has been heavily fictionalized.[10] We also assume that the character with a bare head in each image is the same person, but it would be possible to use these images as illustrations for a novel featuring three men, perhaps brothers, who share an aversion to headgear (most of the other male characters in the book wear hats or caps). Then too we assume there are no gaps in the story, and that consecutive scenes are directly linked; that the woman to whom he proposes (fig. 5.12) is the same as the woman who leaves him (fig. 5.13), and that the bare-headed man at right is in despair (if he is in despair, rather than e.g. being sick) because his offer of marriage has been turned down (if he has made an offer of marriage, and was not e.g. singing a song in the street). If, however, we imagine these two scenes as illustrating separate chapters of a novel, then there does not have to be a direct link between them, and the characters do not need to be thought of as the same people. We try to make sense of what we see, try to guess Masereel's motives. He must, we think, be telling a simple, intelligible, coherent story, and so we construct a story of that kind out of the events he depicts; but many other stories could be written for which these woodcuts would be effective illustrations. A plot can be extracted from the novel, but other plots can be extracted from it, too.

For Thomas Mann, writing the introduction to the German edition of *Mon livre d'heures*,

> [the hero's] classlessness is not utopian; it is a natural gift of fate and genuine at all times. It is this that surrounds him with an atmosphere of purity, strangeness, detachment, something which would once have been called 'saintliness'; and it is this too which, in a world torn apart into classes, into an embittered struggle of class warfare, makes him, the outsider, the uninvolved, the pure guest, ... the only one whom humanity can secretly trust.
> (Masereel 1926, pp. 36–37)

In novels, heroes are usually sympathetic, and Mann assumes that the hero in Masereel's novel is also sympathetic; and yet the hatless man drinks heavily, visits brothels, gets into fights, knocks people's hats off, farts in their faces, expresses his contempt for humankind by pissing on a city[11] and is possibly a paedophile (fig. 5.14) as well as a racist (fig. 5.15). Frans Masereel himself was a lifelong pacifist and antifascist (Hiepe 1989), but the story he created, precisely because he did not narrow the interpretative options by using language, can be read in ways he never intended.

We are back with our comments about the ambiguity of plots, which we discussed earlier in this chapter regarding *De donkere kamer van Damokles*. A plot can be

10 Mann writes (Masereel 1926, 10) that "Masereel depicts himself", but he does not suggest that all the events in the narrative took place in Masereel's life.

11 This woodcut is omitted from some editions.

interpreted in more than one way, and in the end will need to rely on designation if the ambiguities are to be settled. Either the reader decides that the author designated one plot rather than another, or the reader decides, perhaps in the absence of clear indicators of the original designation, to redesignate a plot; but the plot will not (so to speak) designate itself. That there is often widespread agreement among readers and viewers about the events in a plot does not in itself show that the plot has a unique meaning; it shows that we all have a good grasp of narrative conventions and know what we are expected to think.

Comic strips and film have the advantage that they can assign iconographies to images immediately, without the need for prior knowledge on the part of the viewer. To understand what is going on in fig. 1.1 or fig. 1.2 you need to be aware of the contents of Josephus's *Jewish Antiquities* or Shakespeare's *Hamlet*, but to understand what is going on in a comic strip or a film you can simply read the text bubbles or listen to the soundtrack. Since modern images are so often accompanied by texts or soundtracks identifying the characters and explaining the plot, the need for pre-existent iconographic knowledge has lessened with time. While in past centuries the ability to recognize large numbers of images required considerable erudition, now images are interpreted for the viewer by the words that travel with them.

Stories that explain themselves (or seem to explain themselves) have another advantage, in that they can proliferate. If the audience of a comic strip or a film does not need to know the story in advance, then new narrative images can be invented at will, in the knowledge that their iconographies will be decoded by their viewers. And indeed, the number of narrative images has enormously increased in the past century. Today about 3,000 fictional feature films are produced around the world each year, and while not all these films have entirely original plots – because some are remakes, or film versions of pre-existing novels – the great majority do (Albornoz 2016). This can be compared to the c. 10,000 medieval and Renaissance iconographies of myths, legends, fictions and historical events preserved in the Photographic Collection at the Warburg Institute. Although these statistics are rough and ready, it seems probable that, in the past quarter of a century, more new narrative iconographic types have been invented than in the whole period of world history before 1900.

This explosion of plots has had another consequence, which is that fewer stories are held in common. Educated Europeans in the sixteenth century shared a knowledge of a group of narratives, from the Bible and from classical texts by authors such as Homer, Virgil, Ovid and Livy, which meant that they were able to recognize many images that illustrated passages from these books. Nowadays, however, there are fewer widely known narratives, since cultural experience is more individual; we all watch different films and read different novels (Taylor 2022a; Taylor 2022b). Or at least this is true of myths, legends and fictions; the imagery that is still widely known is historical. Photographs of the Russian Revolution, or the assassination of John F. Kennedy, or the release of Nelson Mandela now form our shared stock of readily recognizable iconographies.[12] Historical events before the invention of photography, however, are much less well known; it is as if the camera had brought the past to our attention.

12 I thank Johannes von Müller for this insight.

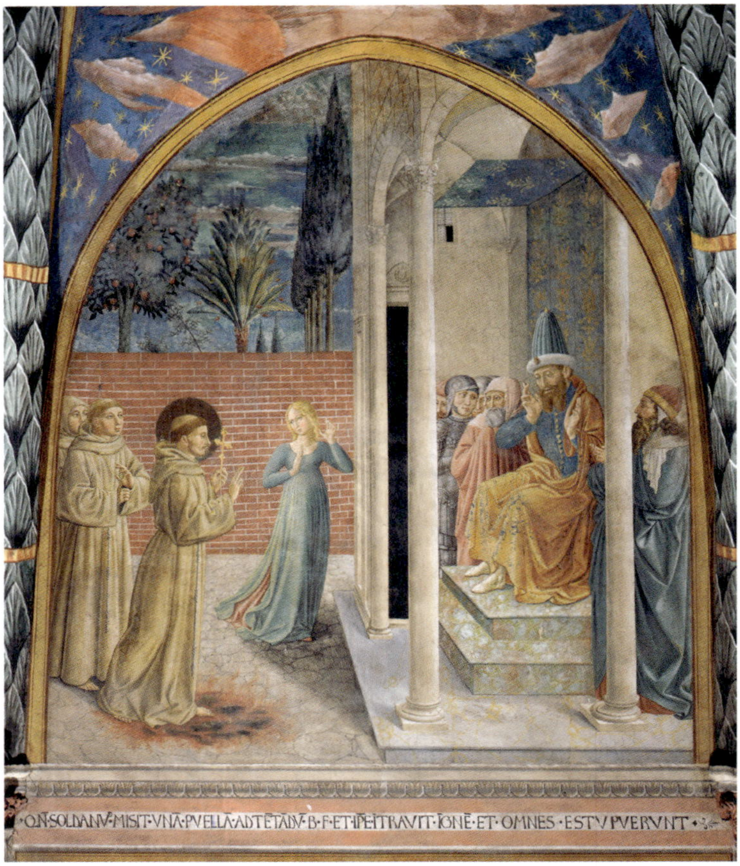

5.16 | Benozzo Gozzoli, St Francis Walking through Fire before the Sultan, 1450–52. San Francesco, Montefalco

Anonymity

Benozzo Gozzoli's fresco of St Francis before the Sultan (fig. 5.16) is accompanied by an inscription that identifies – and fails to identify – the people in the scene: "*Quando Soldanus misit unam puellam ad tentandum Beatum Franciscum et ipse intravit ignem et omnes estupuerunt*" (When the Sultan sent a girl to tempt the Blessed Francis and he entered the fire, and all were astonished). Three of the eleven figures visible in the painting have been given identities, of different kinds. One figure, St Francis of Assisi, has been named. Another figure, the sultan, has been identified by his title. And another figure, 'a girl', has been referred to via an indefinite noun. There are eight other figures in the picture, although one is only visible from what we can see of the very top of his helmet, and three have their faces partially hidden. The viewer might deduce that they are bystanders, whose identity need not concern us. We can infer a few details of their identity from their costume – two are Franciscan friars, three are soldiers, two with beards are presumably meant to be advisers to the sultan – but it is hard to tell, given the visual and textual information Gozzoli provides, if any are important actors in the story.

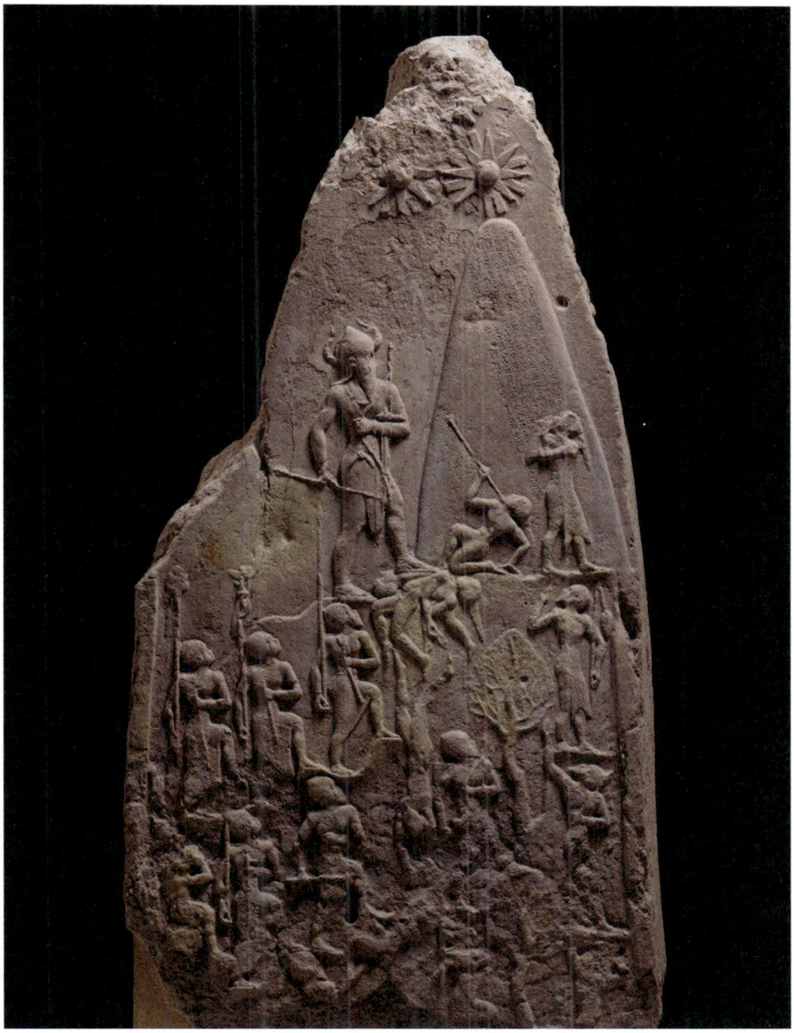

5.17 | Akkadian, Victory Stele of Naram-Sin, c. 2250–2200 BC. Musée du Louvre, Paris

The girl is picked out by the inscription because she plays a significant part in the narrative – she was "sent to tempt the Blessed Francis". But she is not significant enough to be named, nor to be described with any further degree of precision; she is simply 'a girl' who appears in a transaction: she is sent by one individual, the sultan, to tempt another individual, St Francis. Were it not for the inscription, we would not know what to make of her. She might be another bystander, a passing girl put into the picture to enliven the composition, she might be a relative, the wife or daughter of the man in the pointed hat, or she might link with the story in some other way – the reader can invent scenarios.

Narratives of this kind, in which certain figures are specified and others are left nameless and generic, go back a long way in the history of images. The stone stele in

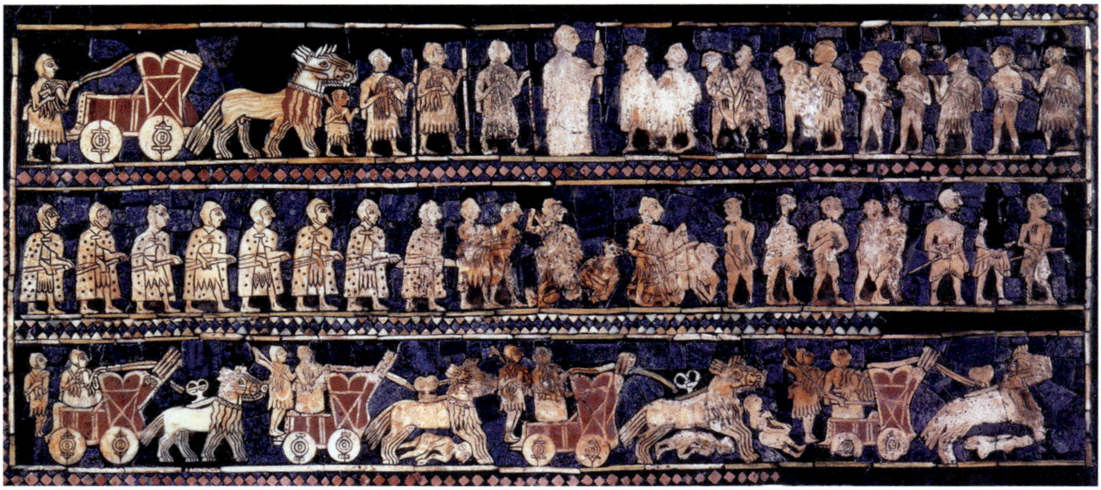

5.18 | Sumerian, Standard of Ur, c. 2600 BC. The British Museum, London

fig. 5.17, from c. 2250–2200 BC, is one of the earliest narrative images in world history for which we can give a name to at least one of the protagonists. The reason we can do so, in this case, is because two inscriptions carved into the stone identify him. One, in Akkadian, tells us that Naram-Sin gained a victory against the Lullubi. We know from other sources that Naram-Sin was king of Akkad, and that the Lullubi lived in the foothills of the Zagros mountains to the east of Mesopotamia. Another inscription, in Elamite, tells us that, a thousand years later, Naram-Sin's stele was captured and taken away as war booty by Shutruk-Nahhunte, king of Elam (Feldman 2009).

The stele shows Naram-Sin leading his troops into the mountains and crushing the Lullubi under his feet. Most of the people in this image are clearly meant to be anonymous; Naram-Sin, who is far larger than anyone else and who is also wearing the horned helmet of a god, is the centre of attention. However, despite his grandiose appearance we only know that Naram-Sin is represented because of the inscriptions; without them the stele would have been nameless. Here we can make a distinction between deliberately nameless narratives and accidentally nameless narratives. We can fail to identify the characters in a narrative because we do not have enough context to be able to give them names. The inscriptions on the stele of Naram-Sin could have been eroded by the elements, and we could have lost his name forever. But he was meant to have a name, as the existence of the inscription shows; and the inscription also shows, or at least strongly suggests, that the soldiers following him were not meant to have names, but were represented as generic soldiers.

We can assume that certain figures on other, earlier images from Mesopotamia, such as the so-called Standard of Ur (fig. 5.18), were originally meant to be understood as having names. Here we see scenes of warfare at the bottom, and captives being led by Sumerian troops in the middle register, with some of these captives being led towards a figure on the upper register who – like Naram-Sin – is noticeably larger than those around him. Presumably he is a man of power, and presumably this work was meant to

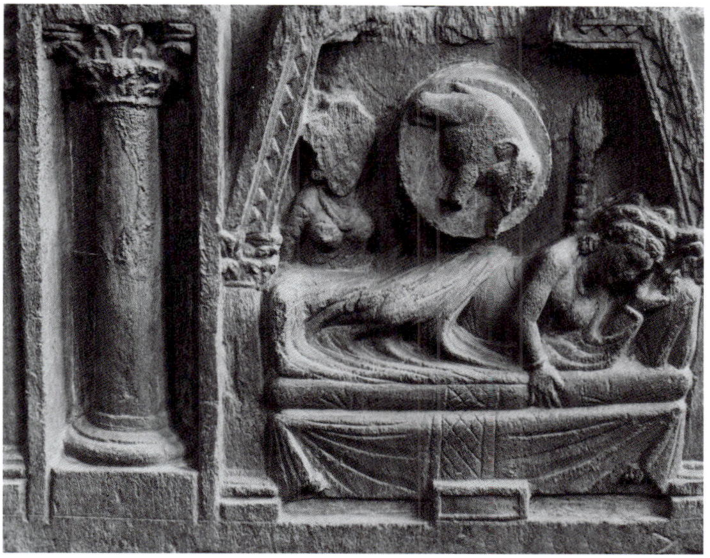

5.19 | Gandharan, Queen Maya's Dream, 1st–3rd century AD. Lahore Museum

honour his victories over his enemies, just like the stele of Naram-sin. But there is no inscription and, as a result, we do not know the Sumerian lord's name (Collins 2015).

In both the Victory Stele and the Standard of Ur the peripheral figures are numerous, but namelessness is not only a feature of crowds. In fig. 5.19, we see one of the most famous and easily recognizable scenes from the life of the Buddha, or rather from just before his life; this is the Buddhist counterpart of the Annunciation to the Virgin Mary. We are told that the bodhisattva entered the womb of his mother, Queen Maya, as a white elephant with six tusks. Some accounts say that she dreamed this, others that it happened in fact. In this small fragment from a Gandharan stair riser we see Maya and the elephant, and we also see an anonymous female attendant who has become even more anonymous due to the loss of her face. Some stories of the conception of the Buddha mention four *devadas* (goddesses), who surround Maya's bed. In art we see figures who watch over Maya as she sleeps, but they do not appear to be goddesses, and their number varies from one to three; quite how many there are seems to have depended on the amount of stone available for carving. Sometimes they hold spears, to guard the queen, sometimes they hold fly whisks, to ensure her sleep is undisturbed. They are not mentioned in Buddhist texts and are unique to the images. There is no reason to think that they were meant to have names; they are just anonymous staffage, like the captives on the Standard of Ur.

Anonymous figures are found in images from the earliest periods of civilization, but when they do appear they are usually subsidiary figures, and other figures in the same images are named. Images in which all the figures are anonymous – human figures, that is, not animals or plants – are rare in Mesopotamian and Egyptian iconography. So far as I am aware there is no history of namelessness in art, but if it is eventually written then the Chinese and Roman empires will play an important role, since it is in

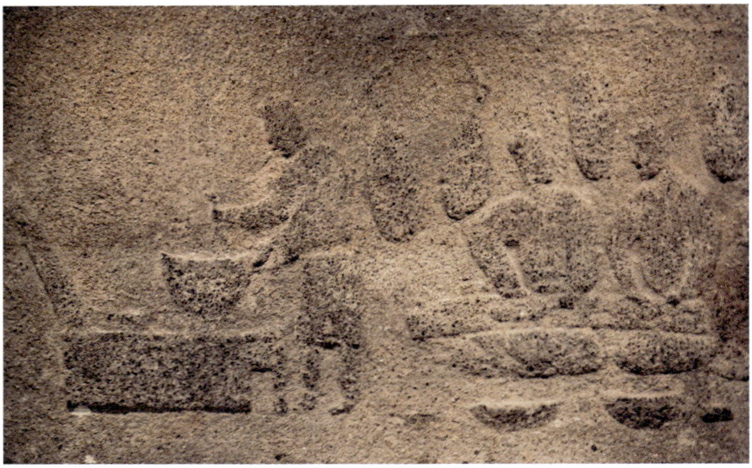

5.20 | Eastern Han, Brick relief with kitchen scene, 25–220 AD.
National Museum of China, Beijing

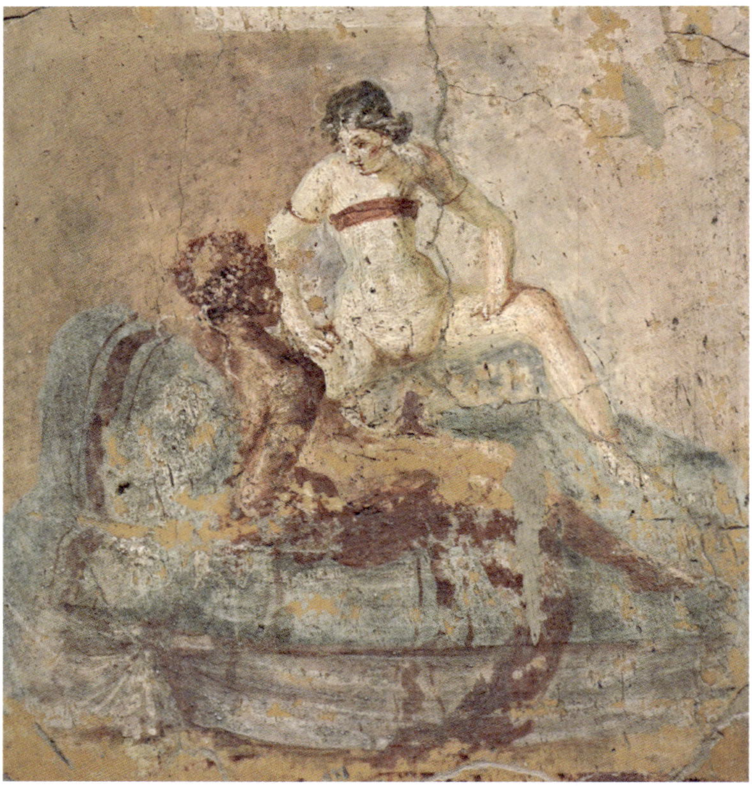

5.21 | Fragment of wall painting with erotic scene from Pompeii, c. 70–79 AD.
Museo Archeologico Nazionale, Naples

these territories that entirely anonymous representations of people became common. In Chinese reliefs of the Han dynasty there are numerous scenes of everyday activities carried out by actors who seem to have no names (fig. 5.20), and the participants in Roman erotic art are probably not representations of people who were well known in the streets of Pompeii (fig. 5.21).

These are only hypotheses; perhaps the female figure in the Pompeian wall relief was meant to represent a famous courtesan or aristocrat, and perhaps the cooks in the Han relief were meant to represent the cooks of the household for which the relief was made. We know too little of the pragmatic contexts to be sure. But it is certainly possible that the figures in these two works were not meant to depict or represent any person indexically; that the figures were simply invented without reference to models or sitters and were intended from the start to represent nameless humans: *some* cooks, *a* woman and *a* man. They were not depictions or representations of people in the real world; they were invented people, figures who looked like flesh and blood humans, but who were not meant to refer to living exemplars. That is, they were conceptual depictions of human beings, but they were not indexical depictions, and they were also not representations of specific personages.

There are different kinds of anonymity, at different levels of reality. If the lovers in fig. 5.21 are indeed fictional characters, then they have no more claim to existence than Horatio or Yorick (fig. 1.2). The nameless characters in the stele of Naram-Sin (fig. 5.17), on the other hand, have a slightly different status. The individual representations of soldiers are probably not meant to be portraits of actual members of Naram-Sin's army, but they are meant to be generic stand-ins for real people, who fought for the Akkadian king. The same can be said for the soldiers and the captives on the Standard of Ur (fig. 5.18). The entourage of the Turkish sultan in Gozzoli's fresco (fig. 5.16) are somewhere betwixt and between. Like Naram-Sin's soldiers they are not portraits of actual people; rather, they are Gozzoli's best guess at the kind of people who might be part of a Sultan's court. Since he had never seen a sultan there is a large amount of invention involved, but the characters are perhaps slightly less fictional than the Pompeiian couple.

Images consisting entirely of anonymous figures are not uncommon in Chinese and Roman art, but the great majority of images – especially religious images – in those two empires contained named figures. The same is true of most images from other epochs and places, but, with the passing of time, the proportion of entirely anonymous images has increased. In most Chinese landscape paintings from the Tang dynasty (618–907) onwards, anonymous, invented people inhabit anonymous, invented countryside, and the same can be said of early modern European landscapes (fig. 5.22). In sixteenth- and seventeenth-century Europe anonymous scenes of everyday life became popular, and by the mid-seventeenth century in Holland well over half of the paintings in private collections were anonymous images of one kind or another – genre, landscape or still life. Paintings with named individuals – from the Bible, from history and from mythology – suffered a sharp fall in popularity (Montias 1982, 237; Fock 2021; Taylor 2025).

This is a tendency that continued in ensuing centuries; anonymous subjects were at the heart of Impressionism (fig. 5.23) and of most of the figurative movements in twentieth-century art. By anonymous subjects here we mean intentionally anonymous representations. The man in Édouard Manet's boating scene above is thought to be an indexical depiction of Rodolphe Leenhoff, the artist's brother-in-law, but that fact is irrelevant to the iconography of the painting, which is presented as some man and some

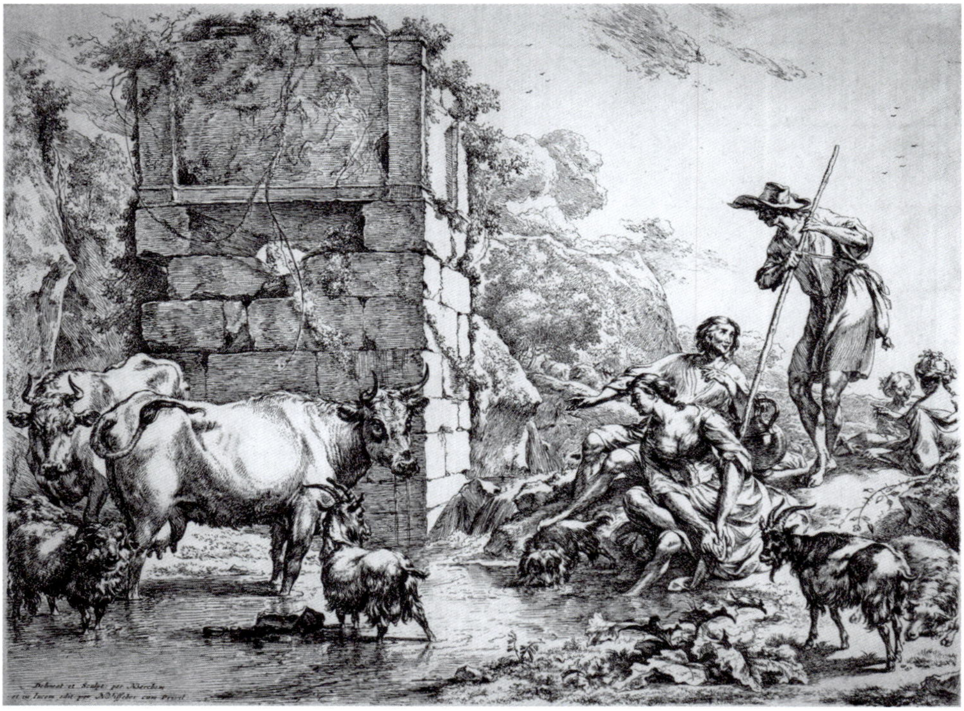

5.22 | Nicolaes Berchem, Landscape with cows, sheep and figures, 1680. Private collection

woman in some boat, somewhere (presumably in France). How do we know this? How do we know that this is not, say, a scene from a French novel? There may well be a passage of Maupassant or Zola to which this painting would make an effective illustration. If we think that this is not a representation of a scene from Maupassant or Zola, that is because we think it was never designated as such. If it had been designated as a literary scene then Manet scholars would surely have discovered the fact, and the Metropolitan Museum's website would tell us which scene, from which novel, is represented. In fact, the painting was exhibited in Manet's lifetime with the title *En bateau*: no attempt was made to give the sitters identities, or to weave a story around the interaction between the two characters.

That a narrative image does not represent a specific narrative is just as much an iconographic fact as that it does represent a specific narrative, and to learn that it is meant to be representationally indeterminate requires the application of iconographic devices. I did not know until I visited the Metropolitan Museum's website that this painting was originally called *En bateau*, but I was not surprised when I learned it. As a museum goer I know that Impressionist paintings are usually given anonymous titles, and I have never come across a Manet described as *A Scene from Maupassant*. If Manet originally designated this painting as an anonymous event, then that information must come to his viewers in later centuries through a process of linkage. Here the linkage is provided by wall texts written by curators who have studied art history at university and have been told there about the iconographic preferences of Impressionist painters

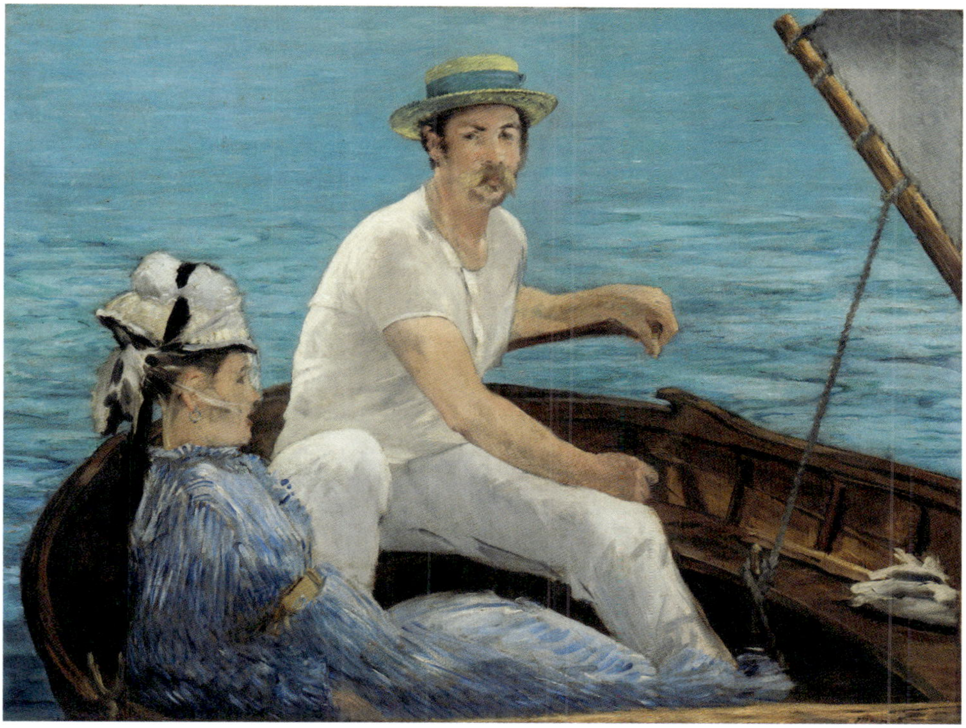

5.23 | Édouard Manet, *En bateau*, 1874. The Metropolitan Museum of Art, New York

by lecturers who have read books on the subject written by scholars who have studied primary sources from the nineteenth century. We have here a community of art historians who share knowledge and impart that knowledge to the public. Since not everyone in the community will have met face-to-face – because they live in different countries, or on different continents – they must communicate through the medium of print, but the process of linkage to the original designation is essentially the same as in an African or Melanesian village.

Anonymity of figure and absence of narrative are widespread features of figurative art today, both of the famous art discussed by art historians, and of the products of unknown artists which decorate homes, hotels and hospitals. Part of the reason for this is surely that, as we said at the end of the previous section, we have fewer stories in common. What we are witnessing is a process of cultural estrangement; as societies become more complex, each of us can only assimilate a small number of the thousands of narratives that have been written. Artists who represent scenes from their favourite novels will make images that are unintelligible to anyone who does not share their literary tastes. So, instead, artists represent events acted out by anonymous figures, and leave it to their viewers to construct narratives around the events. Images drained of reference are easier to understand.

Works of art in small-scale cultures tend to have specific meanings. The larger and more diffuse the culture, the harder it is to convey identities. When artists make no pretence to represent specific people engaged in specific narratives, they make images accessible in a culture where meanings are no longer shared.

Specific and generic representation

Throughout this book I have used the words 'specific' and 'generic' in an informal way, without discussing their implications in detail; perhaps now, after this discussion of anonymity, is the time to think about them more closely. 'Specific and 'generic' can be applied at the levels of both depiction and representation. They have some aspects in common with 'indexical' and 'conceptual', but there are several important differences. To date I have only been applying the latter terms at the level of depiction. Why not speak of indexical or conceptual representation? One answer to that question is that an index, in Peirce's terminology (Atkin 2005), is a sign caused by its referent, and we have taken it to mean that 'there is something out there in the real world that causes the image to come into existence; the image is an index of that something'. A representation is not *caused* in this way, it is the outcome of what we might call a semantic consensus. Another point to make is that 'conceptual' and 'indexical' are not opposites. All indexical depictions are also conceptual depictions (p. 48 above). 'Specific' and 'generic', however, are opposites: generic is non-specific and specific is non-generic. The opposite of 'indexical' is 'non-indexical'. We should not think, however, that 'indexical' means the same thing as 'specific' or that 'non-indexical' means the same thing as 'generic', for the reasons we have just given about causality.

There are images that depict indexically and represent specifically (e.g. Chief Kimano, fig. 4.7); images that depict indexically but represent generically (like Manet's sailor, fig. 5.23); images that depict non-indexically but represent specifically (e.g. Chief Fosia, fig. 3.3); and images that depict non-indexically and represent generically (e.g. the Pompeiian lovers, fig. 5.21). Photographs, too, can represent generically, as in the photograph of the old man walking up the hill in Aljezur (fig. 5.1): we will encounter more examples of this phenomenon in the next chapter.

Another important difference between 'indexical' and 'specific' is that there are many images which are specific, but which are not real. We could hardly say, for example, that the Gandharan relief of Queen Maya (fig. 5.19) is an indexical representation, because it does not represent a real individual; and at the same time we can hardly say that it is a conceptual representation, because it does not represent a generic individual. Depiction is a matter of what the image-maker does in the real world, but representation is often not a matter of the real world, but of imaginary worlds, and since 'indexicality' is tied to the notion of reality, it would be of limited utility when discussing imaginary scenes (even if it did not also include the implication of causality).

But there is another problem. At the time the Gandharan relief was carved, the makers and users of the work thought that Queen Maya existed, and indeed many Buddhists today would share that belief. 'Specific' is a useful word, since it allows us to talk about both existent and non-existent individuals; but its limitation is that it does not allow us to distinguish the two. With our talk of indexical depiction we have made a point of flagging the reality of the depicted motif, but with talk of 'specific representation' we are being agnostic about the reality of the represented motif.

In recent philosophical literature on 'fictional entities' (Voltolini 2006, xiii; Kroon and Voltolini 2018) untrue stories are all described as fictions, and so it might seem tempting to talk of 'fictional representation'; but here too there are difficulties, because the sorts of images encountered by historians of traditional imagery are not usually fictional, if we think of a fiction as being a story invented by an author and known to be untrue from the moment of its creation. Rather they are, typically, myths and legends. In what follows I will call representations of non-existent entities – myths, legends and fictions – fictive representations. These can be either specific (e.g. Apollo and the Muses) or generic (e.g. satyrs and nymphs). We can call representations of existent entities non-fictive representations. These too can be either specific (e.g. Erwin Panofsky) or generic (e.g. the old man in Aljezur). Although 'specific' and 'generic' are opposites, there will be some haziness about the borders between the two concepts. For example, the sultan and the girl in fig. 5.16 are unnamed. Are they specific or generic? We might think that they seem more specific than the anonymous bystanders, but more generic than St Francis. Here I will fall back on a comment I made about borders in Chapter 2 (p. 48 above): there will be a very large number of borderline cases between indexical depictions and non-indexical depictions, but this should not worry us unduly, so long as there are abundant unambiguous cases on either side of the border, and there are.

Fictive representation

In current English, 'myth' and 'legend' are generally taken to mean narratives that are untrue, but here I will be using the words in the sense in which scholars of myth and legend use them, to refer to stories that, though untrue, are nevertheless believed to be true by those who tell them. 'Myth' is generally distinguished from 'legend', with myths said to involve non-humans, in the remote past, in a world unlike that of today, and legends to involve humans, in the recent past, in the world of today (Bascom 1984; cf. Bietenholz 1994). Myths and legends that are no longer believed to have taken place can be called 'fables' (Pettazzoni 1984). 'Myth', 'legend' and 'fable' define one another; a fable is a former myth or legend, and a myth or a legend is a fable in prospect.

Many narrative images before the early modern period, in fact probably most, were representations of myths and legends. The two narrative images in figs. 5.24 and 5.25 show the myth/fable of Perseus and Andromeda. Andromeda is chained to a rock, a sea monster approaches with the intention of eating her and Perseus flies to her rescue. In fig. 5.24 the hero is flying with the aid of winged sandals and holds the head of the Gorgon Medusa, which turns those who see it to stone. In fig. 5.25 he is sitting on a winged horse, without the Gorgon's head. We know that fig. 5.24 was painted before AD 80, since it was found at Pompeii, preserved under volcanic ash from the last eruption of Vesuvius. Fig. 5.25 was made for a German edition of Ovid's *Metamorphoses* published in 1582.

There was no known inventor of the story of Perseus and Andromeda, which was current in Greece by the sixth century BC, and which may have entered the Greek peninsula from the east (Phillips 1968). According to the myth, Perseus and Andromeda were the parents of Perses, from whom the Persian ruling dynasty were descended; Herodotus writes that Xerxes, in a speech delivered by a herald to the Greeks, used this genealogical connection as proof that he too was Greek by descent (*Histories*, 7.150). Whether Xerxes believed this is hard to say, but elsewhere Herodotus recounted the myth of Perses as if it were true (7.61). That Perseus was thought to have existed is suggested by the fact that he was worshipped as a god in various places in the eastern Mediterranean and the Near East, in Hellenistic and Roman times (Sauneron 1962; Mastrocinque 2011).

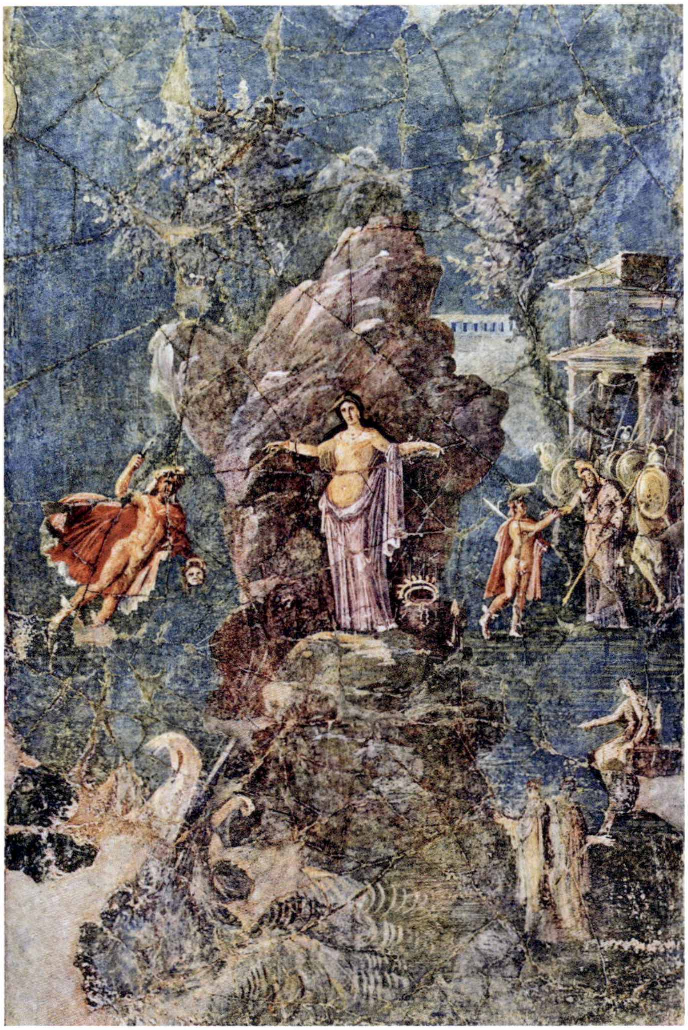

5.24 | Perseus and Andromeda, 20–10 BC. House of the Priest Amandus, Pompeii

Religious faith was waning in Rome by the time Vesuvius erupted. Cicero's *De natura deorum* tells us that some people found ancient myths hard to credit (1.27; 2.24–28; 3.17, 20–23, 31, 34). Whether the owner of the room in which fig. 5.24 was painted believed that Perseus existed, and freed Andromeda from a sea monster, we do not know. The house has 'Sacerdos Amandus' written on the outside wall, which suggests that at some point it was the home of a priest (*sacerdos*); perhaps ancient Roman priests were more likely to believe myths and legends. If Amandus saw the mural, then he may have thought of it as a representation of a true narrative.

However, it is not necessarily a simple matter of true or false. Cicero also tells us (1.42; 2.24–28; 3.24–25) that some people thought the myths of the gods were allegories

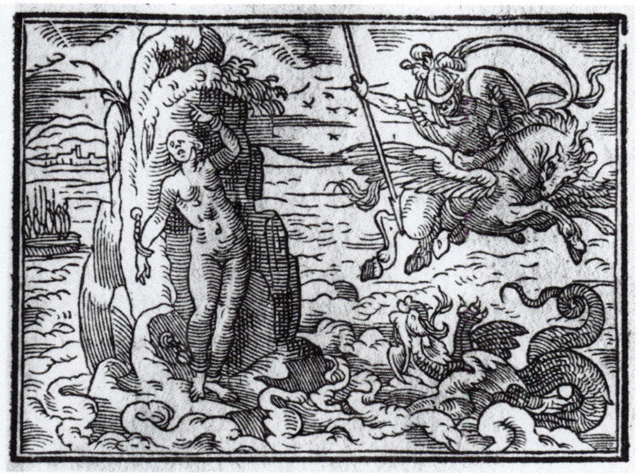

5.25 | German, Perseus and Andromeda (from Ovid, *Metamorphoses*, Leipzig 1582, p. 187)

of arcane wisdom, while others believed them to be based on events that had occurred to actual people who had lived on earth, whose stories had been distorted over time (Seznec 1953, 11–56; Gay 2020, 10, 17–23). On this view there was some man who was the original of Perseus, and this man might have saved the original of Andromeda from some peril or other, an event that, in later centuries, was transformed into this myth. So, the story might have been accepted in part even by those who refused to believe in sea-monsters or winged sandals. The less believable details of the story came to be dismissed as fabulous, but there was thought to be some kernel of truth to the tale.

Quite how interpretations of this kind worked can be seen if we turn to fig. 5.25. By the sixteenth century in Christian Europe no one really believed that Perseus was a god or that he flew on a winged horse to save Andromeda from a sea monster. However, mythographers did still toy with the idea that there might have been some historical events that lay behind the myth and that the myth was describing them in a distorted way, and they also thought, or said they thought, that the fabulous elements of the narrative might have been meant as allegories. In the preface to the 1582 German Ovid from which fig. 5.25 is reproduced, we read the following of Perseus:

> The story of Perseus is known to almost everybody. Greek writers recount that he waged war against the Gorgon people, whose queen was Medusa. But with his actual deeds they mingled others that were fables, such as the tale of the head of Medusa that turned everything to stone, and which he cut off with the help of the gods. Do not these fabulous inventions contain in brief an abundance of lessons, bearing on life and on morals? Suppose you understand Perseus as reason, and Medusa and her sisters as the enticements of pleasure, which deserve to be conquered by reason with the help of divine aid, which is signified by the shield of Minerva, and the sword of Mercury and the helmet of Pluto, with which the poets armed him. Or what if you interpret the Gorgons, who are said to have inhabited the Dorcades islands in the

> Ethiopian Ocean, as the daughters of the sea, the waters themselves, Medusa in fact as the thinner upper layer floating on the surface, Perseus finally as the sun: in such a fable there are ingenious explanations of the wonderful actions of nature and of God the creator, who bestows his power on nature.[13]

Perseus, then, was a real man who really waged war on a people called the Gorgons, led by their queen named Medusa; and all the implausible details of the story were made up by the poets. Nevertheless, those details can be read as moral allegories of reason's struggle with pleasure, or physical allegories of the workings of nature. At some point in the past, the implausible details were also thought to be facts; the Perseus myth has been on a long journey from factuality to fictiveness.

In Europe, Greco-Roman fables were very popular subjects during the 'long Renaissance', from the fifteenth to the eighteenth century.[14] This European practice of deliberately representing fables is an unusual one in world image making. In non-European imagery there are plenty of narratives we would think of as fabulous, such as those in figs. 1.5 and 4.16, but at least in theory these scenes were thought, by those who first viewed them, to have occurred. The European narratives in figs. 3.13 and 5.25, on the other hand, are of scenes that were once thought to have taken place, but were no longer thought to have done so in the period when these images were made. Here fig. 3.13 is a special case, since it is an eighteenth-century print representing a Hellenistic statue. The subject was thought to be a fable by the time the print was made, but when the original statue was carved it was still a widely believed myth. Indeed, in the sixteenth century, when the images of Laocoön in figs. 3.11 and 3.12 were painted, the Trojan War was still thought to have taken place, although the episodes of divine intervention were discounted (Bietenholz 1994, 154–57; Burke 2012, 262, 271).

Hundreds of thousands of images of fables were made in Europe between the fifteenth and the eighteenth centuries. Finding similar representations in non-European art is less easy, although there are some examples, especially in Islamic iconography. In fig. 5.26 we see an example: Rustam, the mythical Persian hero, had been sent on a mission to kill the Akvan *div* (demon), who had been attacking local livestock. After a

---

13 "*Nota est plerisque omnibus Persei historia, quem adversus Gorgonum gentem, quarum regina fuit Medusa, bellum gessisse, Graeci scriptores narrant. Sed huius rebus gestis fabulae cum alia admiscuerunt, tum narrationem de Medusae capite saxifico, Deorum ope ab ipso amputato. Haec fabulosè efficta, quantam in summa brevitate continent doctrinae copiam ad vitam atque mores conferentis; si Perseum scilicet rationem intelligas, Medusam verò unà cum sororibus voluptatum illecebras, quae ratione superari solent divino adiuta auxilio: id quod aegis Minervae innuit cum Mercurii gladio, & Orci galea, quibus poëtae illum armavêre. Quod si Gorgones, quae Dorcadas Oceani Aethiopici insulas habitasse perhibentur, aquas ipsas interpreteris maris filias, Medusam verò partem earum tenuiorem, ac supernatantem, Perseum denique solem: non defuturae sunt in hac ipsa fabula subiectiones ingeniosae de naturae Deique opificis actionibus mirabilibus, qui vires suas naturae impertit.*" Gregor Bersman, 'Praefatio', in Ovid, *Metamorphoseon libri XV*, Leipzig: Steinman, 1582, fols. 4 r–v. My thanks to Elizabeth McGrath for help with the translation.

14 The myths were also known throughout the medieval period, but interest in them multiplied dramatically in the fourteenth and fifteenth centuries. Seznec 1953, 11–147, provides an account of medieval imagery of the gods, claiming (3) that "pagan antiquity, rather than experiencing a 'rebirth' in fifteenth-century Italy, had remained alive within the culture and art of the Middle Ages. Even the gods were not *restored* to life, for they had never disappeared from the memory of imagination of man." This is true but ignores the fact that the imagery of the gods increased fiftyfold between the thirteenth and the seventeenth centuries. The gods may not have been restored to life, but they were raised from a deep coma.

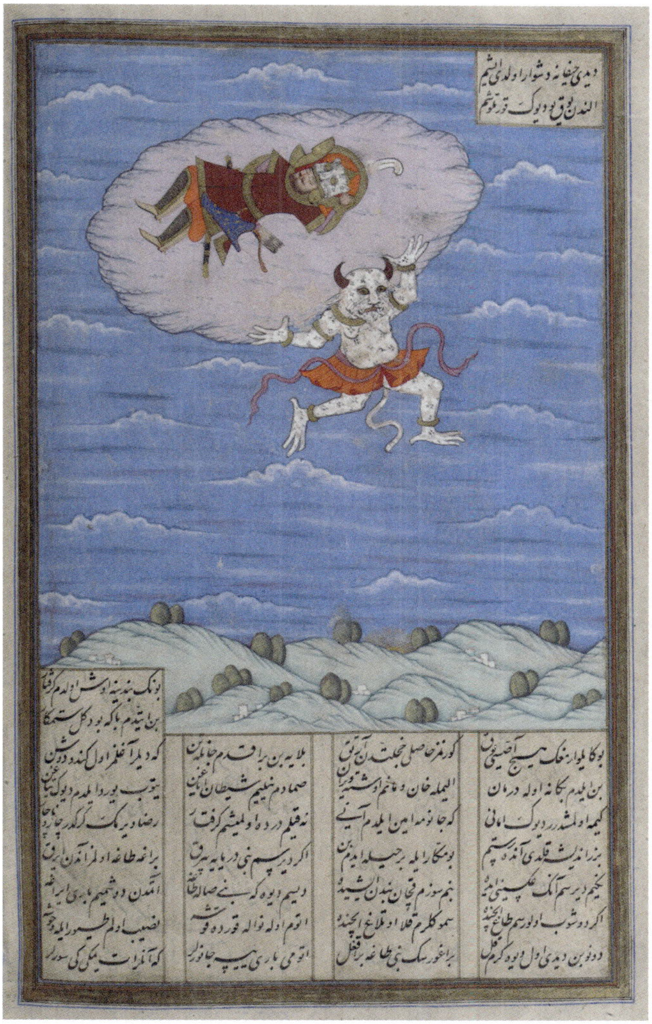

5.26 | The Akvan Div throws Rustam into the Sea, from a Turkish translation of the Shahnameh made in Istanbul, 1616–20. New York Public Library, Spencer MS 1, fol. 62

day and a night of fruitless searching for the *div* he felt tired, and lay down to rest. The demon found him asleep, but, rather than killing Rustam on the spot, he carefully cut out a big lump of soil and took it, with Rustam still asleep on top, down to the shore. Rustam woke up as the *div* was wondering whether to throw him into the sea or into the mountains. Since the hero was now awake, he was offered the choice. Rustam decided that the sea was the safer option, so he asked to be thrown into the mountains. The demon, predictably, threw him into the sea. Rustam swam back to shore, and, after various further adventures, cut off the *div*'s head (Warner and Warner 1908, 272–81).

This tale appears in the *Shahnameh*, a Persian epic poem that chronicles the deeds of the pre-Islamic kings of Iran, written by the tenth- or eleventh-century poet Ferdowsi.

Most of the *Shahnameh* is an account of historical figures, whose lives Ferdowsi researched in chronicles, but the earlier books contain mythical and fabulous material. Ferdowsi explicitly tells us that he considers this tale of the Akvan *div* to be incredible, and he encourages us to read it allegorically. Once the *div*'s head has been cut off, we are told the allegorical sense of the fable, which is that those who do not praise God and who "transgress the ways of manhood" are *divs*, not human beings (Warner and Warner 1908, 273, 281; cf. ibidem, 108; Nöldeke 1896, 36).

Even though Rustam frequently engages in adventures with *divs* and other exotic creatures, in none of which Ferdowsi's readers are likely to have believed, they will have thought that the tales of Rustam were based on a person who actually existed (Shahbazi 1993; Hämeen-Anttila 2017). Like Perseus, Rustam was taken to be a historical figure with fabulous accretions. The various unlikely stories told about Rustam resemble those told about Perseus in that they were not believed, but the difference is that, before Ferdowsi, they were not widely known either. In this they differ from the situation in Europe, where the mythology of an entire religion, which had been familiar to millions across the continent of Europe, fell into almost complete oblivion when Christianity replaced paganism as the official religion of the Roman empire, only to be revived as fable a thousand years later.

With the rise of Christianity, new myths were created, although students of myth would call them legends. Scholars who concern themselves with myths and legends are so used to distinguishing these concepts that, in the words of William Bascom (1984, 17), "they seem so obvious and self-evident that I can only wonder at the disagreements that have arisen". To recap, myths involve non-humans, in the remote past, in a world unlike that of today, while legends involve humans, in the recent past, in the world of today. It is indeed easy to slot certain narratives into these conceptual pigeonholes, so that the scenes in figs. 1.5 and 5.24 are surely myths, whereas those in figs. 5.2–5.4 are legends. But there are plenty of examples that seem to be in a borderland between the two concepts. Is the story of Laocoön (figs. 3.11–3.13) a myth or a legend? Perhaps that depends on how remote the past in which myths are meant to have taken place is thought to be. Non-humans were involved in the story; the snakes were sent by a deity, either Apollo or Athena or Poseidon. And what of fig. 4.15? The two figures on either side of the Buddha are gods, Brahma and Indra, so this should make the scene a myth. However, the Buddha was human, and in fact a human who is still thought to have existed, although his precise dates are controversial. That would make the scene a legend. Many illustrated narratives of the Buddha's life, the so-called *jatakas*, are of his previous lives, when he took on many different forms; in fig. 5.27 we see him reincarnated as a golden deer. Are these legends or myths?[15] Perseus and Rustam were human, but they sometimes engaged in adventures with non-human creatures like gods and *divs*. Should we think that scenes in which Rustam is fighting humans are legends, but that scenes in which he is fighting *divs* are myths?

The difficulty of making a clear distinction between myth and legend comes out if one adopts the point of view of those who believe in myths. For believers, myths are historical, because they were actual events that occurred at some point in time, even if the time in question is too remote to be known. The faithful will see no need

15 Dehejia 1990, 1997 refers to stories involving the Buddha as legends.

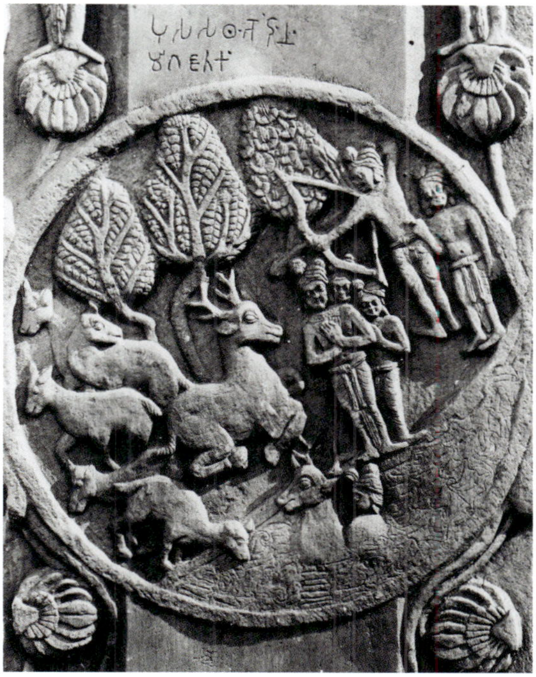

5.27 | Ruru-jataka, from the Stupa of Bharhut, Satna, Madhya Pradesh, 125–100 BC

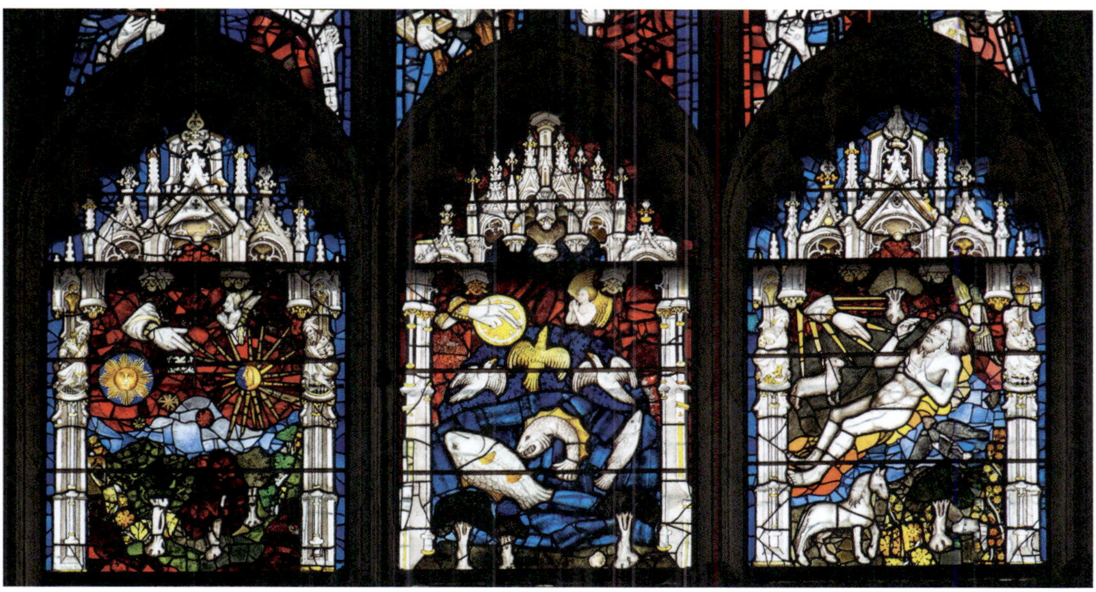

5.28 | The Creation, early 15th century. East Window, York Minster

for a distinction between this-worldly and other-worldly if they believe in the actual existence of the other-worldly. Even an occurrence as decidedly supernatural as the Creation of the World by God (fig. 5.28) was (and still is, by some) considered to be a datable historical event. In early modern Europe, a great deal of scholarly ingenuity was expended on tracing family trees back through mythological figures like Neptune and Wotan to Noah and so to God (Bizzocchi 2009; Trevisan 2018; Trevisan 2020). To draw the myth/legend distinction one must already have decided that the world can be divided into the mythical and the non-mythical, and those who believe in myths – that is, who consider them to be histories – have no incentive to accept such a division.

We will follow the received terminology and will refer to myths that involve human beings who are supposed to have lived in our world and our time as 'legends', even when, as in the scene of the Buddha with Indra and Brahma, they also involve supernatural beings. We will also refer to these events, as we did with myths, as legends while they are believed, but fables when they are no longer believed. As with myths, legends are defined anachronistically; that is, a legendary narrative is distinguished from a historical narrative by its retrospectively fabulous character. In Benozzo Gozzoli's cycle of paintings representing the life of St Francis in Montefalco, the scene of the saint walking through fire before the sultan (fig. 5.16) is now considered a fable, and as a result we think of it as a legend,[16] but the scene in the same fresco cycle of Pope Honorius III confirming the Franciscan Order is not a fable (fig. 5.29), since it is a historically attested event (even if it did not necessarily take place with the saint kneeling before the pope), so was also not a legend.

On the left-hand side of the fresco in fig. 5.29 we see St Francis holding up a collapsing church. This seems like an inherently legendary event, but, in the background, there is a scene of a pope in his bed, sleeping (improbably) in his tiara. The scene of St Francis supporting the collapsing church is not meant to be an actual scene of superhuman strength but a dream sequence, said to have occurred to Pope Honorius's predecessor, Innocent III. This dream may or may not have happened – our earliest evidence for it dates from 30 years after the dream is supposed to have taken place (Gardner 1989; Griego 2011). As a result, it is, so to speak, a legend in limbo. If the dream took place, it is a historical narrative, if the dream did not take place, it is a legend. Note here that when we talk of a legend being a fable or fabulous, we are not claiming that it is incredible or contrary to the laws of nature, although it might be; we are simply saying that it was thought to take place but did not. A current event can also be a legend if it is at first believed and then shown to be untrue – for example, the deliberately manufactured claim that Iraqi soldiers threw Kuwaiti babies out of incubators just before the 1991 Gulf War (MacArthur 2004; cf. Edwards and Cromwell 2006).

Legends can come into existence in various ways. They may emerge due to misunderstanding, or to rumours that take on their own life. They can also be crafted by

16 In fact the scene is doubly fabulous, since it did not occur even in legend. In Gozzoli's fresco the account of Francis's conversion of the Sultan of Babylon, as told in contemporary lives of the saint, is much altered. In the textual narratives Francis did not walk through fire before the sultan, and the sultan did not send a girl to tempt him. For discussion of these tales, their basis in fact, their fabulous elaboration and their representation in art, see Tolan 2009. For the fresco cycle at Montefalco, see Boschetto 1961; Ahl 1996, 23–32.

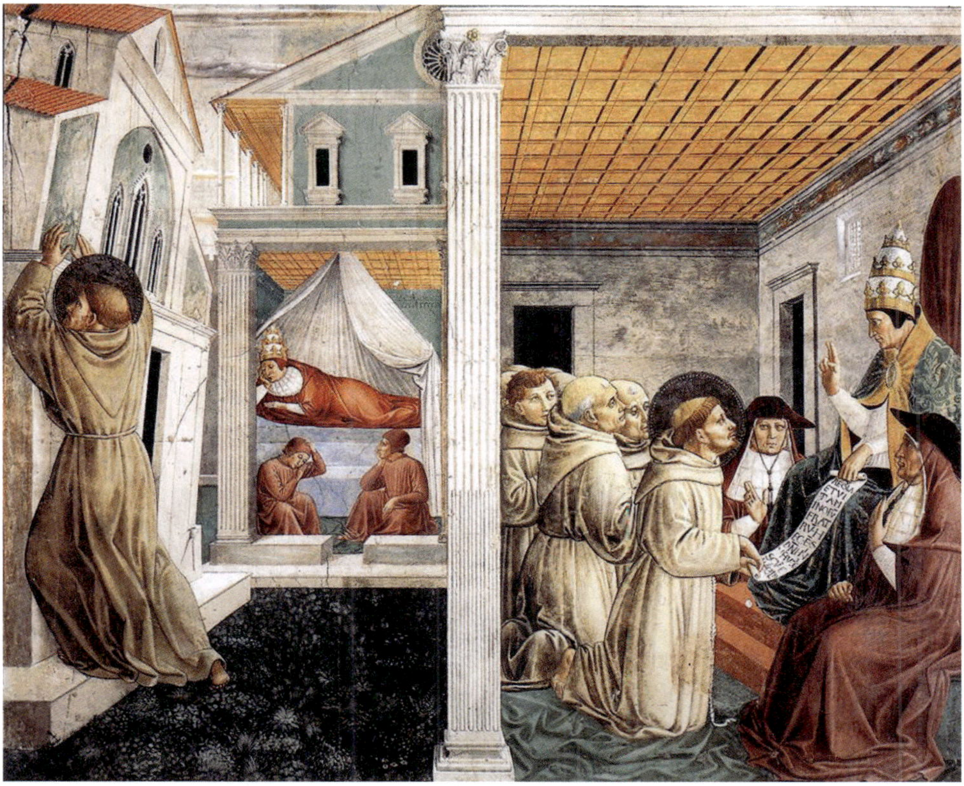

5.29 | Benozzo Gozzoli, The Confirmation of the Franciscan Order, 1450–52. San Francesco, Montefalco

deliberate invention, a narrative version of forgery. The story about Kuwaiti incubators would be one example, and many of the very formulaic stories about the saints were probably made up by hagiographers. St Mammas (fig. 4.23) is said to have been thrown to the lions, who instead of eating him licked him affectionately; the same story is told of so many other saints (p. 136) that it must have been a literary trope, employed by religious writers in an attempt to give their subjects an air of miraculous power. We might think of calling such fraudulent stories 'fictions', since they are consciously and intentionally invented, but they differ from literary fictions in that they purport to be true.

The priest Pero Ser Landi, the reader may recall, was "exceptionally devoted to the glorious saint and martyr St Mammas" (Bacci 1904, 164–45, cited on p. 136). Presumably Ser Landi believed the story about the lions to be historical fact. In his view, the lions' den tale was not a fable and not a legend. The image of the lions' den in Filippo Lippi's predella (fig. 4.23) was, for him (or would have been if he had been miraculously made aware of our jargon) a non-fictive representation. Those who think of the story of Mammas and the lions as a legend will be thinking of the image as a fictive, though specific representation. As with the Hindu story of Krishna and the water serpent (p. 142), there is no need to think of this as two conflicting truths. Pero Ser Landi may have been wrong to believe in this legend, and the Mammas sceptics may be wrong to doubt it.

What these examples show, again, is that merely looking at a depicted event will not allow one to ascertain the represented narrative; also that one and the same image of a depicted event may change meanings over time, as beliefs change. What is taken for a historical fact by observers at a given time can be taken for a myth or a legend at a different time.

Transmitting narratives

We said earlier that Delacroix's print (fig. 1.2) 'looks like' the gravedigger scene from *Hamlet* (p. 159). This seems like an unproblematic statement, but it creates philosophical complexities. One view of pictorial resemblance describes it as involving geometric similarity between an image and the object it resembles. Concepts such as 'occlusion shape' and 'outline shape' are used by philosophers who follow this line of reasoning. The idea is that the shape of the part of a picture that depicts an object must be geometrically similar to the shape of the object, as viewed from a particular angle (Hopkins 1998; Hyman 2006; cf. Kulvicki 2014b, 56–65).

However, when we say that Delacroix's print 'looks like' a scene from *Hamlet* we are saying something rather different. A scene from *Hamlet* cannot be viewed from a particular angle. A performance of the scene, or at least a moment of that performance, can be, but the scene as such is a more abstract notion. There are an indefinite number of dramatic realisations of Shakespeare's text, and these can be viewed from different angles, with actors of different appearances, in different costumes and postures, against different backgrounds and so on. Nevertheless, we can immediately recognize (if we already know the story and are primed by the context to expect Shakespeare) that an image resembles an event from the gravedigger scene, especially if the character of Hamlet is being passed, or is holding, a skull. We extract from images of this scene their narrative content, even though the images themselves differ in appearance from one another in numerous ways.

The 'narrative content' is in fact very slight; most of the marks made by Delacroix are not essential to the story. Neither Horatio nor the gravedigger must have beards, and Hamlet does not need his pair of tights, his broken nose, the feathers on his hat; there does not have to be a castle on a hill in the background, and so on. Should we say that there is a difference between the iconographic narrative and the visual narrative? That is, that this instantiation of the story (the visual narrative) should be thought of as telling an individual version of the (iconographic) narrative? In this sense, the image is something like a performance of a drama: the performance has its own identity. But a difference is that the drama is linked to the performance in the text, while, in a silent image, the text is absent (Goodman 1976, 210–11).

Among philosophers there is talk of the 'natural generativity' of images, by which they refer to the way that, once I have seen an image of a person or a building, I can recognize other images of the person and the building, even from unfamiliar angles (Schier 1996, 43–64; Sartwell 1991). Here we have something similar, but it is a natural generativity that is conceptual rather than illusionistic. To say that something 'looks like' a particular narrative is a kind of shorthand for a more complex claim, that various narrative conditions have been met by a certain image; that figures who can plausibly be read as figures from a particular story have been combined in such a way, and with, if necessary, the relevant props, to match an event (or a selection of events) from the narrative in question. However, as we have seen, to look like a narrative and to be a representation of that narrative are not the same thing. Fig. 1.2 looks like the gravedigger scene from *Hamlet*, but it also looks like other possible narratives. It could for example be a representation of body snatchers at work. If we decide that the print represents Hamlet at the graveside rather than a scene of body snatching, that is because we are assuming the iconography was designated as such by Delacroix and was accepted as such by most of his contemporaries. We are working with a set of meta-iconographic assumptions that are traditional within our society and many others, that the designator (understood to be the person who chose the iconography, not necessarily the artist) is the person who decides the representation of the image. Once again, it is designation that settles the iconographic issue. One can ignore the original act of designation and redesignate the subject at will, but, if so, this will be a fresh act of designation; it is only through designation that a unique representation can emerge from the plural possibilities of depiction.

Narratives are 'transmissive multiples' (p. 88) in that, once we have seen one image of a particular narrative, we will have a good chance of identifying another, if the contextual cues are in place. Since narratives are complex and there are many ways of representing them, with different backgrounds, different compositions, different attributes, or with different numbers of anonymous subsidiary characters (figs. 3.11–3.13), one representation of a particular story may differ from another to such an extent that the underlying narrative similarity is not evident. We are more likely to fail to see a narrative resemblance than a resemblance of attributes, for the simple reason that there are more possibilities for difference.

Narratives are more complex than attributes, but they operate in similar ways. Like attributes, they can be transmissive; and, like attributes, they must rely on designation.

6. Likeness

Likeness and designation

The developing technology of illusionism, from foreshortening and perspective through photography and film to computer generated imagery and virtual reality, has allowed us to see people we have never met, to know what places look like when we have never visited them and to follow events we never saw as if we were watching the action take place before our eyes. These experiences are so vivid that discussions of illusionism often focus on the cognition of visual deception, on the ways in which images can conjure up an absent reality (Gombrich 1960).

But besides creating imaginary sights, illusionistic technology has also had a profound impact on iconography. Photographic imagery can produce such fine-grained differentiation of motifs that it can generate an almost infinite variety of distinguishable images. These differences allow photographs to depict many more identities than traditional, manual methods, and so permit a far greater range of representational meaning. The attribute system of Buddhism allowed 3–4,000 Buddhas and bodhisattvas to be distinguished – imperfectly, as we have seen – but today photographs represent almost all the 8 billion people in the world, and much besides. It is the optical neutrality and precision of the camera that allows customs officials and facial recognition systems to match photographs to faces at borders. If on our identity cards we were all identified by symbolical attributes such as conches and maces, the surveillance society would never have come into being.

Despite this revolution, photographs and manually produced images that provide a good likeness of their subjects have meta-iconographic similarities to figures with attributes. Both photographs and attributes use transmission in order to establish their meanings. To bring this out, we can compare two series of images, one using attributes and the other using likeness as an iconographic device. If you visit churches in southern Germany, you frequently encounter paintings and statues that depict a soldier pouring water on to a blazing building (fig. 6.1a–e). These statues often do not have haloes, but, given that they are located in churches, you will think, rightly, that they represent saints, and you will hypothesize, with caution – remembering the case of Erasmus and Thiemo – that they all represent the same saint. But which saint? If you have not already been told, and if there are no inscriptions beneath the figures, you will not know. You can gaze at the saint for as long as you like, but that will not help. All you know is that there is a soldier saint who pours water onto a blazing building: you have no access to his name. Until, one day, you walk into a church and there you see a soldier pouring water onto a fire, with a banner on which his name is written: S. Florianus (fig. 6.2). From now on, whenever you see this saint performing this action, you will know to call him St Florian.

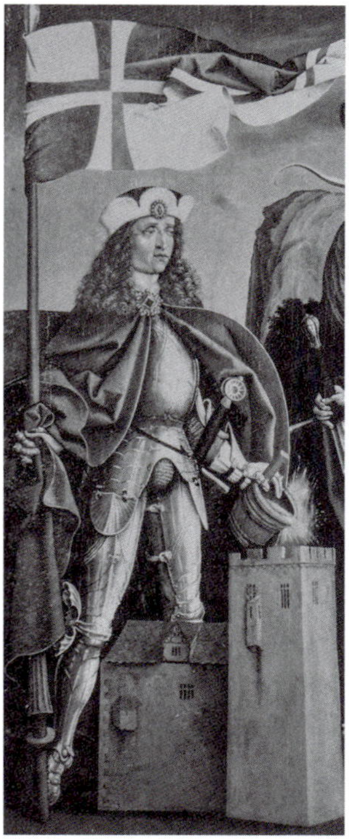
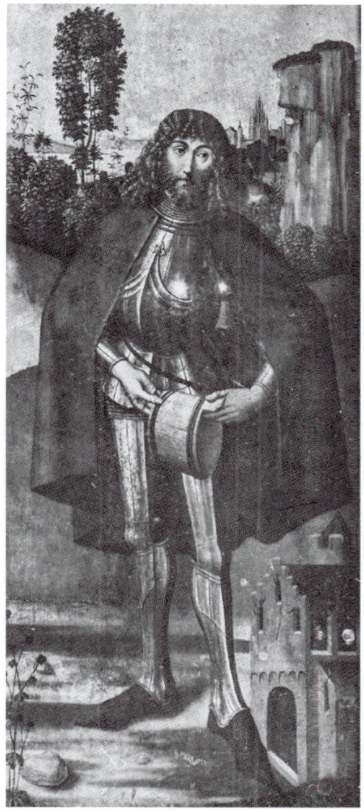
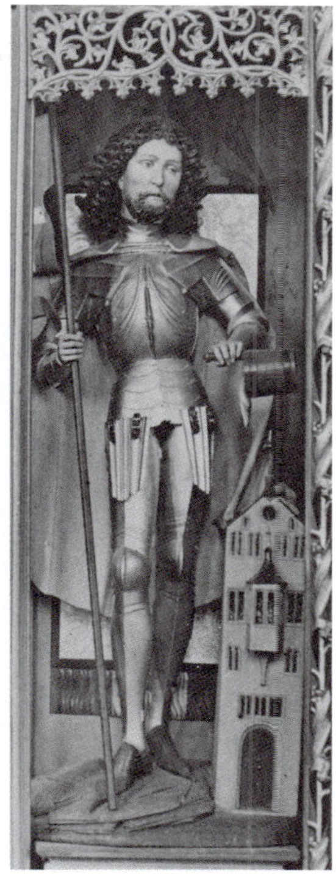
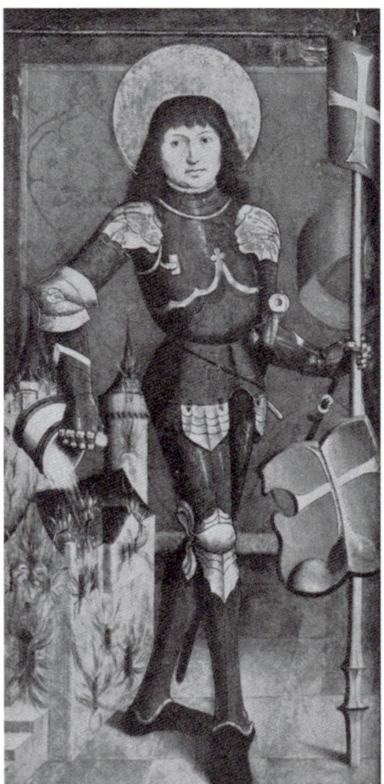
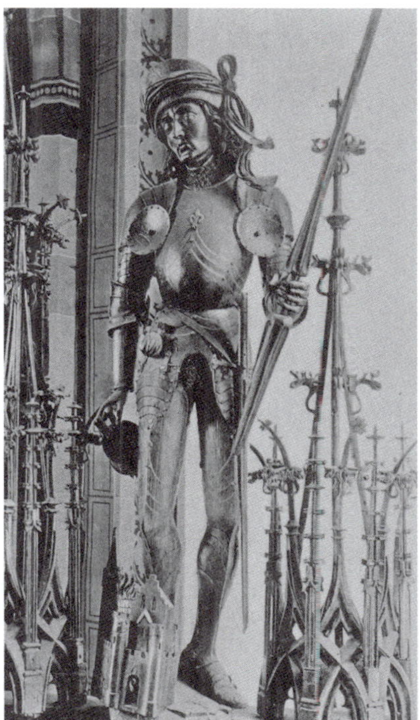
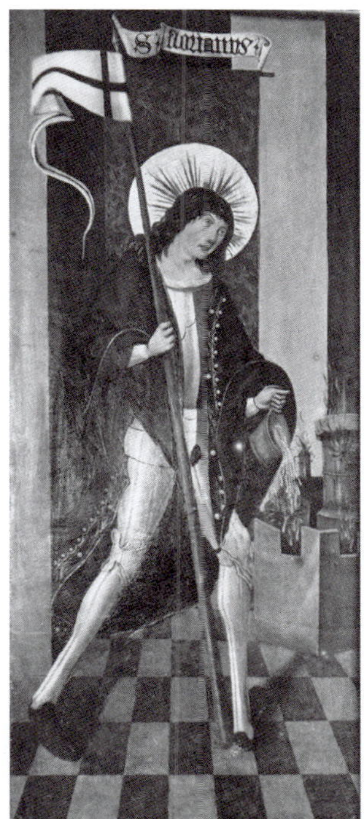

6.1a–e | Soldier saints pouring water on to a building on fire. Various locations, Germany

6.2 | St Florian

This is an example of how attributes are transmissive. An attribute will not, in itself, reveal the identity of the figure that holds it; the image has to be linked to language. Once one figure of a particular iconographic type has been connected with its name, then through the similarity of attributes other figures can also be connected to that name – assuming, again, that there is only one saint who has attributes of the kind. It might be thought that this feature of transmission is an outcome of the fact that saints are identified by attributes: one must learn the conventional meaning of the attribute to identify the saint. For anyone who holds a view like the one with which we began the introduction to this book – that images are no more conventional than mirrors – it might be thought that photographs and other realistic images do not face the same problem, since they give us immediate, non-conventional access to the identities of their subjects. However, transmission is also a feature of likenesses. To show this, consider fig. 6.3a–f. Here we see six portraits of a woman at different stages of her life, from her early twenties to her mid-sixties. It is fairly obvious that it is the same person, although one needs to follow the sequence closely; the second photograph looks like the first, and the third looks like the second, but the third looks less like the first. Nevertheless, her features act, so to speak, as her attribute, and the similarity between them functions like that between the buckets of water held by different statues of St Florian.

But who is she? We are in the same situation as with the unidentified saint. You can look at her face for as long as you like, but it will not tell you what she was called. Names are conventional, and they are given to us by designation; once we have received them, we must rely on the system of linkage to transmit them to others. This linkage can come about by simple oral transmission, as will be the case when our friends and acquaintances learn our name; or it can come about through a combination of text and image, as when our identity cards are checked, or our place of work puts up a board covered with staff photos, or our image appears in a book or on a website: but even then, the identifying caption will only be written next to our faces if we have already communicated our name, so it is an oral form of linkage that initiates the transmissive process. Some people appear in newspapers or books, in films or on television; again, they will need to have a name placed next to their face, or have it mentioned by another participant in the film, if anyone is to know what they are called. There are some people who are so famous that, when we see their face, we immediately know their name, but even superstars cannot be identified *a priori*; there was some day in the past when we learned what they were called for the first time.

The photographs in fig. 6.3a–f indexically depict a woman we have already met (figs. 2.9 and 2.10), Sarah Bernhardt. In the late nineteenth and early twentieth centuries she was the most famous actress in the Western world, and millions of people would have been able to recognize these photographs. Now her name is more famous than her face. Anyone who knows what Bernhardt looked like will normally be able to identify her in a photograph without the help of a caption. However, to do so, they must at some point have seen her name linked to her portrait, in a book, a journal or on a website. Some people will have connected name and face via the spoken word, at an illustrated lecture or on TV, but there must have been an occasion when her name became attached to her face in their minds. It is, again, a case of designation and linkage, with the original act of designation being Bernhardt acquiring her name – not, in this particular case, as an infant, because she was baptized Henriette-Rosine Bernard; she named herself Sarah Bernhardt when she began her acting career.

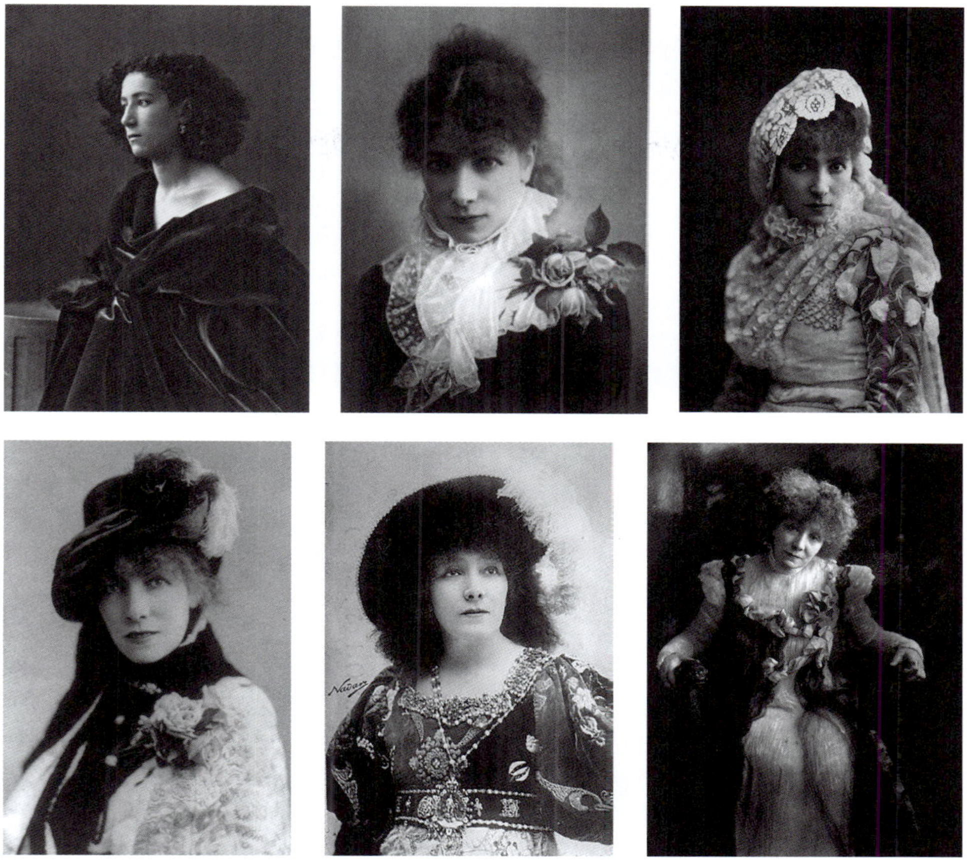

6.3a–f | Portraits to be identified

Is there, then, any difference between attributes and likeness? Yes, there is: from photographs of Bernhardt we learn what the actress looked like, but from images of Florian we do not learn what the saint looked like. Nevertheless, if we are trying to establish the identity of the person depicted in the image, both attribute-images and likeness-images function in similar ways. People's faces act as their personal attributes. Just as we cannot learn an individual's name by looking at their attribute, so too we cannot learn an individual's name by looking at their face.

The meaning of a physical attribute can easily be forgotten, so too face-attributes are frequently – in fact, usually – forgotten. Despite their mechanical reproducibility, photographs are sometimes singles. Fig. 6.4 is an example: this is a photograph I found inside an envelope in the home of my late uncle. Since no name was written on the back, and since this face does not correspond to any man in the captioned images from our family's photo albums, I do not know who the sitter is. Within the context of those photo albums, this photograph is doubly a single; it is the only print of this photograph, and the only photograph of this man. If this is the only photograph ever taken of this man, it

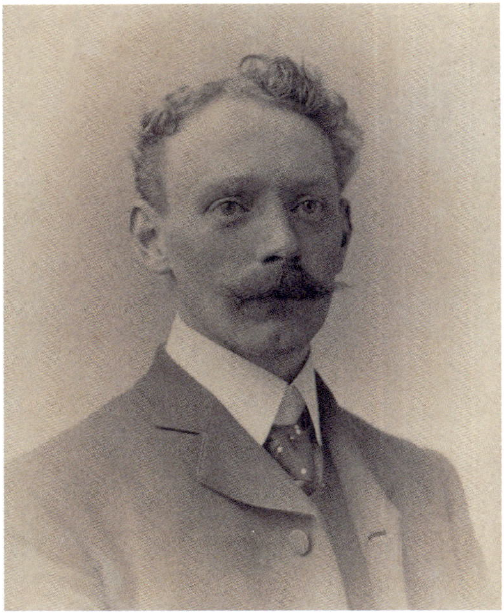

6.4 | English, Portrait of an unknown man, early 20th century

will be impossible for anyone in the world to identify him.

Now that this single has been printed in this book, it is no longer a single. Hundreds of reproductive multiples of the original single have been made. However, this gets us no closer to identifying the individual depicted, because none of the reproduced images is linked to his name.[1]

With an ancestor figure, we could not identify the individual represented without being connected to the chain of linkage to the original act of designation. The ancestor figure, however, did not resemble the individual represented sufficiently closely to allow individuation to take place. The photograph in fig. 6.4 does resemble the represented individual very closely indeed; and yet we find ourselves in the same position. Which suggests that, like attributes and narrative, the iconography of likeness is founded on designation and linkage.

The difference, it might be thought, is that images of Florian, or ancestor figures, need two levels of designation. To know that an ancestor figure represents Moawu, we need to know both the name that Moawu was given at birth and the fact that the ancestor figure represents Moawu. The ancestor figure looks very little like Moawu, so must be designated as Moawu if it is to represent him. The same is not true of the photograph of Bernhardt. Anyone who knows what Bernhardt looks like will know that the photograph represents her.

This is not quite the case, however, because a photograph that depicts Bernhardt does not necessarily represent Bernhardt; and when it does, it is not always a portrait of Bernhardt. In fig. 6.3, for example, four of the photographs show her in role as characters from plays. As such they are not portraits of Sarah Bernhardt, in the way that the other two photographs are. However, the other two photographs, as we will see in the next section, did not have to be portraits either; they could have been fashion photographs or stock photographs or some other kind of generic representation. If they are not, if they

1 In the preface to this book I wrote that "European and Asian imagery could be filed away on analogous principles, but I found it impossible to create a similar iconographic taxonomy for African, Oceanic and much of Amerindian art. This was due in part to the sheer number and variety of non-Eurasian cultures, and also to the scarcity of reliable iconographic information about some of them, but it was also due – although I was unaware of it at the time – to the difference between 'singles' and 'multiples', of which the reader will hear more below." The existence of multiples does not in itself permit iconographic identification to take place, but they are essential if one is trying to construct an iconographic taxonomy like that of pre-photographic Eurasia, since this largely consists of filing away multiples under iconographic headings. See Taylor 2022b.

function as portraits of an individual, that tells us something about their iconography in the context of their making. All six of these photographs could show Bernhardt in role, and if I can claim that two are not role photographs, that is only because I have relied on captions to tell me that they were meant as portraits. Their function was designated, and it has been communicated by linkage through captions.

While likenesses indexically depict individuals, not all likenesses specifically represent individuals. It is not simply a case of establishing an individual's name by linking back to the original act of designation; we also need to ascertain if the image represents a named individual, or an anonymous individual.

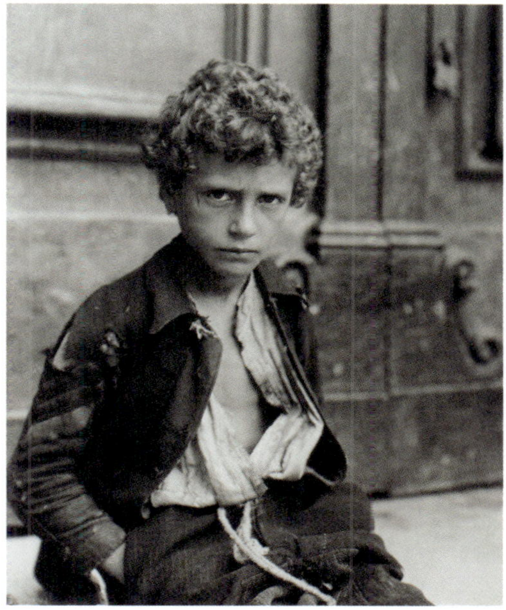

6.5 | Alfred Stieglitz, *Venetian Boy*, 1887 (negative) 1947 (print). The Philadelphia Museum of Art

Anonymous likeness

In the previous chapter we discussed anonymity in narrative imagery (pp. 177–84). All the examples given there were of non-photographic images, and few of the anonymous figures were indexical depictions of actual people (a painting by Manet provided an exception). With the invention of photography, the number of indexical depictions has enormously increased, but even though the individuals depicted by the camera are specific, in photography anonymous and generic representations are nevertheless widespread.

As an example, take fig. 6.5, a photograph by Alfred Stieglitz that is usually captioned *Venetian Boy*, although Stieglitz's original title was the more sentimental *Venetian Gamin* (Hoffman 2004, 84). What this boy's name was, and how he came to be sitting in rags when a passing American took his photograph, are facts unrecorded in the Stieglitz literature, and of course Stieglitz himself may not have known the answers to these questions. Whether the boy was happy to have his photograph taken (was he paid?) we do not know.

There is an important difference between *Venetian Boy* and a portrait that has lost its name. The photographs in figs. 6.4 and 6.5 both depict individuals who had names, but whereas fig. 6.4 seems to have been intended as a portrait and so was meant originally to represent a particular person, and will have been associated with his name by those who saw it, fig. 6.5 was presented by its creator and received by its public as a nameless representation of an individual. With the case of the man represented in fig. 6.4 we are dealing with identity loss, or identity ignorance, but that is not the same thing as representational namelessness – when the subject's name is not considered relevant to the meaning of the image. It is possible that someone, somewhere, has a family photo album that gives the name of the boy in fig. 6.5; or perhaps he could be identified through administrative files in Venice. But if it were discovered that the name of this boy was, say, Giovanni Vianello, that would not turn Stieglitz's photograph into a portrait of

Giovanni Vianello. The photographer and his public took this image to be a picture of a type, a *gamin*, an urchin.[2]

The Venetian boy in fig. 6.5 is presented without a name, but from his ragged clothes and his lively if ambiguous facial expression (a look of unhappiness? an angry glance of reproach?) he engages the viewer's sympathy and is presented to us as a person with a history, even though anonymous. A different presentation of the anonymous subject can be found in a widespread genre of imagery today, the fashion advert. Some adverts depict models who have become celebrities, but in many others, for example fig. 6.6, the name of the model is not widely known.[3] Those who are familiar with the fashion industry may recognize her as the Russian model Sasha Pivovarova, but this knowledge is not needed by those who view the advertisement. Her name is not as important as the brand name of the clothes she is being employed to sell. Anyone who reads the photograph as representing 'a model' wearing Giada clothes has understood the iconography of the image. This may be an indexical depiction of Sasha Pivovarova, but it is not a specific representation of her.[4] It is not merely that she is presented anonymously; her personality is elided by the conventions of the iconographic genre in which she is appearing. Like an actress, she is playing a role. Viewers who are invited to comment on fashion photographs by sociologists frequently discuss the personality of the model, but it is not the personality of the depicted individual that interests them; it is the personality of the character that the model is thought to be adopting (Crane 1999). Figs. 6.5 and 6.6 are both anonymous photographs, anonymous intentionally from the start, but the Venetian boy is represented as himself, while Pivovarova is presented as someone engaging in role play.

If, however, we compare the Giada advert with fig. 2.8, the still photo showing Charles Laughton in role as Rembrandt, or fig. 2.9, the postcard of Sarah Bernhardt in role as Hamlet, we see that role play comes in different forms. I suggested in Chapter 2 that these two photographs of Laughton and Bernhardt represented Laughton and Bernhardt, not Rembrandt and Hamlet. Now I am suggesting that fig. 6.6 does not represent Pivovarova but represents 'a model' playing a role. These intuitions of mine may not be shared by others. However, the models in fashion advertisements are often presented anonymously, whereas the names of actors appear in lights; it is surely right to say that anyone who looks at fig. 6.6 and can recognize Pivovarova does not have a better understanding of what the image is trying to do than someone who does not know her name. But someone who does not grasp that the clothes she is wearing are designed by a company called Giada has missed the iconographic point.

I also made the claim in Chapter 2 that 'when we see a photograph of an actor as Hamlet we tend to see the photograph as representing the actor, playing Hamlet', and added that 'this is true both when the actor is someone very famous whose face we can

---

2 For a nineteenth-century ode to the *gamin* as type, one which Stieglitz may well have read, see Victor Hugo's *Les Misérables*, 3.1.

3 Adverts representing celebrities are more common in some countries than others. My thanks to Fan Baiding for conversations about advertising in China, where celebrity endorsement is very widespread.

4 Cf. Scruton 1981, 579: "if a photograph is a photograph of a subject, it follows that the subject exists, and if x is a photograph of a man, there is a particular man of whom x is the photograph. It also follows, though for different reasons, that the subject is, roughly, as it appears in the photograph." This is true at the level of indexical depiction, but not necessarily at the level of representation.

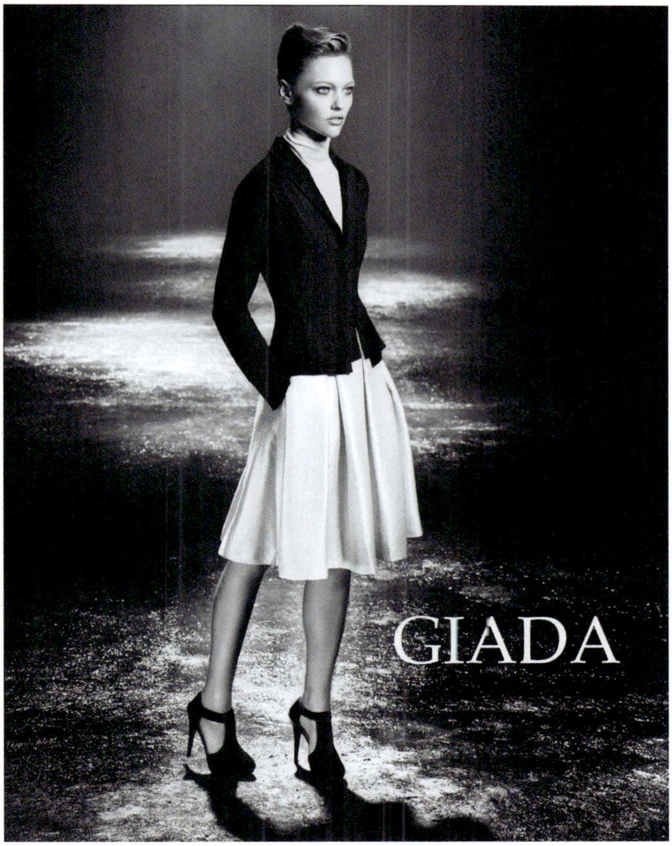

6.6 | Sølve Sundsbø, Giada Advertising Campaign, 2009

recognize and when the actor is someone whose face we do not recognize'. This may sound like a contradiction of the comments I have just made. But anonymity comes in different forms, as we have just seen; there are people whose names we unfortunately do not know (fig. 6.4) and people whose names we are led to believe we do not need to know (figs. 6.5 and 6.6). A photograph of an amateur actor playing Hamlet might fall into the first class, but a stock photo of an unknown person pretending to play Hamlet (fig. 6.7) might fall into the second class. We do not think of a photograph of this kind as a photograph of Hamlet, and we do not think of it, either, as a portrait of a specific person. At the website of Shutterstock, the company that owns this image, the photograph is captioned as follows: '"A romantic young man in a medieval costume with a sword says a Shakespearean monologue. The guy is holding a human skull."[5] The romantic young man has a name, of course, but his name is not of interest to prospective buyers of stock

5 Shutterstock, stock photo ID 1853862016, https://www.shutterstock.com/image-photo/romantic-young-man-medieval-costume-sword-1858460962 (accessed 17 December 2024).

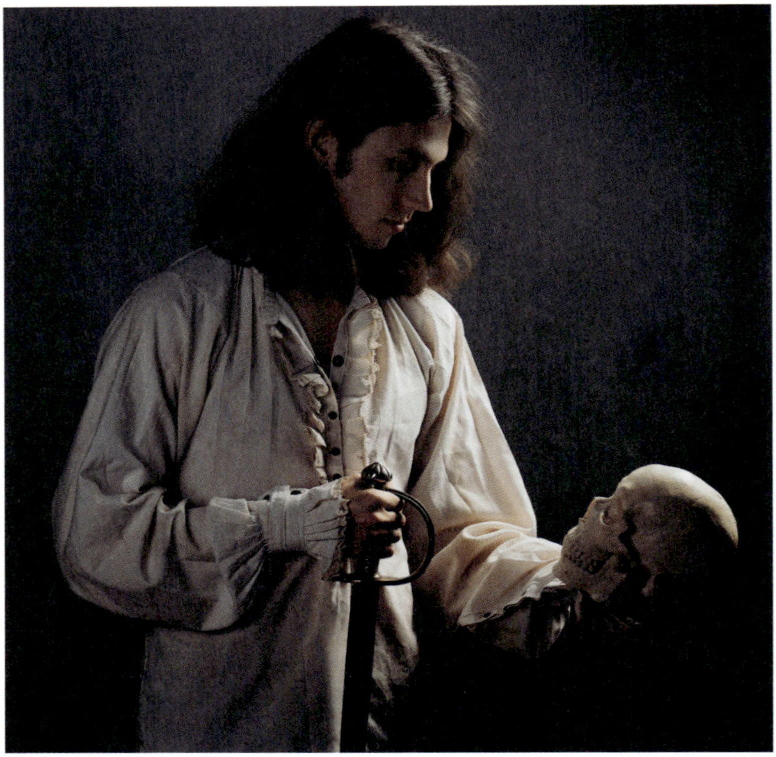

6.7 | Shutterstock stock photo, 'Hamlet'

photos. He doubtless has many photographs in his smartphone and elsewhere that are meant to be portraits of him, but this is not one of them.

Stock photographs do not normally show characters from Shakespeare; instead, they show people engaged in day-to-day activities, as well as places, animals, scenes from nature, material objects and so on. They are ubiquitous on websites, advertising hoardings and book covers, in newspapers, magazines and shops (Aiello 2022). The actors in stock photos are not normally famous enough to be identified. As a result, the photographs have all the generic anonymity of traditional genre paintings. Since they are often contextually ambiguous – just showing someone smiling, looking thoughtful, yawning, without our knowing why they are doing any of these things (although the answer will usually be: because the photographer asked them to) – the photographs can be used in numerous contexts. Indeed, the same photograph can be used with very different agenda. The photograph in fig. 6.8, for example, has appeared on the covers of books about language learning, scheduling, mind mapping, multicultural identity, suicide and Christian theology, as well as in numerous student-related handouts, articles, advertisements and websites. Other photographs of the same model made during a two-day photo shoot in 1996 have been used in over 33 countries around the world (Balliett 2020, 82). The model, Jennifer Anderson, was not a professional, has never modelled since, and was surprised when she began to encounter photographs of

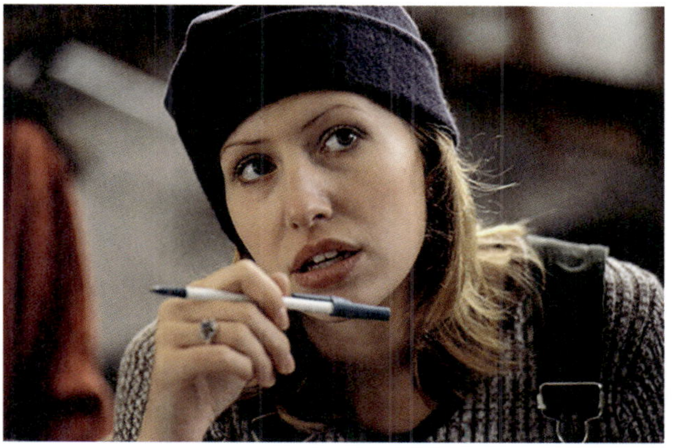

6.8 | Stock photo of Jennifer Anderson, 'The Everywhere Girl', 1996

herself in diverse promotional contexts. Others also became aware of her ubiquity and dubbed her 'The Everywhere Girl'.[6]

All the many published instances of these photographs are indexical depictions of Jennifer Anderson, but it would be strange to think of them as specific representations of her. If they were thought to be specific representations of Anderson, picture editors would not keep selecting these images repeatedly. Indeed, Anderson herself has said of 'The Everywhere Girl' that, in her family, "we always think of her as this other person, like, it's not really me".[7]

Does this photo represent anyone at all? When it appears on the front cover of a book about language, suicide or theology, few readers can suppose that it represents a particular language student, suicide risk or Christian; it is only meant to be a photograph on a cover. The photograph presumably appeals to so many picture editors because, in their view, it looks a bit like a language student, a suicide risk or a Christian, as well as showing a pleasant, youthful face that could attract book buyers. One might think of it as being designated as, and taken to conceptually represent, a generic language student etc., but perhaps even this is too precise. Maybe no representation at all is going on: maybe the photograph functions more like film music, communicating a mood. Those who see it, after all, know that it is a stock photo, of a model who was just posing for a camera.

Any photograph could be a stock photo; it could be sold to some business that wanted to create a particular mood, or to sell a particular product. However, while that is true in theory, some photographs have less possibilities for successful reuse than others. Anonymity, for example, is an important part of the stock photograph's effectiveness; it would be counterproductive to put an image of someone who is famously an atheist on the cover of a book about Christian theology, or someone who is well known for their

6 Anderson tells her own story on Facebook, and gives hundreds of examples of her photographs being reused: The Everywhere Girl, online at https://www.facebook.com/TheEverywhereGirl/ (accessed 17 July 2022).

7 In a vlog on Youtube: https://www.youtube.com/watch?v=jAyepggKyZs (accessed 17 July 2022).

optimistic, happy nature on the front cover of a book about suicide. Jennifer Anderson is a cheerful non-Christian, but fortunately she was a complete unknown when her photograph was chosen to grace theology and suicide books.[8] The models for stock photos are not celebrities, and indeed stock photo companies make it a condition that their models remain relatively anonymous for a number of years.[9] Anonymity increases the image's range of possibilities for reinterpretation.

Anderson was asked to pose in artificial situations, but not all stock photographs involve people acting parts. Some are shots of everyday scenes that find their way into the collections of stock photo websites (fig. 6.9). These can be commissioned from professional photographers or can be uploaded by tourists hoping to sell their holiday snaps. Iconographically, stock photos of unposed scenes, tourist photos (fig. 6.10) and documentary photos of unknowns (fig. 5.1) can be hard to tell apart. They all involve anonymity, but it is anonymity of a rather different kind to that we find in fashion photos or posed stock photos. In figs. 6.6 and 6.8 the anonymity involves the deliberate concealment of identities which are in fact known to the photographer, while in figs. 5.1, 6.5, 6.9 and 6.10 the anonymity is in part an outcome of ignorance, and in part of insouciance. The people depicted are not known because photographers and subjects are strangers to one another; but this is not thought to matter, because the names of the subjects are not needed for the images to elicit a response or fulfil a purpose.

Anonymity, of course, is a relative property. All the people in fig. 6.10 will be known to other people, and some of them appear to be known to one another. The photograph was taken in the Temple of Heaven Park in Beijing, where in the foreground we see someone standing on 'The Heavenly Centre Stone'. A nearby plaque says that "if one speaks standing on the Heavenly Centre Stone, their voice will be particularly resonant and sonorous", and tourists visiting this feature take it in turns to test the stone's acoustic properties. These days they also have their photographs taken on their friends' smartphones, and perhaps by other, passing tourists – including, in this case, the author. I do not know the names of anyone in this photograph, since to me they were all strangers, or perhaps it would be more accurate to say that I was a stranger to them.

What does this photograph represent? We might say that it generically represents tourists at the Heavenly Centre Stone. But given that everyone in the photo has a name and none are adopting anonymous personas, like Sasha Pivovorova and Jennifer Anderson, should we say that it specifically represents (to adopt some common Chinese names) Wang Mengying, Liu Qingqin, Zhou Shuchang and so on? It indexically depicts all these people, of course, but does it also specifically represent them? Clearly, I as the photographer do not think of the image as representing individuals with specific names, and neither do you (unless, as is most unlikely, someone in the photograph is reading this book, and can attach names to some of those shown).

Perhaps we should not worry about who it represents at all. What this example shows (and we have encountered this in other chapters, for instance in our discussion

8 Ibid. Anderson (now Jennifer Kind) is a counsellor and therapist who, on her website, writes that she is "the fearless leader and Happiness Alchemist of The Daring Happiness Revolution". https://www.yourtango.com/experts/jen-kind, (accessed 19 July 2022).

9 S. Woodstock, 'Interview with the most famous stock photography model in history', *Insiderdiva*, https://www.insiderdiva.com/interview-rebecca-givens/(accessed 16 July 2022).

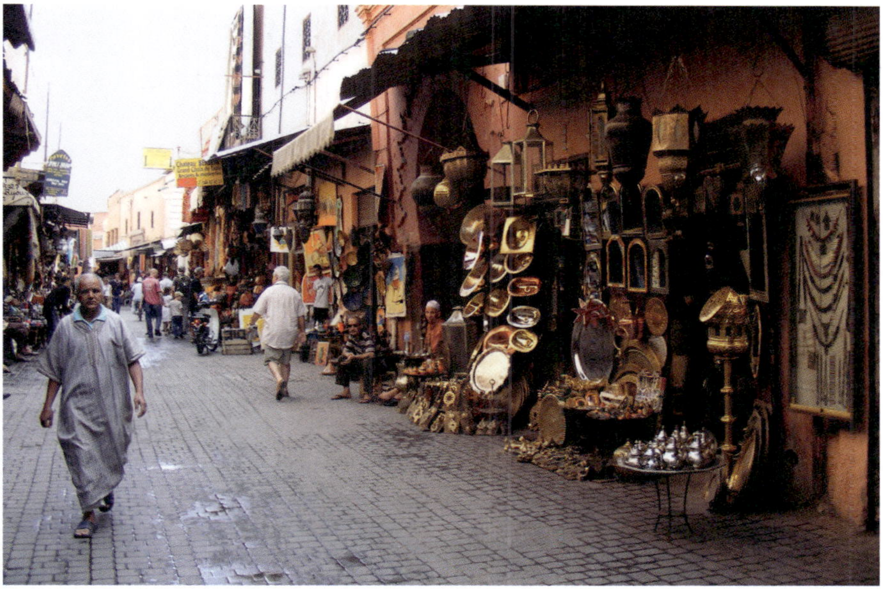

6.9 | Street scene in Morocco, 2017

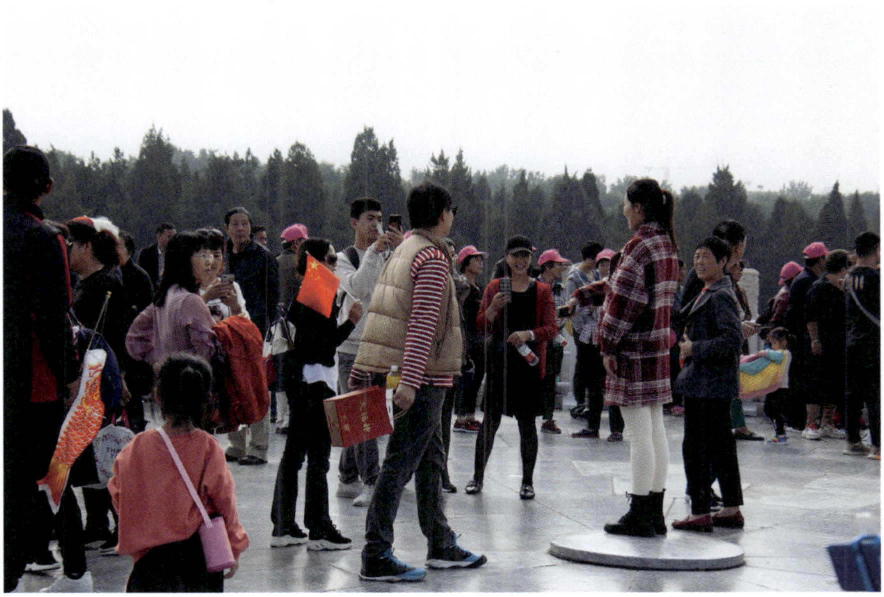

6.10 | Heavenly Centre Stone, Beijing, 10 October 2019

of fetishes in Chapter 3) is that, while the notions of generic and specific representation seem to fit some images well, with others they are not clearly applicable. That does not mean that we do not understand what is going on with images when it is hard to decide whether they represent specifically or generically. In this case we have a perfect understanding of the situation; it is a photograph of people who have names, but whose names we do not know.

Is fig. 6.9 exactly analogous? This is a view of the souk in Marrakech, freely available at various stock photo websites. It is widely used online in contexts concerning both Marrakech and Morocco by tour operators, travel blogs, newspapers, car hire companies and so on. Those who make use of it on their websites do not of course engage in research to discover the names of the various people depicted. Those who look at it online presumably just think of it as a view of the souk in Marrakech, or of a souk in Morocco, and do not spend much time considering the identities of the strangers we can see. From the very contexts in which it is used, in adverts and articles which are meant to be browsed quickly, the image encourages a superficial glance. Like sightseeing tourists, we gaze at the scene without considering the lives of the people before us.

In this case the subjects are presented as anonymous, and only the souk is named. Only the souk, in fact, is important, and the fact that the man at left happened to be walking towards the camera when the shutter was released is an irrelevant coincidence. The photograph would have fulfilled its purpose if he had been somewhere else at the time. Perhaps he provides some compositional balance, but someone else could have done that too. In fact, the photograph has been carefully composed to ensure that nobody is too prominent, because it is the souk, as a site of picturesque commercial transaction, that is the focus of interest. Fig. 6.10 on the other hand shows people interacting in a lively way, and for that reason it would make a poor stock photo of the Heavenly Centre Stone. One would need more stone, fewer distracting people.

As a final example of anonymity, we can consider fig. 6.11. Here we have a street scene with anonymous people in it, and one internationally famous person, Muhammad Ali. He is shown in the small Dutch fishing town of Volendam, signing autographs for two young women wearing traditional Volendam costume.[10] Ali was only in Holland for 24 hours, promoting the Dutch edition of his autobiography. A photograph of his signing for the young women appeared across the Dutch press the next day (Van de Vooren 2022).[11] We are not told their names, nor of the people in the street who clearly recognize Ali – when this photo was taken, in 1976, he had one of the best-known faces in the world. Perhaps if one went to Volendam one could establish some of their identities. But if one did find out their names that would not change the

10 They were not necessarily from Volendam. Just off camera to the right is a photographer's studio, Foto Zwarthoed, which took photographs of tourists in Volendam costume. The young women may have been tourists; or possibly they worked at Foto Zwarthoed but commuted from other towns. At this same studio a traditional fisherman's outfit had been prepared for Ali, in the hope that he would agree to be photographed in it. However, he refused (Rosman 2016).

11 The photograph chosen by the press was one from a few seconds earlier, when only one of the autograph hunters was visible. It also showed two Dutch celebrities, the photographer Ed van der Elsken and the TV sports presenter Ruud ter Weijden. Ter Weijden's leather jacket is visible at right in fig. 6.11. My thanks to Jeroen Stumpel for recognising Van der Elsken. There were too many celebrities in the earlier photograph to suit my discussion.

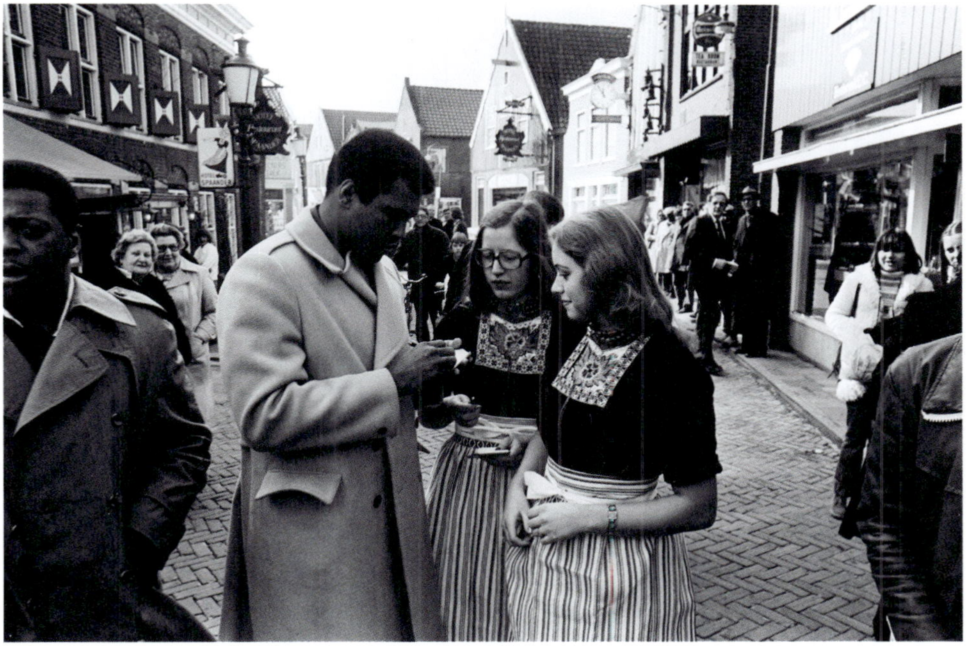

6.11 | Bert Verhoeff, Muhammad Ali in Volendam, 1976

iconography of the photograph, which is about Ali, and about the homage the obscure pay to the famous. The fact that these people are nameless is, in a way, part of the point.

These examples of anonymity show, yet again, that indexical depiction and specific representation do not always align, and that this is true also for images that employ likeness as an iconographic device. Understanding the conventions of anonymity is something one needs to understand not only for traditional sculptures and paintings but also for photographic imagery. Who in an image is understood as named, and who is anonymous? To answer these questions requires an awareness of the conventional ways in which photographs are perceived in different contexts. And there are also subtle differences of anonymity between documentary and tourist photographs on the one hand, and stock or fashion photographs on the other. We might agree that figs. 6.6, 6.7 and 6.8 are generic representations, but figs. 6.10 and 6.11 seem more, if not fully, specific.

In this discussion I have focused on photographs of people, but degrees of anonymity and definiteness can also be applied to photographs of material objects. A photograph can be of a mountain, or a volcano or Mount Damavand; of an Indian meal, or a chicken korma or the chicken korma served to President X; of a watch, or a Rolex or the Rolex worn by Elvis Presley, and so on. Not all objects have names, but they can be described using various levels of indefinite and definite description (Gombrich 1949, 72).

For any photograph, then, we need to establish its degree of definiteness. The same photograph can be of an anonymous thing or person to one viewer and a named or definite thing or person to another viewer. Viewer A might take a photo to be of a woman with a mountain in the distance, where viewer B might take it to be of the actress

Negar Javaherian before Mount Damavand. However, it is not only a question of one's knowledge of identities; in certain contexts, identities will be intended, and will form part of the meaning of the photograph in context. If a photo of Javaherian before Damavand is used as a film poster it will clearly have a different iconographic intent to the same image sold as a stock photo. Iconographies can change from context to context, but most do not, and the viewer needs to understand which of the possibilities were designated (or redesignated) in the context of use. The question then is how the designated meaning can be conveyed. However this takes place, it will not be due to the likeness in itself.

Ignorance

With the invention of the camera, images began to transcend their makers' ignorance. To give an example of this, consider the depiction of trees. Very few artists before the mid-seventeenth century were able consistently to depict botanically identifiable tree species.[12] Trees are very complex to draw; their boughs fork in intricate ways, their bark and trunks differ from species to species, and each of their leaves, which number in the tens of thousands on a full-grown tree, twists and turns at a different angle (Ruskin 1843–60, 1.391). Even the Dutch landscape painter Jacob van Ruisdael, who has impressed modern botanists with his ability to distinguish the characteristics of individual species of tree (Ashton et al. 1982), was reduced to suggesting leafage by scattering dots of paint. And most of his contemporaries, most of the time, depicted generic trees that could be said to be deciduous or coniferous, but little more specific than that.

In a photograph, on the other hand, if it is in focus, the botanist will be able to identify each tree with fair accuracy, even if the photographer (like most of us) can only identify a few species. Painters can try to depict the species they know, by sight or by name, and will probably fail to make a convincing depiction of those; but photographers succeed in depicting species they do not know, whether they like it or not.

Many other forms of information can be captured by the camera despite the photographer's ignorance. Margaret Mead, writing about the uses of photography in anthropology (1963), observed that "Photographs can record a large amount of observation which the anthropologist either lacks the scientific sophistication to record or for which the methods of analysis have not yet been developed .... Photographs taken by one observer can be subjected to continued re-analysis by others". The same is not likely to be true of an 'ethnological' painting, such as this seventeenth-century Dutch representation of a native dance in what is now Brazil (fig. 6.12) (Brienen 2006, 95–129). If the painting were to be "subjected to continued re-analysis by others", the artist would have had to have made an accurate rendition of the dance. Given the vagueness of the plant and armadillo depictions, and the strange aimlessness of the dance itself, it is hard to have much faith in the artist's veracity, and this is not surprising. When faced with a complex and unfamiliar set of actions performed by people whose language one does not understand, it is almost impossible to draw what is happening with complete fidelity, even if one is trying to do so.

---

12 For an amusingly scathing analysis of seventeenth-century tree painting, see Ruskin 1843–60, 1.380–99. To give the flavour: "But the old masters are not satisfied with drawing carrots for boughs. Nature can be violated in more ways than one, and the industry with which they seek out and adopt every conceivable mode of contradicting her is matter of no small interest" (385).

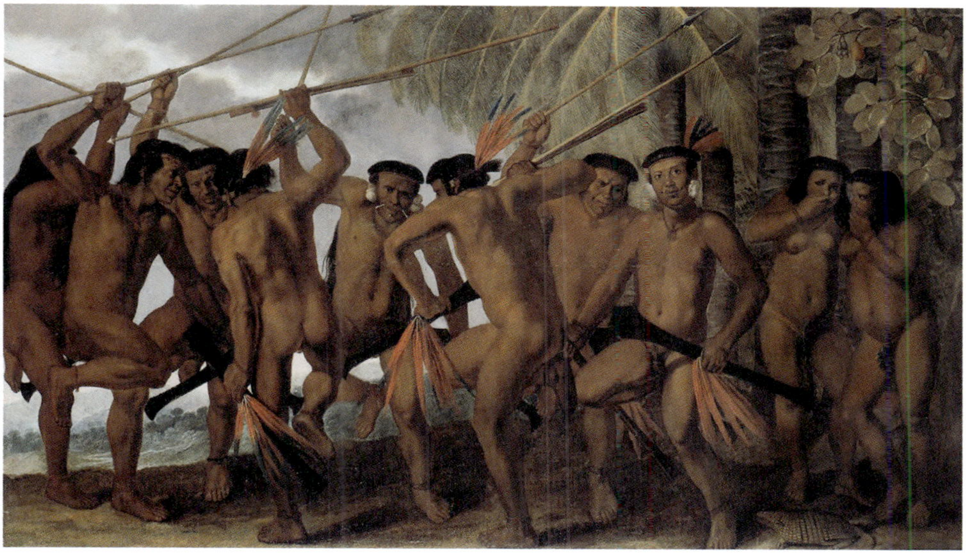

6.12 | Albert Eckhout, Tupayu Dancers, 1643. Nationalmuseet, Copenhagen

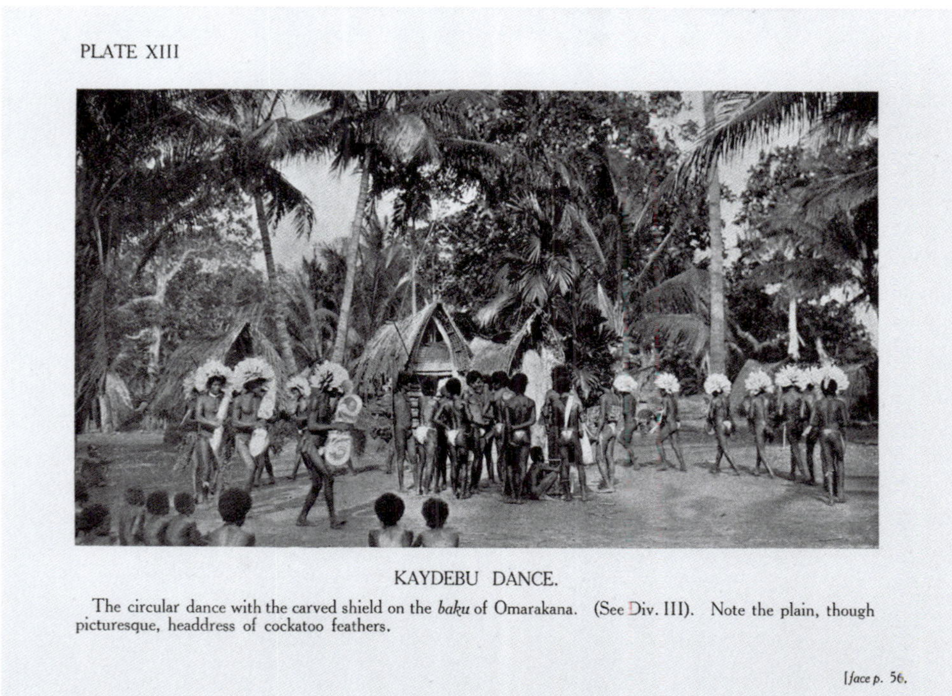

PLATE XIII

KAYDEBU DANCE.

The circular dance with the carved shield on the *baku* of Omarakana. (See Div. III). Note the plain, though picturesque, headdress of cockatoo feathers.

[*face p.* 56.

6.13 | Bronisław Malinowski, 'Kaydebu dance' (Malinowski 1922, pl. XIII)

Anthropologists photographing a dance may also not have an entire understanding of what they are witnessing, but with a camera in their hand they have a good chance of recording it accurately. Bronisław Malinowski included a couple of photographs of Trobriand Island dances in his *Argonauts of the Western Pacific* (fig. 6.13). In the caption to this one we are told that the photograph shows a *kaydebu* dance "on the *baku* of Omarakana": the *baku* is a central space, or village green, and Omarakana is a village. In the text itself we are not told much more, but in a different publication, 'Baloma; the Spirits of the Dead', Malinowski described such dances in more detail (Malinowski 1916, 380–81).[13] It becomes clear from the account in 'Baloma' that the captions in *Argonauts* are confusing, and that this may reflect some confusion on Malinowski's part. We are told in the *Argonauts* captions that the '*kaydebu* dance' is "the circular dance with the carved shield", as if the dance's official name was *kaydebu* and there was only one of them. However, the *kaydebu* was the 'carved shield' itself. A number of different dances were performed with the *kaydebu*, none of which seem to have been called *kaydebu*. It does not appear that Malinowski knew the names or significance of all of these dances, and it is also not clear that he knew exactly what a *kaydebu* was, or what it signified. More recent scholars call these objects 'dance paddles' or 'dance wands'; they do not look like Trobriand war shields and were not used in warfare, so there seems little point in calling them shields (Young 1998, 92–94; Young and Beran 2016; Beran 2011). But despite this atypically hazy area of Malinowski's ethnological knowledge, his photographs are important documentation for anyone interested in the history of Trobriand dances and *kaydebu* carvings, and this accords with his view on the value of the camera to the ethnologist. In some criticisms of his own anthropological method, he wrote that "I treated photography as a secondary occupation and a somewhat unimportant way of collecting evidence. This was a serious mistake. In writing up my material on gardens I find that the control of my field notes by means of photographs has led me to reformulate my statements on innumerable points" (Malinowski 1965, 461; Poignant 1992, 65).

It would be easy to give more examples of photographs that tell more than their maker knew; in fact, it would be hard to find one that did not. There will always be an observer who knows more about some aspect of a photograph than the photographer. Where does this leave the theory of iconographic designation? The answer surely is that photographs of this kind are operating in a way which is similar to the representations of anonymity we discussed in the previous section. In fig. 6.13 the village is named and the dance is named (generically), but the people are not named, the trees are not named and the specific dance that is taking place is not named. This is what we expect from a photograph; we do not think that every person or object has to be identified: we accept fuzzy representation. Malinowski has designated the iconography of his photograph as being a '*kaydebu* dance', and most readers of his book will not trouble to redesignate the photograph to extract more information. But some will, and they may give it a new caption, and say that what we see here is in fact a *gumagubu* dance (Malinowski 1916, 380; Young 1998, 92–93). And perhaps too the photograph may fall into the hands of botanists, who for reasons of their own may find the trees in the background of interest, and who may publish it as a representation of early twentieth-century Trobriand

13 This publication appeared six years before *Argonauts of the Western Pacific*; I do not know why the later publication seems less well informed on these dances.

arboriculture. The photograph can have any number of representations attached to it, depending on the interests of the viewer or user, but it will never be taken to represent every individual and every tree in the shot. Conceivably, it could be, but in practice the iconography of photographs always allows a certain indeterminacy. Part of designation is deciding how much indeterminacy to allow.

Identity

When we consider a likeness, we need to ask what it is a likeness of. This may seem like a question with an obvious answer, and some theorists of the photograph have suggested that it is indeed obvious. Roland Barthes, in a famous essay on 'the photographic message', proposed that a photograph transmits a scene in a direct, unmediated way, providing "a perfect *analogon*" of reality, but that, through various strategies of treatment and rhetoric, the *analogon* can become invested with cultural connotations (Barthes 1961, 128, 130). There is no doubt that photographs are replete with cultural connotations, but the cultural construction already occurs at the most basic meta-iconographic level, because we think of photographs as reproducing not reality, but reality as conceived in particular ways.

We cannot transmit a scene in a direct, unmediated way, because when we think of a photograph as representing an object we think of it as doing more than it is in fact doing. To give an example, a photograph of a tree is not a photograph of the whole tree, including its roots and heartwood and sapwood; these parts of the tree are hidden from sight by earth and bark. If the tree is in leaf its branches and shoots are also invisible behind the foliage. And one can only photograph one side of the tree; the rest of the tree is hidden from sight. So to say that a photograph depicts a tree is perhaps a kind of shorthand; what we mean to say is that the photograph depicts as much of a tree as can be seen from a particular vantage point. And yet this seems wrong: we tend to think that a photograph of a tree is a photograph of a tree, as if the plant's whole identity were captured in the image.[14]

Similarly, a photograph of a person is not merely a record of what they look like. People are more than their appearance, and someone who only knows what Sarah Bernhardt looked like, but does not know that she was a famous actress, had many lovers, was a talented painter and sculptor, wrote two novels, an autobiography and a book on acting technique, and so forth, does not know much about her. Someone who knows a great deal about Bernhardt's biography but, by some strange chance, has never seen a photograph of her, has a fuller conception of her identity than a Parisian shop owner with no interest in the theatre, who lived in Bernhardt's neighbourhood and knew her by sight but did not know her name, or even that she was an actress.

Our imaginary Parisian shop owner might be able to identify all of the photographs in fig. 6.3 as depicting the person who sometimes came in to buy items from his shop, but these photographs do not represent the person who bought from his shop. They represent Sarah Bernhardt. It might also be said that they represent the author of *L'Art du théâtre*, even though all six photos show her at a time of her life when she had not yet started writing that book (Bernhardt 1923). A photograph of Bernhardt in her early

14 A photograph of a tree in a biology textbook might be taken to represent not that tree, but any specimen of that particular species (Jonas 1961, 167–68).

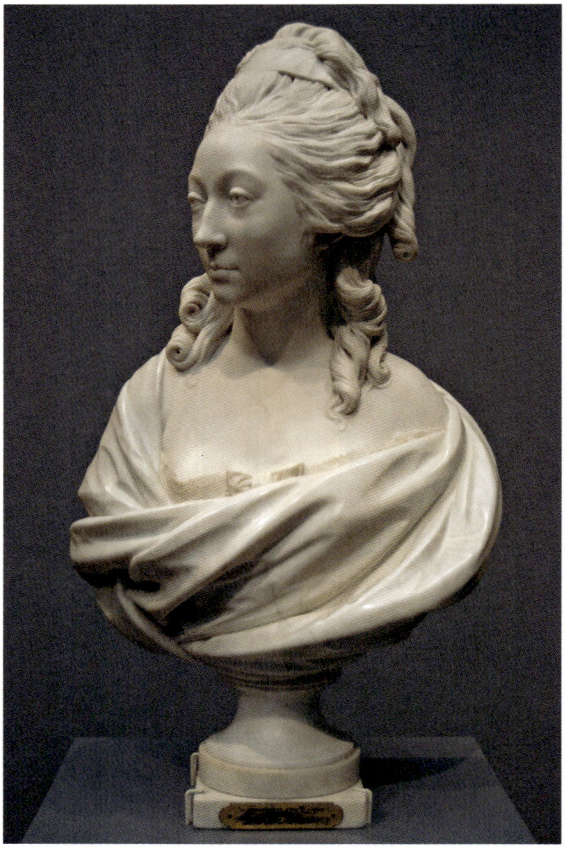

6.14 | Jean Antoine Houdon, Bust of Anne-Marie-Louise Thomas de Domangeville de Sérilly, Comtesse de Pange, 1780. Art Institute of Chicago

twenties is just as much a photograph of Bernhardt as a photograph of her as an old woman, even though, at the time the former was made, she still had her adult life and achievements before her. Photographs represent individuals, and when we look at them we do not suppose that they are just captured reflections of a face at one particular instant, even though that is what, in fact, they are.

This also applies to physical objects. Take the photograph of the sculpture by Jean-Antoine Houdon in fig. 6.14. This photograph, which I took myself, came into existence on 1 November 2015, in the 42nd second of the minute beginning 2.52 pm, Central Standard Time. This precise information, however, is of no interest to anyone. If I had taken it five minutes earlier, ten days later, or fifteen years earlier it would have looked much the same. And it is not merely a matter of visual similarity. We do not think of photographs as being images of how something looked at a particular instant. This is a photograph of Houdon's bust of the Comtesse de Pange. We do not take it to be a photograph of Houdon's bust of the Comtesse de Pange at 2.52.42 CST on 01/11/2015, even though that is what it is. Photographs, so to speak, represent more of things than we can see; we take them to be representations not of a state of affairs *s* at micro-second *t*, but of things that have some identity over time.[15]

It is rare for the details of where and when a photograph was made to matter. The camera is usually invisible in the images it produces, so it is easy to forget that it was there. Looking at photographs as, so to speak, half a scenario, with the photographer and the camera in the other unseen half, is not so easy to do, and most of us imagine ourselves viewing the motif as if there was empty space where the camera once was.

The point of these examples is to show that an image that is a likeness of an individual is not merely reproducing the appearance of a person or thing. At the level of indexical depiction, it could be thought of as a likeness of a particular individual or object made at a specific time, but at the level of representation it takes on a different sense. A photograph represents aspects of its subject's identity, and which aspects are represented will be governed by conventional, meta-iconographic attitudes.

In this respect, likenesses and attributes are performing very similar functions. The attribute and the likeness both pick out personages, and the resultant image represents that personage. An image of Bernhardt as a young woman or Bernhardt as an old woman both represent Bernhardt; and an image of St Florian with or without facial hair represents St Florian. The fact that we do not know what St Florian looked like, nor indeed if he existed, and that any image of him is almost certain to be an inaccurate rendition of his appearance (if he had one), does not stop an image of the saint representing him. One might argue that the saint as represented is not identical with the historical person (if there was an historical person) who was killed for his Christian beliefs and on whom the saint's identity was based, and the same perhaps is true even when a saint was in fact an historical personage, such as St Paul or St Jerome. But a non-existent saint is also an individual, since even specific fictive entities are individuals.

Our intuitions about how images represent things and individuals are complex and may shift from person to person, object to object, but it is not a simple matter of the image reproducing a motif. The motif needs to be conceptualized (cf. the discussion of conceptual depiction on p. 44 above). That is true even when we are dealing with images, like photographs, that have a direct, optical relationship with a motif; the physical simplicity and fidelity of the process by which the photograph is made do not alter the fact that the resultant image is taken to have a conceptually rich relationship to the subject it depicts and represents.

Iconology of photography

With some images, we take the maker's intention to establish its iconography. For example, there has in the past been a debate in the art historical literature about whether the man in the painting by Rembrandt in fig. 2.11 represents Aristotle, Apelles, Virgil, Albertus Magnus, Ludovico Ariosto, Torquato Tasso or Pieter Cornelisz Hooft (Liedtke 2007, 630–54).[16] Scholars who have taken part in this debate have assumed that the issue at

---

15 For a different view, that "the sense of the moment is seldom lost in photography", but that portrait painting "aims to capture the sense of time and to represent its subject as extended in time", see Scruton 1981.

16 Most scholars today hold to the Aristotle theory.

stake is who Rembrandt intended the figure to be. Rembrandt is thought, so to speak, to own the iconography, to take the decisions on the identities of the figures he created.

It is not always, or perhaps often, the case that the artist's intention settles the representation, as we have seen (p. 43 above). A factor in this process is the conventionality of the iconography. Rembrandt's subject of a man contemplating the bust of Homer is extremely rare, so nobody looking at the painting can be expected to identify the man without some connection to the original chain of designation and linkage. With a painting such as Leonardo's Last Supper (fig. 1.1), on the other hand, the iconography is widely known, and nobody needed to ask Leonardo what he meant by it. This has a further corollary, which is that if Leonardo had had unusual ideas about what the iconography meant – a scenario we imagined in passing in Chapter 1 (p. 30) – nobody at the time would have revised their view of the painting's iconography in the light of the artist's opinions. Painted on the wall of a Dominican refectory, a painting that looked just like a Last Supper would be a Last Supper. According to the iconological attitudes of the time, it was the Church, not the artist, who had the authority to decide such matters. Similarly, in Vasari's *Lives* we read that Leonardo's contemporary Pietro Perugino "was a person of very little religion, and he could never be made to believe in the immortality of the soul" (Vasari 1568, 1.515),[17] and, if this is true, then when he painted the Virgin or Christ he presumably held heretical views about the figures he was painting; but when they were hung up in churches they were thought to represent the Virgin or Christ as understood by ecclesiastical orthodoxy, because Perugino's opinions, whatever they were, were not relevant to their identity.

Similar processes govern photographs: iconological convention can overrule the photographer's conception of their own photograph's iconography. I took the photograph in fig. 6.10, but if I were to claim that it represents a scene from a play that I had written, called *The Adventure of the Stone of Heaven*, and if I were to give names to the people in the photograph after the fictional characters in my play, then I would meet a certain amount of iconological resistance, because people would expect its representation to align more closely with its depiction. It depicts not characters from my play, nor actors acting the parts of the characters in my play, but a group of people who have never heard either of me or of my play, and so people would tend to think, given the iconological conventions surrounding photographs in our society, that it cannot have the dramatic meaning I tried to give it. Rembrandt, on the other hand, could in theory have been illustrating a scene from a play he had written; if correspondence in his own hand were discovered in which he claimed to have done so, art historians would take it seriously, but they would not take my claim about my photograph seriously (even if I had in fact written the play).

Rembrandt entirely invented his own subject; he created every inch of the image (possibly with the assistance of his workshop). This gives him a power of designation that the photographer does not have. The photographer is capturing an image of a scene in the real world, which has its own meaning, and this – again, within the iconological conventions of our time – limits the iconographic scope of the photo.

17 For arguments to suggest that, on this occasion, Vasari can perhaps be trusted, see Guidoni 2004.

This does not mean that I have no designatory power over the photograph; it is just more restricted than it would be if I were painting a picture. I have given fig. 6.10 the caption 'The Heavenly Centre Stone, Beijing', but I could have called it 'Tourists in Beijing' or 'An Overcast Day in Beijing'. In different contexts, if for example it were used to illustrate magazine articles, it might be captioned 'Crimson is this Year's Colour in China', 'Smartphones Capture Fifty Billion Photos A Day' and so on. In all five of these captions the anonymity of the people depicted is taken for granted, in two of them the anonymity of the city is taken for granted and in one of them the anonymity of the country is taken for granted. If I had known some of the people in the shot, I might have pencilled on the back of the photograph 'Zhou Shuchang snaps Wang Mengying', turning it from an anonymous image into a portrait. I have some iconographic leeway, but less than Rembrandt.

Iconological convention governs representation, controlling what is iconographically permissible. Since what is permissible is what is expected, it can also be used to generate deception. It is not merely that viewers of photographs tend to assume that they indexically depict what they are said to represent, and will assume that, to return to an earlier example (p. 157), a film purporting to represent Libyans rejoicing at the death of Muammar Gaddafi does not depict a scene at an Indian political rally. Genre conventions can also be used to mislead. Take the aerial photograph of the 'Al-Mamoun Solid-Propellant Production Plant' in fig. 6.15, which appeared in a C.I.A. white paper in October 2002. According to the accompanying text (C.I.A. 2002), the photograph showed that buildings that had been used to manufacture solid propellant for rocket motors and had been destroyed in the first Gulf War had been rebuilt, and that "the only logical explanation for the size and configuration of these mixing buildings is that Iraq intends to develop longer-range, prohibited missiles". In response to this claim, UN weapons inspectors visited the Al-Mamoun plant, but found no evidence of prohibited activity (Drogin and Farley 2003). The fact of their visit reveals the guile of the photograph. The C.I.A. published an aerial photo of the site, when they did not need to. Iraq was open to UN weapons inspectors; as the American inspector David Kay observed, "Al-Mamoun is a facility that inspectors can go to and sit on top of. You can be sure whether castings are being made for non-approved missiles" (Watt and Pallister 2002). C.I.A. agents could have driven there and photographed it from the ground. By publishing a photograph from the air, they gave the impression that they were forced to acquire information surreptitiously; that the Iraqis had something to hide. The strong implication was that the photograph both represented and indexically depicted a solid-propellant production plant, rather than a former solid-propellant production plant.

It might be questioned whether the conventions associated with military aerial photographs are iconological or logical. From the fact that a photograph was taken from the air it may be concluded that one could not have been taken from the ground due to the territory being in hostile hands. Is that an iconological convention, or a practical deduction? It is not easy to draw a clear distinction; when we decide that Leonardo's Last Supper does not represent a group of characters who like to make ceramic facsimiles of foodstuffs which they enter into competitions, we are surely basing this conclusion on our iconological assumptions about the kinds of iconography we might expect in a Dominican refectory; but is this not also a practical deduction? We might think of iconology as being the practical deductions we make about the effects of

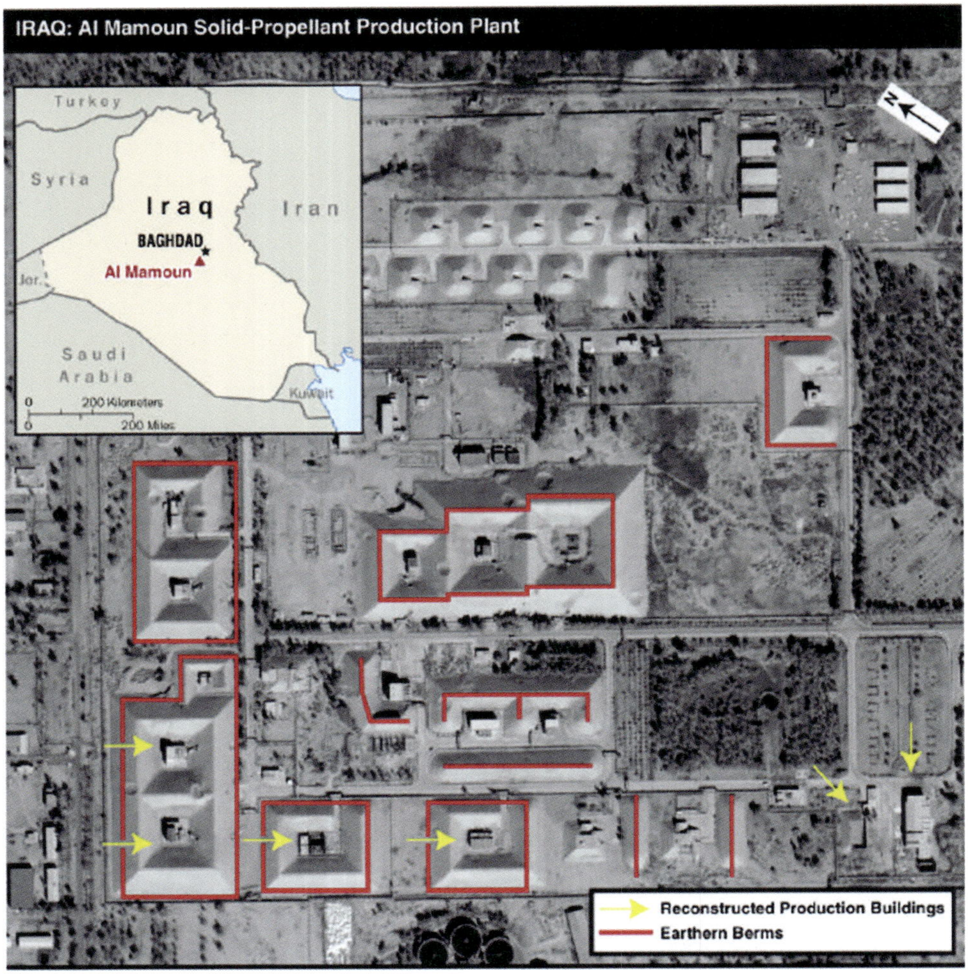

6.15 | Aerial photograph of the 'Al-Mamoun Solid Propellant Production Plant', from C.I.A., *Iraq's Weapons of Mass Destruction Programs,* White Paper Iraq, 3 October 2002, p. 21

context on images. Issues like these can perhaps be described as 'meta-iconology' and could form the theme for a different book.[18]

Film and transmission

With the invention of film soundtracks, transmission has once again become an oral phenomenon. The character in a fictional screenplay is typically designated with a name by the scriptwriter/s, and that name is transmitted to the watchers of the film by other characters in the film. We first learn that the character played by Ingrid Bergman in *Casablanca* is called Ilsa when Sam the piano player calls her 'Miss Ilsa'; we learn that

18 I thank Behailu Mihirete and Mónica Uribe Flores for discussing this topic with me.

her surname is Lund when her husband, Victor Laszlo, introduces her formally, and so on. This, of course, is the same process as in a theatrical drama, where each character is introduced to the audience by one of the other characters in the play. The manner of the introduction may be carefully considered; Macbeth is introduced to the audience by one of the three witches, Hamlet by his father's murderer. The minor characters also need their introductions, and the procedure by which it is done needs skill if names are to be remembered and the naming is not to seem unnatural and obtrusive.

The designation of the characters' names occurs offscreen, and not only because scriptwriters invent them. Even in the fictional world, the characters already have names. Ilsa was called Ilsa when she entered Rick's bar; she acquired it at her fictional christening, and so when she is first named by Sam this is a transmission, not a designation. This is the case both in the fictional world of the film and in the real world of the script, its invention and performance.

Not all the characters in *Casablanca* have names. There are numerous walk-on parts: drinkers and gamblers and shoppers in the bazaar who are never identified. These characters are designated as anonymous figures in the script and in the final disposition of the performance, and their lack of identity is transmitted by the fact they are never named. In fact, those who watch films and pick up on their cues will know that most of these people never will be named. If they were to play a significant part in the story, they would be drawn to our attention in some way.

These remarks apply also to films that deal with real characters – documentaries and TV programmes (news, quiz, music, sport) featuring people appearing under their own names. Usually their identities will be transmitted in a less natural and more direct way, by an announcer or interviewer, or by a floating caption. Of more interest from our point of view are the anonymous parts (passers-by, people in the background, studio or stadium audience). Their anonymity within the film is established by the script, or by the outcome of the editorial process. In a quiz show, for example, there may be no script; the participants may be speaking off the cuff. The audience in the studio is nevertheless intentionally anonymous; no attempt is made to introduce them to the audience watching the broadcast. Editorial control over the outcomes of a film is in itself a form of scriptwriting, or at least a way of expressing intentionality.

Computer-generated images

The image in fig. 6.16 was generated at the website thispersondoesnotexist.com, which uses 'generative adversarial networks' (GANs) to create photographs that seem to be portraits of real people, but are instead computer-generated composites of photographs of people. By going to the website and hitting the refresh button one can create new faces that have never existed before. Fig. 6.16 is not a portrait, nor even a stock photo; it is not an indexical depiction of anyone, any more than Leonardo's Christ in the Last Supper is an indexical depiction of anyone. It resembles a woman so convincingly that most people would take it to be a photograph of a woman. These GAN images do sometimes trip up and give themselves away, especially in the backgrounds and the peripheries. Sometimes weird mutant shapes appear next to the central portrait, and details at the edges can go slightly awry. In this example, the hair at left looks like it has just been snipped by some invisible scissors, and the earring seems unsure if it is silver or hair. Forensic experts on GAN imagery (a new profession has arisen) are also able to identify computer-generated photos from tiny details like the virtual reflections

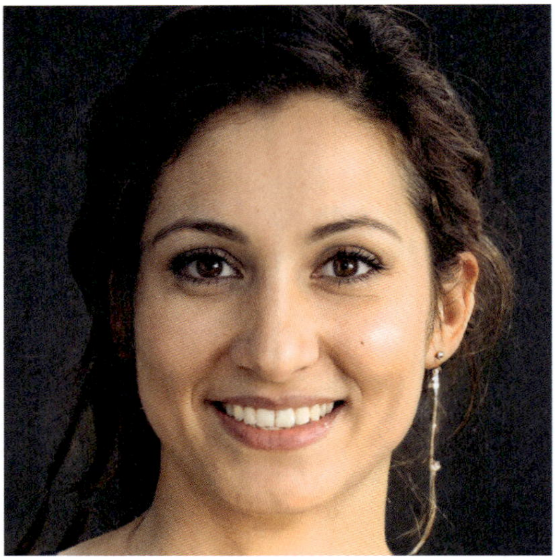

6.16 | Computer-generated image, from thispersondoesnotexist.com

on virtual teeth. But although the deception is not yet completely undetectable, we are heading towards the point where even experts will be unable to tell a photograph from a fake, or, for that matter, a film from a fake (Schick 2020; Grothaus 2021).

Fig. 6.16 resembles a woman. Does it also make sense to think of the image as conceptually depicting a woman, given that it was generated by a computer that can surely not be credited with intentionality? It probably does, because the scientists who wrote the code for this programme were trying to make the computer generate images of men or women or children, but not all three at once. There was, then, an intention to produce intentionality, and people looking at the image respond to that intention.

What about representation? Is this an anonymous photograph, like those we discussed in a previous section? A difference here, perhaps, is that there can only be anonymity when a name is withheld, and this fictional character never had a name in the first place. And can we say that it represents 'a woman', when it does not represent any particular woman? Fig. 6.8 represents a woman and indexically depicts Jennifer Anderson; the fact that her identity is withheld does not detract from the fact that the photograph both indexically and conceptually depicts and represents a woman. But then again, fig. 4.2 also indexically depicts no one, and yet it conceptually depicts a woman and represents St Catherine of Alexandria. Is there, then, any reason to refuse representation to our computer-generated image?

Computer-generated imagery is much like the artificial imagery of painters and sculptors, in that indexicality is not necessary for conceptual depiction. If we nevertheless wonder if representation is really permissible for these images, that is surely because of two centuries of training that the photograph represents the real world, and not an invented world. That, however, is an attitude we may have to unlearn, as photographic-style imagery is increasingly created by artist-programmers.

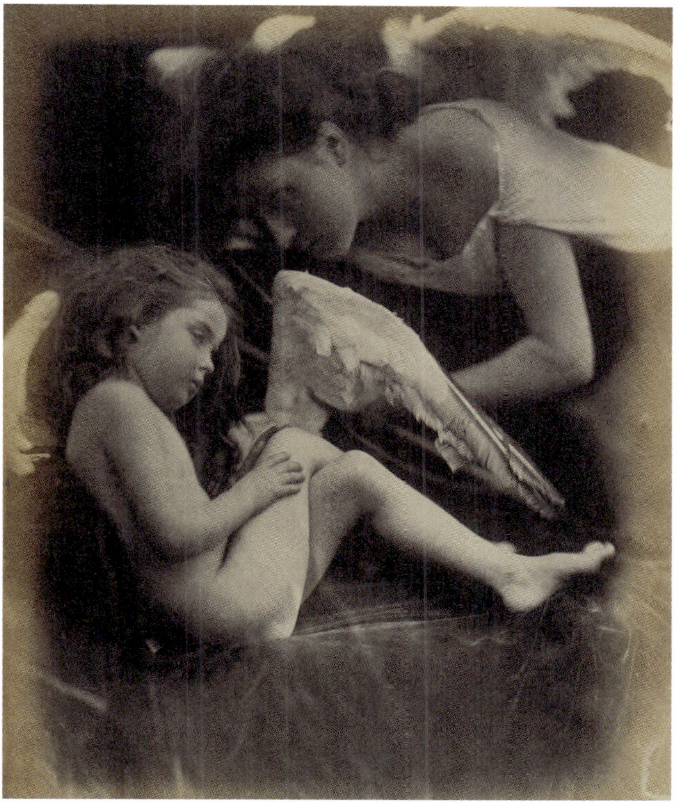

6.17 | Julia Margaret Cameron, *Venus Chiding Cupid and Depriving Him of His Wings,* 1872. Minneapolis Museum of Art

Photographic imagery, especially in motion pictures, can conjure up fictive worlds of many kinds, but there are some types of image to which they are less well-suited: in particular, religious and mythological scenes. Julia Margaret Cameron's attempts to represent traditional subjects from European iconography struggle to escape from their indexicality. Cameron called this image (fig. 6.17) *Venus Chiding Cupid*, but it is hard not to think of it as a representation of a woman and a child posing with fake wings in Victorian England. With non-indexical artificial images, we are somehow more willing to accept pictures of gods and myths, but with photographs they are less convincing. Perhaps, however, with the rise of the computer-generated photograph-style image this will change. Freed from the shackles of indexicality, we may be able to accept photographically convincing deities, saints and angels as representations.

Iconography, intentionality and language

Readers with good memories may recall that, in Chapter 2, we left to one side a problem that we promised to return to at the end of Chapter 6. The people of Lascaux, we noted (p. 44), may not have thought of fig. 2.2 as a depiction of a horse, because they may not have had a word for 'horse'. I added that "perhaps they had a word which referred to large quadrupeds with furry pelts, like deer, horses and bison, which they did not differentiate verbally".

In itself, this may not seem like much of a problem, but contained within it is a problem worth our attention. Could the people of Lascaux have thought the image depicted a horse, even though they did not have a word corresponding to 'horse'? If they had no word for horse, they may still have been able to pick out horses using other words (e.g. 'the hornless large furry creature with the hairy tail'). They may also have been able to think of horses as types without reference to specific words, just as we can recognize breeds of dog or species of plant without always knowing their names. A cave-dweller may have thought of our painting as depicting 'one of those creatures', without having to provide a word or a description for the type of creature. This shows that, while words are of very great importance in meta-iconography, it is not invariably the case that the meaning of an image needs to be expressed in linguistic terms, so long as an intentionality can be conveyed.

In cases like these, we are assuming that intentionalities are reliant on a background of language, but some sort of image content recognition is also possible for minds that do not use language. Even insects can be trained to recognize, or at least consistently respond to, black and white photographs. Bees will avoid a photograph of a face associated with quinine and approach a photograph of a face associated with honey (Dyer et al 2005). Whether this is the same thing as grasping the intentionality of the image, however, is not so clear. In the experiment on which this finding is based, the bees were able to distinguish between photos of faces, but they were always shown the same photo of each face; they were not presented with photographs of the same face from different angles or in different lighting, let alone with different hairstyles or at different ages.[19] They presumably saw the photograph as a configuration of shapes and tones, "a strange flower in the shape of a human face" (Chittka 2022, 110), rather than as an image. This, then, appears to be pre-pre-iconography.

Experiments with primates get us further up the iconographic scale. Chimpanzees and – with considerably more training – rhesus monkeys, if rewarded with gifts of fruit juice when they get the right answer, are able to match different photos, taken from different angles and in slightly different lighting conditions, of the faces of individuals from their own species (Parr et al 2000). They seem to have grasped that two photographs show a particular individual. What is more, chimpanzees are able to differentiate photographs of familiar and unfamiliar individuals, both chimpanzee and human, and at least one chimp has been trained to use symbolic language to refer to them (Tomonaga et al. 1993). This suggests an ability to grasp something of the distinction between the named and the anonymous, or at least the specific and the generic, which we have discussed in this chapter.

It seems, then, that iconography is not solely the province of those with the power of speech. It is sometimes argued (Gombrich 1982a, 24–25; Gombrich 1982c, 286–87) that the ability of some animals to interpret some images is a strong argument against the idea that images are conventional or symbolic. Perhaps at the level of resemblance this is right, but it seems less probable that animals are able to grasp depiction or representation. It would not be very difficult to deceive even the brainiest chimpanzee

19 They were presented with photographs turned through 180 degrees and were unable to recognize them.

with a trick photo – we can deceive humans too – and the pertinent question is whether chimps would have any concept of what being deceived might mean. If they have answered the question of which two faces resemble one another and do not get their gift of fruit juice, they might with reason feel puzzled or angry. Could they understand that one photograph was an indexical depiction of a chimpanzee, and the other was not? That one represented Frodo, a chimp individual, and the other was a digital fraud that only resembled Frodo?

We return to Nelson Goodman's assertion (1978, 5) that "a picture, to represent an object, must be a symbol for it, stand for it, refer to it; and that no degree of resemblance is sufficient to establish the requisite relationship of reference". A photograph does not simply resemble an object, it refers to it, and in so doing it makes a claim about its identity and character. A photograph of a chimpanzee both indexically and conceptually depicts a chimpanzee, and it represents either a particular or a generic chimpanzee. These are claims with logical consequences, which go beyond questions of mere resemblance. A GAN photo may look like a chimp, and may conceptually depict a chimp, but it does not indexically depict a chimp, and arguably does not represent a chimp.

Is it possible to express the assertions of intentionality and logical entailment that form part of human iconographic conceptualization without the help of language? This question takes us into the crossfire of current philosophical debate (Haugeland 1998; Brandom 2014; Griffin 2018; Nelson 2019). Perhaps we do not need to risk an assertion one way or the other: the fact remains that our understanding of images is drenched in linguistic concepts.

7. Iconographic diversity

Learning iconography

As many scholars have noted, it is hard to understand how small children can learn languages so perfectly and with such little effort. In Noam Chomsky's words:

> A human language is a system of remarkable complexity. To come to know a human language would be an extraordinary intellectual achievement for a creature not specifically designed to accomplish this task. A normal child acquires this knowledge on relatively slight exposure and without specific training. He can then quite effortlessly make use of an intricate structure of specific rules and guiding principles to convey his thoughts and feelings to others, arousing in them novel ideas and subtle perceptions and judgments. For the conscious mind, not specially designed for the purpose, it remains a distant goal to reconstruct and comprehend what the child has done intuitively and with minimal effort.
> (Chomsky 1975, 4)

If children are outstanding linguists, they are not such gifted artists. At an age when they can hold grammatically and syntactically correct conversations on a wide variety of topics, they are still drawing the world around them as scribbles, blobs and tadpoles (Kerschensteiner 1905; Arnheim 1974; Golomb 1992).[1] Even when we have grown up, few of us are good at drawing; this is a practice at which some people are extremely gifted and most of us mediocre or bad. The camera has levelled the playing field, allowing all of us to make accurate images, but here too some display more ability than others. A talented photographer will manage to incorporate more pertinent information than an ungifted amateur, and even the talented discard many unsatisfactory photographs when choosing the most memorable shot.

Although we are generally poor at making images, we are much better at reading them, and this from an early age (Hochberg and Brooks 1962). Or, rather, we are very good at seeing what images resemble, and we can quickly learn what some kinds of images represent and depict. Children can understand the tens of thousands of frames in a cartoon or a simple film without difficulty, and can interpret them at both the depictive and representational levels – that is, they will know all the characters in *Beat Bugs* or *Paw Patrol* and will be able to recognize their actions. This sort of competence

1 Arnheim objects to the term tadpoles: 1974, 197–99.

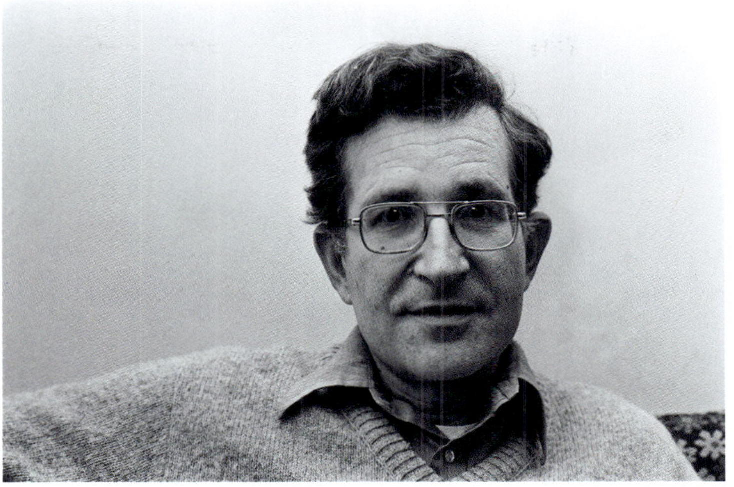

7.1 | Hans Peters, Portrait of Noam Chomsky, 8 December 1977

they can, of course, only acquire because they have already mastered spoken language: through the voices of the protagonists in films young viewers learn the representational identities of characters, and the stories in which they are involved.

Children can follow films because they are assisted by the soundtrack, but once this is removed from the iconographic process, interpreting images becomes more challenging. To be sure, even small children can recognize much of the depictive content of photographs, but in order to learn their representations a vast knowledge of people, places and things is required. This knowledge can only be acquired motif by motif. It is true that once we have seen one image of, for instance, a building, we have a remarkable ability to recognize other images of that building, even when seen from unfamiliar angles. That will not help us to recognize images of other buildings, however; knowing what the Taj Mahal looks like is of no use if we are looking at a photograph of Tbilisi Cathedral, or a row of shops in Buenos Aires.

Just as no person in the world can speak more than a fraction of the world's languages, so no person in the world can recognize more than a fraction of the world's iconographies. It is often said that images are much easier to learn than languages. Theorists who make this claim (e.g. Hochberg 1983; Stumpel 1993; Lopes 1995; Abell 2005; Dilworth 2005) are not thinking iconographically. While it is true that we can look at an image and can come up with ideas about what it resembles, and, if we know the depictive rules of the genre, can make a good guess at its conceptual depiction, we can recognize very few of the representations we encounter. To say of this photograph (fig. 7.1) that it shows a middle-aged man in a shirt and V-neck jumper looking at the camera through metal-rimmed spectacles is something that almost anyone who can identify a shirt, a V-neck jumper and a pair of spectacles could say, and it is perfectly accurate at the depictive level; but that is not the same thing as to identify its representation, as a portrait of Noam Chomsky. If 'learning images' consists in learning how to recognize conceptual depictions then yes, we are very good at it. But we do not

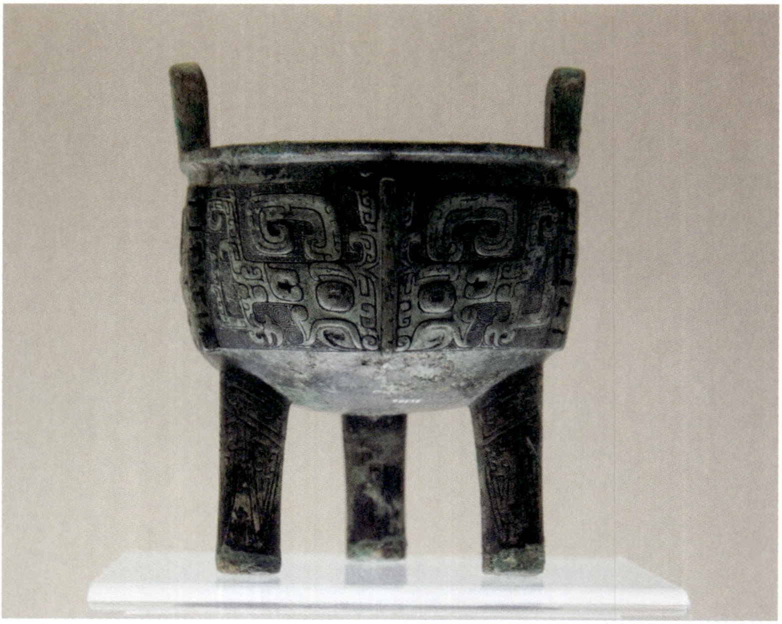

7.2 | Shang bronze, 1300–1100 BC. Shanghai Museum

know the representations of more than a tiny handful of the billions of images made each week.

With some years of application and a reasonable talent for languages you could learn Chinese well enough to be able to make Chinese friends, enjoy Chinese books and hold down a job in China. But however hard you worked, you would never learn the iconography of every Chinese image, for the simple reason that you could not identify the photos of every boyfriend, mother, friend and neighbourhood in every Chinese smartphone.[2] And you would also have to understand the photographs in the press, in academic journals, in book illustrations, as well as all the traditional images, the Daoist, Buddhist and Confucian saints and sages, the woodcuts in old books, the stories in traditional paintings, and strange images in bronze from ancient China like the *taotie* (fig. 7.2), which no one today can understand (Bagley 1993). A hundred lifetimes would not suffice. It would be vastly more difficult than learning all the Chinese characters.

Here it may be thought that we are not comparing like with like; there are billions of images, but only tens of thousands of Chinese characters. So which would be easier to learn; 10,000 characters or 10,000 iconographies? That would depend on the nature of the image. A stock photo of 'a woman' (fig. 6.8) is fairly easy to learn, once one understands the conventions for the use of stock photography, although one may need to know enough of the textual context in which it appears (book on learning,

2 To talk of 'photographs' being 'in' smartphones is a form of shorthand. For the intricacies of photographic ontology, see Wilson 2021.

Christianity, suicide etc) to appreciate the intended meaning (a learner, a Christian, a suicide risk etc). The same need for an understanding of textual context is required when trying to understand fashion imagery. If one cannot read the name 'Giada' in fig. 6.6 then one does not understand the function of the image, and one must of course have the background knowledge of why images of thin, beautiful women appear in magazines, a knowledge that Panofsky's Australian, or a medieval European, would need to acquire.

A photo of a specific individual is harder to grasp at the representational level; it requires knowledge of the individual's name and something of their history. To learn that a photograph of a burly man with dark skin and short curly hair is a representation of Muhammad Ali is not enough, you need to know who Ali was, both as a 'boxer' and a 'figure in the civil rights movement'. You also needs to know that he was very 'famous', and 'signing an autograph' for two young women in 'traditional Dutch costume' (the inverted commas are there to show concepts that need extensive background cultural knowledge) before you can understand the iconography of fig. 6.11. Is that easier or more difficult than to learn the Chinese characters 拳师, *quánshī* (boxer), or the Dutch word *bokser*?

And these are the easy examples. If you want to know the iconographies of figs. 1.1, 1.2 and 1.6 you would need to learn something of the contents of texts by Flavius Josephus, the Four Evangelists and William Shakespeare. In the traditional iconography of pre-modern Europe there are thousands of similar examples. As I noted in the preface, in the Photographic Collection of the Warburg Institute we have around 18,000 iconographic types. Is it possible to learn all of them? After 33 years of work in that room, I think I can claim an ability to recognize most of these iconographies, but no more than that. I have never met anyone who could claim to recognize them all. It is too complex a task, too large a feat of memory. And that is just European iconography; we are not claiming to know much about Islamic, Chinese or Mesoamerican iconography. I probably know over 25,000 words in English, and a few thousand in some other European languages, but I certainly cannot recognize that many traditional iconographies.

Suppose one took 5,000 words at random from the Oxford English Dictionary and asked a native speaker to identify their meanings. They would not recognize them all, since our active vocabulary is much smaller than the full lexicon of English (c. 600,000 words). Suppose one then took 5,000 images at random, from books and magazines and websites, both photographs and traditional images. To make the two experiments comparable, one would have to ensure that no text was visible next to any of the images, to give the iconography away. Would the subjects of this experiment be able to identify the meanings of more words, or more images? My money is on more words, but we need an experimental iconographer to test the claim.

Learning iconographies is not only about learning the names of depicted figures. You also have to understand what is being depicted, and that is frequently far from straightforward, especially when you are dealing with representations from the past, or from distant cultures. To know what an angel or a bodhisattva or a totem is requires some general education. In Aboriginal painting humanoid figures can sometimes be used to depict humans and sometimes spirits, and also different types of spirits, for example disincarnate and never incarnate (Macintosh 1977, 194; Taylor 1996, 182–91). Objects can also present difficulties. Some of the attributes of Christian saints, Hindu deities or Buddhist bodhisattvas are unfamiliar to Christians, Hindus and Buddhists; we cannot all recognize a curry comb, an elephant goad or a three-stalked staff. The difficulties of recognition can become severe when we approach unfamiliar styles of depiction; besides the *taotie* already mentioned, there are complicated images like the *lanzón* of Chavín de Huantar (Burger 1995), or the so-called Assyrian Sacred Tree (Giovino 2007), or New Ireland *malagan* images, or the many seemingly abstract patterns that are given depictive readings mentioned in Chapter 1 (pp. 36–37).

We noted in Chapter 1 that an Australian Aboriginal would find it very difficult to read the objects in Leonardo da Vinci's Last Supper and that Erwin Panofsky would have found it very difficult to interpret a caveful of Aboriginal rock art. The Australian anthropologist N.W.G. Macintosh (1952, 1977) carefully transcribed Aboriginal images in an Arnhem Land cave, and then compared his own interpretations of the images with those of an Aboriginal elder called Lamderod. He found that he had misidentified 90% of the motifs; misread the gender of some of the figures; failed to differentiate humans and spirits, and types of spirits; confused a wombat with a cat, a kangaroo with a possum, a wallaby with a pademelon and a woman with a lizard. He concluded that "the mental code of the artists' schematisation cannot be cracked without keys provided by highly initiated informants".[3] And this was an attempt to interpret the 'outside' meanings of the images; the 'inside' meanings were of course lost on him.

Iconographic diversity

Languages expand, as we invent new words for new purposes. This can be seen on the shelves of any humanities library: the vocabularies of ancient Greek and Latin can fit into one-volume dictionaries, while the modern European languages require dictionaries of ten volumes or more.[4] And yet this growth is as nothing when compared to the sudden eruption of iconographies over the past five centuries, as first print and then photography and digital imagery have left a thick deposit of images all over our societies. In this new age of mass imagery, iconographic meanings have come vastly to outnumber lexicographic meanings. And yet, in the past, lexicographic complexity was far greater than iconographic complexity. Any language will contain tens of thousands of words, but traditional small-scale societies in Africa, Oceania and the Americas would often carve or paint no more than twenty or thirty iconographic types.

As iconographies expand, so there is less chance that the members of a society will be able to recognize every representation within that society. When there are billions of portraits on smartphones, of course no one can be expected to recognize the identities of every sitter; but even in much smaller iconographies, like that of Europe in the Renaissance, there were numerous saints who were unrecognizable outside the small region within which they were worshipped, there were numerous narrative scenes illustrating stories that were not universally known (in the more obscure parts of the Old Testament, or in Greco-Roman mythology, or in poems that were only read by the educated), there were numerous landscapes and portraits known only to a few, and there were numerous allegories that were barely intelligible even to those who had

3 Macintosh assumed throughout that Lamderod's readings were correct.

4 This is not to deny that all languages are equally structurally complex; see Webb and Kembo-Sure 2000, 66, 156.

them painted on their ceilings. And there was a sizeable iconographic class difference, between those who could stock up on iconographic motifs because they could afford books and had the literacy and leisure time to read them, and those whose reading was more restricted. An anecdote told by the painter, poet and biographer Karel van Mander in his *Schilder-boeck* of 1604 is revealing, whether or not it is true. It concerns a painting by Cornelis Ketel, of Jupiter descending on Danaë as a shower of gold:

> I think that this composition is still in his home, hanging in the hallway: about which there is a funny story concerning a peasant, who saw this piece as he was passing, and who asked Ketel's wife if he could look at the painting: for he thought that he understood it, and it appealed to him, saying: Madam, can you make something like this? You will certainly earn your keep:[5] standing speculating in this way, he said, I bet I know what this painting means, it is the Angelic greeting, when the holy Angel made the Annunciation to our dear Lady, and he congratulated himself on his good judgement and understanding: seeing a flying Cupid as the Angel, and Danaë, who was lying naked on a beautifully furnished bedstead with her legs apart, as Mary, and so he left, with all his coarse understanding, just as wise as he had come.
> (Van Mander 1604, 279v–280r)

Ancient fables like that of Danaë were read by those who studied Latin in school, and paintings of these tales were expensive and reserved for the better-off, so it is not surprising that a peasant would be unable to recognize the story and would be forced to interpret it in terms of the religious iconography that was more familiar to him.

Knowledge of iconography did not only divide along class lines. Van Mander himself had a hazy grasp of the iconography of some paintings made by his friends, including Ketel (Taylor 2002, 147). Iconographic competence is a less universal phenomenon than linguistic competence. There are many images that only a small number of people can be expected to recognize – family photos, photos of colleagues, views of streets in a neighbourhood. Then there will be images that are known to a particular subculture – musicians of varying kinds, or scenes from TV programmes, or illustrations from books. Relatively few images will be recognizable to almost everyone: they might include portraits of well-known political figures, photographs of the Pyramids or the Eiffel Tower, views of the earth or the moon. Of course, in language there are many words that are only intelligible to a handful of specialists or word game enthusiasts, but there are thousands that pretty much every language user will know and use.

The size of a society will make a difference to the number of images it is likely to produce. A small village will be unable to support a very large iconography, while a civilization of tens of millions of people is likely to generate a very diverse body of images (Taylor 2006). But it is not just a matter of the number of images; the size of a society will also have an effect on the ways by which images mean. In a village, the iconographies of images can be chosen on the spot and shared by word of mouth; but in a large society, with little face-to-face contact, other mechanisms must be found to produce and convey representational meanings. And to create a larger number of meanings, images must themselves be more varied, more differentiable; the more

5 He appears to assume that Ketel's wife painted the picture. Miedema in Van Mander 1998, 159.

'functional contrast' there is between images, the easier it is to generate representations. In this regard, images are like language, which also requires a clear differentiation of phonemes to generate the tens of thousands of words present in a typical vocabulary (Saussure [1916] 1995, 2.4.§4; Lyons 1977, 230–38).

The possibilities for variety in images are even greater than the possibilities for variety in language. The latter relies on a finite number of phonemes and characters, and, while these elements can be combined in an indefinite number of ways, an image can create new semantic possibilities by minute alterations of line, tone or colour (Goodman 1976, 225–41; Lopes 1995, 66–68; Kulvicki 2006, 29–48). Names are repetitive, but every passport photograph is different.

This is to think of likenesses, rather than representations identified by designation, attributes or narratives. In likenesses, far more of the image is brought into iconographic play. A row of Jain saints can be identical, with their representations given by the attributes carved on their bases. From the point of view of iconographic individuation, only the attributes are significant since the rest of the statue is generic. In a sequence of photographs of the people who worship these idols, however, the shapes and colours of every feature will figure in the process of determining their identification. It is precisely because a greater proportion of the image is being used to assign representation that the possibilities for iconographic differentiation so dramatically increased when likeness was introduced as an iconographic device.

Afterword: Iconography and AI

If humans find it hard to learn iconography, will computers be able to do better? I wrote in the previous chapter that "however hard you worked, you would never learn the iconography of every Chinese image, for the simple reason that you could not identify the photos of every boyfriend, mother, friend and neighbourhood in every Chinese smartphone". And that is indeed so, but, while you could not do it, the computer systems of the Chinese state could. The same is true, of course, for every solvent state, even if the Chinese have, for now, gone further down this road than other nations (Tyler 2022). Not that the rest of the world is far behind; anyone who travels by air will have encountered facial recognition systems, which speed up the process of sieving out the legally, medically, politically or economically proscribed. Since these systems have enormous reservoirs of stored memory, they can match the millions of faces that pass through their video gates with names.

Of course, artificial intelligence can only achieve this feat if, at some point in the past, the face has been designated in the system. Computers have vast resources of memory, but, like human beings, they cannot deduce someone's name merely by scanning their features; names are arbitrary additions to our identities. Unfortunately, namelessness is an increasingly rare and precious resource in the twenty-first century. Given the ubiquity of computers and cameras, it is hard for anyone who does not live in a desert or a rainforest to avoid being tagged by the surveillance state, and once one's face and name are linked on some server it is practically impossible to escape back into anonymity.

There is, however, a further obstacle that would need to be crossed by a machine iconographer, as opposed to a surveillance system. A facial recognition scanner looking at fig. 6.8 could identify the sitter as Jennifer Anderson, but this image does not represent Jennifer Anderson. It indexically depicts her, but it represents an anonymous model. To know the meaning of an image one needs to know both what is named and what is not named. The machine iconographer would need to suppress parts of its own knowledge in order to identify the iconography as humans understand it. Perhaps it could give a name to each brand of her clothing, or the make of the biro in her hand; but if it offered up this information it would not be giving us a facsimile of human intelligence, which does not need irrelevant details.

To mimic human iconographic requirements, AI will need to become sensitive to styles of photography. It is not easy to verbalize why we humans can immediately recognize that fig. 6.8 is a stock photo while fig. 7.1 is a portrait, but the machine iconographer would not have to verbalize this either; it would simply have to learn how to discriminate them, and computers have shown themselves very receptive to this kind of training. Once it has classified the pictorial genre it can move on to identify the iconography: 1) a stock photo of a woman holding a biro, 2) a portrait of Noam Chomsky. Fig. 6.11, in which Muhammad Ali is named and the others are anonymous, would create further complications, but the machine could be given a course in human attitudes towards celebrities and their iconographic implications. A difficulty here, in fact, is the architecture. A computer would have no problem recognizing the street as Haven in Volendam in Holland, but should it offer this information, and how much of it should it offer? The answer is to be found within the specific communicative context of the photograph. In the Dutch newspapers which showed this scene the identity of the town was considered relevant and was mentioned, because the two autograph hunters were wearing Volendam costume, something which Dutch readers might be expected to recognize; but the identity of the street was passed over as irrelevant. If the same photograph had been shown in a non-Dutch newspaper, the identity of the town could also have been ignored. The computer would need to know how and to whom the photograph was being presented before it could describe its iconography in human terms.

Computers may be able to guess some such pragmatic contexts, but others require information that a machine could not guess. Take fig. 6.10, my photograph of the Heavenly Centre Stone in Beijing. An AI scanner could not know, merely by uploading the photograph, who took it, but its meaning depends very much on the taker. It might have been made by a relative of the woman standing on the stone and her friend in the black cap, in which case the photograph would have been meant as portraits of those people, with their names. For me it is a tourist snap of anonymous people only because all these people were unknown to me, a foreigner in China. The machine iconographer could call the photograph 'Tourists at the Heavenly Centre Stone' or 'Mengying and Shuchang on holiday in Beijing'; either description might be correct, or incorrect, depending on who held the camera: and it is precisely this fact which cannot be deduced from a scan of the image itself. With many photographs, the identity of the photographer does not matter. The iconographic content of fig. 7.1 is Noam Chomsky, and we do not need to know who pressed the button on the camera. But sometimes, the meaning of the image depends on its author.

When AI is applied to traditional works of art it can no longer rely on its almost infinite ability to identify faces. We do not recognize Vishnu, St Erasmus or Rustam by their facial features. Here the computer is up against the same metaiconographic constraints as those we discussed in chapters 4 and 5; it needs to identify attributes and distinctive narratives.

At present, internet search engines rely heavily on captions and text. All images on the web are accompanied by texts (or numbers) of some kind – this accompanying information is known as 'metadata' – and the search engine will look for the metadata rather than the image itself. If you type 'Virgin and Child' into a search engine you will be shown many images of the Virgin Mary with the Christ Child. If you type 'Madonna and Child' into a search engine you will be shown many more images of the Virgin Mary with the Christ Child. However, you will find that there are very few images in common between the two sets, even though they are iconographically identical. This is because the search engine was not searching for an iconography; it was searching for a phrase of text. This means that, besides having the iconography that interests you split into two

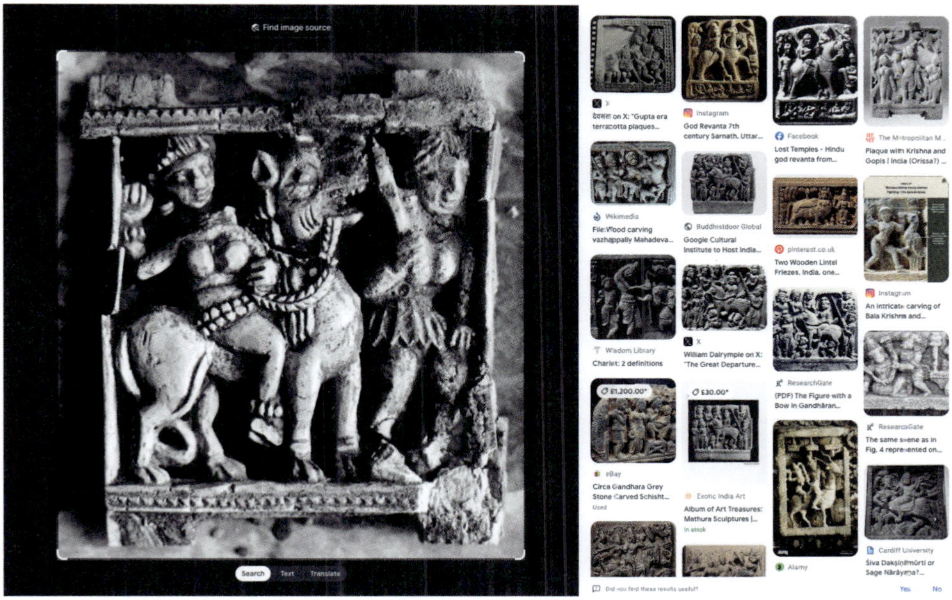

8.1 | Indian ivory from the Begram Hoard, 1st century AD, and related Google Lens search

camps, you will also only find images of the Virgin/Madonna and Child that appear on English-language websites. Images filed as '*Virgen con el Niño*' or 'Дева с младенцем' will not show up. If search engines were able to look for iconographies, rather than textual descriptions of iconographies, then they would greatly expand the searchable range of images.

Not all searches are textual – you can also use an image search engine. If you take a photograph of a painting in a museum and drop it straight from your camera into an image search engine, with no identifying metadata attached, the search engine will find the same picture on the website of the museum, or on any other website that happens to reproduce it. However, the image search engine can of course only do this if the painting is on the web. If you take an image that has never been uploaded onto the internet and drop it into an image search engine, you will find that the search engine gives you instead a number of visually similar images, which may or may not be of use to you.

Take the first-century Indian ivory in fig. 8.1, for example. This seems not to be on the internet at the time of writing, because when I dropped a digital image of it into Google Lens the search engine did not manage to find this exact plaque; instead, I was given a range of images that resemble it to some extent. All of the images were of Indian reliefs, which shows an impressive ability to recognize style; but only half of the images managed to identify the pre-iconography as being of a person on the back of a quadruped, and in each case the person in question was clothed and male, whereas in our ivory she is nude and female. The search engine is failing at the depictive level.

Alt text generators, which use artificial intelligence to create captions for images, do no better and no worse than search engines in this regard. If you ask one to write a

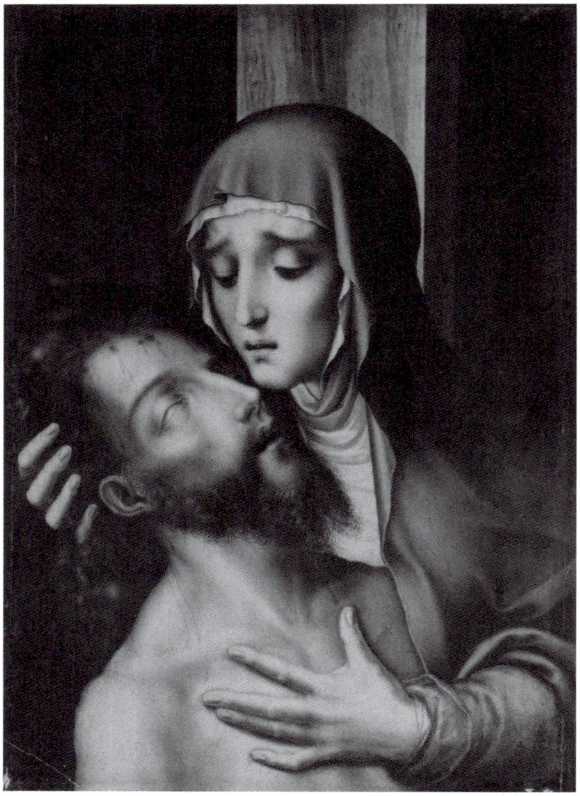

8.2 | Luis de Morales, The Virgin Embracing the Dead Christ at the Foot of the Cross, 1565–70. Villar-Mir Cultural Fund, Madrid

caption for an artwork that has appeared on the internet, then it will give an accurate iconographic description at the representational level, using the metadata available online. So, for example, when I put this image (fig. 8.2) into an online alt text generator, alttext.ai, it was described accurately enough as "Black and white photo of a painting depicting mary holding jesus after his crucifixion, showing a tender and sorrowful embrace". But if you ask it to write a caption for an artwork that has never been uploaded to the web, it will be much less precise. I was told by alttext.ai that fig. 8.1 is an "Ancient relief depicting a centaur fighting a human, illustrating detailed carvings in a mythological scene on a square stone panel". It is true that it is an ancient relief, but everything else is false or unknown; it does not depict a centaur, no fight is taking place, the figure at right may or may not be a human, the carvings are not particularly detailed, the panel is not made of stone, and whether the scene is mythological, legendary, religious or something else remains to be seen.

So far, then, AI is a very effective iconographic mimic, but when it is left to its own devices it is less impressive. We can be sure that, with time, it will become better able to distinguish pre-iconographic motifs and will accurately characterize this relief as a nude female riding a four-legged creature. But could it not do better than that? Could it not identify the creature, name the woman, say what she is doing, what the person walking ahead of her is holding and so on?

If AI can do this, then it will be acting on its own, since we humans cannot, at present, identify this female figure, or the creature she is riding, or the object held by her companion. If this ivory represents a mythological, legendary or religious scene, we do not know what it is; and it is quite possible that it does not represent any particular scene at all. The ivory was found in a cave at Begram in Afghanistan, where it formed part of a hoard with around 200 other Indian ivories, as well as Roman sculpture and glassware and a few pieces of Chinese lacquerware (Hackin et al. 1954; Stone 2008). These works of art from opposite ends of Eurasia appear to have been left in the cave in the first century AD, since an Indian ivory of a very similar style has been excavated from Pompeii (Levi d'Ancona 1950). It is possible that the hoard belonged to a trader travelling the Silk Route, who was selling Indian carvings in Europe and Roman artefacts in India. The Indian ivories do not seem to show Hindu or Buddhist religious iconography, but concentrate instead on ornament, plants, animals, monsters, hunting scenes and, in over half the examples, buxom young females wearing jewellery and little else, as in fig. 8.1. Similar females appear in Buddhist and Hindu art, where they represent *yakshis*, nature spirits; but it is not clear that they have the same significance in the Begram ivories, where they are shown dancing, playing or interacting in courtly environments. It seems possible, though it cannot be proved, that they were deliberately drained of specific cultural meanings so that they would appeal to buyers outside India. These ivories may be early scenes of anonymous figures that emphasize nudity on purpose, having been designed for the Roman market.

This, however, is speculation; and despite the general absence of iconographic specificity in the Begram ivories, the scene in fig. 8.1 is more likely than most to represent a particular narrative. It appears to be a multiple; another Begram ivory shows very similar figures walking in the opposite direction (fig. 8.3). Here the four-legged creature looks more like a horse (despite its sharp teeth), and the implement held by the walking figure seems to be a spear. Another ivory shows a scenario of the same kind, except that the mount has a human head and the figure walking ahead is a semi-nude female of the *yakshi* type (fig. 8.4). If any of these images had been found in a Buddhist temple rather than the Begram hoard one would feel confident that they were meant to represent a religious story; they have the feel of the Buddhist *jatakas* (p. 192), and it would be easy to imagine that the *yakshi*'s mount is meant to be one of the previous incarnations of the Buddha. I do not know of a *jataka* that involves a *yakshi* riding the Bodhisattva, but that does not of course mean that it does not exist.

We are surely not far from the stage when AI will be able to help solve problems of this kind. Translated texts of all the Buddhist *jatakas* are available online, and it should take an AI system a fraction of a second to survey all of them, and to tell us if one describes a scenario similar to that we see here. Of course, the computer will first have to be able to look at the image and distinguish the *yakshi* riding a horse, but we are on the verge of such technology (Stork 2023, ch. 10). Identifying narratives is one field of investigation where AI should be able to outstrip human iconographers, since computers can read much more than us, in a tiny fraction of the time we need. Once all texts have been uploaded onto the internet, the sum of human narrative will be available for the computer to browse.

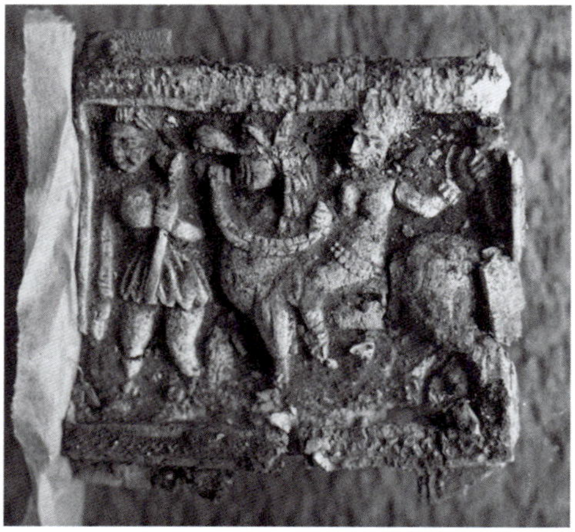
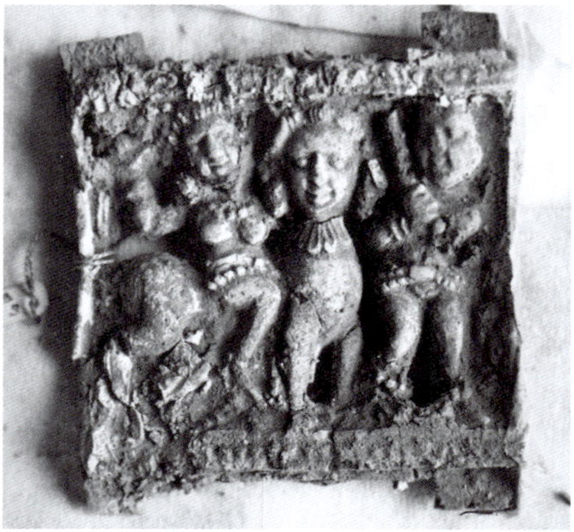

8.3, 8.4 | Second and third Indian ivory from the Begram Hoard, 1st century AD

Would a machine iconographer have been able to help me to interpret the scene by Frans Caucig of Herod and his mother (fig. 1.6)? The scene is very obscure and may well be a visual single, and if so, the computer could not go looking for other images on the internet which resembled it. What it could do - or rather, what computers may be able to do in the near future - is to hunt through all the digitised literature in the world and find a match between the original passage of text in Josephus and the image. Of course, this will involve a great deal of iconographic feedback, with the computer having to decide how ambiguous elements of the image – such as Herod waving his sword – should be read. But similar problems face AI in the translation of texts, and these problems, which only twenty years ago seemed insurmountable, have largely been overcome.

The drawing by Caucig has the advantage that, once the solution has been found, it is hard to deny that the passage from Josephus fits the image so well that it must be the text Caucig was meaning to illustrate. Some other puzzles that iconographers have been trying to solve for many decades (Elkins 1999) – such as Piero della Francesca's Flagellation (Ginzburg 1985; Hope and Taylor 1992; Israëls 2020), Giorgione's Tempest (Holberton 1995; Paoli 2011; Holberton 2021) or Rembrandt's early history painting in Leiden (Stumpel 2000; Taylor 2011; Hecht 2018) – have received numerous iconographic interpretations, none of which have been accepted by all art historians. It is, however, possible that the iconographies of these paintings have in fact been solved, but that the relationship between picture and interpretation was not so watertight that it left no space for disagreement. If an AI system were to scan the whole of the relevant primary literature and alight on a text that made the best possible fit with a particular image, human iconographers might still decide to reject its findings. The attempts of AI systems to contribute to the field of art attribution have also not always succeeded in persuading the experts (Alberge 2011).

Another problem is that figures are often portrayed without specific attributes or narrative context (pp. 113, 119, 134). When they can be identified at all it is through nearby captions, or through archival references or descriptive texts from the period: the image itself does not contain information that will settle its representational identity.

Perhaps the computer will also be able to uncover references in a database of archival texts, but where these do not exist such figures will have to remain anonymous.

Anonymity is another issue; as we have seen, many images, even in textual cultures, are supposed to be representations of anonymous characters who have never appeared in any written narrative (figs. 5.20–5.23). That does not mean that there is no text that was available to the maker of the image, and which tells a story that fits the image exactly. Should AI uncover some forgotten French novel of the nineteenth century that features a man dressed in white at the tiller of a yacht in which a woman in blue is seated, then a machine iconographer might well conclude that Manet had read that book (fig. 5.23), and was trying to illustrate the passage in question. The Manet experts might prove sceptical: their arguments against the finding would have to involve much careful balancing of iconological evidence.

In these examples the machine iconographer is working to interpret the imagery of textual cultures, but when it is dealing with oral cultures that have left no traces for historians to use as evidence, it will be unable to provide well-grounded interpretations. It may generate suggestive hypotheses, but AI systems will not identify the protagonists of Moche iconography (fig. 4.16), nor the subjects of African and Oceanic sculptures when their original semantic context has been lost. Some other cultures, such as Shang dynasty China (fig. 7.2), have left us literary remains, but too few to provide us with the iconographic evidence we need (Bagley 1993; Bagley 2008). Intelligent computers can perform many tasks more quickly and effectively than we can, but even for them, such questions will remain insoluble. Here AI will be able to do no better than human researchers, and no worse.

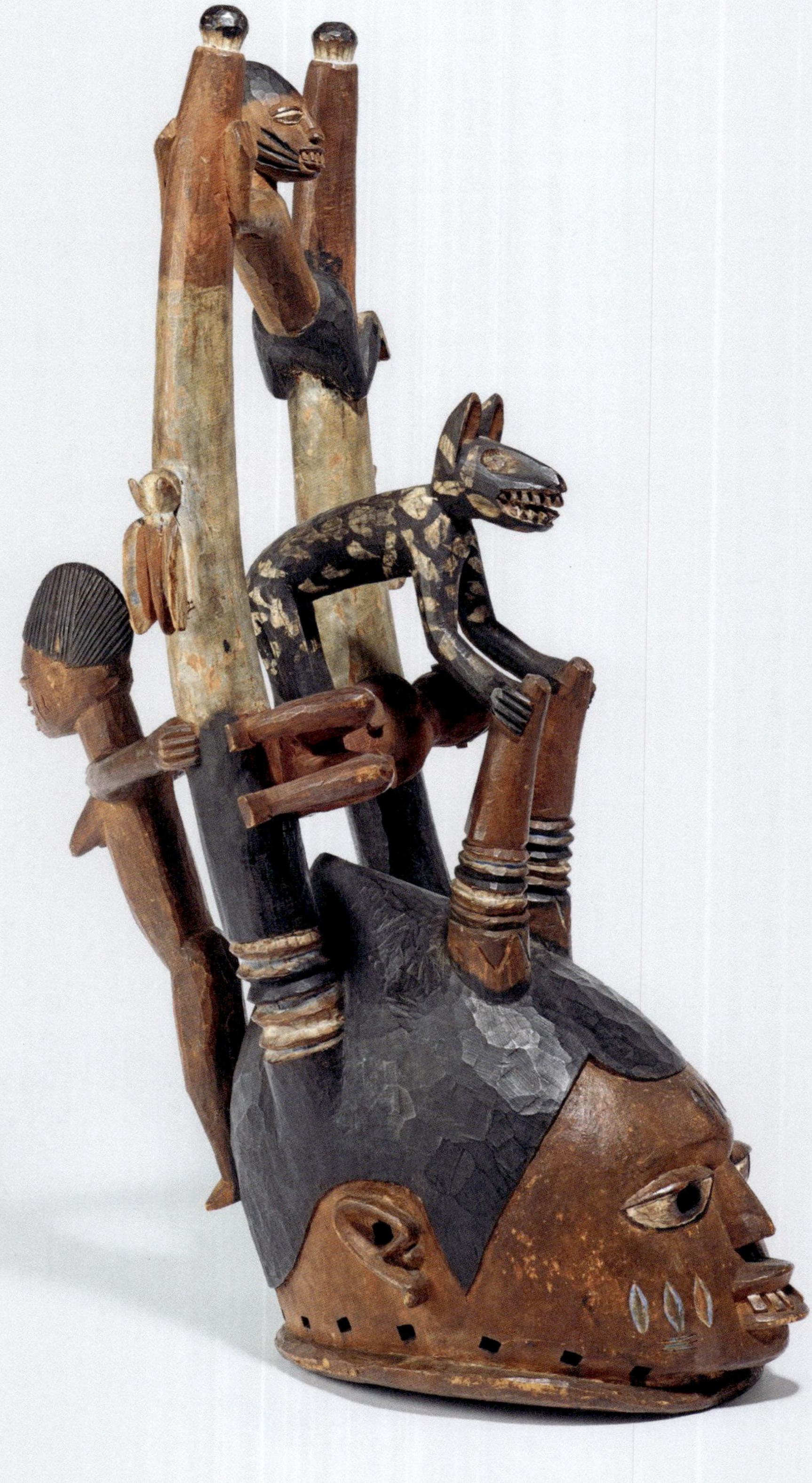

Bibliography

Abell, C. 2005. 'Against Depictive Conventionalism', *American Philosophical Quarterly* 42/3, 185–97

Abíódún, R. 2013. 'Àkó-graphy: Òwò Portraits', in *Portraiture and Photography in Africa*, edited by J. Peffer and E. Cameron, Bloomington: Indiana University Press, 341–62

Addison, J. 1718. *Remarks on several parts of Italy, &c. in the years 1701, 1702, 1703*, 2nd edn (1st edn 1705), London: J. Tonson

Adler, A. 1998. 'Des rois et des masques. Essai d'analyse comparative (Moundang du Tchad, Bushong de l'ex-Zaïre)', *L'Homme* 145, 169–203

Ahl, D.C. 1996. *Benozzo Gozzoli: Tradition and Innovation in Renaissance Painting*, New Haven and London: Yale University Press

Aiello, G. 2022. 'Perfect Strangers in the City: Stock Photography as Ambient Imagery', in *Seeing the City Digitally: Processing Urban Space and Time*, edited by G. Rose, Amsterdam: Amsterdam University Press

Ainsworth, M. 2007. 'Text and Image: How St Jerome Sees the Trinity', *The Burlington Magazine* 149/1247, 95–96

Alberge, D. 2021. 'Was famed Samson and Delilah really painted by Rubens? No, says AI', *The Guardian*, 26 September; https://www.theguardian.com/artanddesign/2021/sep/26/was-famed-samson-and-delilah-really-painted-by-rubens-no-says-ai

Albert, J.-P. and A. Kedzierska-Manzon. 2016. 'Des objets-signes aux objets-sujets', *Archives de sciences sociales des religions* 61/174, 13–25

Albornoz, L. 2016. *Diversity and the Film Industry: An Analysis of the 2014 UIS Survey on Feature Film Statistics*, Montreal: UNESCO Institute for Statistics; http://dx.doi.org/10.15220/978-92-9189-190-0-en

Alva, W. and C. Donnan. 1993. *Royal Tombs of Sipán*, Los Angeles: Fowler Museum

Ambrose, K. 2017. 'Émile Mâle', in *The Routledge Companion to Medieval Iconography*, edited by C. Hourihane, Abingdon: Routledge, 65–74

Ariel, M. 2010. *Defining Pragmatics*, Cambridge: Cambridge University Press

Arney, P. 2007. 'The *Bade Shikshapatra*: A Vallabhite Guide to the Worship of Krishna's Divine I', in *Krishna: A Sourcebook*, edited by E.F. Bryant, Oxford: Oxford University Press, 505–36

Arnheim, R. 1974. *Art and Visual Perception*, Berkeley and Los Angeles: University of California Press

Ashton, P., A. Davies and S. Slive. 1982. 'Jacob van Ruisdael's Trees', *Arnoldia* 42/1, 2–31

Atkin, A. 2005. 'Peirce on the Index and Indexical Reference', *Transactions of the Charles S. Peirce Society* 41/1, 161–88

Ayotte, M. and C. Ayotte. 2002. *Sociolinguistic Language Survey of Ngwe*, Dallas: SIL International

Baaren, T.P. van. 1968. *Korwars and Korwar Style: Art and Ancestor Worship in North-West New Guinea*, Paris and The Hague: Mouton & Co.

Babb, L. 1988. 'Giving and Giving Up: The Eightfold Worship among Śvetāmbar Mūrtipūjak Jains', *Journal of Anthropological Research* 44/1, 67–86

Bacci, P. 1904. 'La "Trinità" del Pesellino della National Gallery di Londra: Nuovi documenti', *Rivista d'arte* 2, 160–77

Bach, K. 2006. 'The Excluded Middle: Semantic Minimalism without Minimal Propositions', *Philosophy and Phenomenological Research* 73, 435–42

Bagley, R. 1993. 'Meaning and Explanation', in *The Problem of Meaning in Early Chinese Ritual Bronzes*, edited by R. Whitfield, London: School of Oriental and African Studies, 34–55

Bagley, R. 2008. 'Interpreting Prehistoric Designs', in *Iconography without Texts*, edited by P. Taylor, London and Turin: Warburg Institute and Nino Aragno, 43–68

Bagley, R. 2009. 'Anyang Mold-Making and the Decorated Model', *Artibus Asiae* 69/1, 39–90

Bahn, P. 2008. 'Holding onto Smoke? Wishful Thinking vs Common Sense in Rock Art Interpretation', in *Iconography without Texts*, edited by P. Taylor, London and Turin: Warburg Institute and Nino Aragno, 15–24

Bal, M. and N. Bryson. 1991. 'Semiotics and Art History', *Art Bulletin* 73/2, 174–208

Balliett. A. 2020. *Killer Visual Strategies: Engage Any Audience, Improve Comprehension, And Get Amazing Results Using Visual Communication*, Hoboken: Wiley

Bamford, G. 1993. 'Popper's Explications of Ad Hocness: Circularity, Empirical Content, and Scientific Practice', *The British Journal for the Philosophy of Science* 44/2, 335–55

Yoruba Gelede mask, before 1924 (fig. 5.10)

Bantinaki, K. 2008. 'The Opticality of Pictorial Representation', *Journal of Aesthetics and Art Criticism* 66, 183–92

Barbier de Montault, X. 1898. *Traité d'iconographie chrétienne*, Paris: Société de Librairie Ecclésiastique et Religieuse

Barthes, R. 1961. 'Le message photographique', *Communications* 1, 127–38 (English translation: 'The Photographic Message', in R. Barthes, *Image-Music-Text*, translated by S. Heath, London: Fontana, 1977, 15–31)

Barthes, R. 1968. 'La mort de l'auteur', *Manteia* 5, 12–17 (English translation: 'The Death of the Author', in R. Barthes, *Image-Music-Text*, translated by S. Heath, London: Fontana, 1977, 142–48)

Barthes, R. 1970. *S/Z*, Paris: Éditions du Seuil (English translation: R. Barthes, *S/Z*, translated by R. Miller, Oxford: Blackwell, 1990)

Bascom W. 1984. 'The Forms of Folklore: Prose Narratives', in *Sacred Narrative: Readings in the Theory of Myth*, edited by A. Dundes, Berkeley and Los Angeles: University of California Press, 5–29

Basedow, H. 1925. *The Australian Aboriginal*, Adelaide: F.W. Preece and Sons

Bastin, M.-L. 1976. 'On Tshibinda Ilunga', *African Arts* 10/1, 95–97, 100

Bastin, M.-L. 1978. *Statuettes tshokwe du heros civilisateur Tshibinda Ilunga*, Arnouville-lès-Gonesse: Arts d'Afrique noire

Bastin, M.-L. 1984. 'Ritual Masks of the Chokwe', *African Arts* 17/4, 40–45, 92–93, 95–96

Bateman, J. 2014. *Text and Image: A Critical Introduction to the Visual/Verbal Divide*, Abingdon: Routledge

Baxandall, M. 1988. *Painting and Experience in Fifteenth Century Italy*, 2nd edn, Oxford: Oxford University Press

Bedaux, J.B. 1986. 'The Reality of Symbols: The Question of Disguised Symbolism in Jan van Eyck's *Arnolfini Portrait*', *Simiolus: Netherlands Quarterly for the History of Art* 16, 5–28

Belting, H. 1994. *Likeness and Presence: A History of the Image before the Era of Art*, translated by E. Jephcott, Chicago: University of Chicago Press

Bender, K. 2015. 'Distant Viewing in Art History: A Case Study of Artistic Productivity', *DAH-Journal* 1, 94–104

Bender, K. 2018. *The Italian Venus Revisited*, Morrisville: Lulu; https://archive.org/details/Vol1.2ItalianVenusRevisited/

Benjamin, W. [1936] 1980. 'Das Kunstwerk im Zeitalter seiner technischen Reproduzierbarkeit', in *Gesammelte Schriften*, vol. 1, Frankfurt am Main: Suhrkamp, 471–508

Bentley W.H. 1900. *Pioneering on the Congo*, London: The Religious Tract Society

Beran, H. 2011. 'The Iconography of the War Shields of the Trobriand Islands of Papua New Guinea: An Interpretation Recorded by Malinowski and Explained by Paramount Chief Pulayasi', *Pacific Arts*, N.S. 11, 33–45

Bergman M. and S. Paavola. 2014. *The Commens Dictionary: Peirce's Terms in His Own Words*, new edn; http.//www.commens.org/dictionary

Berlejung, A. 1997. 'Washing the Mouth: The Consecration of Divine Images in Mesopotamia', in *The Image and the Book: Iconic Cults, Aniconism, and the Rise of Book Religion in Israel and the Ancient Near East*, edited by K. van der Toorn, Leuven: Peeters, 45–72

Bernhardt, S. 1923. *L'Art du théâtre. La Voix, le geste, la pronunciation*, Paris: Éditions Nilsson

Bhattacharyya, B. 1958. *The Indian Buddhist Iconography*, Kolkata: K.L. Mukhopadhyay

Białostocki, J. 1963. 'Iconography and Iconology', in *Encyclopedia of World Art*, vol. 7, edited by B. Myers, New York: McGraw-Hill, 769–85

Bidyabinod, P. [1920] 1998. *Varieties of the Vishnu Image*, Janpath, New Delhi: Archaeological Survey of India (reprint of 1920 edn)

Biebuyck, D. 1973. *Lega Culture: Art, Initiation and Moral Philosophy among a Central African People*, Berkeley and Los Angeles: University of California Press

Biebuyck, D. 1977. 'Schemata in Lega Art', in *Form in Indigenous Art*, edited by P. Ucko, Canberra: Australian Institute of Aboriginal Studies, 59–65

Bietenholz, P. 1994. *Historia and Fabula: Myths and Legends in Historical Thought from Antiquity to the Modern Age*, Leiden: Brill

Billings, D. 2007. 'New Ireland Malanggan Art: A Quest for Meaning', *Oceania* 77/3, 257–85

Binkley D. and P. Darish. 2009. *Kuba*, Milan: 5 Continents

Bizzocchi, R. 2009. *Genealogie incredibili. Scritti di storia nell'Europa moderna*, Bologna: Il Mulino

Black, J. and A. Green, 1992. *Gods, Demons and Symbols of Ancient Mesopotamia: An Illustrated Dictionary*, London: British Museum Press

Blumson, B. 2014. *Resemblance and Representation: An Essay in the Philosophy of Pictures*, Cambridge: Open Book Publishers

Blurton, T.R. 1992. *Hindu Art*, London: British Museum Press

Boas, F. 1927. *Primitive Art*, Oslo: H. Aschehoug & Co.

Bober H. 1978. 'Editor's Preface', in É. Mâle, *Religious Art in France, the Twelfth Century*, Princeton: Princeton University Press, v–xxi

Bober, P.P. and R. Rubinstein. 1986. *Renaissance Artists and Antique Sculpture*, London: Harvey Miller

Bocher. S. 2006–07. 'Reconstructing Votive Cult Practices in Early Greek Sanctuaries – The Example of the Geometric Votive Bronzes from Olympia', *Anodos. Studies of the Ancient World* 6–7, 85–91

Böhm, B. 1976. 'Thiemo von Salzburg', in *Lexikon der Christlichen Ikonographie*, vol. 8, edited by E. Kirschbaum and G. Bandmann, Rome: Herder, 468

Borg, E. 2004. *Minimal Semantics*, Oxford: Oxford University Press

Borg, E. 2012. 'Semantics without Pragmatics?', in *The Cambridge Handbook of Pragmatics*, edited by K. Allan and K Jaszczolt, Cambridge: Cambridge University Press, 513–28

Boschetto, A. 1961. *Benozzo Gozzoli nella chiesa di San Francesco a Montefalco*, Milan: Istituto editoriale italiano

Boucher, D. 2008. 'Is There an Early Gandhāran Source for the Avalokiteśvara Cult?', *Journal Asiatique*, 296/2, 297–330

Bourgeois, A. 2014. *Yaka*, Milan: 5 Continents

Bouttiaux, A.-M. 2009. *Persona: Masks of Africa. Identities Hidden and Revealed*, Milan: 5 Continents

Bouttiaux, A.-M. 2016. *Guro*, Milan: 5 Continents

Boyer, A.-M. 2008. *Baule*, Milan: 5 Continents

Boyer, A.-M. 2016. *Les Yohouré de Côte d'Ivoire. Faire danser les dieux*, Lausanne: Éditions Ides et Calendes

Boyer, A.-M. 2019. *We*, Milan: 5 Continents

Brain, R. and A. Pollock. 1971. *Bangwa Funerary Sculpture*, London: Duckworth

Brandom, R. 2014. 'Intentionality and Language', in *The Cambridge Handbook of Linguistic Anthropology*, edited by N.J. Enfield, P. Kockelman and J. Sidnell, Cambridge: Cambridge University Press, 347–63

Braun, J. 1943. *Tracht und Attribute der Heiligen in der deutschen Kunst*, Stuttgart: J.B. Metzler

Breckenridge, J.D. 1968. *Likeness: A Conceptual History of Ancient Portraiture*, Evanston: Northwestern University Press

Bredekamp, H. 2010. *Theorie des Bildakts. Frankfurter Adorno-Vorlesungen 2007*, Berlin: Suhrkamp (English translation: *Image Acts: A Systematic Approach to Visual Agency*, translated by E. Clegg, Berlin and Boston: De Gruyter, 2021)

Bredekamp, H. 2014. 'The Picture Act: Tradition, Horizon, Philosophy', in *Bildakt at the Warburg Institute*, edited by S. Marienberg and J. Trabant, Berlin and Boston: De Gruyter, 3–32

Breniquet, C. 1996. 'Du fil à retordre: réflexion sur les "idoles aux yeux" et les fileuses de lépoque d'Uruk', in *Collectanea Orientalia. Histoire, arts de l'espace et industrie de la terre. Études offertes en hommage à Agnès Spycket*, edited by H. Gasche and B. Hrouda, Neuchâtel-Paris: Recherches et publications, 31–53

Brennan, A. 2017. 'Necessary and Sufficient Conditions', in *Stanford Encyclopedia of Philosophy*, edited by Edward N. Zalta; https://plato.stanford.edu/archives/sum2017/entries/necessary-sufficient/

Brienen, R.P. 2006. *Visions of Savage Paradise: Albert Eckhout, Court Painter in Colonial Dutch Brazil*, Amsterdam: Amsterdam University Press

Burger, R. 1995. *Chavin and the Origins of Andean Civilization*, London: Thames and Hudson

Burgess A. and B. Sherman, eds. 2014. *Metasemantics: New Essays on the Foundations of Meaning*, Oxford: Oxford University Press

Burke, P. 2012. 'History, Myth and Fiction: Doubts and Debates', in *The Oxford History of Historical Writing*, edited by J. Rabas, M. Sato, E. Tortarolo and D. Woolf, Oxford: Oxford University Press, 261–81

Burke, P. 2014. 'Gombrich's Search for Cultural History', in *Meditations on a Heritage: Papers on the Work and Legacy of Sir Ernst Gombrich*, edited by P. Taylor, London: Paul Holberton, 14–21

Burke, S. 1998. *The Death and Return of the Author: Criticism and Subjectivity in Barthes, Foucault and Derrida*, 2nd edn, Edinburgh: Edinburgh University Press

Cadbury, T. 2008. 'A Trader in Central Africa: The Dennett Collection at the Royal Albert Memorial Museum, Exeter', *Journal of Museum Ethnography* 20, 109–19

Cadman, H. 1922. *An Assessment Report on the Bangwa Tribal Area in the Mamfe Division of the Cameroon Province, Dec 19th 1922*, Buea: National Archives, File No. Af 13, Original File No. E.P. 6859; www.lebialem.info

Cahier, C. 1867. *Caractéristiques des saints dans lart populaire*, Paris: Poussielgue Frères

Cameron, E. 2001. *Art of the Lega*, Los Angeles: Fowler Museum

Camille, M. 1989. *The Gothic Idol: Ideology and Image-Making in Medieval Art*, Cambridge: Cambridge University Press

Cappelen H. and E. Lepore, 2005. *Insensitive Semantics*, Oxford: Blackwell

Carroll, P. 1977. 'Mimi from Western Arnhem Land', in *Form in Indigenous Art*, edited by P. Ucko, Canberra: Australian Institute of Aboriginal Studies, 119–30

Casati, R. 2004. 'Methodological Issues in the Study of the Depiction of Cast Shadows', *Journal of Aesthetics and Art Criticism* 62, 163–74

Cassidy, B. 1993. 'Introduction', in *Iconography at the Crossroads*, edited by B. Cassidy, Princeton: Department of Art and Archaeology, 3–15

Caubet, A. 2006. 'Des yeux et des lunettes', *Syria* 83, 177–81

Central Intelligence Agency. 2002. *Iraq's Weapons of Mass Destruction Programs*; https://irp.fas.org/cia/product/Iraq_Oct_2002.pdf

Central Intelligence Agency. 2023. *The World Factbook: Angola;* https://www.cia.gov/the-world-factbook/countries/angola/

Chambers, E. 1728. *Cyclopaedia*, London: James and John Knapton et al.

Chilver, E.M. 1967. 'The Bangwa and the Germans: A Tailpiece', *Journal of the Historical Society of Nigeria* 4/1, 155–60

Chittka, L. 2022. *The Mind of a Bee*, Princeton: Princeton University Press

Chomsky, N. 1975. *Reflections on Language*, New York: Random House

Choul, G. du. 1556. *Discours de la religion des anciens Romains*, Lyon: Guillaume Roville

Christian, K.W. 2006. 'Poetry and "Spirited" Ancient Sculpture in Renaissance Rome', in *Aeolian Winds and the Spirit in Renaissance Architecture*, edited by B. Kenda, London and New York: Routledge, 103–24

Clark, W.E. 1965. *Two Lamaistic Pantheons*, New York: Paragon

Clercq, F.S.A. de. 1893. *Ethnographische beschrijving van de West- en Noordkust van Nederlandsch Nieuw-Guinea*, Leiden: P.W.M. Trap

Cobo, B. [1653] 1990. *Inca Religion and Customs*, translated and edited by Roland Hamilton, Austin: University of Texas Press

Cohn, N., ed. 2016. *The Visual Narrative Reader*, London: Bloomsbury

Cole, H. 2013. *Igbo*, Milan: 5 Continents

Colleyn, J.-P. 2009. *Bamana*, Milan: 5 Contients

Collinet-Guérin, M. 1961. *Histoire du nimbe. Des origines aux temps modernes*, Paris: Nouvelles éditions latines.

Collins, S. 2015. *The Standard of Ur*, London: British Museum Press

Collon, D. 1982. *Catalogue of the Western Asiatic Seals in the British Museum. Cylinder Seals, Vol. 2: Akkadian/Post-Akkadian/Ur III Periods*, London: British Museum Publications

Collon, D. 1987. *First Impressions: Cylinder Seals in the Ancient Near East*, London: British Museum Press

Corbey, R. 2019. *Korwar: Northwest New Guinea Ritual Art According to Missionary Sources*, Leiden: Zwartenkot

Corbin, G.A. and S. Fabricant. 1979. 'Some Notes on Kairak Baining Night Dance Headdresses and Masks', *Pacific Arts Newsletter* 9, 2–5

Cort, J. 1994. 'Following the Jina, Worshiping the Jina: An Essay on Jain Rituals', in *The Peaceful Liberators. Jain Art from India*, edited by P. Pal, Los Angeles: County Museum of Art, 39–54

Cort, J. 1995. 'Genres of Jain History', *Journal of Indian Philosophy* 23/4, 469–506

Crane, D. 1999. 'Gender and Hegemony in Fashion Magazines: Women's Interpretations of Fashion Photographs', *The Sociological Quarterly* 40/4, 541–63

Cunningham, A. 1879. *The Stûpa of Bharhut*, London: W.H. Allen et al.

Curchin, L. 1995. 'Literacy in the Roman Provinces: Qualitative and Quantitative Data from Central Spain', *The American Journal of Philology* 116/ 3, 461–76

Curtis, M.Y. 2018. *Baga*, Milan: 5 Continents.

Daniélou, A. 1964. *Hindu Polytheism*, New York: Bollingen

Dearden, C.W. 1975. 'The Poet and the Mask Again', *Phoenix* 29/1, 75–82

Dehejia, V. 1990. 'On Modes of Visual Narration in Early Buddhist Art', *Art Bulletin* 72/3, 374–92

Dehejia, V. 1997. *Discourse in Early Buddhist Art: Visual Narratives of India*, New Delhi: Munshiram Manoharlal

Delaporte, L. 1920. *Musée du Louvre. Catalogue des cylindres, cachets et pierres gravées de style oriental*, Paris: Hachette

Deleuze, G. 1984. *Cinéma. Vol. 1: L'Image-mouvement*, Paris: Éditions de Minuit

Denner, A. 2006. 'Images from Over the Sea: The Meaning and Use of Masks on Anir, New Ireland, Papua New Guinea (Part I)', *Pacific Arts*, N.S. 2, 20–29

Denner, A. 2008. 'Images from Over the Sea: The Meaning and Use of Masks on Anir, New Ireland, Papua New Guinea (Part II)', *Pacific Arts*, N.S. 7, 12–23

Dennett, R.E. 1902. 'The Religion of the Fjort or Fiote: "Mavungu"', *Journal of the African Society* 1, 452–54

Deręgowski, J.B. 2017. 'Cross-Cultural Studies of Illusions', in *The Oxford Compendium of Visual Illusions*, edited by Arthur Shapiro and Dejan Todorović, New York: Oxford University Press, 38–53

Derlon, B. 1990/1991. 'L'objet Malanggan dans les anciens rites funéraires de Nouvelle Irlande', *RES: Anthropology and Aesthetics* 19/20, 178–210

Derlon, B. 1994. 'Droits de reproduction des objets de culte, tenure foncière et filiation en Nouvelle-Irlande', *L'Homme* 34/130, 31–58

Díaz del Castillo, B. [1568] 1870. *Historia verdadera de la conquista de la Nueva España*, Mexico City: Escalante

Diderot, D. [1767] 1963. *Salons III, 1767*, edited by J. Seznec and J. Adhémar, Oxford: Clarendon Press

Diderot D. and J. d'Alembert, eds. 1765. *Encyclopédie, ou dictionnaire raisonné des sciences, des arts et des métiers*, vol. 8, Neufchâtel: Samuel Faulche

Didi-Huberman, G. 2002. *L'Image survivante. Histoire de l'art en temps des fantômes selon Aby Warburg*, Paris: Éditions de Minuit

Didron, A.-N. 1843. *Iconographie chrétienne. Histoire de Dieu*, Paris: Imprimerie royale

Dijk, J.J.A. van. 1957. 'Gott', in *Reallexikon der Assyriologie und vorderasiatischen Archäologie*, vol. 3, edited by M. Falkner, Berlin and New York: De Gruyter

Dilworth, J. 2005. 'A Double Content Theory of Artistic Representation', *Journal of Aesthetics and Art Criticism* 63/3, 249–60

Dobbins, K.W. 1968. 'Two Gandhāran Reliquaries', *East and West* 18, 151–62

Donnan, C.B. 1978. *Moche Art of Peru: Pre-Columbian Symbolic Communication*, Los Angeles, UCLA Museum of Natural History

Donnan, C.B. 2004. *Moche Portraits from Ancient Peru*, Austin: University of Texas Press

Donnan, C.B. and D. McClelland, 1999, *Moche Fineline Painting*, Los Angeles: Fowler Museum

Douglas, M. 1966. *Purity and Danger: An Analysis of the Concepts of Pollution and Taboo*, London: Routledge

Drogin, B. and M. Farley. 2003. 'Hard Claims But Only Soft Proof So Far in Iraq', *Los Angeles Times*, 26 January; https://www.latimes.com/archives/la-xpm-2003-jan-26-fg-inspect26-story.html

Dummett, M. 1981. *Frege: Philosophy of Language*, 2nd edn, Cambridge, MA: Harvard University Press

Dunstan, E. 1965. 'A Bangwa Account of Early Encounters with the German Colonial Administration', *Journal of the Historical Society of Nigeria* 3/2, 43–413

Dupeux, C., P. Jezler and J. Wirth, eds. 2001. *Iconoclasme. Vie et mort de l'image médiévale*, Paris: Somogy

Dyer, A.G., C. Neumeyer and L. Chittka. 2005. 'Honeybee (*Apis mellifera*) Vision Can Discriminate between and Recognise Images of Human Faces', *The Journal of Experimental Biology* 208, 4709–14

Dyer, C.L. 2005. *The French Explorers and the Aboriginal Australians, 1772–1839*, St Lucia: University of Queensland Press

Eck, C. van. 2015. *Art, Agency and Living Presence: From the Animated Image to the Excessive Object*, Boston and Berlin: De Gruyter

Eco, U. 1976. *A Theory of Semiotics*, Bloomington: Indiana University Press

Edwards, D. and D. Cromwell. 2006. *Guardians of Power: The Myth of the Liberal Media*, London: Pluto Press

Eire, C. 1986. *War Against the Idols: The Reformation of Worship from Erasmus to Calvin*, Cambridge: Cambridge University Press

Ekroth, G. 2012. 'Pelops Joins the Party: Transformations of a Hero Cult within the Festival at Olympia', in *Greek and Roman Festivals: Content, Meaning and Practice*, edited by J.R. Brandt and J.W. Iddeng, Oxford: Oxford University Press, 95–137

Elkins, J. 1999. *Why Are Our Pictures Puzzles? On the Modern Origins of Pictorial Complexity*, New York: Routledge

Ellen, R. 1988. 'Fetishism', *Man*, N.S. 23, 213–35

Erizzo, S. 1568. *Discorso sopra le medaglie de gli antichi*, Venice: Giovanni Varisco

Evans, G. 1973. 'The Causal Theory of Names', *Aristotelian Society: Supplementary Volume* 47, 187–203

Evans, G. 1982. *The Varieties of Reference*, edited by John McDowell, Oxford: Oxford University Press

Evans-Pritchard, E.E. 1937. *Witchcraft, Oracles and Magic among the Azande*, Oxford: Oxford University Press

Evans-Pritchard, E.E. 1940. *The Nuer: A Description of the Modes of Livelihood and Political Institutions of a Nilotic People*, Oxford: Oxford University Press

Evans-Pritchard, E.E. 1951. *Social Anthropology*, London: Cohen and West

Evans-Pritchard, E.E. 1953. 'The Nuer Conception of Spirit in Its Relation to the Social Order', *American Anthropologist* 55/2, 201–14

Evans-Pritchard, E.E. 1954. 'A Problem of Nuer Religious Thought', *Sociologus*, N.S. 4/1, 23–42

Evans-Pritchard, E.E. 1956. *Nuer Religion*, Oxford: Clarendon Press

Evans-Pritchard, E.E. 1965. *Theories of Primitive Religion*, Oxford: Clarendon Press

Ezcurdia M. and R. Stainton, 2013. 'Introduction', in *The Semantics-Pragmatics Boundary in Philosophy*, edited by M. Ezcurdia and R. Stainton, Peterborough, ON: Broadview, xiii–xxxiv

Fan, B. 2022. 'The Birth of the Photographic Collection at the Warburg Institute', *World* 3/5, 132–51 (in Chinese)

Faris, J.C. 1972. *Nuba Personal Art*, London: Duckworth

Feldman, M. 2009. 'Knowledge as Cultural Biography: Lives of Mesopotamian Monuments', *Studies in the History of Art* 74, 40–55

Felli, C. 2006. 'Lugal-Ušumgal: An Akkadian Governor and his Two Masters', in *The Iconography of Cylinder Seals*, edited by P. Taylor, London and Turin: Warburg Institute and Nino Aragno, 35–50

Fernandez, J. 1973. 'The Exposition and Imposition of Order: Artistic Expression in Fang Culture', in *The Traditional Artist in African Societies*, edited by W. d'Azevedo, Bloomington: Indiana University Press, 194–220

Fienup-Riordan, A. 1996. *The Living Tradition of Yupik Masks*, Seattle: University of Washington Press

Fineman, M. 2012. *Faking It: Manipulated Photography before Photoshop*, New Haven and London: Yale University Press

Fock, C.W. 2021. 'Art Ownership in Leiden in the Seventeenth Century', *Journal of Historians of Netherlandish Art* 13/1; https://jhna.org/articles/art-ownership-in-leiden-in-the-seventeenth-century/

Forge, A. 2017a. 'Art and Environment in the Sepik', in *Anthony Forge: Style and Meaning. Essays on the Anthropology of Art*, edited by A. Clark and N. Thomas, Leiden: Sidestone Press, 51–69

Forge, A. 2017b. 'Style and Meaning in Sepik Art', in *Anthony Forge: Style and Meaning. Essays on the Anthropology of Art*, edited by A. Clark and N. Thomas, Leiden: Sidestone Press, 87–110

Forge, A. 2017c. 'The Problem of Meaning in Art', in *Anthony Forge: Style and Meaning. Essays on the Anthropology of Art*, edited by A. Clark and N. Thomas, Leiden: Sidestone Press, 111–21

Forge, A. 2017d. 'Learning to See in New Guinea', in *Anthony Forge: Style and Meaning. Essays on the Anthropology of Art*, edited by A. Clark and N. Thomas, Leiden: Sidestone Press, 123–37

Foucher, A. 1900. *Étude sur l'iconographie Bouddhique de l'Inde*, Paris: Leroux

Foucher, A. 1905. *L'Art Gréco-Bouddhique du Gandhâra*, vol. 1, Paris: Imprimerie nationale

Foucher, A. 1918. *L'Art Gréco-Bouddhique du Gandhâra*, vol. 2.1, Paris: Imprimerie nationale

Foucher, A. 1922. *L'Art Gréco-Bouddhique du Gandhâra*, vol. 2.2, Paris: Imprimerie nationale

Fracassi, L. 2024. 'Ambiguity and Polyvalence in Rubens's Allegories', MA thesis, London: Warburg Institute

Frangenberg, T. 2003. '"One could invent not one, but a hundred further meanings": Francesco Bracciolini on an Early State of Pietro da Cortona's Barberini Ceiling', in *The Enduring Instant: Time and the Spectator in the Visual Arts / Der bleibende Augenblick: Betrachterzeit in den Bildkünsten*, edited by A. Roesler-Friedenthal and J. Nathan, Berlin: Gebr. Mann

Frankfort, H. 1954. *The Art and Architecture of the Ancient Orient*, New Haven and London: Yale University Press

Frankfort, H. 1955. *Stratified Cylinder Seals from the Diyala Region*, Chicago: University of Chicago Press

Frazer, J.G. 1910. *Totemism and Exogamy*, London: Macmillan

Frazer, J.G. 1912. *The Golden Bough*, 3rd edn, New York and London: Macmillan

Freedberg, D. 1986. 'Art and Iconoclasm, 1525–1580: The Case of the Northern Netherlands', in *Kunst voor de beeldenstorm. Noordnerlandse kunst, 1525–1580*, edited by J.P. Filedt Kok, W. Halsema Kubes and W.T. Kloek, Amsterdam: Rijksmuseum, 39–84

Freedberg, D. 1989. *The Power of Images: Studies in the History and Theory of Response*, Chicago: University of Chicago Press

Frege, G. [1892] 1977. 'On Sense and Reference', in *Translations from the Philosophical Writings of Gottlob Frege*, 4th edn, edited by P. Geach and M. Black, Oxford: Blackwell, 56–78 (1st edn: 'Über Sinn und Bedeutung', *Zeitschrift für Philosophie und philosophische Kritik* 100 (1892), 25–50)

Fresnoy, C.A. du. 1668. *L'Art de peinture*, translation and commentary by R. de Piles, Paris: Nicolas l'Anglois

Friend, S. 2017. 'Elucidating the Truth in Criticism', *Journal of Aesthetics and Art Criticism* 75/4, 387–99

Friesen, I. 2001. *The Female Crucifix: Images of St Wilgefortis since the Middle Ages*, Waterloo: Wilfrid Laurier University Press

Fussman, G. 2012. 'The Genesis of Avalokiteśvara Iconography: About Two Statues in the Pritzkers Collection', in *The Early Iconography of Avalokiteśvara / L'Iconographie ancienne d'Avalokiteśvara*, edited by G. Fussman and A.-M. Quagliotti, Paris: Boccard, 34–36

Gabriele, M., C. Galassi and R. Guerrini, eds. 2013. *L'Iconologia di Cesare Ripa. Fonti letterarie e figurative dall'antichità al Rinascimento*, Florence: Olschki

Gagliardi, S.E. 2015. *Senufo Unbound: Dynamics of Art and Identity in West Africa*, Milan: 5 Continents

Gardner, J. 1989. 'Päpstliche Träume und Palastmalereien. Ein Essay über mittelalterliche Traumikonographie', in *Träume im Mittelalter. Ikonologische Studien*, edited by A. Paravicini Bagliani and G. Stabile, Stuttgart: Belser, 113–24

Garlake, P. 1995. *The Hunter's Vision: The Prehistoric Art of Zimbabwe*, London: British Museum Press

Gay, L. 2020. 'The French Renaissance of the Pagan Gods. French Manuscript Illuminations 1320–1420', PhD thesis, London: Warburg Institute

Gazda, E. 2002. *The Ancient Art of Emulation: Studies in Artistic Originality and Tradition from the Present to Classical Antiquity*, Ann Arbor: University of Michigan Press

Geimer, P. 2007. 'Image as Trace: Speculations about an Undead Paradigm', *Differences: A Journal of Feminist Cultural Studies* 18, 7–28

Gell, A. 1988. *Art and Agency: An Anthropological Theory*, Oxford: Clarendon Press

Getty, A. 1914. *The Gods of Northern Buddhism: Their History, Iconography and Progressive Evolution through the Northern Buddhist Countries*, Oxford: Clarendon Press

Giehlow, K. 1915. 'Die Hieroglyphenkunde des Humanismus in der Allegorie der Renaissance', *Jahrbuch der Kunsthistorischen Sammlungen des Allerhöchsten Kaiserhauses* 32, 1–232 (English translation: *The Humanist Interpretation of Hieroglyphs in the Allegorical Studies of the Renaissance*, translated by R. Raybould, Leiden: Brill, 2015)

Gilbert, C. 1952. 'On Subject and Not-Subject in Italian Renaissance Pictures', *Art Bulletin* 34, 202–16

Gilligan, I. 2008. 'Clothing and Climate in Aboriginal Australia', *Current Anthropology* 49/3, 487–95

Ginzburg, C. 1985. *The Enigma of Piero*, London: Verso

Giovino, M. 2006. 'Assyrian Trees as Cult Objects', in *The Iconography of Cylinder Seals*, edited by P. Taylor, London and Turin: Warburg Institute and Nino Aragno, 110–25

Giovino, M. 2007. *The Assyrian Sacred Tree: A History of Interpretations*, Fribourg and Göttingen: Academic Press and Vandenhoeck & Ruprecht

Goffen, R. 1979. '*Nostra Conversatio in Caelis Est.* Observations on the *Sacra Conversazione* in the Trecento', *Art Bulletin* 61/2, 198–222

Golomb, C. 1992. *The Child's Creation of a Pictorial World*, Berkeley and Los Angeles: University of California Press

Gombrich, E.H. 1941. 'Introduction to the Study of Iconography in Medieval and Modern European Art. 2: Secular Iconography', Unpublished typescript, Warburg Institute Archive, Gombrich Papers (Cf. Kurz 1939)

Gombrich, E.H. 1949. 'Review of C. Morris, *Signs, Language and Behaviour*', *The Art Bulletin* 31, 68–73

Gombrich, E.H. 1960. *Art and Illusion: A Study in the Psychology of Pictorial Representation*, Oxford: Phaidon

Gombrich, E.H. 1963. 'Meditations on a Hobby Horse', in E.H. Gombrich, *Meditations on a Hobby Horse and Other Essays on the Theory of Art*, London: Phaidon, 1–11

Gombrich, E.H. 1965. 'The Use of Art for the Study of Symbols', *American Psychologist* 20/1, 34–50

Gombrich, E.H. 1966. 'The Renaissance Theory of Art and the Rise of Landscape', in E.H. Gombrich, *Norm and Form*, Oxford: Phaidon, 107–21

Gombrich, E.H. 1970. *Aby Warburg: An Intellectual Biography*, Oxford: Phaidon

Gombrich, E.H. 1971. 'Personification', in *Classical Influences in European Culture*, edited by R.R. Bolgar, Cambridge: Cambridge University Press, 247–57

Gombrich, E.H. 1972a. 'Introduction: Aims and Limits of Iconology', in E.H. Gombrich, *Symbolic Images: Studies in the Art of the Renaissance II*, Oxford: Phaidon, 1–25

Gombrich, E.H. 1972b. '*Icones symbolicae*: Philosophies of Symbolism and their Bearing on Art', in E.H. Gombrich, *Symbolic Images: Studies in the Art of the Renaissance II*, Oxford: Phaidon, 123–91

Gombrich, E.H. 1978. 'The Logic of Vanity Fair: Alternatives to Historicism in the Study of Fashions, Style and Taste', in E.H. Gombrich, *Ideals and Idols*, London: Phaidon, 60–92

Gombrich, E.H. 1982a. 'Visual Discovery through Art', in E.H. Gombrich, *The Image and the Eye: Further Studies in the Psychology of Pictorial Representation*, Oxford: Phaidon, 1982, 11–39

Gombrich, E.H. 1982b. 'The Visual Image: Its Place in Communication', in E.H. Gombrich, *The Image and the Eye: Further Studies in the Psychology of Pictorial Representation*, Oxford: Phaidon, 1982, 137–61

Gombrich, E.H. 1982c. 'Image and Code: Scope and Limits of Conventionalism in Pictorial Representation', in E.H. Gombrich, *The Image and the Eye: Further Studies in the Psychology of Pictorial Representation*, Oxford: Phaidon, 1982, 278–97

Gombrich, E.H. 1984. *The Sense of Order: A Study in the Psychology of Decorative Art*, 2nd edn, London: Phaidon

Goodman, N. 1949. 'On Likeness of Meaning', *Analysis* 10, 1–7

Goodman, N. 1976. *Languages of Art: An Approach to a Theory of Symbols*, 2nd edn (1st edn 1968), Indianapolis: Hackett

Goodman, N. 1978. *Ways of Worldmaking*, Indianapolis: Hackett

Gopinatha Rao, T.A. 1914–16. *Elements of Hindu Iconography*, Madras: Law Printing House

Gorakshakar, S. 1994. 'Meditating Female', in *The Peaceful Liberators: Jain Art from India*, edited by P. Pal, Los Angeles: County Museum of Art, 139

Gordon, R. and S.S. Douglas. 2000. *The Bushman Myth: The Making of a Namibian Underclass*, Boulder, CO: Westview Press

Green, L. 2016. "And do not say 'tis superstition": Shakespeare, Memory, and the Iconography of Death', *Comparative Drama* 50, 249–70

Griaule, M. 1963. *Masques Dogons*, 2nd edn, Paris: Institut d'Ethnologie

Griego, H. 2011. 'Pastoral Care, Inquisition, and Mendicancy in the Medieval Franciscan Order', in *The Origin, Development, and Refinement of Medieval Religious Mendicancies*, edited by D. Prudlo, Leiden: Brill, 117–56

Griffin, N. 2018. 'Brandom and the Brutes', *Synthese* 195/12, 5521–47

Grosz, P.G., E. Kaiser and F. Pierini. 2021. 'Discourse Anaphoricity and First Person Indexicality in Emoji Resolution', *Proceedings of Sinn und Bedeutung* 25, 340–57

Grothaus, M. 2021. *Trust No One: Inside the World of Deepfakes*, London: Hodder and Stoughton

Grzankowski, A. 2015. 'Pictures Have Propositional Content', *Review of Philosophy and Psychology* 6/1, 151–63

Guidoni, E. 2004. 'Tra incredulità e devozione. La religiosità di Pietro Perugino', in *Pietro Vannucci, il Perugino*, edited by L. Teza, Perugia: Volumnia, 441–48

Gunn, M. 1987. 'The Transfer of Malagan Ownership on Tabar', in *Assemblage of Spirits: Idea and Image in New Ireland*, edited by L. Lincoln, New York: George Braziller in association with the Minneapolis Museum of Art, 74–83

Gunn, M. 1992. 'Malagan Ritual Art on Tabar, New Ireland, Papua New Guinea', PhD thesis, Dunedin: University of Otago

Hackin, J. et al. 1954. *Nouvelles recherches archéologiques à Begram, ancienne Kâpicî, 1939–1940. Rencontre de trois civilisations, Inde, Grèce, Chine*, Paris: Imprimerie nationale

Haddon, A. 1921. *Magic and Fetishism*, London: Constable & Co.

Hämeen-Anttila, J. 2017. 'Rustam in Arabic Literature and the Middle Persian *Khwadāynāmag*', *Wiener Zeitschrift für die Kunde des Morgenlandes* 107, 27–58

Harpur, Y. 1986. 'The Identity and Positions of Relief Fragments in Museums and Private Collections: The Reliefs of R'-ḥtp and Nfrt from Meydum', *The Journal of Egyptian Archaeology* 72, 23–40

Harris, W.V. 1989. *Ancient Literacy*, Cambridge, MA: Harvard University Press

Hart, J. 1993. 'Erwin Panofsky and Karl Mannheim: A Dialogue on Interpretation', *Critical Inquiry*, 19/3, 534–66

Harter, P. 1990. 'Royal Commemorative Figures in the Cameroon Grasslands: Ateu Atsa, a Bangwa Artist', *African Arts* 23, 70–77

Haugeland, J. 1998. 'The Intentionality All-Stars', in J. Haugeland, *Having Thought: Essays in the Metaphysics of Mind*, Cambridge, MA: Harvard University Press, 127–70

Hecht P. 2018. 'Could This Be It? Rembrandt's Leiden History Painting of 1626 Depicts Orestes and Pylades before King Thoas in Tauris'. *Simiolus: Netherlands Quarterly for the History of Art* 40/4, 292–301

Heck, T. 1999. 'The Evolving Meanings of Iconology and Iconography: Towards Some *Descriptive* Definitions', in *Picturing Performance: The Iconography of the Performing Arts in Concept and Practice*, edited by T. Heck, Rochester, NY: University of Rochester Press, 7–41

Heintze, D. 1987. 'On Trying to Understand some Malagans', in *Assemblage of Spirits: Idea and Image in New Ireland*, edited by L. Lincoln, New York: George Braziller in association with the Minneapolis Museum of Art, 42–55

Helmsdörfer, G. 1839. *Christliche Kunstsymbolik und Ikonographie*, Frankfurt am Main: J.C. Hermann

Herles, M. 2006. *Götterdarstellungen Mesopotamiens in der 2. Hälfte des 2. Jarhtausends v. Chr*, Münster: Ugarit-Verlag

Hermans, W.F. 1958. *De donkere kamer van Damokles*, Amsterdam: G.A. van Oorschoot (English translation: *The Darkroom of Damocles*, translated by I. Rilke, London: Pushkin Press, 2020)

Hermerén, G. 1969. *Representation and Meaning in the Visual Arts*, Lund: Berlingska Boktryckeriet

Hersak, D. 2010a. 'Reviewing Power, Process and Statement: The Case of Songye Figures', *African Arts* 43/2, 38–51

Hersak, D. 2010b. 'There Are Many Kongo Worlds: Particularities of Magico-Religious Beliefs among the Vili and Yombe of Congo-Brazzaville', *Africa: Journal of the International African Institute* 71/4, 614–40

Hiepe, R. 1989. 'Aus dem Dunkel ans Licht. Frans Masereel und der Sozialismus', in *Frans Masereel (1889–1972). Zur Verwirklichung des Traums von einer freien Gesellschaft*, edited by K.-L. Hofmann and P. Riede, Saarbrucken: Verlag der Saarbrucker Zeitung, 256–65

Hilton, A. 1987. 'European Sources for the Study of Religious Change in Sixteenth and Seventeenth Century Kongo', *Paideuma* 33, 289–312

Himmelheber, H. 1964. 'Sculptors and Sculptures of the Dan', in *Proceedings of the First International Congress of Africanists, Accra 11th–18th December 1962*, edited by L. Brown and M. Crowder, London: Longmans, 243–55

Hochberg, J. 1983. 'Problems of Picture Perception', *Visual Arts Research* 9/2, 7–24

Hochberg, J. and V. Brooks. 1962. 'Pictorial Recognition as an Unlearned Ability: A Study of One Child's Performance', *The American Journal of Psychology*, 75/4, 624–28

Hoff, J. 1977. 'Aboriginal Carved and Painted Human Figures in North-east Arnhem Land', in *Form in Indigenous Art*, edited by P. Ucko, Canberra: Australian Institute of Aboriginal Studies, 156–64

Hoffman, K. 2004. *Stieglitz: A Beginning Light*, New Haven and London: Yale University Press

Holberton, P. 1995. 'Giorgione's *Tempest* or 'little landscape with the storm with the gypsy': More on the Gypsy, and a Reassessment', *Art History* 18/3, 383–404

Holberton, P. 2021. *A History of Arcadia in Art and Literature*, 2 vols, London: Ad Ilissum

Holly, M.A. 1984. *Panofsky and the Foundations of Art History*, Ithaca and London: Cornell University Press

Hope, C. 1980. 'Problems of Interpretation in Titian's Erotic Paintings', in *Tiziano e Venezia*, edited by N. Pozza, Vicenza: N. Pozza, 111–24

Hope, C. 1990. 'Altarpieces and the Requirements of Patrons', in *Christianity and the Renaissance*, edited by T. Verdon and J Henderson, Syracuse: Syracuse University Press, 535–71

Hope, C. 2007. 'Il concetto di Historia nelle arti visive prima di Alberti', in *Alberti e la tradizione. Per lo smontaggio dei mosaici Albertiani*, edited by R. Cardini and M. Regoliosi, Florence: Edizioni Polistampa, 533–44

Hope, C. 2014. 'Vasari's *Vite* as a Collaborative Project', in *The Ashgate Research Companion to Giorgio Vasari*, edited by D.J. Cast, Farnham: Ashgate, 11–21

Hope C. and P. Taylor. 1995. 'Piero's *Flagellation* and the Conventions of Painted Narrative', in *Incontri del Dizionario Biografico degli Italiani. Piero della Francesca*, edited by A. Uguccioni, Rome: Istituto della Enciclopedia Italiana, 48–101

Hopkins, R. 1998. *Picture, Image and Experience*, Cambridge: Cambridge University Press

Horton, R. 1965. *Kalabari Sculpture*, Lagos: Department of Antiquities

Houston, S. 1994. 'Literacy among the Pre-Columbian Maya: A Comparative Perspective', In *Writing without Words: Alternative Literacies in Mesoamerica and the Andes*, edited by E.H. Boone and W. Mignolo, Durham and London: Duke University Press, 1994, 27–49

Houston S. and K. Taube. 2008. 'Meaning in Early Maya Imagery', in *Iconography without Texts*, edied by P. Taylor, London and Turin: Warburg Institute and Nino Aragno, 127–44

Howitt, A.W. 1904. *Native Tribes of South-East Australia*, London: Macmillan

Huang, Y. 2014. *Pragmatics*, Oxford: Oxford University Press

Hubert, H. and M. Mauss. 1902–03. 'Esquisse d'une théorie générale de la magie', *L'année sociologique* 7, 1–146

Huis, A. van. 2017. 'Cultural Significance of Termites in Sub-Saharan Africa', *Journal of Ethnobiology and Ethnomedicine* 13, 8; https://doi.org/10.1186/s13002-017-0137-z

Huisstede, P. van. 2017. 'Aby M. Warburg: Iconographer?', in *The Routledge Companion to Medieval Iconography*, edited by C. Hourihane, Abingdon: Routledge, 75–88

Humphrey, C. and J. Laidlaw. 1994. *The Archetypal Actions of Ritual: A Theory of Ritual Illustrated by the Jain Rite of Worship*, Oxford: Clarendon Press

Hyman, J. 1993. 'The Meaning Theory of Pictures', *Iyyun: The Jerusalem Philosophical Quarterly* 42, 149–63

Hyman, J. 2006. *The Objective Eye: Color, Form and Reality in the Theory of Art*, Chicago: University of Chicago Press

Hyman, J. 2012. 'Depiction', *Royal Institute of Philosophy Supplement* 71, 129–50

Hyman J. and K. Bantinaki. 2017. 'Depiction', in *Stanford Encyclopedia of Philosophy*, edited by Edward N. Zalta; https://plato.stanford.edu/archives/sum2017/entries/depiction/

Imperato, P.J. 1970. 'The Dance of the Tyi Wara', *African Arts* 4/1, 8–13, 71–80

Ingold, T. 2000. 'Totemism, Animism and the Depiction of Animals', in T. Ingold, *The Perception of the Environment: Essays on Livelihood, Dwelling and Skill*, Abingdon, Routledge, 111–31

Ishii, M. 1994. 'The Noh Theater: Mirror, Mask, and Madness', *Comparative Drama* 28/1, 43–66

Islam F. and G. Baggio. 2020. 'Kripkeans of the World, Unite!', *Journal of Semantics* 37, 297–309

Israëls, M.B. 2020. *Piero della Francesca and the Invention of the Artist*, London: Reaktion Books

Jacob, P. 2019. 'Intentionality', in *Stanford Encyclopedia of Philosophy*, edited by Edward N. Zalta; https://plato.stanford.edu/archives/win2019/entries/intentionality/

Jacobsen, T. 1989. 'God or Worshipper', in *Essays in Ancient Civilization presented to Helene J. Kantor*, edited by A. Leonard and B.B. Williams, Chicago: The Oriental Institute, 125–30

James L. and R. Webb. 1991. "To Understand Ultimate Things and Enter Secret Places": Ekphrasis and Art in Byzantium', *Art History* 14/1, 1–17

James, E.O. 1959. *The Cult of the Mother-Goddess: An Archaeological and Documentary Study*, London: Thames and Hudson

Jameson, A. 1848. *Sacred and Legendary Art*, London: Longman, Brown, Green and Longman

Jędrej, M.C. 1980. 'A Comparison of Some Masks from North America, Africa, and Melanesia', *Journal of Anthropological Research* 36/2, 220–30

Jędrej, M.C. 1986. 'Dan and Mende Masks: A Structural Comparison', *Africa: Journal of the International African Institute* 56/1, 71–80

Jonaitis, A. 2006. 'Sacred Art and Spiritual Power: An Analysis of Tlingit Shamans' Masks', in *The Anthropology of Art: A Reader*, edited by H. Morphy and M. Perkins, Oxford: Blackwell, 358–73

Jonas, H. 1961. 'Homo pictor und die differentia des Menschen', *Zeitschrift für philosophische Forschung* 15/2, 161–76

Kadowaki, Y. 2014. 'Noh Drama and the Samurai', *Bulletin of the Detroit Institute of Arts* 88/1, 104–13

Kaftal, G. 1952. *Iconography of the Saints in Italian Painting, 1, Iconography of the Saints in Tuscan Painting*, Florence: Sansoni

Kalinowski, L. 2024. 'Iconology or Iconography?The Term Iconology in Erwin Panofsky's Research on Art', in *Art Historiography and Iconologies Between West and East*, edited by W. Bałus and M. Kunińska, New York: Routledge, 29–57

Kaplan, D. 1989. 'Afterthoughts', in J. Almog, J. Perry and H. Wettstein, eds., *Themes from Kaplan*, Oxford: Oxford University Press, 565–614

Kendon, A. 1988. *Sign Languages of Aboriginal Australia: Cultural, Semiotic and Communicative Perspectives*, Cambridge: Cambridge University Press

Kendon, A. 2004. *Gesture: Visual Action as Utterance*, Cambridge: Cambridge University Press

Kerr B. and J. Kerr. 2005. 'The "Way" of God L: The Princeton Vase Revisited', *Record of the Art Museum, Princeton University* 64, 71–79

Kerschensteiner, G. 1905. *Die Entwickelung der zeichnerischen Begabung*, Munich: Carl Gerber

Kidson, P. 1987. 'Panofsky, Suger and St Denis', *Journal of the Warburg and Courtauld Institutes* 50, 1–17

Kjørup, S. 1978. 'Pictorial Speech Acts', *Erkenntnis (1975-)* 12, 55–71

Korshak, Y. 1987. 'The Liberty Cap as a Revolutionary Symbol in America and France', *Smithsonian Studies in American Art* 1, 52–69

Korta K. and J. Perry, 2020. 'Pragmatics', in *Stanford Encyclopedia of Philosophy*, edited by Edward N. Zalta; https://plato.stanford.edu/archives/spr2020/entries/pragmatics/

Kraus, F.X. 1882. 'Archäologie, christliche', in *Real-Encyklopädie der Christlichen Alterthümer*, edited by F.X. Kraus, 2 vols, Freiburg im Breisgau: Herder, 1.76–87

Kripke, S. 1981. *Naming and Necessity*, 2nd edn, Oxford: Blackwell

Kroon F. and A. Voltolini. 2018. 'Fictional Entities', in *Stanford Encyclopedia of Philosophy*, edited by Edward N. Zalta; https://plato.stanford.edu/archives/win2018/entries/fictional-entities/

Kubler, G. 1962. *The Shape of Time: Remarks on the History of Things*, New Haven and London: Yale University Press

Küchler, S. 1987. 'Malangan: Art and Memory in a Melanesian Society', *Man*, N.S. 22, 238–55

Küchler, S. 1988. 'Malangan: Objects, Sacrifice and the Production of Memory', *American Ethnologist* 15/4, 625–37

Küchler, S. 2002. *Malanggan: Art, Memory and Sacrifice*, Oxford: Berg

Kulvicki, J. 2006. *On Images: Their Structure and Content*, Oxford: Oxford University Press

Kulvicki, J. 2014a. 'Beholders' Shares and the Language of Art', in *Meditations on a Heritage: Papers on the Work and Legacy of Sir Ernst Gombrich*, edited by P. Taylor, London: Paul Holberton, 127–38

Kulvicki, J. 2014b. *Images*, Abingdon: Routledge

Kulvicki, J. 2020. *Modeling the Meanings of Pictures*, Oxford: Oxford University Press

Kunzle, D. 1973. *The Early Comic Strip: Narrative Strips and Picture Stories in the European Broadsheet from c. 1450 to 1973*, Berkeley and Los Angeles: University of California Press

Kurz, O. 1939. 'Introduction to the Study of Iconography in Medieval and Modern European Art. 1: Religious Iconography', Unpublished typescript, Warburg Institute Archive, Gombrich Papers (Cf. Gombrich 1941)

Lacombe, J. 1752. *Dictionnaire portatif des Beaux-Arts*, Paris: La Veuve Estienne et fils and Jean-Th. Herissant

LaGamma, A. 2007. 'Catalogue: Central African Reliquaries', in *Eternal Ancestors: The Art of the Central African Reliquary*, edited by A. LaGamma, New York: Metropolitan Museum of Art, 122–323

LaGamma, A. 2011. *Heroic Africans: Legendary Leaders, Iconic Sculptures*, New York: Metropolitan Museum of Art

Laidlaw, J. 1995. *Riches and Renunciation: Religion, Economy and Society among the Jains*, Oxford: Oxford University Press

Lambert, W.G. 1997. 'Sumerian Gods: Combining the Evidence of Texts and Art', in *Sumerian Gods and Their Representations*, edited by I. Finkel and M. Geller, Groningen: STYX Publications, 1–10

Lane, B.G. 1988. 'Sacred versus Profane in Early Netherlandish Painting', *Simiolus: Netherlands Quarterly for the History of Art* 18 106–15

Lavin, I. 1993. 'Iconography as a Humanistic Discipline', in *Iconography at the Crossroads*, edited by B. Cassidy, Princeton: Department of Art and Archaeology, 33–42

Lawal, B. 1996. *The Gèlèdé Spectacle: Art, Gender, and Social Harmony in an African Culture*, Seattle: University of Washington Press

Lawal, B. 2012. *Yoruba*, Milan: 5 Continents

Lawton, C. 2017. *The Athenian Agora. Vol. 38: Votive Reliefs*, Athens: American School of Classical Studies

Layton, R. 1977. 'Naturalism and Cultural Relativity in Art', in *Form in Indigenous Art*, edited by P. Ucko, Canberra: Australian Institute of Aboriginal Studies, 33–43

Layton, R. 1985. 'The Cultural Context of Hunter-Gatherer Rock Art', *Man*, N.S. 20, 434–53

Le Blant, E. 1878. *Étude sur les sarcophages chrétiens antiques de la ville d'Arles*, Paris: Imprimerie nationale

Lehuard, R. and A. Lecomte. 2010. *Babembe*, Milan: 5 Continents

Leon-Portilla, M., ed. and tr. 1992. *The Broken Spears: The Aztec Account of the Conquest of Mexico*, Boston: Beacon Press

Leonard, T. 2013. 'The Front Line in our Living Room: Pro-Nato Journalism', in T. Leonard, *Definite Articles: Selected Prose 1973–2012*, Okehampton: Etruscan Books, 207–09

Le Quellec, J.-L. 2004. *Rock Art in Africa: Mythology and Legend*, translated by Paul Bahn, Paris: Flammarion

Levi d'Ancona, M. 1950. 'An Indian Statuette from Pompeii', *Artibus Asiae* 13/3, 166–80

Levinson, S. 1983. *Pragmatics*, Cambridge: Cambridge University Press

Lévi-Strauss, C. 1964. *Totemism*, translated by Rodney Needham, London: Merlin Press

Lewis, P. 1969. *The Social Context of Art in Northern New Ireland*, Chicago: Field Museum of Natural History

Liedtke, W. 2007. *Dutch Paintings in the Metropolitan Museum of Art*, New York: Metropolitan Museum of Art

Lockhart, V. 1994. *A Socio-Historical Study of Social Change among the Bangwa of Cameroon*, Edinburgh: University Centre of African Studies

Lopes, D. 1995. *Understanding Pictures*, Oxford: Oxford University Press

Loran, E. 1970. *Cézanne's Composition: Analysis of his Form with Diagrams and Photographs of his Motifs*, Berkeley and Los Angeles: University of California Press

Luczanits, C. 2005. 'The Bodhisattva with the Flask in Gandharan Narrative Scenes', *East and West* 55/1, 163–88

Lyons, J. 1977. *Semantics*, Cambridge: Cambridge University Press

MacArthur, J.R. 2004. *The Second Front: Censorship and Propaganda in the 1991 Gulf War*, Berkeley and Los Angeles: University of California Press

MacDonald, G. 1999. *Haida Art*, Vancouver: Douglas & McIntyre

MacGaffey, W. 1977. 'Fetishism Revisited: Kongo *Nkisi* in Sociological Perspective', *Africa: Journal of the International African Institute* 47/2, 172–84

MacGaffey, W. 1990. 'The Personhood of Ritual Objects: Kongo *Minkisi*', *Etnofoor* 3, 45–61

MacGaffey, W. 1994. 'African Objects and the Idea of the Fetish', *RES: Anthropology and Aesthetics* 25, 123–31

MacGaffey, W. 2015. 'Franchising *Minkisi* in Loango: Questions of Form and Function', *RES: Anthropology and Aesthetics* 65/66, 148–57

Machery, E., R. Mallon, S. Nichols and S. Stich. 2004. 'Semantics, Cross-cultural Style', *Cognition* 92, B1–B12

Macintosh, N.W.G. 1952. 'Paintings in Beswick Creek Cave, Northern Territory', *Oceania* 22/4, 256–74

Macintosh, N.W.G. 1977. 'Beswick Creek Cave Two Decades Later: A Reappraisal', in *Form in Indigenous Art*, edited by P. Ucko, Canberra: Australian Institute of Aboriginal Studies, 191–97

Macrae, A. 2019. *Discourse Deixis in Metafiction: The Language of Metanarration, Metalepsis and Disnarration*. New York and Abingdon: Routledge

Maerle, R. van. 1931–32. *Iconographie de l'art profane au Moyen-Âge et à la Renaissance*, The Hague: Martinus Nijhoff

Makowski, K. 2005. 'La deidad suprema en la iconografía Mochica: ¿cómo definirla?', in *Moche. Hacia el final del milenio*, edited by S. Uceda and E. Mujica, Lima: Universidad Nacional de Trujillo, 1.343–81

Mâle, É. 1898. *L'Art religieux du XIIIe siècle en France. Étude sur l'iconographie du moyen âge et sur ses sources d'inspiration*, Paris: Leroux (English translation: *Religious Art in France: The 13th Century*, translated by M. Mathews, Princeton: Princeton University Press, 1984)

Mâle, É. 1908. *L'Art religieux de la fin du moyen âge en France. Étude sur l'iconographie du moyen âge et sur ses sources d'inspiration*, Paris: Armand Colin (English translation: *Religious Art in France: The End of the Middle Ages*, translated by M. Mathews, Princeton: Princeton University Press, 1986)

Mâle, É. 1922. *L'Art religieux du XIIe siècle en France. Étude sur les origines de l'iconographie du moyen âge*, Paris: Armand Colin (English translation: *Religious Art in France, the Twelfth Century: A Study of the Origins of Medieval Iconography*, translated by M. Mathews, Princeton: Princeton University Press, 1978)

Mâle, É. 1927a. 'La clef des allégories peintes et sculptées au XVIIe et au XVIIIe siècle, 1: En Italie', *Revue des deux mondes*, 7th ser. 39/1, 106–29

Mâle, É. 1927b. 'La clef des allégories peintes et sculptées au XVIIe et au XVIIIe siècle, 2: En France', *Revue des deux mondes*, 7th ser. 39/1, 375–94

Malinowski, B. 1916. 'Baloma; The Spirits of the Dead in the Trobriand Islands', *The Journal of the Royal Anthropological Institute of Great Britain and Ireland* 46, 353–430

Malinowski, B. 1922. *Argonauts of the Western Pacific*, London: Routledge & Kegan Paul Ltd

Malinowski, B. 1965. *Coral Gardens and Their Magic, Vol. 1: Soil-Tilling and Agricultural Rites in the Trobriand Islands*, Bloomington: Indiana University Press

Mallowan, M. 1947. 'Excavations at Brak and Chagar Bazar', *Iraq* 9, 1–259

Mander, K. van. 1604. *Het Schilder-boeck*, Haarlem: Paschier van Wesbusch

Mander, K. van. 1998. *The Lives of the Illustrious Netherlandish and German Painters*, vol. 5, translated with a commentary by H. Miedema, Doornspijk: Davaco

Maniura, R. and R. Shepherd, eds. 2006. *Presence: The Inherence of the Prototype Within Images and Other Objects*, Aldershot: Ashgate

Maraszak, E. 2017. 'Adolphe-Napoléon Didron', in *The Routledge Companion to Medieval Iconography*, edited by C. Hourihane, Abingdon: Routledge, 47–56

Marshall, C.W. 1999. 'Some Fifth-Century Masking Conventions', *Greece & Rome* 46/2, 188–202

Masereel, F. 1919. *Mon livre d'heures*, Geneva: Albert Kundig

Masereel, F. 1926. *Mein Stundenbuch*, Munich: Kurt Wolff Verlag

Massing, J.M. 2007. 'Crosses and Hunting Charms: Polysemy in Bakongo Religion', in *Encompassing the Globe: Portugal and the World in the 16th & 17th Centuries. Vol. 3: Essays*, edited by J. Levenson, Washington, D.C.: Smithsonian Institution, 87–95

Mastrocinque, A. 2011. 'Kronos, Shiva, and Asklepios: Studies in Magical Gems and Religions of the Roman Empire', *Transactions of the American Philosophical Society* 101/5, 1–130

Mazzucco, K. 2002. 'On the Reverse: Some Notes on Photographic Images from the Warburg Institute Photographic Collection', *Aisthesis* 5, 217–32

Mazzucco, K. 2011. 'Mnemosyne, il nome della memoria. *Bilderdemonstration, Bilderreihen, Bilderatlas*. Una cronologia documentario del progetto warburghiano', *Quaderni del Centro Warburg Italia* 3/4–5, 139–203

Mazzucco, K. 2012. 'L'Iconoteca Warburg in Amburgo. Documenti per una storia della Photographic Collection del Warburg Institute', *Quaderni storici* 141/3, 857–87

McCloud, S. 1993. *Understanding Comics: The Invisible Art*, New York: Harper Collins

McGinnis, N. 2017. 'Taking the "Cognitive Turn" in Experimental Philosophy of Language', *Teorema: Revista Internacional de Filosofía* 36/3, 61–94

McGrath, E. 1998. 'Von der "Erdbeeren" zur "Schule von Athen". Titel und Beschriftungen von Kunstwerken der Renaissance', *Vorträge aus dem Warburg-Haus* 2, 117–88

Mead, M. 1963. 'Anthropology and the Camera', in *The Encyclopedia of Photography*, 20 vols, edited by W. Morgan, New York: Greystone Press, 1.166–84

Mello e Souza, M. 2007. 'Central African Crucifixes: A Study of Symbolic Traditions', in *Encompassing the Globe: Portugal and the World in the 16th & 17th Centuries. Vol. 3: Essays*, edited by J. Levenson, Washington, D.C.: Smithsonian Institution, 97–101

Merrill, M. 2004. 'Masks, Metaphor and Transformation: The Communication of Belief in Ritual Performance', *Journal of Ritual Studies* 18/1, 16–33

Mitchell, W.J.T. 1994. 'Metapictures', in W.J.T. Mitchell, *Picture Theory*, Chicago: University of Chicago Press, 35–82

Mitchell, W.J.T. 1996. 'What Do Pictures *Really* Want?', *October* 77, 71–82

Miyaji, A. 2008. 'Iconography of the Two Flanking Bodhisattvas in the Buddhist Triads from Gandhāra: Bodhisattvas Siddhārtha, Maitreya and Avalokiteśvara', *East and West* 58/1, 123–56

Molanus, J. 1618. *De historia SS. imaginum et picturarum pro vero earum usu contra abusus, libri IIII*, Antwerp: Gasparus Bellerus

Montagu, J. 1968. 'The Painted Enigma and French Seventeenth-Century Art', *Journal of the Warburg and Courtauld Institutes* 31, 307–35

Monteiro, J.J. 1875. *Angola and the River Congo*, vol. 1, London: Macmillan

Montias, J.M. 1982. *Artists and Artisans in Delft: A Socio-Economic Study of the Seventeenth Century*, Princeton: Princeton University Press

Morphy, H. 1991. *Ancestral Connections: Art and an Aboriginal System of Knowledge*, Chicago: University of Chicago Press

Morphy, H. 1999. 'Manggalili Art and the Promised Land', in *Painting the Land Story*, edited by L. Taylor, Canberra: National Museum of Australia, 53–74

Müller, M. 2015. 'Iconography and Symbolism', in *A Companion to Ancient Egyptian Art*, edited by M. Hartwig, Oxford and Chichester: Wiley Blackwell, 2015, 78–97

Munn, N. 1973. 'The Spatial Presentation of Cosmic Order in Walbiri Iconography', in *Primitive Art and Society*, edited by A. Forge, London: Oxford University Press, 193–220

Munn, N. 1986. *Walbiri Iconography: Graphic Representation and Cultural Symbolism in a Central Australian Society*, 2nd edn, Chicago: University of Chicago Press

Nagel, A. and L. Pericolo, eds. 2010. *Subject as Aporia in Early Modern Art*, Aldershot: Ashgate

Nakassis, C.V., W.J.T. Mitchell, M. Barker, E. Edwards, C. Ball, T. Kolich and D. Morgan. 2020. 'Opening up the Indexicality of the Image, Again: A Virtual Roundtable', *Semiotic Review* 9; https://semioticreview.com/ojs/index.php.st/article/view/62

Natali, A. and A. Cecchi. 1989. *Andrea del Sarto. Catalogo completo dei dipinti*, Florence: Cantini

Ndobegang, M.M. and F. Bowie. 2009. 'Azi since Conrau: Anthropological and Historical Perspectives', in *Encounter, Transformation and Identity*, vol. 1, edited by I. Fowler and V.G. Fanso, New York and Oxford: Berghahn, 93–109

Nelson, E. 2019. 'What Frege Asked Alex the Parrot: Inferentialism, Number Concepts, and Animal Cognition', *Philosophical Psychology* 33/2, 206–27; 10.1080/09515089.2019.1688777

Noel, W. 1995. *The Harley Psalter*, Cambridge: Cambridge University Press

Nöldeke, T. 1896. *Das Iranische Nationalepos*, Strassburg: Karl J. Trübner, 1896

Nukariya, K. 1913. *The Religion of the Samurai: A Study of Zen Philosophy and Discipline in China and Japan*, London: Luzac

O'Byrne, E. 2017. *Fighting Fake News*, Cork: Institute of Technology; https://thereadonlyfiles.wordpress.com/1-defining-and-re-defining-fake-news/

Ong, W. 1982. *Orality and Literacy: The Technologizing of the Word*, London and New York: Methuen

Osborne, R., ed. 2004. *The Object of Dedication*, Special Issue of *World Archaeology* 36/1

Ossa-Richardson, A. 2019. *A History of Ambiguity*, Princeton and Oxford: Princeton University Press

Ottenberg, S. 1975. *Masked Rituals of Afikpo: the Context of an African Art*, Seattle and London: University of Washington Press

Pal, P. 1994a. 'Introduction', in *The Peaceful Liberators: Jain Art from India*, edited by P. Pal, Los Angeles: County Museum of Art, 13–37

Pal, P. 1994b. 'An Altarpiece with Multiple Jinas', in *The Peaceful Liberators: Jain Art from India*, edited by P. Pal, Los Angeles: County Museum of Art, 150

Pal, P. 2006. 'Reflections on the Gandhāra Bodhisattva Images', *Bulletin of the Asia Institute* 20, 101–15

Panofsky, E. 1932. 'Zum Problem der Beschreibung und Inhaltsdeutung von Werken der bildenden Kunst', *Logos* 21, 103–19 (English translation: 'On the Problem of Describing and Interpreting Works of the Visual Arts', translated by J. Elsner and K. Lorenz, *Critical Inquiry* 38, 2012, 467–82)

Panofsky, E. 1934. 'Jan van Eyck's *Arnolfini Portrait*', *The Burlington Magazine* 64, 117–27

Panofsky, E. 1939a. 'Introductory', in E. Panofsky, *Studies in Iconology*, Oxford and New York: Oxford University Press, 3–17

Panofsky, E. 1939b. 'The Neoplatonic Movement in Florence and North Italy', in E. Panofsky, *Studies in Iconology*, Oxford and New York: Oxford University Press, 131–60

Panofsky, E. 1953. *Early Netherlandish Painting: its Origins and Character*, Cambridge, MA: Harvard University Press

Panofsky, E. 1955. 'Iconography and Iconology: An Introduction to the Study of Renaissance Art', in E. Panofsky, *Meaning in the Visual Arts*, Garden City, NY: Doubleday, 26–54

Panofsky, E. 1969. *Problems in Titian, Mostly Iconographic*, London: Phaidon

Paoli, M. 2011. *La 'Tempesta' svelata: Giorgione, Gabriele Vendramin, Cristoforo Marcello e la 'Vecchia'*, Lucca: Pacini Fazzi

Paris, C. et al. 2019. 'Les Gisements gravettiens d'Amiens-Renancourt 1 et 2 (Somme, France). Premières données palethnologiques', in *Préhistoire de l'Europe du Nord-Ouest. Mobilités, climats et identités culturelles (28e Congrès préhistorique de France (Amiens, 30 mai - 4 juin 2016)*, edited by C. Montoya, J.-P. Fagnart and J.-L. Locht, Paris: Société Préhistorique française, 97–115

Parkinson, R. 1907. *Dreißig Jahre in der Südsee*, Stuttgart: Strecker & Schröder

Parpola, A. 1994. *Deciphering the Indus Script*, Cambridge: Cambridge University Press

Parr, L.A., J.T. Winslow, W.D. Hopkins and F.B.M. de Waal. 2000. 'Recognizing Facial Cues: Individual Discrimination by Chimpanzees (*Pan troglodytes*) and Rhesus Monkeys (*Macaca mulatta*)', *Journal of Comparative Psychology* 114/1, 47–60

Peek, P. 2008. 'Couples or Doubles? Representations of Twins in the Arts of Africa', *African Arts* 41/1, 14–23

Peekel, G. 1927. 'Die Ahnenbilder von Nord-Neu-Mecklenburg. Eine kritische und positive Studie (Schluß)', *Anthropos* 22/1, 16–44

Peirce, C. S. [1909] 1998. 'A Sketch of Logical Critics', in *The Essential Peirce: Selected Philosophical Writings, Volume 2 (1893–1913)*, edited by N. Houser and the Peirce Edition Project, Bloomington and Indianapolis: Indiana University Press, 451–62

Perrois, L. 2006. *Fang*, Milan: 5 Continents

Perrois, L. 2012. *Kota*, Milan: 5 Continents

Perry, E. 2005. *The Aesthetics of Emulation in the Visual Arts of Ancient Rome*, Cambridge: Cambridge University Press

Pettazzoni, R. 1984. 'The Truth of Myth', in *Sacred Narrative: Readings in the Theory of Myth*, edited by A. Dundes, Berkeley and Los Angeles: University of California Press, 98–109

Phillips, K.M. 1968. 'Perseus and Andromeda', *American Journal of Archaeology* 72/1, 1–23

Picton, J. 1990. 'What's in a Mask?', *African Languages and Cultures* 3/2, 181–202

Pietz, W. 1985. 'The Problem of the Fetish I', *RES: Anthropology and Aesthetics* 9, 5–17

Pietz, W. 1987. 'The Problem of the Fetish II: The Origin of the Fetish', *RES: Anthropology and Aesthetics* 13, 23–45

Pietz, W. 1988. 'The Problem of the Fetish IIIa: Bosman's Guinea and the Enlightenment Theory of Fetishism', *RES: Anthropology and Aesthetics* 16, 105–23

Pintchman, T. 2005. *Guests at God's Wedding: Celebrating Kartik among the Women of Benares*, Albany: State University of New York Press

Poignant, R. 1992. 'Surveying the Field of View: The Making of the RAI Photographic Collection', in *Anthropology and Photography, 1860–1920*, edited by E. Edwards, New Haven and London: Yale University Press, 42–73

Pois, A. Le. 1579. *Discours sur les medalles et graveures antiques, principalement romaines*, Paris: Mamert Patisson

Pongratz-Leisten, B. 2015. 'Imperial Allegories: Divine Agency and Monstrous Bodies in Mesopotamia's Body Description Texts', in *The Materiality of Divine Agency*, edited by B. Pongratz-Leisten and K. Sonik, Berlin: De Gruyter, 119–41

Pool, R. 1990. 'Fetishism Deconstructed', *Etnofoor* 3, 114–27

Powdermaker, H. [1933] 1971. *Life in Lesu: the Study of a Melanesian Society in New Ireland*, New York: W.W. Norton

Poynor, R. 1987. 'Ako Figures of Owo and Second Burials in Southern Nigeria', *African Arts* 21/1, 62–63, 81–83, 86–87

Prézel, H.L. de. 1756. *Dictionnaire iconologique*, Paris: T. de Hansy

Prządka-Giersz, P. 2015. 'Ai Apaec: ¿una divinidad suprema prehispánica o una manipulación en la traducción intercultural?', *Politeja* 38, 7–16

Quilter J. and M. Koons. 2012. 'The Fall of the Moche: A Critique of Claims for South America's First State', *Latin American Antiquity* 23/2, 127–43

Quine, W.V. 1960. *Word and Object*, Boston: MIT Press

Quine, W.V. 1987. 'Indeterminacy of Translation Again', *Journal of Philosophy* 84, 5–10

Radowitz, J. von. 1834. *Ikonographie der Heiligen*, Berlin: F. Dümmler

Rattray, R.S. 1923. *Ashanti*, Oxford: Clarendon Press

Rattray, R.S. 1927. *Religion and Art in Ashanti*, London and Accra: Oxford University Press

Ravenhill, P. 1996. *Dreams and Reverie: Images of Otherworld Mates among the Baule*, Washington, D.C.: Smithsonian Institution Press

Recanati, F. 2004. 'Pragmatics and Semantics', in *The Handbook of Pragmatics*, edited by L. Horn and G. Ward, Oxford: Blackwell, 442–62

Recanati, F. 2010. *Truth-Conditional Pragmatics*, Oxford: Clarendon Press

Recht, R. 2013. *L'Iconologie avant Warburg. Images Re-vues* 4, 2013; https://doi.org/10.4000/imagesrevues.2898

Rhi, J. 2005. 'Images, Relics, and Jewels: The Assimilation of Images in the Buddhist Relic Cult of Gandhāra: or Vice Versa', *Artibus Asiae* 65/2, 169–211

Ripa, C. 1593. *Iconologia overo descrittione dell'imagini universali cavate dall'antichità et da altri luoghi*, Rome: Heredi di Gio. Gigliotti

Ripa, C. 1645. *Iconologia*, Venice: Cristoforo Tomasini

Roberts, M.N. and A. Roberts. 2007. *Luba*, Milan: 5 Continents

Robinson, A. 2009. *Lost Languages. The Enigma of the World's Undeciphered Scripts*, London: Thames and Hudson

Rose, D.B. 2013. 'Common Property Regimes in Aboriginal Australia: Totemism Revisited', in *The Governance of Common Property in the Pacific Region*, edited by P. Larmour, Canberra: ANU Press, 127–44

Rose, S. 2022. *Interpreting Art*, London: UCL Press

Rosman, C. 2016. 'Een Volendamse broek aan, dát vertikte Ali', *Algemeen Dagblad*, 6 June; https://www.ad.nl/nieuws/een-volendamse-broek-aan-dat-vertikte-ali~a9a411c6/?

Roy, C. 2015. *Mossi*, Milan: 5 Continents

Rudy, S. 1972. 'Cameroon Grasslands Royal Sculpture', in *African Art and Leadership*, edited by D. Fraser and H. Cole, Madison: University of Wisconsin Press, 123–35

Ruskin, J. 1843–60. *Modern Painters*, 6 vols, London: Smith, Elder & Co.

Ruskin, J. 1851–53. *The Stones of Venice*, 3 vols, London: Smith, Elder & Co.

Salmazo, A. de Nicolo. 2000. 'Le reliquie di San Luca e l'abbazia di Santa Giustina a Padova', in *Luca Evangelista. Parola e immagine tra Oriente e Occidente*, edited by G. Canova Mariani, Padua: Il Poligrafo, 155–86

Salmon, N. 1986. *Frege's Puzzle*, Cambridge, MA: MIT Press

Samperi, P. 1645. *Iconologia della Gloriosa Vergine Madre di Dio Protettrice di Messina*, Messina: Giacomo Matthei

Sandrart, J. von. 1680. *Iconologia Deorum, oder Abbildung der Götter*, Nuremberg: C.S. Froberger

Sartwell, C. 1991. 'Natural Generativity and Imitation', *British Journal of Aesthetics* 31/1, 58–67

Sauneron, S. 1962. 'Persée, dieu de Khemmis (Hérodote II, 91)', *Revue d'Egyptologie* 14, 53–57

Saussure, F. de [1916] 1995. *Cours de linguistique générale*, edited by C. Bally and A. Sechehaye, Paris: Payot

Schellhas, P. 1904. 'Representations of Deities of the Mayan Manuscripts', *Papers of the Peabody Museum of American Archaeology and Ethnology, Harvard University* 4/1 (Original edition: *Die Göttergestalten der Mayahandschriften. Ein mythologisches Kulturbild aus dem alten Amerika*, Dresden: R. Bertling, 1897)

Schick, N. 2020. *Deep Fakes and the Infocalypse: What You Urgently Need to Know*, London: Octopus

Schier, F. 1986. *Deeper into Pictures*, Cambridge: Cambridge University Press

Schlosser, J. von. 1896. 'Giusto's Fresken in Padua und die Vorlaüfer der Stanza della Segnatura', *Jahrbuch der Kunsthistorischen Sammlungen des Allerhöchsten Kaiserhauses* 17, 13–100

Schnell, W. 1989. 'Das Kind als Ziel. Hans von Marées' suche nach den Anfängen', *Wallraf-Richartz-Jahrbuch* 50, 219–49

Schnürer G. and J.M. Ritz. 1934. *Sankt Kümmernis und Volto Santo. Studien und Bilder*, Düsseldorf: L. Schwann

Schwarz, M.V. 1998. 'Beckmann, Klaus Mann, Thomas Mann. Weltbilder im Gegenlicht', *Marburger Jahrbuch für Kunstwissenschaft* 25, 165–81

Scopacasa, R. 2015. 'Moulding Cultural Change: A Contextual Approach to Anatomical Votive Terracottas in Central Italy, Fourth-Second Centuries BC', *Papers of the British School at Rome* 83, 1–27, 343–44

Scruton, R. 1981. 'Photography and Representation', *Critical Inquiry* 7/3, 577–603

Searle, J. 1978. 'Literal Meaning', *Erkenntnis* 13, 207–24

Searle, J. 1992. *The Rediscovery of the Mind*, Cambridge, MA: MIT Press

Sears, E. 2015. 'A Diarist's View: Roger Hinks on the Warburg Institute "25 years after its settling in London"', *Vorträge aus dem Warburg-Haus* 12, 71–95

Sears, E. 2024. 'Iconology vs. Iconography: G.J. Hoogewerff's Seminal Distinctions', in *Art Historiography and Iconologies Between West and East*, edited by W. Bałus and M. Kunińska, New York: Routledge, 58–73

Seler, E. 1902–04 and 1908. *Gesammelte Abhandlungen zur amerikanischen Sprach- und Alterthumskunde*, 3 vols, Berlin: A. Asher & Co. and Berlin: Behrend & Co.

Seznec, J. 1953. *The Survival of the Pagan Gods*, Princeton: Bollingen (Original edition: *La Survivance des dieux antiques*, London: Warburg Institute, 1940)

Shahbazi, A.S. 1993. 'The Parthian Origins of the House of Rustam', *Bulletin of the Asia Institute*, N.S. 7, 155–63

Shearman, J. 1965. *Andrea del Sarto*, Oxford: Clarendon Press

Siroto, L. 1968. 'The Face of the Bwiti', *African Arts* 1/3, 22–27, 86–89, 96

Siroto, L. 1979. 'On the Cultural Context of Terracotta Statuettes from Mali', *African Arts* 13/1, 20–23

Sivaramamurti, C. 1955. 'The Weapons of Vishnu', *Artibus Asiae* 18, 128–36

Slive, S., ed. 1989. *Frans Hals*, London: Royal Academy of Art

Snape, S. 2014. *The Complete Cities of Ancient Egypt*, London: Thames & Hudson

Spencer, B. 1914. *Native Tribes of the Northern Territory of Australia*, London: Macmillan

Spooner, B. 1988. 'Weavers and Dealers: the Authenticity of an Oriental Carpet', in *The Social Life of Things: Commodities in Cultural Perspective*, edited by A. Appadurai, Cambridge: Cambridge University Press, 1988

Stafford, E. and J. Herrin 2005. *Personification in the Greek World: From Antiquity to Byzantium*, Abingdon: Routledge

Stone, E.R. 2008. 'Some Begram Ivories and the South Indian Narrative Tradition: New Evidence', *Journal of Inner Asian Art and Archaeology* 3, 45–59

Stork, D.G. 2024. *Pixels and Paintings: Foundations of Computer-Assisted Connoisseurship*, Hoboken: John Wiley & Sons

Strathern, A. and M. Strathern. 1971. *Self-Decoration in Mount Hagen*, London: Duckworth

Strother, Z.S. 2008. *Pende*, Milan: 5 Continents

Stumpel, J. 1990. 'A Raphael by Raphael: The Story of the *Madonna of the Fish*', in J. Stumpel, *The Province of Painting*, Utrecht: The Author, 26–58

Stumpel, J. 1993. 'Hobby Horses in Lascaux: On pictures and Semiosis', *Argumentation* 7, 103–17

Stumpel, J. 1995. 'Review of K. Moxey, *The Practice of Theory: Poststructuralism, Cultural Politics, and Art History*', *Simiolus: Netherlands Quarterly for the History of Art* 23/4, 280–84

Stumpel, J. 1996. 'The Vatican Tazza and Other Petrifications: An Iconological Essay on Replacement and Ritual', *Simiolus: Netherlands Quarterly for the History of Art* 24/3, 111–27

Stumpel, J. 2000. 'A Twelfth Attempt: The Subject of Rembrandt's "History Piece" in Leiden', *Simiolus: Netherlands Quarterly for the History of Art*, 28/1–2, 44–50

Stumpel, J. 2014. 'Pattern and Portrayal: Remarks on the Concept of "Schema" in Gombrich', in *Meditations on a Heritage: Papers on the Work and Legacy of Sir Ernst Gombrich*, edited by P. Taylor, London: Paul Holberton, 109–26

Swanton, J. 1905. 'Contributions to the Ethnology of the Haida', *Memoirs of the American Museum of Natural History* 8/1, 1–300

Taube, K. 1992. 'The Major Gods of Ancient Yucatan', *Studies in Pre-Columbian Art and Archaeology* 32, 1–160

Taylor, J. 2018. *What Did Jesus Look Like?*, London: Bloomsbury

Taylor, L. 1996. *Seeing the Inside: Bark Painting in Western Arnhem Land*, Oxford: Oxford University Press

Taylor, P. 1995. *Dutch Flower Painting 1600–1720*, New Haven and London: Yale University Press

Taylor, P. 2002. 'Review of K. van Mander, *The Lives of the Illustrious Netherlandish and German Painters*, with a commentary by H. Miedema, 6 vols, Doornspijk: Davaco, 1994–99', *Oud Holland* 115/2, 131–54

Taylor, P. 2006a. 'Introduction', in *The Iconography of Cylinder Seals*, edited by P. Taylor, London and Turin: Warburg Institute and Nino Aragno, 1–5

Taylor, P. 2006b. 'The Warburg Institute's Photographic Collection and the Diversity of Mesopotamian Iconography', in *The Iconography of Cylinder Seals*, edited by P. Taylor, London and Turin: Warburg Institute and Nino Aragno, 9–18

Taylor, P. 2008a. 'Introduction', in *Iconography without Texts*, edited by P. Taylor, London and Turin: Warburg Institute and Nino Aragno, 1–14

Taylor, P. 2008b. 'Moche Libation Bottles', in *Iconography without Texts*, edited by P. Taylor, London and Turin: Warburg Institute and Nino Aragno, 145–60

Taylor, P. 2010. 'Images and Stories', *The Monist* 93, 368–81

Taylor, P. 2011. 'Rembrandt's *Injustice of Piso*', *Oud Holland* 124, 112–18

Taylor, P. 2014. 'Gombrich and the Idea of Primitive Art', in *Meditations on a Heritage: Papers on the Work and Legacy of Sir Ernst Gombrich*, edited by P. Taylor, London: Paul Holberton, 90–108

Taylor, P. 2015. *Condition: The Ageing of Art*, London: Paul Holberton

Taylor, P. 2022a. 'Iconography in the Age of Mechanical Reproduction', *ARJ – Art Research Journal: Revista de Pesquisa em Artes* 9/1; https://periodicos.ufrn.br/artresearchjournal/article/view/29648/15924

Taylor, P. 2022b. 'From the Rise of Civilization to the Rise of Capitalism: The Warburg Institute's Photographic Collection', *World 3* 5, 2–16 (in Chinese)

Taylor, P. 2025. 'Iconography and Investment: Private Art Collections in Seventeenth-Century Holland', in *The Oxford Handbook of Historical Privacy Studies*, edited by M. Birkedal Bruun and S. Nauman, Oxford: Oxford University Press

Tenney, J. 2017. 'Babylonian Populations, Servility, and Cuneiform Records', *Journal of the Economic and Social History of the Orient* 60/6, 715–87

Thompson, R.F. 1973. 'Yoruba Artistic Criticism', in *The Traditional Artist in African Societies*, edited by W. d'Azevedo, Bloomington: Indiana University Press, 19–61

Tolan, J. 2009. *Saint Francis and the Sultan: The Curious History of a Christian-Muslim Encounter*, Oxford: Oxford University Press

Tomonaga, M., S. Itakura and T. Matsuzawa. 1993. 'Superiority of Conspecific Faces and Reduced Inversion Effect in Face Perception by a Chimpanzee', *Folia Primatologica* 61, 110–14

Travis, C. 1997. 'Pragmatics', in *A Companion to the Philosophy of Language*, edited by B. Hale and C. Wright, Oxford: Blackwell, 87–107

Trever, L. et al. 2017. *The Archaeology of Mural Painting at Pañamarca, Peru*, Washington, D.C.: Dumbarton Oaks

Trevisan, S. 2018. *Mythical Ancestry in World Cultures, 1400–1800*, edited by S. Trevisan, Turnhout: Brepols

Trevisan, S. 2020. *Royal Genealogy in the Age of Shakespeare*, London: D.S. Brewer in association with The British Library

Tuzin, D. 1980. *The Voice of the Tambaran: Truth and Illusion in Ilahita Arapesh Religion*, Berkeley and Los Angeles: University of California Press

Tuzin, D. 1997. *The Cassowary's Revenge: The Life and Death of Masculinity in a New Guinea Society*, Chicago: University of Chicago Press

Tyler, H. 2022. 'The Increasing Use of Artificial Intelligence in Border Zones Prompts Privacy Questions', *Migration Information Source. The Online Journal of the Migration Policy Institute*, 2 February; https://www.migrationpolicy.org/article/artificial-intelligence-border-zones-privacy

Valeriano, P. 1556. *Hieroglyphica, sive de sacris Aegyptiorum literis commentarii*, Basle: Michel Isengrin

Vansina, J. 1964. *Le Royaume Kuba*, Tervuren: Musée Royal de l'Afrique Centrale

Vansina, J. 1972. '*Ndop*: Royal Statues among the Kuba', in *African Art and Leadership*, edited by D. Fraser and H. Cole, Madison: University of Wisconsin Press, 41–55

Vansina, J. 1978. *Children of Woot: A History of the Kuba Peoples*, Madison: University of Wisconsin Press

Vasari, G. 1550. *Le vite de più eccellenti architetti, pittori, et scultori italiani, da Cimabue insino a tempi nostri*, Florence: Lorenzo Torrentino

Vasari, G. 1568. *Le vite de più eccellenti pittori, scultori ed architettori*, Florence: I Giunti. (English translation: *Lives of the Most Eminent Painters, Sculptors and Architects*, translated by G. de Vere, London: Philip Lee Warner, 1912)

Velden, H. van der. 1997. 'Petrus Christus's *Our Lady of the Dry Tree*', *Journal of the Warburg and Courtauld Institutes* 60, 89–110

Velden, H. van der. 2000. *The Donor's Image: Gerard Loyet and the Votive Portraits of Charles the Bold*, Turnhout: Brepols

Vico, E. and A. Zantani, 1548. *Le imagini con tutti i riversi trovati et le vite de gli imperatori tratte dalle medaglie et dalle historie de gli antichi*, Parma: Enea Vico

Vogel, S. 1973. 'People of Wood: Baule Figure Sculpture', *Art Journal* 33, 23–26

Volp, R. and L. Kaute. 1968. 'Attribute', in *Lexikon der Christlichen Ikonographie*, vol. 1, edited by E. Kirschbaum and G. Bandmann, Rome: Herder, 197–201

Voltolini, A. 2006. *How Ficta Follow Fiction: A Syncretistic Account of Fictional Entities*, Dordrecht: Springer

Vooren, J. van de. 2022. 'Het bliksembezoek van Muhammad Ali aan Volendam', *Sportsgeschiedenis.nl*, 7 March https://sportgeschiedenis.nl/overige-sport/vechtsporten/8-maart-1976-muhammad-ali-in-volendam/

Vries, L. de. 1999. 'Iconography and Iconology in Art History: Panofsky's *Prescriptive* Definitions and Some Art-Historical Responses to Them', in *Picturing Performance: The Iconography of the Performing Arts in Concept and Practice*, edited by T. Heck, Rochester, NY: University of Rochester Press, 42–64

Walker, C. and M. Dick. 2001. *The Induction of the Cult Image in Ancient Mesopotamia: The Mesopotamian Mīs Pî Ritual*, Helsinki: Neo-Assyrian Text Corpus Project, Institute for Asian and African Studies, University of Helsinki, 2001

Walton, K. 1990. *Mimesis as Make-Believe*, Cambridge, MA: Harvard University Press

Walton, K. 2008. 'Transparent Pictures: On the Nature of Photographic Realism', in K. Walton, *Marvelous Images: On Values and the Arts*, New York: Oxford University Press, 79–116

Warburg, A. 1932. *Gesammelte Schriften*, Leipzig: B.G. Teubner. (English translation: *The Renewal of Pagan Antiquity*, translated by D. Britt, Los Angeles: Getty, 1999)

Ward, B. 1956. 'Some Observations on Religious Cults in Ashanti', *Africa: Journal of the International African Institute* 26/1, 47–61

Warner, A. and E. Warner, 1908. *The Sháhnáma of Firdausí, done into English*: London: Kegan Paul, Trench, Trübner & Co., 1908, 3.272–81

Warner, M. 1976. *Alone of All Her Sex: The Myth and Cult of the Virgin Mary*, London: Weidenfeld and Nicolson

Warner, M. 1985. *Monuments and Maidens: The Allegory of the Female Form*, London: Vintage Books

Wastiau, B. 2006. *Chokwe*, Milan: 5 Continents

Waterworth, J. 1848. *The Canons and Decrees of the Sacred and Ecumenical Council of Trent*, London: Dolman

Watt, N. and D. Pallister. 2002. 'Sifting the Old Claims from the New and Suspicions from Assertions of Fact', *The Guardian*, 25 September; https://www.theguardian.com/politics/2002/sep/25/uk.iraq7

Webb, V. and Kembo-Sure. 2000. *African Voices: An Introduction to the Languages and Linguistics of Africa*, Oxford: Oxford University Press

Webster, T.B.L. 1965. 'The Poet and the Mask', in *Classical Drama and Its Influence: Essays Presented to H.D.F. Kitto*, edited by M.J. Anderson, London: Methuen, 5–13

Wentzel, H. 1937. 'Attribut', in *Reallexikon der deutschen Kunstgeschichte*, vol. 1, edited by O. Schmitt, Stuttgart: J.B. Metzler, 1212–20

Williams, G. 1985. 'Reactions on Cook's Voyage: In *Seeing the First Australians*', edited by I. Donaldson and T. Donaldson, Sydney: George Allen & Unwin, 35–50

Wilson, D. 2021. 'Invisible Images and Indeterminacy: Why We Need a Multi-Stage Account of Photography', *Journal of Aesthetics and Art Criticism* 79/2, 161–74

Wind, E. 1931. 'Warburgs Begriff der Kulturwissenschaft und seine Bedeutung für die Ästhetik', *Beilageheft zur Zeitschrift für Ästhetik und allgemeine Kunstwissenschaft* 25, 163–79. (English translation: 'Warburg's Concept of *Kulturwissenschaft* and its Meaning for Aesthetics', in E. Wind, *The Eloquence of Symbols: Studies in Humanist Art*, edited by J. Anderson, Oxford: Clarendon Press, 1983)

Winter, I. 1985. 'After the Battle Is Over: The "Stele of the Vultures" and the Beginning of Historical Narrative in the Art of the Ancient Near East', *Studies in the History of Art* 16, 11–32

Winter, I. 1986. 'The King and the Cup: Iconography of the Royal Presentation Scene on Ur III Seals', in *Insight through Images: Studies in Honor of Edith Porada*. edited by M.K. Buccellati, P. Matthiae and M. van Loon, Malibu: Undena Publications, 253–68

Winter, I. 2000. '*Le Palais Imaginaire*: Scale and Meaning in the Iconography of Neo-Assyrian Cylinder Seals', in *Images as Media: Sources for the Cultural History of the Near East and the Eastern Mediterranean (1st millennium BCE)*, edited by C. Uehlinger, Fribourg: Fribourg University Press, 51–87

Wirth, J. 2001. *L'Image à la fin du Moyen Âge*, Paris: Cerf

Wittgenstein, L. 1953. *Philosophical Investigations*, translated by G.E.M. Anscombe, Oxford: Blackwell

Wood, C. 2011. 'The Votive Scenario', *RES: Anthropology and Aesthetics* 59/60, 206–27

Woods, C. 2004. 'The Sun-God Tablet of Nabû-apla-iddina Revisited', *Journal of Cuneiform Studies* 56, 23–103

Woolf, G. 2015. 'Mass Illiteracy?', *Bulletin of the Institute of Classical Studies* 58/2, 31–42

Wright, T. 1992. 'Photography: Theories of Realism and Convention', in *Anthropology and Photography, 1860–1920*, edited by E. Edwards, New Haven and London: Yale University Press, 18–31

Wuttke, D. 1979. *Aby M. Warburg: Ausgewählte Schriften und Würdigungen*, Baden-Baden: Koerner

Wuttke, D. 2017. 'Erwin Panofsky (1892–1968)', in *The Routledge Companion to Medieval Iconography*, edited by C. Hourihane, Abingdon: Routledge, 105–22

Yeazell, R.B. 2015. *Picture Titles: How and Why Western Paintings Acquired Their Names*, Princeton: Princeton University Press

Young, M. 1998. *Malinowski's Kiriwina: Fieldwork Photography 1915–1918*, Chicago: University of Chicago Press

Young, M. and H. Beran. 2016. 'Malinowski on Primitive Art: Art Notes and Suggestions', *Pacific Arts* 16/1, 5–32

Zeller, R. 1912. *Die Goldgewichte von Asante (Westafrika). Eine ethnologische Studie* (*Baessler-Archiv*, Beiheft 3), Leipzig and Berlin: B.G. Teubner

Zwalf, W. 1996. *A Catalogue of the Gandhara Sculpture in the British Museum*, London: British Museum Press

Index

Photographic Credits

Archive.org, 3.16; Author photo, page 6, 2.1, 2.4, 2.5, 3.20, 4.23, 5.2, 5.5, 5.20, 5.22, 6.4, 6.10, 6.14, 7.2; Berlin, Ethnologisches Museum, 3.3, 3.4, 3.7, 4.1; Canberra, National Museum of Australia, 1.5; Central Intelligence Agency, 6.15; Flickr: 0.1 (KarentheBrit2); Geheugen.nl, 2.8; Kress, Berthold, 4.12; Lima, Museo Larco, 1.8, 1.9, 4.16; London, British Museum, 3.27, 4.15, 4.33, 5.9, 5.10, 5.18; London, Warburg Institute: 2.3, 3.2, 3.13, 3.17, 3.19, 4.5, 4.6, 4.13, 4.14, 4.17, 4.25, 4.30, 4.31, 5.3, 5.4, 5.12, 5.13, 5.14, 5.15, 5.17, 5.19, 5.24, 5.25, 5.27, 5.28, 6.1a-e, 6.2, 6.13, 8.1, 8.3, 8.4; Los Angeles, Fowler Museum, 3.21; Minneapolis, Museum of Art, 6.17; Neale, Andy, 5.1; New York, Brooklyn Museum, 3.10, 3.14, 3.15, 3.24, 4.8; New York, Metropolitan Museum of Art: 1.2, 1.7, 2.6, 2.7, 2.11, 4.2, 4.3, 4.20, 4.22, 4.28, 5.23; Paris, Musée du Quai Branly, 3.6; Philadelphia, Museum of Art, 6.5; Scala, 5.16; Shutterstock, 6.7; thispersondoesnotexist.com, 6.16; Victoria BC, City of Victoria Archives, 3.25; Vienna, Akademie der bildende Künsten, 1.6; Washington D.C., Library of Congress, 2.9, 4.26; Wikimedia: 1.1, 1.3, 1.10, 2.2, 2.9, 3.5, 3.9, 3.11, 3.12, 3.18, 3.22, 3.23, 3.26, 3.28, 4.4, 4.7, 4.9, 4.10, 4.11, 4.18, 4.19, 4.21, 4.24, 4.27, 4.29, 4.32, 5.7, 5.8, 5.11, 5.21, 5.26, 5.29, 6.3a–f, 6.6, 6.8, 6.9, 6.11, 6.12, 7.1, 8.2